REPUTATION

REPUTATION

Realizing
Value
from the
Corporate
Image

CHARLES J. FOMBRUN

HARVARD BUSINESS SCHOOL PRESS
BOSTON, MASSACHUSETTS

Printed in the United States of America

05 04 03 02   10 9 8 7 6

Library of Congress Cataloging-in-Publication Data

Fombrun, Charles J.
  Reputation : realizing value from the corporate image / Charles J. Fombrun.
    p.   cm.
  Includes index.
  ISBN 0-87584-633-5
  1. Corporate image.   2. Corporate image—Case studies.   I. Title.
  HD59.2.F66   1996
659.2—dc20   95-20172
                                                                  CIP

The paper used in this publication meets the requirements of the American
National Standard for Permanence of Paper for Printed Library Materials
Z39.49-1984

For Michael, Carole, and Marie-Alice,
in a league of their own

CONTENTS

ACKNOWLEDGMENTS

Part of the research I report in this book was supported by a grant from the Bank Financial Analysts Association in 1990–91. The grant provided me with that most luxurious of commodities, time—time to think, time to do, time to write. I am grateful to the association and to my colleagues Ingo Walter and Ed Altman for their patience in seeing some of the reputational returns from that investment.

Naturally, I have benefited from the assistance of many people in putting together the ideas presented here. The initial spark for this work came from creative interactions with Mark Shanley, the former Wharton student, now a colleague at Northwestern University, with whom I carried out the first quantitative analyses of *Fortune* magazine's reputational data. I hope we'll get to work together again in the future.

At New York University, Violina Rindova quickly moved from research assistant to able colleague, coauthor, and critic. Her enthusiasm for the material was energizing, and I expect her to extend the study of corporate reputations in valuable ways. Luis Martins has also proved his mettle as a reader and astute commentator here and elsewhere. John Mezias made writing the Salomon chapter easier thanks to his prep work. Maxine Garvey stimulated me to put pen to paper about some of my experiences in the fashion industry and spared me painful legwork by sharing some of her research. Batt Vadlamani's occasional interest in investment banks and law firms periodically stimulated my own. Various other students also helped along the way, including Santosh Kurup and Lawton Harper. Marc Murray was instrumental in getting me to spend time at Goldman Sachs.

The "citizenship" team that Noel Tichy formed in the fall of 1990 got me to think more about the relationship between reputation and "doing good." Special thanks to Charles Kadushin for starting things off and to Laurie Richardson for keeping the project alive.

Finally, a special note of gratitude to the many executives who made time to talk to me about the reputations of their companies and about the work they do. They include Hildy Simmons, Oliver Wesson, and their staffs at J. P. Morgan; Clive Chajet, Connie Birdsall, and Kate Moran at Lippincott & Margulies; Susan Black at the Dilenschneider Group; Jim Taylor and John Berard at Hill & Knowlton; Tom Schick at American Express; Frank Zarb at Smith Barney (Primerica); Herb Allen at Allen & Company; Larry Zicklin at Neuberger & Berman; Jim Butler at Spear, Leeds; Johaness Frey at UBS Securities; and Ed Markie-wicz at Goldman Sachs. Along the way, I gained much from Bryan Thomlison's (Church & Dwight) infectious enthusiasm. Thanks also to Harold Goldberg at Moody's, Ralph Dickerson at the United Way, Meena Pachapakesan at *Financial World*, Nancy Hass at *Newsweek*, and many others who spoke to me without attribution.

I am indebted to all of these colleagues, associates, and friends for insight and inspiration. Sadly, however, I must insist on being the only one whose reputation is in any way tarnished by whatever improper interpretations were made.

REPUTATION

The purest treasure mortal times afford
Is spotless reputation; that away,
Men are but gilded loam or painted clay.

—*William Shakespeare*
   Richard II

Why Reputations Matter

Do YOU recall the last time you hired a contractor to make improvements to your house or apartment? Or the last time you called on a travel agent for assistance in planning a trip? Or those less than happy times when you required the advice of a lawyer, accountant, dentist, or doctor? Think about how you came to choose that particular contractor, travel agent, lawyer, accountant, dentist, or doctor.

If you're like most people, chances are you didn't just pick their names out of a phone book. You probably went to them because they were recommended to you by a family member, friend, or someone else you trust. *If so, you hired them based on their reputation.*

Consider Fischer Travel Enterprise, a small premier travel agency on Manhattan's East Side. Launched by founder Bill Fischer in the early 1970s, the 12-member agency exploits a unique and lucrative niche in the industry: luxury and exotic travel. To support its claim to exclusivity, Fischer Travel never advertises, has an unlisted phone number, and distributes business cards that carry only the agency's name and address—no phone number. Clients come in through personal referrals, and Fischer Travel lays claim to a select clientele of 500 or so "big names" in the worlds of business and entertainment. They include TV journalist Diane Sawyer and her director husband, Mike Nichols; record mogul Quincy Jones and composer Marvin Hamlisch; insurance tycoons Saul Steinberg and Sandy Weill; celebrity bankers Bruce Wasserstein and Joe Perella; fashion designer Donna Karan; basketball legend Magic Johnson; hotelier Jonathan Tisch; society figure Anne Bass; and artist Brice Marden—not to mention numerous scions of the Vanderbilt, Johnson, and Rockefeller fortunes. According to Mr. Fischer, that's because "we've got the reputation that when it's impossible, we make it possible." The agency obviously relies on that reputation to generate business.[1]

Or consider the Connaught Hotel in London, thought by many to be the world's most exclusive. So successful is the Connaught that it never advertises for customers and its managers go out of their way to avoid the press. Why? Because the hotel relies on its reputation for delivering unique and thorough service. As one journalist reports:

> If the Connaught is about nothing else, it is indeed about tradition and a genteel way of life that, in many quarters, has become only a memory. You sense it everywhere—from the size of the hotel (only ninety rooms and twenty four suites) and the conservative dress of the staff (and clientele) to the tranquility of the small lobby and public areas and chef Michel Bourdin's ultraclassic French and English menu, served in the majestic restaurant and cozy Grill Room. Here one finds no footmen in knee breeches, no shops or dazzling display cases, no tinkling piano, no pool or health spa, no minibars, no mints on the pillows, no special weekend rates, nobody milling about in jeans or jogging suits—nothing, in fact, to suggest the larger more commercial hotels where tourists and businessmen have a different set of expectations.[2]

London's Connaught hotel and New York's Fischer Travel are just two of many businesses that rely on their reputations to compete. Companies like them are generally the first to tell you that friends and relatives provide the best kind of advertising for their products and services. In fact, just ask any lawyer, doctor, dentist, chiropractor, accountant, or travel agent: Each one will probably confirm that word-of-mouth referrals are the sine qua nons of success; that a solid reputation is worth its weight in gold.

In private life, most of us regularly solicit recommendations for the people we hire, whether to build our shelves, to organize our vacations, to do our taxes, to treat our illnesses, or to defend us in court. Given a choice between someone who is well regarded and one about whom we know nothing, most of us opt to do business with the more reputable professional. A reputation embodies the history of other peoples' experiences with that service provider. Good reputations increase credibility, making us more confident that we'll really get what we're promised.

I have often observed how much weight a board of directors will put on "reputation" in determining which supplier to pick. Whereas to pick the low bidder was once common practice, now the inclination is to rely on word of mouth and reputation as the basis for selecting a service provider. In part, it's because a supplier's reputation acts as an equalizer. A good reputation substitutes for differences among board members in personal experience with contractors and reduces the ever-present fear of a shareholder suit should things go wrong. In other words, the contractor's reputation acts as a warranty. It signals the likelihood that our dealings with them will be up to snuff—that they will meet our expectations.

In similar ways, managers often rely on the personal reputations of their employees to make personnel decisions. To avoid the subjectivity of a supervisor's evaluations, for instance, some top companies judge an employee's value by culling information from a wide range of informed observers. A case in point is the industrial giant General Electric. The company has become well known for conducting "360-degree appraisals"—investigative reports based on data obtained not only from an employee's supervisors but from subordinates, clients, suppliers, and others who have had contact with the employee. Similarly, prestigious universities regularly poll peers and professionals in rival colleges before granting lifetime tenure to a member of the faculty. In essence, they create reputational profiles of their employees and base crucial promotion and compensation decisions on those profiles.

Marketers and advertisers are well aware that the reputations of individuals can cast a long shadow over the products they want to promote. Some ads rely on explicit endorsements by well-known personalities like basketball's Michael Jordan or tennis's Andre Agassi. Others rely on the implicit endorsements of supermodels like Cindy Crawford, Naomi Campbell, or Christy Turlington. These endorsements cast a halo over products that increases sales. Psychologically, we create a mental bond between the product, the famous face, and the company that justifies higher prices. Often we willingly pay more money for endorsed products because they promise us both quality and status and ease our fears of a negative experience. Which is why Jordan and Agassi earn millions of dollars in endorsements every year. It's also why superstar models are paid upward of $6,000 a day, or more than $1.5 million a year. In economic terms, such a per diem represents the rental value of the model's fame. It means that a model's reputation is roughly equivalent to having about $22 million in the bank on which you earn a 7 percent rate of interest.

The process of building a reputation is obviously central to the marketing of everyday products like soap, cereal, clothing, cars, and cosmetics. Makers of consumer goods, like Unilever or Procter & Gamble, are experts at converting ordinary products into recognizable "brands" through advertising and promotion. By differentiating products, they create what marketers call "brand equity"—a hidden asset for the company that generally goes unrecorded on its balance sheet.[3] Implicitly, then, a company's reputation embodies the hidden wealth in its portfolio of brands.

In fact, reputations are useful earmarks not only for individuals and products but even for the largest companies. Corporate reputations influence the products we choose to buy, the securities in which we invest our savings, and the job offers we accept. In part, it's because fame is an intoxicating lure; it attracts us to those who have achieved it. That's why so many of us readily lay out bigger bucks to eat in French restaurants, to sleep in Marriott's top-of-the-line hotels, to drive a BMW, to wear designer clothes, to carry an American Express Platinum Card, and to live in Paris or New York. A good reputation is a drawing card. It brings in customers and investors; it commands our respect.

Just as we prefer to hire better-regarded professionals, so too do we favor working for better-regarded companies. After all, for equal pay, why work for a company that gets a bad rap for the products it makes, for the plants it operates, or for the way it treats its people? In the health-conscious, environmentally aware, and civic-minded decade of the 1990s, companies heavily involved in the so-called sinful industries (tobacco, liquor, and gaming), in businesses that unduly pollute the environment or that exploit employees and local communities, are increasingly hard-pressed to defend their dubious reputations to investors, creditors, and prospective hires. But occasionally even a "bad" reputation can act to a company's strategic advantage. In a study of the Mafia-controlled garbage industry in New York, for instance, one researcher showed how the investigation and prosecution of racketeers actually helped to strengthen the unsavory reputation of the industry, thereby deterring entry by honest entrepreneurs and increasing the market power and profitability of organized crime.[4] A perverse outcome, to be sure, but one that supports the view of reputation as a source of competitive advantage.

In most competitive situations, of course, the lack of a good reputation can mean lost sales. After all, for similarly priced products, which company would you choose to buy from: company X or the better-regarded company Y? Surely your choice would be Y. That's why there's not a computer hacker in sight who isn't slightly apprehensive of ordering a computer clone from a little-known company rather than one from a well-regarded company like IBM, Apple, Compaq, Dell, Hewlett-Packard, or Sun Microsystems. Who knows how good the unknown company's product is? Can we trust its warranty claims? Will the company be around if something goes wrong with the machine? These are natural concerns that drive us to favor branded products. The well-known companies that make them have built up a reservoir of credibility and reliability that we trust.

But a reputation is not indestructible. In truth, even among computer companies, few of us could deny not having become slightly suspicious of IBM's computer products after the public knocks the company took for falling behind the times in the late 1980s. You'd better offer large discounts, many buyers told IBM, if you want us to buy your products. Not surprisingly, the large volume of bad press meant not only a downturn in the company's reputation and sales but a nosedive for its stock—one measure of its reputational capital. In 1992 alone, IBM's market value dropped by more than 50 percent.

The point is this: A reputation is valuable because it informs us about what products to buy, what companies to work for, or what stocks to invest in. At the same time, a reputation is of considerable strategic value because it calls attention to a company's attractive features and widens the options available to its managers, for instance, whether to charge higher or lower prices for products and services or to implement innovative programs.

BUILDING REPUTATION

Long ignored, intangible assets are now gaining increased notice. In the last few years, those of us who study corporate strategies have begun to recognize that intangible assets may well provide companies with a more enduring source of competitive advantage than even patents and technologies; the venerable names of companies like 3M, Procter & Gamble, McKinsey & Company, and Johnson & Johnson are, quite literally, as good as gold.

Although many managers today are willing to admit that intangible assets like reputations do have value, most still demonstrate inconsistent attention to the practices necessary to sustain corporate reputations. In this book, I demonstrate how great the economic returns to reputation really are. I also show that in companies where reputation is valued, managers take great pains to build, sustain, and defend that reputation by following practices that (1) shape a unique identity and (2) project a coherent and consistent set of images to the public. Examples of these practices include:

- designing advertising campaigns that promote the company as a whole, not just its products and brands.
- carrying out ambitious programs that champion product quality and customer service with an eye to keeping consumers happy.
- maintaining control systems that carefully screen employee activities for their possible reputational side effects.
- demonstrating sensitivity to the environment, not only because it's socially responsible but because actions that safeguard the environment also dovetail with marketing programs to generate sales.
- hiring internal staff and retaining specialized public relations agencies to safeguard communications through the media.
- demonstrating "corporate citizenship" through philanthropy, pro bono activities, and community involvement.

These efforts are "enlightened" investments. They reflect a commitment to long-term reputation building as well as short-term self-interest. They create economic value because they reinforce a company's competitive position and improve its long-run chances of achieving and maintaining success.

The proliferation of such subjective rankings as "best managed," "most innovative," and "most admired" attests to the growing popularity of reputation as a tool for assessing companies. Every year since 1983, for instance, the widely read business magazine *Fortune* has published a survey of analysts and managers that ranks the top 10 firms in each of 32 industries on various dimensions. The annual issue describing the most admired companies in the United States is consistently a best-seller. It indicates the widespread, almost voyeuristic interest that we take in such corporate pageants and horse races. Operating as most of us do in a cloud of uncertainty about what the "true" performance of a company is, we find ourselves eagerly drawn to these summary appraisals. The rankings crystallize for us on the outside what everybody else thinks about the "net" performance of the company. As *Fortune* writer Rahul Jacob notes, "There's a neat circular logic at work here: CEOs value reputation because it defines a company and motivates its people."[5] In turn, it creates a yardstick that makes CEOs like Jamie Houghton of Corning claim that winning a place among the top 10 companies in *Fortune*'s survey is one of the company's goals.

Questions of reputation are of particular concern to knowledge-based institutions like consulting firms, law firms, investment banks, hospitals, and universities; their most valuable assets—the services they provide—are largely intangible. Economists call the services of these groups "credence goods"—goods that are bought on faith, that is to say, on reputation. In the late 1980s, growing rivalry and declining economic conditions forced service groups to compete for clients. They began to recognize that they relied on their reputations to attract customers and market their services; that their reputations were a significant form of capital that went unrecorded on their balance sheets. In the last few years, professional service firms have come to see exploiting, sustaining, and defending reputation as more vital strategic concerns.

A case in point is the scrambling for position now under way at graduate schools of business in the United States. For years, an accepted ranking distinguished business schools based in the older Ivy League universities from those in lesser schools. In the late 1980s, however, demographics hit hard. Increased rivalry for a declining population of students heightened interest in what those business degrees were really worth. When *Business Week* published its first ranking of business schools in November 1988, the issue was an instant best-seller. As chapter 10 shows, these rankings created unprecedented turmoil in the country's leading business schools.

In part, business schools were caught by surprise because prior ratings had gauged schools' relative performance primarily from assessments made by deans—truth be told, not an unbiased group. Instead, *Business Week* offered a ranking of schools based on surveys of former students and recruiters, two constituencies whose opinions had never before been solicited systematically. For the first time, schools could be ranked on client perceptions, that is, on reputation. The scores proved influential. They had a marked effect on the number of applications received by schools in the following year, and so lit a fire under previously complacent faculties and administrators. In turn, savvy business school deans slowly turned their attention to the underlying factors that build, sustain, and defend reputation. Concerned schools like the University of Chicago, University of Maryland, and New York University actually hired public relations firms to help them strategize.

In recent years, many prominent companies also found their reputations sullied, and so called attention to the importance of protecting and defending reputational capital. Consider the icon of modern business, IBM, a company with a computer franchise that once seemed impregnable and management pratices that appeared beyond reproach. For much of this century, IBM consistently ranked among the best-managed companies in the world, a place employees were enormously proud to work. In the late 1980s, however, much changed: The reputation of the company affectionately known as "Big Blue" took a nosedive; in *Fortune*'s survey of America's most admired companies, IBM fell from number 1 in 1986 to number 7 in 1987 to 32 in 1988. By 1994, IBM was ranked a pedestrian 354 in the magazine's annual survey, and connection to the company had become a source more of embarrassment than pride to customers, suppliers, and employees as the press repeatedly detailed the company's mishaps.

Or look closely at auto behemoth General Motors, a company with a far-flung empire that once seemed invulnerable; or even retail king Sears Roebuck, with a stranglehold on the American shopper that once seemed unbreakable. In 1972, all three companies—IBM, GM, and Sears—had sterling reputations and were among the world's six most valuable companies. Twenty years later, the three of them were ranked a lowly 206, 268, and 300, respectively, in *Fortune*'s survey of corporate reputations. The decline of these once heroic companies suggests how important it is for managers to learn not only how to sustain competitiveness through strategic positioning but also how to preserve reputational capital.

Various accidents and scandals have also helped to magnify the hidden value of a company's reputation and called attention to its defense. One example is investment banker Salomon Brothers. In 1991, Salomon was struck by a scandal that threatened the bank's hard-won franchise in trading government bonds—and, indeed, its very existence. It took considerable savvy on the part of Salomon's board of directors to shore up the bank's reputation with regulators, clients, and employees. Exactly how the bank's adroit strategy of self-defense ultimately preserved its reputational capital is described in chapter 15. If top executives are to sustain their companies' intangible wealth, they will have to master just such judo-like skills.

FROM FAME TO FORTUNE

Reputation: Realizing Value from the Corporate Image examines how managers and companies compete—not only for market share through classic strategic positioning but also for the esteem of their key constituents—for reputation. To achieve prestige requires a long-term outlook toward building competitive advantage. Companies develop winning reputations by both creating and projecting a set of skills that their constituents recognize as unique. For some companies, that means differentiating themselves through *innovation*—nurturing good ideas, translating them into products, and marketing them well. In other companies, uniqueness comes from developing *operational excellence*—a low-cost position with excellent distribution systems—or *closeness to the customer*—distinct strength in servicing customers and solving problems.[6] Whatever form differentiation takes, achieving uniqueness requires routine actions that demonstrate credibility and earn the trust of key constituents.

This book shows that better-regarded companies build their reputations by developing practices that integrate economic and social considerations into their competitive strategies. They not only do things right—they do the right things. In so doing, they act like good citizens. They initiate policies that reflect their core values; that consider the joint welfare of investors, customers, and employees; that invoke concern for the development of local communities; and that ensure the quality and environmental soundness of their technologies, products, and services.

Reputation confers clear-cut advantages and privileges on companies. We trust those companies that we respect, so we grant them the benefit of the doubt in ambiguous situations. Often we willingly pay handsomely for their products, believing those products are more likely to fulfill our expectations than the products of lesser-known companies. A good reputation builds a competitive advantage against rivals. It proves difficult to imitate, and it limits what rivals can do. Which makes *Reputation* a book about why companies come to be highly regarded, about the factors that build favorable word of mouth about a company, its products, and its practices.

At the same time, reputations create responsibilities. The raised expectations of a company's many audiences constrain the actions of its managers. To be held in high esteem creates obligations that managers and companies must live up to, whether in meeting the personal standards of employees, the quality standards of customers, the ethical standards of the community, or the profitability standards of investors. Companies that become well regarded sustain their reputations by building strong and supportive relationships with all of their constituents.

Most important, this book makes clear that every company has a greater or lesser amount of *reputational capital*. A company's reputation is a fragile, intangible asset that we must learn to exploit at least as well as we do the more tangible assets of financial capital or plant and equipment. Indeed, learning to actively manage reputational capital— and the human and intellectual assets it encompasses—may be the most crucial and strategic task that our executives face as they struggle to compete in today's increasingly competitive, information-rich business environment.

A focus on corporate reputation stimulates us to rethink the traditional fragmentation of activities that now separates line from staff in most companies, be it advertising from marketing or public relations from specialists in community relations, investor relations, and government relations. To "manage" reputation is to insist on building closer ties between staff groups and to exploit the latent commonalities of interest that they share. After all, a common thread links these segmented functions: a core commitment to capitalize on a company's hidden store of reputational capital.

MANAGING REPUTATION: A FRAMEWORK

This book is divided into two parts. The first part explains how companies compete for reputation. Much like athletes in Olympic competition, their success rests on their ability to develop and project a unique set of skills—a unique *identity*. A company's name is one component of its identity. It conveys to us the company's most distinctive traits and influences our behavior. When a company serves its constituents well, its name becomes a valuable asset. It creates *reputational capital*—a form of intangible wealth that is closely related to what accountants call "goodwill" and marketers term "brand equity." A company with a large stock of reputational capital actually gains a competitive advantage against rivals because its reputation enables it to charge premium prices for its products, to achieve lower marketing costs, and to benefit from greater freedom in decision making. In other words, reputation building is a form of "enlightened self-interest."

At heart, a company's reputation therefore derives from its identity. It can be traced to managerial practices that make a company a good workplace for its employees, a good provider of products and services for its customers, a good investment for its shareholders, and a good citizen in its local communities. Because traits like these build reputational capital, they give a company the Midas touch. At number 3 in *Fortune*'s 1995 survey of corporate reputations, Coca-Cola is among the few companies to have developed the Midas touch. Coca-Cola's top man, Roberto Goizueta, recognizes the link between identity and reputation: "A CEO is ultimately responsible for the growth of a company as evidenced by its financial performance, its capacity for self-renewal, and its character. The only way you can measure character is by reputation."[7]

But reputations also develop as companies try to build up favorable images of themselves. It's obvious, for instance, that managers regularly manipulate their presentations to reporters and financial analysts—they put a spin on things. They also try to control the propagation of rumors and inuendo that invariably takes place throughout the business community. Reputations are therefore partly a reflection of a company's identity, partly a result of managers' efforts to persuade us of their excellence.

When managers do a good job of safeguarding the reputations of their companies, their efforts can often pay off with prizes and awards. Favorable ranking in reputational surveys like *Fortune*'s is one tool companies rely on to confirm their status. Such a ranking creates intangible barriers to competition that lesser rivals find difficult to overcome.

The first part of the book concludes with a chapter describing the "reputational audit"—a systematic process designed to help managers identify, assess, and exploit their reputational capital. The audit is a powerful tool that can help a company to confront its reputational strengths and weaknesses, to unify its diverse images, and to more closely relate its identity to its reputation. The last chapter in part 1 also emphasizes the importance of a strong executive role in managing reputation, and makes recommendations as to how companies can better capitalize on their intangible assets. Particularly critical to building, sustaining, and defending a company's reputation, I suggest here, is a closer coordination of traditional fiefdoms: employee relations, public relations, customer relations, investor relations, and media relations. Because most companies have historically allowed these functions to be ruled by separate chieftains, linking them is no simple task.

The second part of the book discusses how reputations are actually managed in practice, exploring how companies try to fuse their multiple images in ways that build reputational capital. Six case studies detail how a mix of companies and industries actually build, sustain, and/or defend their reputations through a variety of identity-shaping and image-making practices.

One case study looks at the fashion industry, a world that brings together a large number of companies, each of which is heavily concerned with reputation. We'll closely examine the persistent efforts of these enterprises to build and maintain prestige, the fountain of wealth that strong reputations bring to exclusive designer labels.

A second case study focuses on the reputation-building efforts of U.S. business schools. As just mentioned, declining enrollments and increased competitive pressure have forced leading MBA academies to recognize that their success depends heavily on how well alumni and recruiters perceive and rate them. In the 1990s, we find business schools actively strategizing to enhance their reputations. Most of them are hard at work reinventing themselves, placing greater emphasis on teaching and on outreach activities to strengthen the esteem with which students and employers regard their alma maters.

Wherever money is to be made, consultants appear, and reputation building is no exception. We therefore examine at length the segment of the consulting industry that calls attention to *corporate identity*—a key element in the construction of favorable corporate images. In particular, we discuss the operations of Lippincott & Margulies—the original consultancy that has helped to shape the identities of many of our largest companies.

Turning to consumer goods, where reputation is at the heart of creating successful brands, I focus on Church & Dwight. In recent years, the well-known maker of Arm & Hammer products has taken great strides to exploit its famous brand name and build a reputation as an environmentally friendly producer, despite the aggressive tactics of its far larger rivals Procter & Gamble and Unilever. Church & Dwight's success in this uphill battle testifies to the marketing benefits that can derive from actively managing reputation.

Much as fashion businesses, business schools, and consumer goods companies are hard at work building reputations for their institutions, so too are professional groups. Their performance depends heavily on their clients' *perceptions* of their services. The final chapters of the book examine investment banking, a knowledge-based industry with features common to many other professional services. Investment banks are particularly interesting because their core activities expose them not only to high levels of credit and capital risk but also to extraordinary *reputational risks* that threaten their very existence. I therefore examine how top bankers conceive, monitor, and control the reputational risks to which they are open on a daily basis. Later, I also show how a large bank like J. P. Morgan participates in a portfolio of external practices that help to broaden its visibility in New York City. In addition to its philanthropic gifts, a program of active support for nonprofit groups involves employees of the highly regarded bank in volunteer activities that project Morgan's polished image out to its constituents and help the bank sustain its reputation. The second part of the book ends with a detailed analysis of the scandal that plagued prominent banker Salomon Brothers in 1991. Salomon's example provides a valuable lesson in the defensive art of corporate judo.

Ultimately, fame places its own constraints on those firms that achieve it. In 1994, Intel, the highly regarded maker of silicon chips, experienced these constraints firsthand when a design flaw was uncovered in its top product, the Pentium processor. Intel's managers responded to the crisis with typical engineering arrogance; they initially denied that a flaw existed and, when confronted with mounting criticism, minimized its significance to the average user. They thereby failed to recognize the reputational damage that the *perceived* flaw in the chip was inflicting on the company. Not only did the debacle cost the company money in lost sales, but it temporarily eroded valuable reputational capital. The market value of the company fell by close to 15 percent. I therefore conclude the book with a closer look at the burden that being well regarded imposes on companies and their managers.

THE HIDDEN VALUE OF A GOOD REPUTATION

If one's reputation is a possession, then of all my possessions, my reputation means most to me. . . . I can no more easily renounce my concern with what other people think of me than I can will myself to stop breathing.

—*Arthur Ashe*
  Days of Grace

As
Good
as
Gold

OURS IS an age that celebrates greatness. We value aptitude, worship talent, exalt brilliance, and revere genius. We bask in the reflected radiance of our idols, and for that we gladly confer on them not only transient fame but lasting fortune. Those few people lucky enough to earn such acclaim, be they musicians, artists, writers, athletes, or actors, we endow with inordinate status—stardom and superstardom. Not content that they should merely display their talents, we often assign to them near mythical, demigod status and expect perfection in return.

So it is with our best companies. As producers of the products we consume, as investors of our capital, as employers of our labor, large companies have become the modern icons of our mass society. Not only do we dance to the tune of their decisions, but we increasingly worship at the high altar of their fame.

The pivotal role such companies play in the economy has raised their public profile to levels ordinarily reserved for movie stars. Everywhere we look, whether on billboards, on television, on T-shirts, or on food cartons, we are bombarded with their logos, their jingles, their ads. So much so that we recognize many of them by convenient shorthands, acronyms like IBM, GE, AT&T, GM, and J&J. They are as familiar to us as members of our own families.

In turn, heightened visibility has made a company's every move increasingly subject to the scrutiny of a demanding audience. More than ever before, they are in the limelight. Like the traveling artists, troubadours, and musicians of earlier times, modern-day companies perform for the attention and support of patrons. They compete not only for the approval of consumers but also for that of investors, suppliers, distributors, politicians, and local communities.

In our time, competition for reputation operates as never before. The rise of a mass market for information has made possible ever greater levels of prestige and wealth for the exceptional artist, the exceptional athlete, and the exceptional company. For the individual, perhaps nowhere are the wealth-generating effects of reputation more apparent than in athletic competition, and nowhere more so than at the Olympics.

In 776 B.C., the Greeks held the first Olympic Games. Hordes of spectators converged on the city of Olympia from every part of Greece, Asia, and Africa. Athletes came to compete in five sports: running, leaping, wrestling, javelin throwing, and boxing. Poets, musicians, and playwrights also took advantage of the games to present their productions to a public hungry for entertainment. Following the games, the fame of victorious athletes and favored artists spread far and wide. The tradition continues. Today athletes from around the world gather every four years amid much fanfare for all-out competition. When the dust settles, three Olympians are left standing in each sport. For this achievement, each gets a medal: gold for the winner, silver for the runner-up, and bronze for third place.

As in the games of ancient Greece, contemporary Olympians receive no monetary awards. To receive a medal, however, is to take home a far more valuable, albeit intangible, asset—a reputation. Once established, a reputation brings publicity, and that's one thing all shrewd marketers know how to convert to cash, and lots of it. Indeed, when fame comes calling, fortune is seldom far behind. Today an Olympic gold medal can be worth many millions of dollars in licensing and commercial fees. And the Olympic motto—*Cittius, Altius, Fortius,* or faster, higher, stronger—although intended for athletes, could just as well describe the flow of money that swirls around them.

Ask speed skater Dan Jansen. Having faltered in two previous Olympic tries, his heartwarming gold medal win at the 1994 winter Olympics was expected to bring him more than $2 million in endorsement deals. Or speak to figure skater Nancy Kerrigan. After receiving a blow to the knee in early 1994 in an attack that turned out to have been masterminded by the camp of rival skater Tonya Harding, Kerrigan's earning power grew dramatically. Win or lose, Kerrigan's highly publicized plight virtually guaranteed that she would obtain lucrative endorsement deals with prominent corporate sponsors like Walt Disney and Revlon. After her silver-medal finish, market hounds estimated that the publicity surrounding her ordeal would bring her upward of $10 million.[1]

Much as athletic competition crowns champions and builds wealth, so too do fame and fortune accrue to companies skillful at winning in the highly contested terrain of business. After all, in the twentieth century's market economies, business is probably the biggest sport of all. Companies try to outdo rivals on a daily basis by being the first to market new products, to hire the best job candidates, to win customers, and to show profitability. As in competitive sports, the losers in the economic arena far outnumber the winners, and the corporate landscape is littered with the remains of those outdone in the epic struggle for market share and profitability.

Consider CBS, the network that broadcast the 1994 winter Olympics. In 1993, the network's reputation was severely bruised by defecting shows, loss of its football franchise to archrival ABC, and lackluster programming. Many critics claimed that CBS had overbid for the right to broadcast the Olympics. The critics were proved wrong. In January 1994, the Kerrigan-Harding figure-skating saga drew such large audiences that the ratings helped to reinvigorate CBS's sagging fortunes and repair its reputation. Indeed, in the aftermath of Olympic coverage, many CBS shows gained market share—and the trend held: In March 1994, the *CBS Evening News*, for one, took away the top spot in the ratings from ABC's newscast for the first time in 76 weeks—a side benefit the company attributed directly to the Olympic broadcast. Unfortunately the advantage was short-lived; lacking strong programming, CBS soon deteriorated in the ratings.

The battle to make and market products and services confers on winning companies—as it does on Olympians—a heady dose of fame. Partly because of their products, partly because of their practices, we come to regard winners as being somehow "better" than others. These are the companies we come to know best. They are frequently cited in surveys of the best companies in America to work for: Campbell Soup, Eastman Kodak, H. J. Heinz, Procter & Gamble, Sara Lee, Wal-Mart, Xerox—these names are recognizable across America and even around the world. These companies exhibit their reputations much as gladiators once displayed their laurels. In logos, ads, jingles, labels, and commercials, they proclaim their hard-earned record of victories in the economic arena.

Who among us could fail to associate the Walt Disney Company with Mickey Mouse, family movies, and theme parks? Or the American Express Company with its prestigious credit card? Or Avon with the home selling of women's cosmetics? Over the years, each of these companies has developed a distinct reputation, one that crystallizes for us the essence of what the company does and what it stands for. We probably would be surprised and profoundly shocked were Disney to suddenly produce X-rated films, American Express to buy a discount retailer, or Avon to make farm equipment. And such initiatives would likely fail. In fact, Avon tried its hand at prestige retailing in 1979 by purchasing Manhattan's famed Tiffany store, only to resell it five years later at a loss. American Express tried its hand at broad-based financial services with the purchase of investment bankers Lehman Brothers and brokers E. F. Hutton and Shearson, only to find itself extended into ventures worlds apart from its traditional business. In part, both Avon and American Express failed in their diversification efforts not only because they entered businesses they did not know how to manage but because those businesses projected images incompatible with their established reputations. Managers, customers, employees, and investors were never able to bridge the reputational gap.

LET THE GAMES BEGIN

We generally describe companies in mundane terms—as rivals struggling to improve their market shares and profitability levels. In fact, companies are actually engaged in mortal combat for the respect and trust of consumers, investors, employees, and the public at large. Respect and trust build reputation, and that's what creates a competitive advantage. By attracting investors to a company's securities, customers to its products, and employees to its jobs, a favorable reputation improves a company's profitability and enhances its chances of surviving the competitive fray.

Where then do corporate reputations come from? Why do some companies regularly capture the gold in corporate olympiads? What kinds of management practices produce first-rate corporate reputations? And how do highly regarded companies like Merck, Coca-Cola, and Walt Disney manage not only to scale Olympic heights but to stay on top?

Before we look at companies, it may be instructive to look at individuals. Similar questions are often asked of them. What brings some athletes a gold medal while others struggle in vain to make a mark? How do some writers and their publishers come to win a Pulitzer Prize while others get only passing mention? Why do so few painters, sculptors, or musicians achieve reknown while most toil in near total obscurity? And what earns one person a Nobel prize, an Oscar, a Tony, or a Grammy while other hopefuls are overlooked?

Most of us adhere to an individualistic view of success. Whether speaking of athletes, artists, performers, writers, political leaders, or scientists, we like to ascribe their success to a God-given talent or "natural gift." Since we can't change what we're born with, this view absolves most of us of any real responsibility for failing to achieve greatness. You are what you are; don't try to become what you are not. Great leaders, we seem to think, whether Olympians or Nobelists, are born, not made.

To hold an individualistic view, however, is to ignore the social world that helps some people to succeed and thereby gain reputation. It disregards the contributions to success that a collectivity of constituents—peers, patrons, and audience—makes to a work or a performance, and so to the reputation of the artist, the actor, or the athlete. As one observer of the world of art put it:

> The artist . . . works in the center of a network of cooperating people, all of whose work is essential to the final outcomes. . . . Works of art, from this point of view, are not the products of individual makers, "artists" who possess a rare and special gift. They are, rather, joint products of all the people who cooperate via an art world's characteristic conventions to bring works like that into existence. . . . All these participants in art worlds produce the circumstances in which artists define the problems they work on and find the solutions, embodied in works, which contribute, for good or bad, to their reputations.[2]

Or take Olympic athletes. Consistent with an individualistic bias, most people marvel at the athletic prowess of medal contenders and ascribe to medalists a combination of innate ability and hard work. We assume that star contestants outperform everybody else because they're endowed with that elusive something we call "talent." While talent is critical, it's not everything. Detailed studies of Olympians show that they are unique not in what they *are* but in what they *do*.[3] For one, they compete in a world different from that of the run-of-the-mill athlete. For another, they develop a style and technique that is uniquely theirs.

Watch Olympic swimmers at close range, doing, say, the breaststroke. Ordinary athletes generally pull their arms back too far beneath the body, kick their legs out too wide without bringing them together at the finish, and lift themselves too high out of the water. They fail to take a long pull underwater after turning, and often touch the edge of the pool at the finish with only one hand. In contrast, Olympic swimmers scull their arms out to the side and sweep back in (never actually pulling back), kick narrowly with their feet finishing together, stay low on the turns, take a long underwater pull after the turn, and always touch at the finish with both hands. As one observer puts it: "Not only are the strokes different, they are so different that the 'C' swimmer may be amazed to see how the 'AAAA' swimmer looks when swimming. The appearance alone is dramatically different, as is the speed with which they swim."[4] It's true of champion downhill skiers, speed skaters, tennis players, and figure skaters as well. Their competitive success derives from having developed unique, qualitatively different combinations of style and technique.

Just as "C" athletes differ in style and technique from "AAAA" athletes, so do individual Olympians competing in the same sport. Faced with the same downhill course, tennis court, or skating rink, champions take dramatically different approaches to performance. Which helps explain our fascination with these competitive events. Winners achieve their lofty levels of excellence through widely differing original means. And winners and losers are separated by negligible differences, a few points here and there in tennis, basketball, or baseball, hundredths of a second in speed sports, and hundredths of a rating point in judged sports like gymnastics or figure skating.

To achieve Olympic success also requires absorbing the points of view, strategies, and lifestyles of top rivals. Listen to top athletes and performers. They invariably compare themselves with their chief competitors. When asked to recollect the factors that spurred them to achieve, they allude to a great rivalry. In professional tennis, for instance, longtime champion Chris Evert invariably speaks of her career-long jousts with Martina Navratilova; John McEnroe recalls how his tense struggles with Bjorn Borg and Jimmy Connors forced him to new heights; Pete Sampras and Andre Agassi fuel each other's success. In basketball, the decade-long rivalry between Magic Johnson and Larry Bird spurred these players to greater feats on the court. Similar contests are the stuff of lore in baseball and football; they make for vivid theatricality in the volatile world of professional sports. Top guns in every field compare themselves with the very best and then continue at great effort to *distinguish* themselves from their chief rivals. In corporate-speak, they *benchmark* their activities against their toughest peers.[5]

Moreover, what seems extraordinary to us about Olympic athletes turns out to be quite mundane to them. That's because Olympians demonstrate excellence by doing systematically a host of quite ordinary things. For instance, if Olympic swimmers swim faster than everyone else, that's because they've mastered the flip turn, they know how to streamline their push-off by squeezing their arms together over their heads, and they know how to place their hands in the water so no air is cupped in them. They also know how to lift weights to properly build strength, what are the right foods to eat, and what are the best suits to wear in a race. And on and on. Each of these bits of knowledge, small in itself, allows the athlete to do things just a little bit better, a little bit faster, a little bit longer. Having learned and consistently practiced all of them together, that athlete becomes top-notch and gets to compete at the Olympic Games. Winning a medal involves the synthesis of a countless number of little things, each one done very well indeed.[6]

In short, fame—like a sterling reputation—is hard-earned. It derives from developing a unique style; from comparing oneself with "the best" in a particular field of endeavor; from sustaining ingrained habits that consistently produce high-quality performances. Few can put it together "just right," which is why there are so few stars, so many unknown hopefuls.[7]

As in athletic competition, so it is in business. Our best-regarded companies rise above the rest in prestige, status, and fame because they prize, pursue, and achieve *uniqueness*.[8] They do so by developing management practices that reinforce their uniqueness and foster consistent images of the company as credible, reliable, responsive, and trustworthy. Insofar as those images are benchmarked against top peers, communicated persuasively to a company's constituents, perceived by those constituents to cohere, and maintained over time, they enhance the company's reputation and build competitive advantage.

Reputations are therefore both products and by-products of competition. They rest on the foundation of a company's uniqueness—its ability to chart a course that separates it from the pack. The best-regarded companies love to proclaim their uniqueness. They actively rate themselves against a prominent peer group of rivals. They also practice assiduously some relatively mundane routines that help their products and services stand out, even in crowded and competitive industries.

CREATING UNIQUENESS

The Morgan Motor Company is the world's oldest privately owned car maker. Since its founding in 1909, the British company has built open-topped sports cars with a vintage 1930s look on hand-built frames made of 100-year-old ash. Every year, the company's 130 employees put out just 480 cars, half of which are sold abroad. Every Morgan is unique and reflects a particular customer's personal choices from among 35,000 body colors, with matching leather upholstery, and from options on such things as door handles and hood straps. Despite customization, the company's flagship Plus Eight model sells for a relatively affordable £26,000 (under $30,000) and is known to hold its value well.[9]

The company's reputation derives from its unique product. In turn, the product's uniqueness calls for management practices that stress product quality and customer service. One such practice is Morgan Motor's standing invitation to customers to visit the factory and watch their car being made, a process that can take up to seven weeks. Recognizing the motivational benefits of pride in and ownership of one's work, the Morgan Motor factory eschews specialization and delegates responsibility to individual workers for large parts of each car; the wooden frame is assembled entirely by one person, while the body is fully paneled by another. The reputational effects are crystal clear. Demand far outstrips supply, and there's a six-year waiting list of buyers. Pretax profits for 1992 were close to £1 million on sales of £7.8 million. Obviously, Morgan Motor's uniqueness serves it well.

In similar ways to Morgan Motor, the reputations of large companies like Eastman Kodak in photography, Xerox in photocopying, Wal-Mart in retail, Coca-Cola in soft drinks, and Boeing in aircraft also derive from their success in developing, producing, and marketing a unique product or service that suits many consumers. Of the 50 largest companies in the United States, for instance, more than half are easily identified with the products they originated. Their reputations are product based, and their celebrity rests on a distinctive innovation, frequently traceable to a single founder: Henry Ford at Ford Motor Company, Thomas Edison at General Electric, Edwin Land at Polaroid.

If a reputation delineates the uniqueness of a company to outside observers, it also personifies the singular identity of the company to its employees. Strong founders imprint their companies with their personal characteristics. Over time, founders force their companies to adopt distinctive practices that make each look different from the other. For many years, IBM's formality in dress, control of office decor and architecture, work manner, and ceremonial style stood in stark contrast to Apple's laid-back street smarts and informality. Each company is uniquely itself, and its evolving identity has reinforced its external image. Which is why IBM's announcement in February 1995 came as such a surprise: To convey an image of competitiveness with Apple, IBM decided to abandon its dress code of white shirts and dark suits in favor of a more informal, casual look.

Uniqueness is also key to reputation building and competitive advantage among professional service firms. Investment banker Salomon Brothers, for instance, is a company that has carved its reputation in its trading franchise, which it maintains through a plethora of corporate practices that fuel individual competitiveness. In contrast, the mystique of banking's premier firm Goldman Sachs is built around a core set of values that emphasize customer service, team-based interactions, and a strong culture of checks and balances.

Likewise, McKinsey & Company stands out from the field of management consultants. It commands a pristine reputation for delivering expert advice to senior executives from a host of *Business Week*'s Global 1000 firms. To do so, the firm tries hard to recruit the best. It's populated by talented people with big salaries and even bigger egos. With 62 offices in 31 countries, the 3,000-member firm's reputation rests on its ability to bring unparalleled analytic power to bear on a client's problems. That reputation is reinforced by a set of image-making practices that sustain the McKinsey "mystique" in the business schools where the company recruits (principally Harvard) and in the press (which it avoids).

Or consider law firms. Many people think that all law firms look alike. As it turns out, they don't. A group of former Harvard law students interviewed lawyers working in their first jobs as junior associates around the country and compiled profiles of leading law practices. Their book, *The Insider's Guide to Law Firms,* presents a dramatically different account of law firms as extraordinarily diverse in character and reputation.[10] Some are depicted as starchy and traditional, others more relaxed and friendly; some highly conservative, others downright radical.

To what, then, do these law firms ascribe their reputations? In 1989, attorney Erwin Cherovsky pointed out that "one should never confuse the outward similarities of firms with their inner reality which, in fact, determines their culture, reputation, and destiny."[11] He later wrote in his *Guide to New York Law Firms* that "anyone who truly knows these firms—their personnel, tradition, governance, expertise, and clients— appreciates that they are in key respects very different institutions from the ways in which they have been portrayed."[12]

In periodic surveys sponsored by the *American Lawyer,* junior lawyers regularly describe their law firms on various dimensions. A few years ago, I studied their responses and found that young attorneys make a twofold distinction: one between law practices where reputations are built on a unique competence in more or less specialized areas of corporate law; another between law firms where enduring character is regarded as more or less work driven or collegial. The law practice of Wachtell, Lipton, Rosen & Katz is a case in point. The Park Avenue firm is well known for its profitability. During the merger boom of the 1980s, the firm built a reputation as a skilled specialist with strong technical expertise in the design of innovative instruments to finance takeovers. In doing so, it also developed a reputation for maintaining an internal climate where only the smartest, fittest, workaholic associates could survive. Bill Starbuck, a professor at NYU, explored the factors that made Wachtell so successful and concluded—like Cherovsky and the junior lawyers surveyed in *The Insider's Guide to Law Firms*—that the firm owes much of its reputation to its idiosyncratic character:

Wachtell's extraordinary success derives from its individuality. Not only does [it] differ in important ways from all organizations, it differs in important ways from the mass of law firms and . . . from other highly successful law firms. Wachtell is quite distinctive, and other law firms have not imitated its distinctive properties. . . . Wachtell's success with M&A cases arose partly from its ability to innovate, partly from its use of team-

work, partly from its willingness to practice law 168 hours a week, partly from its self-confidence, and partly from the personalities and abilities of its founders.[13]

In short, Wachtell's homegrown characteristics have made it unique, and the firm's uniqueness is the heart and soul of its hardy reputation. These comments reinforce the point that in law firms and consulting firms—as in all companies—uniqueness is a prized commodity that builds reputation.

BENCHMARKING THE BEST

Being unique, credible, and consistent breeds imitators and spurs competition. That's why most managers of well-regarded companies are quite self-conscious about how they are seen on the outside—especially by customers and investors—and rightly so. Like athletes, they too gauge their results against other Olympian companies. In his 1990 book *New and Improved,* Harvard historian Richard Tedlow recounts how the evolution of business in this century involved dynamic rivalries between a handful of players: for soft-drink maker Coca-Cola, the rival was Pepsi; for Ford, it was General Motors; for Sears, it was Montgomery Ward. Managers made comparisons between them to justify not only strategic investments but also decisions about advertising budgets, charitable contributions, bonuses, and other resources that could improve a company's public image. Each benchmarked the other in its struggle to gain prestige or to retain parity.[14]

Benchmarking has become popular in recent years as a powerful tool for encouraging change. It helps companies imitate good management practices as well as build valuable reputational capital. Comparisons with rivals explain how deeply managers commit their companies to investments in plant and equipment or to research and development. Anyone who has ever received multiple job offers can testify to the comparability of their pay packages; companies generally tie their offers to those of their principal rivals. Managers also do it in new product development, in facilities planning, in manufacturing, and in philanthropic initiatives. Take highly regarded banker J. P. Morgan, a company we examine more closely in chapter 14. In deciding how much to contribute to charitable causes, bank officers could look to a wide range of financial institutions that includes brokers like Merrill Lynch or investment bankers like Goldman Sachs. As J. P. Morgan's head of community relations suggests, however, the bank's donations are typically benchmarked against the efforts of Bankers Trust, a rival that Morgan more closely resembles as it diversifies into investment-banking services.

Whenever a company becomes known for being "good" at something, it becomes an especially attractive target for imitators. Take companies best known for the quality of their products—say Xerox in photocopiers, Caterpillar in farm equipment, Home Depot in home improvement, the Marriott Corporation in hotel services. Rivals benchmark their activities against these high-fliers by (a) observing their administrative practices; (b) identifying the kinds of relationships they maintain with employees, suppliers, distributors, and the business media; and (c) imitating their best practices. Imitation fuels an ever-tightening spiral of competitive rivalry as companies vie for attention, that is, as they compete for reputation.

In recent years, various popular prizes and awards have provided managers with even more visible symbols to target—benchmarks to rate themselves against. The Malcolm Baldrige National Quality Award, for instance, provides one of the more prominent reference points for assessing the internal quality of a company's management programs. Although participation is costly, competition for such awards is intense; the payoff for the winner is enormous publicity. Companies benefit from ensuing gains in reputation, as attested by past winners Motorola, Xerox, and GM. Awards bring visibility to outstanding companies and encourage managers to benchmark their companies against better-regarded rivals, fostering an upward spiral of achievement.[15]

A reputation develops from a company's uniqueness and from identity-shaping practices—maintained over time—that lead constituents to perceive the company as credible, reliable, trustworthy, and responsible. In turn, a company's established reputation helps to protect it from rivals trying hard to imitate its practices. Reputation builds strategic value for a company by granting it a competitive advantage that rivals have trouble overcoming. To achieve that advantage, however, a company must develop appropriate practices, or character traits, as it were, that rivals find difficult to imitate.

PRACTICING MUNDANE MANAGEMENT

A strong reputation may originate in a unique product, but it is either reinforced or negated by an array of managerial practices that project image and identity. In combination, these practices signal the company's relative merits to observers and build up or deflate the reputational halo around a company's products and activities.

Long ago, management guru Peter Drucker recognized the simple artfulness of corporate excellence. He concluded that success in business "does not require special gifts, special aptitude, or special training. Effectiveness as an executive demands doing certain—and fairly simple—things. It consists of a small number of practices."[16]

He was right. Our best-regarded companies achieve their reputations by systematically practicing *mundane management*. They adhere rigorously to practices that consistently and reliably produce decisions that the rest of us approve of and respect. Faced with crises or accidents, their actions are governed by values, systems, and processes that sanction justifiable responses. By increasing our faith and confidence in the company's actions, credibility and reliability create economic value.

Few large firms have built as much reputation in the last decade as pharmaceutical giant Johnson & Johnson. Most of the company's reputation derives from the reactions of its managers to seven cases of cyanide poisoning attributed to ingestion of the company's number 1 pain reliever, Tylenol, in 1982 and 1986. After one victim died, the company immediately recalled all outstanding Tylenol inventory, set up hotlines, launched an advertising campaign, and offered rewards for information leading to the arrest of the murderer. These active steps earned the company enormous public sympathy and consumer trust, enabling recapture of more than 90 percent of its former customers. J&J's actions set a model for the industry in its social responsiveness, creating virtually overnight a favorable reputation for the company. It was, in fact, a seemingly miraculous comeback for a brand that analysts and investors had all but condemned. When asked, managers later explained their decisive actions on the basis of the company's core values, enshrined in "The Credo," a set of widely shared principles that specify the company's obligations to consumers, employees, local communities, and stockholders and that form the core of the company's identity.[17]

Contrast J&J's actions with those of the Exxon Corporation following its 11-million-gallon spill of North Slope crude oil into Prince William Sound, off the shores of Valdez, Alaska, in March 1989. After the spill, investors depreciated Exxon's stock by 10 percent, or some $6 billion. Since then, the company has been castigated on multiple fronts, especially for its (a) failure to take quick and decisive action, (b) lack of credible concern for victims, (c) reluctance to take responsibility, and (d) poor communication with the media.[18] Probing below the surface, one can easily trace these reactions to the "Exxon Way," a ponderous, insular culture that champions analysis over action and so moves slowly; that centralizes decision making and so constrains local responsiveness; that eschews visibility and so shuns publicity.

The differences between J&J and Exxon are stark. They call our attention to the everyday practices that compel managerial decisions that we either applaud or condemn. As is the case for individual athletes, *details* are what separate Olympian companies from mere mortals. By doing the little things well on a consistent basis, companies like J&J improve the likelihood that they will act responsibly when faced with a crisis and so will earn a favorable reputation.

In its heyday, Sears Roebuck was a company known for its effortless ability to perform. But a rash effort to diversify out of hard-goods retailing and into fashion merchandising and financial services in the 1970s and 1980s destroyed much of the valuable reputational capital Sears had created in its proud history, placing it well behind Wal-Mart in most reputational rankings of retailers. By 1994, Sears had divested itself of many of those unrelated businesses and was busily returning to its roots. Today, with its reputation resurging, it seems entirely possible that the 1990s could replicate the 1960s. Its managers might want to note that in 1964 a *Fortune* article praised Sears in these terms: "How did Sears do it? In a way, the most arresting aspect of its story is that there was no gimmick. Sears opened no big bag of tricks, shot off no skyrockets. Instead, it looked as though everybody in its organization did the right thing, easily and naturally."[19] When you come down to it, building reputation is downright mundane.

GOING FOR THE GOLD

When delegates to the International Olympic Committee gathered in Monte Carlo in September 1993, they faced an important decision: who would host the games in the year 2000. The vigorous campaign pitted five cities against one another for the honor: Istanbul, Berlin, Manchester, Sydney, and Beijing. None competed more aggressively than China's capital city of Beijing. Its bid took on political priority as Communist Party leaders saw symbolic meaning in the start of a new millenium.

Hosting the games in 2000 would return China to the international stage after years of isolation following the events in Tiananmen Square, where in June 1989 the government crushed the student-led democratic movement.

Throughout the first three rounds of balloting, Beijing led the way, eliminating in quick succession Istanbul, then Berlin, then Manchester. In the final round, only Sydney and Beijing remained. In both cities, crowds stood poised, with bated breath, waiting for the announcement. Suddenly, miscued by the speech of the committee president, millions of Chinese standing in auditoriums and by their television sets exploded into cheer—only to fall into despair as seconds later they realized their error: Sydney had beat out Beijing by a close vote of 45 to 43.

Like the Olympics itself, the contest to host the games builds reputation. In the short run, the Olympic Games are always a financial loss for the host country and city. In the long run, however, enormous visibility, prestige, and recognition accrue to a host, attracting tourism, business, and capital. Just as individual athletes become famous from their victories in competition, so too do cities and states gain a competitive edge on the global stage from hosting the games. After winning the bid for the 1996 Olympics, the city of Atlanta acknowledged its lack of a clear identity and embarked on a massive effort to define itself to the outside world. The hope? To shape a stronger sense of the city's values—its sense of self—for the purpose of highlighting key traits that might form the basis of a full-blown publicity campaign.

Similar concerns fuel rivalry among the four TV networks ABC, CBS, NBC, and Fox for the contract to broadcast the Olympic Games. In the past, CBS has consistently won out for the winter Olympics, while ABC has held out for the summer Olympics. Economics explains a good part of the value CBS and ABC attach to winning the contract, but not all of it. For instance, at every auction, observers like to proclaim that the winning network has overbid for the deal and will lose money—the so-called winner's curse.[20] In fact, they are probably not overbidding at all. Prior experience gives the winning network marginally more information and better estimates than any rival about the benefits to be derived from coverage. For another, the winner's higher bid incorporates the greater reputation-building side effects that it attaches to its broadcast role. The strong ratings CBS obtained for broadcasting the 1994 winter Olympics, for instance, cast a welcome halo over the network's other programs and brought in unanticipated revenues. Obviously, the bids are risky. But because of the hidden reputational gains, winners have higher expected returns on their investments than might be apparent.

In recent years, managers and researchers have begun to recognize that competitive advantages based on reputation can prove even more enduring than those that result from traditional strategic positioning or from the development of proprietary standards. Reputation is both a product and a by-product of competition. It is produced directly as a firm builds competitive advantage in pursuing uniqueness, as it differentiates itself from rivals. At the same time, reputation is a signal. It informs investors, employees, and customers, and so has real economic value for the firm. In many companies, reputation is a hidden asset. It complements—and sometimes surpasses—the value of the more tangible material and financial assets that managers routinely worry about.

Different companies will deploy different strategies to build a strong reputation. Some companies want to make their presence known—they seem ever present in the public eye. Others prefer to hide from the press—they keep a low profile. Either strategy can help produce a resilient reputation and build economic value. Those firms that favor low profiles generally want to avoid the downside of prestige and fame. Much as star athletes and performers complain of the rigorous demands of popularity, so do some companies worry about performing in the spotlight, their actions a constant source of commentary. As the late tennis great Arthur Ashe put it, "No matter what I do, or where or when I do it, I feel the eyes of others on me, judging me."[21]

The eyes of the world gaze steadfastly on Olympian companies. With fame also come grave responsibilities: the duty to respond to the demands not only of shareholders but of all constituents. And that requires a closer look at the roots of reputation in the company's identity.

C H A P T E R   T W O

Our names are labels, plainly printed on the bottled essence of our past behavior.

—*Logan P. Smith*
  Afterthoughts

What's in a Name?

NAMES GIVE us legal status and distinguish us from one another. In time, some names gain greater visibility and prestige. In the United States, a Kennedy or Rockefeller gets instant recognition, as does a Churchill or Thatcher in England. Advertisers spend a wealth of energy gauging the drawing power of individual names as well as of product names and corporate names. Various consultants specialize in nomenclature and offer naming services to companies struggling to come up with identifying names for new products, divisions, or businesses. Ultimately, a name crystallizes reputation: It anchors public perceptions about a company and its products and activities. This chapter examines the relationship between names and reputations and explores the ways in which they reflect a company's character, its sense of identity.

MARQUEE NAMES

In June 1989, the well-known industrialist J. B. Fuqua sold his 1.3 million shares in Atlanta-based Fuqua Industries and retired. The old-line conglomerate's reputation was at an all-time high, as was the company's market value of $600 million. By 1993, however, the company's stock had plummeted to less than $175 million. Charged with mismanagement, its reputation tarnished, Fuqua Industries was forced to withdraw a bond offering in the summer of 1992. In July 1993, the 75-year-old entrepreneur offered the company a cool $1 million to retrieve his name. As Mr. Fuqua put it, "I'm doing it to protect my name and reputation." Starved for capital, Fuqua Industries accepted and was soon reborn as the Actava Group.

Fuqua's attachment to his name is understandable. In pursuit of immortality, he had given nearly $20 million to Duke University's business school in 1980, in exchange for which it was promptly renamed the Fuqua School of Business. In 1993, within weeks of retrieving his name from the company he had founded, he announced a donation of $10 million to the Prince Edward Academy in Farmville, Virginia, a private school. In turn, the school was renamed—you guessed it—the Fuqua School. As he said: "If a school has my name on it, you can be assured that my family and I will always be interested in it."

Schools are not the only institutions to play the name game. Increasingly they find themselves competing with libraries, concert halls, and museums. At New York's Metropolitan Opera, for instance, patrons who donate $10,000 can get their name inscribed on a plaque on the back of an orchestra seat. But that's small potatoes when you consider what fashion designer Bill Blass's $10 million donation to the New York Public Library got him in January 1994. Within days of announcing the gift, the library emblazoned his name in gilt over the entrance to its public catalogue room. If value is measured by size, however, New York real estate developer Samuel LeFrak may have gotten an even better deal. For the same $10 million bequest he made that month, the Guggenheim Museum named the entire building after him and his wife, Ethel.

Why these gifts in the name of the giver? Because names have great psychological value. Having our name on an enduring structure appeals to us because it buys a piece of immortality. Being themselves in the business of money making, it's probably safe to presume that J. B. Fuqua, Bill Blass, and Samuel LeFrak hope to benefit from the indirect reputational gains that will result from having their names associated with high-profile institutions. In shifting their names from the business sphere to the social sphere, they follow in a long tradition of U.S. philanthropists like Andrew Carnegie, J. Pierpont Morgan, Henry Ford, and John Rockefeller, whose enlightened worldviews admitted no incompatibility between altruism and self-interest. Like their forebears, the Fuqua,

Blass, and LeFrak names now adorn monuments and institutions in ways that will reinforce the value of the companies owned by their descendents.

Names are important because they convey tacit information. They create initial impressions in the minds of consumers and investors that predispose us to feel better or worse. If you've ever tried to come up with a name for a new product or a new business, you'll know how agonizing it can be to pick just the "right" name. Names evoke images, convey personality, and impart identity. They are powerful symbols that define for others who we are and what we can become. All parents know this. That's why they fret and fuss so much before deciding on names for their offspring. For children, names often pack a tremendous punch. They convey to strangers important cues about their family's religion, race, and origins.

In a market society like ours, it's clear that names—and the reputations we associate with them—have economic value. Having a "good" name can be worth big bucks. Ask Michael Jordan. In 1992, the basketball legend was named first in a survey of the 10 most wanted corporate spokespersons. Even after he unexpectedly left basketball in 1993 and took up a lackluster baseball career, Jordan continued to bring in top endorsement income from companies like Nike, Hanes, General Mills, and Quaker Oats, who pay him an estimated $13 million a year. When he returned to basketball in March 1995, the CBS network, which broadcast his first game, drew its highest rating of all time. Other athletes whose names have the Midas touch include golfers Jack Nicklaus, Arnold Palmer, and Greg Norman; quarterback Joe Montana; hockey player Wayne Gretzky; and the colorful tennis pro Andre Agassi. In 1994, it's estimated that each collected well over $5 million in annual income from lending their names to corporate products—far more than their yearly earnings from their sport itself.

If celebrity endorsements cast a welcome halo over corporate products and generate sales, the reverse is also true: Celebrity scandals can depress sales. Much fuss was made over media giant Time Warner's decision not to renew the record contract of rap performer Ice-T after his controversial song "Cop Killer" spurred calls for a boycott of Time Warner products. Similarly, when singer Madonna's hit song "Like a Virgin" was attacked for its blasphemous use of religious symbols, PepsiCo dropped its planned multimillion dollar advertising campaign with the pop icon. And most visibly, despite 10 years of endorsements from superstar Michael Jackson, the company severed its lucrative ties with the entertainer in

August 1993 following allegations that he had sexually abused a child—even though no legal charges had been filed. As *Nightline* newscaster Ted Koppel put it at the time, "Often it's not the reality but the perceptions that count most." By dropping Michael Jackson, PepsiCo recognized the need to minimize the impact of the scandal on the company's reputation. As Clive Chajet, chairman of the identity consulting firm Lippicott & Margulies, told us: "I really admire Pepsi's handling of Michael Jackson. They have always recognized that the brand is the real star. Nobody goes into a store to ask for a Michael Jackson drink. They ask for a Pepsi. Just as it does for Coke, the brand name overwhelms the name of the spokesperson, and that's hitting a home run."

Names obviously convey images. When a name is popular, it can stimulate product sales. When a name becomes controversial, it can hurt a company and its products. Recall the sad saga of the Helmsley Palace Hotel, the crown jewel in the Helmsley real estate empire. Throughout the 1980s, the hotel enjoyed an enviable reputation for luxury, quality, and service, fanned by a national advertising campaign that featured Leona Helmsley as the self-styled "queen" of New York's hotel industry. In 1989, after Helmsley had been arrested, tried, and sentenced to a four-year prison term for tax evasion, the hotel's reputation was severely tarnished. Occupancy rates fell below 30 percent, to less than half the industry average. In 1992, the hotel went into receivership and was rechristened the New York Palace. In November 1993, the royal family of Brunei purchased the troubled property for what was widely considered a bargain price of $202 million.[1]

SOME DEFINITIONS

Figure 2-1 shows the relationship between a company's identity and its name, image, and reputation. *Corporate identity* describes the set of values and principles employees and managers associate with a company. Whether widely shared or not, a corporate identity captures the commonly understood features that employees themselves use to characterize how a company approaches the work it does, the products it makes, and the customers and investors it serves. Corporate identity derives from a company's experiences since its founding, its cumulative record of successes and failures. It describes the features of the company that appear to be central and enduring to employees.[2] On a day-to-day basis, corporate identity appears in the managerial practices managers employ

Figure 2-1 FROM IDENTITY TO REPUTATION

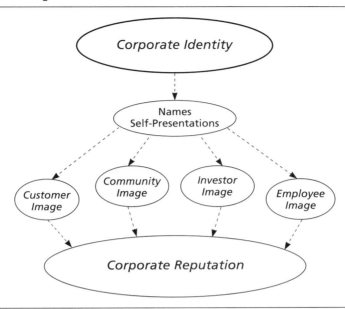

in their dealings internally with employees and externally with other constituents.

Every one of us, however, regularly recognizes a company by its name and by the many presentations it makes to describe its actions, its plans, and intentions. We interpret those self-presentations more or less favorably and form mental images of the company. Sometimes a *corporate image* accurately mirrors the company's identity; more often than not, the image is distorted (a) as the company tries to manipulate its public through advertising and other forms of self-presentation, or (b) as rumors develop from the unofficial statements of employees to peers, analysts, and reporters. In due course, different images form, some consistent, some less so.

As evaluators rate a company against a peer group of others, an overarching reputation crystallizes from the plethora of images produced. Based on the *American Heritage Dictionary*'s description of the word "reputation," we define a *corporate reputation* as the overall estimation in which a company is held by its constituents. A corporate reputation represents the "net" affective or emotional reaction—good or bad, weak or strong—of customers, investors, employees, and the general public to the company's name.

THE NAME GAME

Marketing Evaluations is a small Long Island outfit that consults to the entertainment industry. Seven times a year, the company surveys a nationwide panel of respondents and asks them to rate some 1,500 public personalities. Each performer is assigned a Q(uotient)-rating that gauges his or her mass appeal. The rating divides an individual's popularity—how much a performer is liked—by familiarity—how widely the person is recognized. Table 2-1 lists the top 10 stars of 1991 and 1992 based on their Q-ratings. Obviously, the list is dominated by star performers on hit television series. Although he didn't make it into the top 10 in 1992, basketball's Michael Jordan remains the highest Q-rated athlete.

In the movie industry, similar ratings are used to distinguish so-called superstars from run-of-the-mill stars in their ability to bring in larger audiences—their marquee value, their box office draw. The salaries of those performers are commensurate with their popular appeal. Across both the TV and movie industries, a horde of reporters, agents, and publicists work hard to build and sustain the ratings and economic value of those individual names. When actors win prestigious industry awards like Oscars or Emmies, their ratings rise, as do their clout and income.

In the 1980s, many corporate chieftains starred in television commercials in an attempt to personalize their companies. Chrysler's Lee Iacocca,

Table 2-1 THE TOP 10 STARS

Rank	In 1991	In 1992
1	Jaleel White	Bill Cosby
2	Bill Cosby	Jimmy Stewart
3	Estelle Getty	Clint Eastwood
4	Whoopi Goldberg	Steven Spielberg
5	Michael Jordan	Robin Williams
6	Mary Kate and Ashley Olsen	Whoopi Goldberg
7	Robin Williams	Billy Crystal
8	Kevin Costner	Mel Gibson
9	Ted Danson	Damon Wayans
10	Carroll O'Connor	Tim Allen

Source: Adapted from *New York Times*, July 6, 1992, 31, and *Advertising Age*, August 31, 1992, 3.

Remington's Victor Kiam, and Wendy's Dave Thomas were among the decade's more visible media personalities. In recent years, the Q-ratings of these executives have dropped precipitously, leading some to speculate as to whether overexposure of corporate spokesmen breeds contempt.[3]

PRODUCT NAMES

Like individuals, product names have legal standing. In the United States, trademarks and patents provide their owners with virtual monopoly protection for some 17 years. When products go off patent, they become "generics," at which point it's a free-for-all in the marketplace as competitors spring up from nowhere. Many companies manage a stable of trademarks, especially in the consumer goods industries and the chemical and pharmaceuticals industries. For instance, ask giant Du Pont about the value of its trademarks. The company invests aggressively in building up its product names, even after imitators enter the marketplace. Nylon and Lycra are among the trademarked products the chemical company has made famous. Despite rivalry from substitute products, Du Pont still controls the lion's share of the market for synthetic fibers. Or take the company's famous Lycra, the original fiber whose generic name is spandex. Although the 31-year-old product's patent has long since expired, savvy marketing has enabled Du Pont to retain its hold over two thirds of the world market for spandex.

Most consumer products, however, are difficult to protect from imitation. Maintaining the value of a product's name requires aggressive action. A case in point is Rollerblade, the Minnesota company that virtually invented in-line skating. Since its founding in 1981, the company has seen its name become virtually synonymous with the sport. When that happens, a company can lose its competitive advantage to rivals who simply copy the product and offer it at a lower price. To defend itself against the influx of lower-priced generics, Rollerblade has been extremely aggressive in the courts, most recently suing some 33 competitors in February 1993 for undermining the company's high-profile brand name. Clearly, this is a company that recognizes the dollar value of the intangible equity hidden behind its brand name.

Preventing imitation of brand names requires extensive advertising and promotion. Makers of consumer products are among the largest advertisers, and their aim is not only to attract customers to their branded products but to shut out rivals. The cereal industry, for instance, is dominated by the Big Four: General Mills, Kellogg, Post, and Quaker Oats. Through intensive advertising and coupon promotions, the Big Four maintain the visibility of their brands and prevent rivals from acquiring shelf space in supermarkets. Branding sustains market share and enhances profitability. As most shoppers know, it enables the Big Four to charge premium prices for their cereals.

In 1978, noted packaged foods manufacturer H. J. Heinz spent $120 million to buy Weight Watchers, the frozen-dinner business. Heinz managers took the next decade to improve the quality of Weight Watchers' offerings and the reputation of the brand—just in time to capitalize on the health-conscious 1980s. By 1989, Heinz had put the Weight Watchers name on more than 200 of its food products, and the brand boasted annual sales of more than $1.3 billion. As Heinz showed, a name and reputation like Weight Watchers, if well managed, can be quickly converted into revenues.

Most companies involved in selling prestige products worry about diluting their brand names. When credit card giant American Express introduced its lower-status revolving charge card Optima in 1987, it was heavily criticized for having damaged the company's "exclusive" franchise. The card subsequently failed, got pulled, and was reintroduced in 1994.

In the fashion industry, apparel designer Halston sent out a warning signal when he sold his name to mass distributor J. C. Penney. The designer name lost prestige in the eyes of consumers and virtually disappeared from the marketplace. Rivals learned from Halston's mistake. Most are now careful to retain ownership of their names and sell off only the right to attach that name to a narrow category of products. For instance, in January 1994, designer Calvin Klein sold his underwear business for $64 million to retailer Warnaco. The fragrance, jeans, and apparel businesses, however, are still under his control.

Many products carry protected names that they license for use. In 1980, retail sales of all licensed products totaled $10 billion. By 1990, licensing revenues had grown astronomically to $66.5 billion. Of these, well-known corporate trademarks accounted for the lion's share of royalties, with cartoon characters like Mickey Mouse and Teenage Mutant Ninja Turtles taking second place, and sports figures third. Table 2-2 indicates the enormous revenues generated when well-known names are put on consumer products. It helps explain the considerable interest that consumer products companies have in associating with high-profile

Table 2-2 NAMES THAT MEAN SALES

Type of Name	Retail Licensing Revenues in 1990 ($ billions)
Art	$ 5.7
Cartoon characters	13.0
Celebrities	3.0
Designers	6.3
Music	1.3
Publishing	1.7
Sports	10.0
TV programs	1.7
Movies/plays	2.3
Brand names/trademarks	21.6
Total	66.5

Source: Karen August, *The Licensing Letter,* Brooklyn, New York.

entertainers and sports figures. Celebrity endorsements and other tie-ins invariably fuel sales.

CORPORATE NAMES

In recent years, many food and consumer goods companies have introduced lower-priced generic versions that are of comparable quality to the more expensive, branded products sold by high-end firms. These generic products have heightened popular concern with the costs of branded products and reduced their appeal. They've led managers to ponder the possible value of investing, not only in their product names, but also in their corporate names. After all, companies themselves are granted names and afforded legal protection. A company's name symbolizes its reputation. Good names become more valuable; bad names lose value. Increasingly, managers wonder if the company's overall reputation might not prove more valuable than owning a stable of brand names in building reputational capital.

It's a question that might be asked of the makers of Arm & Hammer baking soda. Most of us know the product well for its many uses in the kitchen. Recently, the multipurpose product has also found its way into detergents and toothpaste. Yet few people would recognize the company that makes Arm & Hammer brand products. Should they? Well, consider this: The trademark is owned by Princeton-based Church & Dwight. With about $800 million in annual sales, the company just about makes it onto lists of the 1,000 most valuable firms in the United States. As rival products and brands attack the company's core market, however, one wonders whether Church & Dwight might not capitalize even further by building its corporate identity around its trademark name. Perhaps a corporate name change? Adopt the Arm & Hammer label and logo company-wide? Explore ways of more systematically projecting a positive image to constituents? Give to charitable causes? Create a foundation? These are some of the upside possibilities that Church & Dwight could explore to boost its reputational capital. Chapter 12 examines how the company is currently exploiting the A&H logo.

The downside of associating a product with a company name, of course, is that a corporate name can also detract from a company's success at promoting itself and its products. Consider Delaware State College of Dover, Delaware. For the first 50 years of its 102-year existence, the school was known as the State College for Colored Students. As cultural values changed, the college's name got in the way of student recruitment. Recognizing this, the college opted for a name change in the 1940s. In August 1993, the state legislature approved yet another costly change of name, this time to Delaware State University. Why? The hope that as a full-fledged university the school would increase its stature, thereby gaining greater recognition, better financing, and more corporate grants and private donations.

A name essentially describes how a company is perceived on the outside. It signals to outside observers what a company stands for, the quality of its products. When the value-priced cosmetics maker Avon tried to improve its reputation by purchasing the prestige retailer Tiffany's in 1979, most doubted the wisdom of the move. That's why it came as no surprise when five years later Avon sold off the operation. Not only did owning Tiffany's fail to add luster to Avon, but negative publicity about Avon ownership was rapidly tarnishing Tiffany's reputation. To consumers, Tiffany's operates in a world of privilege and prestige far removed from the one Avon trades in.

By raising or lowering expectations about what a company stands for, a corporate name can also make or break a new business. Healthcare giant Pfizer recognized that fact when in May 1993 the company announced a name change for its Specialty Chemicals Division. The division would henceforth be known as the more consumer friendly Food Science Group, a move designed to refocus the division on new and healthful foods and to back its newest product, a fat substitute called Dairy-Lo. The name change was effective in building reputation. Soon thereafter, *Food Engineering* magazine gave the division an award for excellence in marketing.

Established companies worry about whether their names convey the right impression to potential customers. In September 1993, three operating companies of the investment bank First Boston announced a worldwide name consolidation to convey the strategic integration of the company. Exhibit 2-1 reproduces the announcement sent to clients,

Exhibit 2-1 **AN INVESTMENT BANK'S QUEST FOR IDENTITY**

Going Forward We Are

CS FIRST BOSTON
Worldwide

To our clients:

Our three operating companies—The First Boston Corporation in the Americas, Financière Credit Suisse-First Boston in Europe, and CS First Boston Pacific, Inc. in the Pacific—will be operating as one under the name of CS First Boston. Our mission is to serve our clients worldwide in the most efficient and effective manner. After a thorough study by the Firm's leadership, we concluded that your needs as well as the dynamics of the marketplace required this change. We are committed to serving you better by building on our unique long-standing regional capabilities in the Americas, in Europe, and in the Pacific.

As a member of the CS Holding Group we continue to maintain our strong alliance with Credit Suisse, one of the world's largest and soundest financial services groups, which means that you can count on the stability and global reach of a truly international firm.

Our Firm is having the most successful year in its history in terms of operating earnings, levels of activity, landmark transactions, and after-tax profits. We have recorded a return on equity which has been one of the highest on Wall Street over the last two years. We appreciate your continued support.

One Firm   One Name   One Mission

 CS FIRST BOSTON

AMERICAS: New York, Atlanta, Boston, Chicago, Dallas, Houston, Los Angeles, Miami, Philadelphia, San Francisco, San Juan
EUROPE: London, Amsterdam, Budapest, Frankfurt, Geneva, Madrid, Milan, Paris, Prague, Zug, Zurich
PACIFIC: Tokyo, Auckland, Beijing, Hong Kong, Melbourne, Osaka, Singapore, Sydney, Wellington

Reprinted by permission.

displaying the firm's new title and its new logo: "One Firm . . . One Name . . . One Mission."[4] The logo clearly signals a desire to project a stronger, more coherent identity to customers and to capitalize on the marquee value of the bank's name.

The same thing happened in January 1994 when two Bell companies announced that they were retiring the names of their telephone subsidiaries New Jersey Bell and New York Telephone. Both companies launched cheerful ad campaigns that affirmed their new identities under their respective parents' names and logos: Bell Atlantic and NYNEX.

And it happened to financial services behemoth Primerica. Scarcely had Primerica completed its acquisition of Shearson—the American Express brokerage subsidiary—when it announced a deal with Travelers, the insurance giant, in fall 1993. After the merger, Primerica adopted the Travelers name to capitalize on the strength of the established insurance franchise. The decision reflected CEO Sandy Weill's awareness of the minimal stock of reputational capital tied to the old Primerica name. Before the merger, the company's two principal subsidiaries had operated under their own monikers as Smith Barney Shearson in the brokerage business and as Commercial Credit Corporation in consumer finance. In contrast, the Travelers name and trademark red umbrella were high-visibility imprints. Weill clearly intends to make the Travelers umbrella at least as familiar to consumers as Merrill Lynch's bull and Prudential's rock.

Meanwhile, American Express, has been actively consolidating its remaining businesses in an effort to become, according to the company's latest vision statement, "the world's most respected service brand." Having divested Shearson and Lehman Brothers, among others, the firm sent out this announcement to customers in January 1995 about the name change of its IDS subsidiary:

> For years . . . you've known us as IDS Financial Services. Today, I'm writing to share some important and exciting news: On January 1, IDS will be renamed American Express Financial Advisors. . . . The reason for the name change is basically a business one. . . . We've been part of the American Express family for over a decade. Therefore, we decided that it would be appropriate for us to start using the same name. In addition, because American Express is among the nation's most well-known and respected companies, we think the name will increase recognition of our business throughout the United States.

American Express is one of the world's most familiar service brands. In 1992, the company was reeling from its failed efforts at diversification into financial services. Under its new chairman Harvey Golub, the company opted to rebuild the company around its American Express brand name. Pictured here is Martha Stewart, spokesperson for the company's revitalized Optima True Grace Card and the centerpiece of their promotions. (©1994 American Express Travel Related Services.)

The familiarity, visibility, and cachet of a corporate name send a signal to consumers, investors, and other constituents about the likely credibility and reliability of the company and its products. By allaying fears of a bad experience, a corporate name—and the reputation it implies—breeds loyalty and fuels sales.

REGIONAL NAMES

Like companies, regions benefit from a good name. Wine enthusiasts like me, for instance, regularly pay premium prices for French wines.

We shell out larger sums for an aged Cabernet Sauvignon from Bordeaux, for a Riesling from Alsace, for the sparkling wines of Champagne, and for the dessert wines of Sauternes.

Realizing the value of its regional names, France exercises close control over affiliated products. Since 1935, the French Institut National des Appellations d'Origine des Vins et Eaux-de-Vie (National Institute of Place-Names of Wines and Spirits) has governed name usage among French wine producers. Strict laws control every factor that contributes to the wine's flavor, including the geographical composition of the soil, the permissible grapevines, the minimum alcoholic content, the viticultural practices for handling the vines, the amount of permissible harvest, and the wine-making practices. Control prevents dilution of the name and improves the reputation of all producers associated with it. As noted enologist Alexis Lichine points out: "In the case of every Appellation Contrôlée that has gone into effect, the result has been an immediate and marked increase in quality. Passage of a control law cut out the lesser wines and the grower—conscious that his efforts would be reimbursed—strove for high quality."[5]

Not only are wine producers strictly controlled, but they hold assigned status rankings. To this day, France recognizes an official hierarchy of wine makers that dates back to 1855. It identifies five principal tiers of producers, ranked from first to fifth growth. Producers Chateau Margaux and Chateau Lafite Rothschild are among the five top-ranked names of Bordeaux. Chateau d'Yquem makes what is probably the world's most famous dessert wine. Table 2-3 describes the major wineries rated in the original classification.

As consumers, we pay a premium for the better-rated wines. Although dated in its ability to signal the true quality of a wine, the first-growth rating of the producers in the Pauillac or Margaux regions still commands higher market prices at retail than the *cru bourgeois* wines of lesser-ranked producers. A 1991 bottle of Burgundy's fabled Domaine de la Romanée-Conti was priced at $500 in January 1995. In essence, established reputations are effective barriers that differentiate producers in the marketplace and deter rivals.

Even in the United States, a hierarchy of region and producer conveys a winery's status. Enophiles invariably impute greater prestige to California's wineries than to those of upstate New York or Long Island. Among California wines, those produced in Napa Valley are more highly prized than those from other regions. Much as their Pauillac location confers

Table 2-3 FRANCE'S LEADING WINERIES

The Top Wineries of the Haut-Médoc
Chateau Lafite-Rothschild
Chateau Latour
Chateau Mouton-Rothschild
Chateau Margaux
Chateau Haut-Brion

The Top Wineries of Saint-Emilion
Chateau Ausone
Chateau Cheval Blanc
Chateau Beauséjour-Bécot
Chateau Beauséjour-Duffau-Lagarosse
Chateau Bélair
Chateau Canon
Chateau Figeac
Clos Fourtet
Chateau La Gaffelière
Chateau La Magdelaine
Chateau Pavie
Chateau Trottevieille

The Top Wineries of Sauternes
Chateau d'Yquem
Chateau Guiraud
Chateau La Tour-Blanche
Chateau Lafaurie-Peyraguey
Chateau de Rayne-Vigneau
Chateau Sigalas-Rabaud
Clos Haut-Peyraguey
Chateau Coutet
Chateau Climens
Chateau Suduiraut
Chateau Rieussec

Source: Based on the Official Classification of the Great Growths of the Gironde of 1855. Adapted from Alexis Lichine's *New Encyclopedia of Wines and Spirits,* 5th ed. (New York: Alfred A. Knopf, 1987).

to first-growth French wines like those of Chateau Latour and Chateau Lafite-Rothschild a top ranking among France's elite wineries, so does location in the Rutherford-Oakville region of Napa Valley confer celebrity on wine producers Robert Mondavi, Heitz Cellar, and Beaulieu Vineyard. Not coincidentally, they are among the wine labels that regularly fetch the highest market prices, both at auction and at retail.

Wine making aside, a given locale can have greater or lesser appeal for numerous reasons. In 1992, *Fortune* sponsored a survey of more than 900 executives across the United States to rate cities on various criteria. The magazine used these data to rank urban areas according to their attractiveness to business. Topping the list were Seattle, Houston, San Francisco, and Atlanta. At about the same time, *Business Week* countered with a review of the nation's fastest growing regions, corridors of innovation like Silicon Hills around Austin, Optics Valley near Tucson, the Golden Triangle around San Diego, Laser Lane near Orlando, and the Princeton Corridor. Each region is earning a reputation as a hotbed of entrepreneurship in specific industries, with vast consequences for the well-being of the region—its ability to attract talent, to generate tax revenues, and to build wealth.

Some products benefit from being associated with particular regions, others lose. Consider a survey of the hottest food products of 1991. Some 47 new food products chose to identify with Texas, while Dakota appeared on 13 brands; two products took the name of New York State, while five adopted New York City. None bore the name New Jersey—and for a very good reason. According to Ira N. Bachrach, president of Namelab, the San Francisco–based consulting firm that helped to name products like Honda's Accord, and the Compaq computer: "I can't imagine ever naming any foodstuff or life-style product like clothing or perfume after New Jersey because the general impression outside New Jersey is that it is a crowded, crime-ridden state. The general impression of New Jersey isn't that it is the sort of place that is the paragon of bucolic splendor."[6]

Sadly, it seems that New Jersey's slumping reputation won't even sell cranberries. According to the *New York Times,* New Jersey is second only to Massachusetts in producing cranberries. Yet while Massachusetts sends much of its fresh cranberry crop to market under the name Cape Cod, New Jersey's fresh cranberries are sold generically and at a lower price. Clearly the state's reputation doesn't help sell its products.

Or attract students. Take Rutgers, the well-known university. Few people know that the school's official name is actually Rutgers, the State University of New Jersey. Upset at its inability to capitalize on the strong reputation of Rutgers, in February 1994 the state's senate considered a proposal to drop the Rutgers name entirely. By more closely identifying the university with New Jersey, politicians hoped to boost the state's reputation. Predictably, the proposal "touched off a minor firestorm among Rutgers students and alumni, who say changing the name would diminish prestige, erase national name recognition and wipe out 227 years of the school's history."[7] In the long run, New Jersey would probably gain from the name change. In the short run, however, the new name would surely wreak havoc with the university's identity and reputation, discouraging alumni donations and alienating student and faculty applicants.

Cities, states, and countries regularly contend for reputation and status as they try to attract prestigious companies that promise tax revenues and good jobs. A city such as New York dreads the departure of a company's headquarters, not just because it means lost jobs and tax revenues but because it signals a loss of reputation for the city as a business hub. The frenzied efforts of local mayors to retain companies sometimes appear irrational to the public, particularly when a city gives more in tax breaks than it receives in terms of revenues and jobs. Here too, however, the city's reputational capital remains unaccounted for. Presumably, the city's reputational gain from retaining a large company generates returns from other sources that more than compensate for the tax breaks it provides.

Consider an ad for the state of Pennsylvania, published in *Fortune* magazine in 1993. The ad's explicit purpose was to cast on Pennsylvania the prestige of Merck, Rubbermaid, and Wal-Mart, the top three companies praised in the magazine's annual survey of companies in 1992. It also served to associate *Fortune* magazine itself, a prominent symbol of corporate America, with the Commonwealth of Pennsylvania—and to attract more prestigious companies.

People who bought Japanese products before the 1970s remember well that the label Made in Japan signaled low prices and poor quality. How quickly the country's reputation changed. Much of Japan's turnaround can be traced to the systematic reputation-building efforts of MITI, Japan's activist Ministry of Trade and Industry. In the United States, the massive publicity campaign of the mid-1980s in support of the Pride in America label was a concerted effort to rebuild America's sagging reputation and to promote pride, morale, and credibility among American consumers and workers.

As with a country's name, so goes its economic burden. Investment banks regularly assess the value of a country's debt offerings (especially in developing nations) based on subjective views of the country's political and social stability—its reputation. At Salomon Brothers, for instance, the group researching emerging markets routinely travels the world to collect information about political and economic developments. They then use those data to make predictions about the value of that country's debt, both for Salomon's traders and it's clients. In 1992, Salomon traded about $40 billion in Third World debt. Clearly, a country's name value has economic consequences for that country's ability to marshall financial resources.

In fact, names, like flags, are symbols that convey identity. Much as national identification can inspire intensely patriotic feelings, so in the corporate world can a company's name stir a sense of commitment in employees. Those who identify strongly with a company's objectives work harder, better, and longer. A company's name can also inspire trust in consumers and investors insofar as it connotes integrity and signals credibility. Watchdog groups like the Better Business Bureau actively monitor the trustworthiness of companies and the credibility of their claims. In its published ads, the bureau put it well:

> *When times are uncertain, people need to be even more certain about the companies they do business with. They need to be certain about the honesty and integrity of a company. And that business will be conducted to the highest standards. The Better Business Bureau is a symbol of those high standards. And this is why the undersigned members support it. Please join these and other fine companies in the Better Business Bureau. Because today, it's not just your business reputation at stake. It could be your business.*[8]

NAMES AND IMAGES CONVEY IDENTITY

The reputation we associate with a name communicates a company's core traits to customers and patrons; it defines the company's identity for its employees. In early 1994, the former Ma Bell—the American Telephone and Telegraph Company—announced that it was seeking approval from its shareholders for a name change to its initials—AT&T. The move reflected an awareness that the company's 109-year-old name was technologically outdated. Nonetheless, many of the company's directors and employees expressed considerable feelings of nostalgia for the old name, seeing the change as a symbolic break with the past.

Or consider the giant entertainment company Walt Disney. The company's commitment to family values is deeply anchored in its internal systems as well as its marketing practices. When a stagnant Disney Studios sought to apply its movie-making expertise to more adult fare in the early 1980s, it was terribly worried about the negative impact on its reputation as a provider of family-based entertainment. To avoid diluting the Disney name, the company distanced itself from its R-rated movies by introducing them under a new label, Touchstone Pictures. The strategy worked: Touchstone's hit movies allowed the division to blossom, and Disney's involvement went largely unnoticed.

To change names is a complex matter. It requires a complete reassessment, not only of the image a company presents to the outside world but, more critically, of its core objectives and character traits. Consider the plight of the National Audubon Society. In 1991, the 105-year-old naturalist group was worried about its image. It hired the consulting firm of Landor Associates to find out what people associated with its name. The bad news came back: "Birds." Moreover, the consultants added, the society was regarded as old-fashioned and exclusive, and its mission less than compelling. This, despite the fact that the society's $42 million annual budget was spent on causes ranging from preserving wildlife to controlling pesticides use to promoting alternative energy sources. Concerned about the society's ability to compete with other environmentalist organizations for money and support, Audubon's president chose not to change the group's name but to embark on a campaign to alter its image. First to go was the egret, traditional centerpiece of the society's logo. In its place, a plain blue flag. Next, the group censored the corporate lingo of bird-based imagery. Instead, it called for a younger, fresher writing style in memos as well as in the society's famed *Audubon* magazine. The result: an identity crisis within the society as staff members feared the demise of a long tradition of nature writing, not to mention the loss of their jobs.[9]

As consumers, corporate names have value to us because they provide lots of tacit information about a company and its products. The retail business is a case in point. In mid-1993, the advertising agency BBDO wondered about the reputations of various Manhattan retail stores. It asked 100 female Manhattan residents with household incomes exceeding $35,000 per year what psychological factors compelled them to shop at a particular store. Figure 2-2 diagrams the perceptual map inferred from the interviews. It suggests that each store has a distinct reputation and that customers differentiate very well between them on two key dimensions: (1) luxury-thriftiness and (2) tradition-innovation. According to BBDO's director of research, "The thing that I found most interesting was the distinctiveness of the images of the stores in consumers' minds."[10]

Bergdorf Goodman's reputation for luxury and sophistication contrasts sharply with the reputation of A&S and Macy's for stocking affordable, family-oriented merchandise. Similarly, Lord & Taylor's image as a stodgy, traditional store stands opposed to Barney's carefully cultivated reputation for creativity and innovativeness. Although deceptively simple, the map suggests to marketers that established reputations act as a competitive barrier between stores. It's not necessarily differences in merchandise that influence the ability of a store to attract a clientele;

Figure 2-2 MAPPING A STORE'S REPUTATION

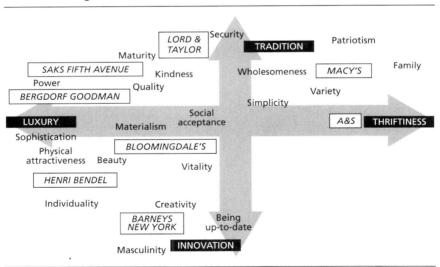

Source: Stephanie Strom, "Image and Attitude are Department Stores' Draw," New York Times, Sunday, August 12, 1993, Business section, D1, based on a study conducted by BBDO, a New York market research and advertising firm. Copyright © 1993 by the New York Times Company. Reprinted by permission.

rather it's the reputation of the store that determines its ultimate profitability. In a world where stores increasingly carry the same merchandise, where designer lines like Calvin Klein, Donna Karan, and Anne Klein are equally available, product no longer differentiates the stores; it's the reputation of the stores that distinguishes them to customers and brings them in to shop. The onus is therefore put increasingly on managing reputation. For stores, that means asking the all important identity-defining questions: Who are we? What do we want to be?

Wal-Mart is well known for both its discount prices and its unique identity. With strong sales and profitability, the company has built up more reputational capital than any other Fortune 500 firm. If you go inside the company, the reason is obvious: Employees are about as involved as it's possible to be, whether through family-style picnics, grassroots meetings, weekly store meetings, employee newsletters, or extensive training offered at the Walton Institute of Retailing and through in-store seminars. Wal-Mart's reputation and its identity are closely related.

The link between identity and reputation extends well beyond the retail sector.[11] Managers rely on their grasp of a company's identity to justify decisions. Being "on top of things," for instance, seems to be a desirable character trait for many U.S.-based companies. In annual reports, managers regularly use language that tries to convey to investors that they are in control of environmental forces—even when it's clear that they are not.[12] Research also suggests that managers try to influence prospective employees' perception of their companies by putting a positive spin on compensation and human resource policies as presented in employment brochures.[13] These studies tell us that actively projecting image is a key concern when you want to build reputation with employees, investors, and other constituents. It's the choice of which images to project that reflects a company's identity—the common theme that crystallizes from the many faces a company intentionally and inadvertently presents.

Moreover, a company's identity and reputation compel managers to make decisions and take action in ways that are mutually consistent. Consider the New York Port Authority, a large private organization that manages some of New York's most prominent real estate, including its midtown bus terminal, its three airports, and the famed World Trade Center. The Port Authority has a solid reputation for being a can-do, high-quality, problem solver. Over the last decade, its managers have struggled to cope with the rising tide of homeless people that threatens to overwhelm its facilities. A few years ago, two of my colleagues, Jane Dutton and Janet Dukerich, studied the actions taken by the Port Authority to deal with the problem in the late 1980s. As they reported, managers had grown extremely distressed over the growing inconsistency between the Port Authority's reputation for problem solving and its inaction vis-à-vis the homeless: "The resigned admission that the organization had to take action on the issue was accompanied by a great deal of emotion about the unfavorable image the Port Authority had in the press, a sense of outrage that those responsible were not doing their job, and a sense of embarrassment and anger generated by negative press coverage of Port Authority actions on homelessness."[14]

In time, managers of the Port Authority mobilized to tackle the unpleasant problem. Organizationally, they recognized that the problem was larger than they could handle on their own. So they sought local and regional partnerships with companies facing similar problems. Financially, they provided $2.5 million to renovate two drop-in centers. By 1989, Port Authority managers were aggressively involved in providing information about homelessness to many in the transportation industry and to the press as part of an active effort to minimize the negative publicity surrounding the issue. In the end, managers increasingly acted in ways that confirmed the organization's reputation as a humane and first rate problem solver. The Port Authority's reputation reflected its core character traits and drove managers to comport themselves accordingly.

Recent hoaxes perpetrated on soft-drink maker PepsiCo present a high-profile illustration of the link between reputation and identity. In June 1993, a dozen or so complaints of needles and other objects in cans of Pepsi-Cola suddenly swept the country. The Associated Press identified at least 50 reports of tampering in 23 states. Nearly all involved cans of Diet Pepsi, and objects claimed to have been found in the cans included syringes, a crack vial, a bullet, and a glob of glue as well as needles.

To PepsiCo managers, this was no laughing matter. Product tampering had nearly destroyed Johnson & Johnson's Tylenol brand in 1982 and 1986. Whereas J&J managers reacted with an extensive show of concern for consumers, followed by a quick and costly product recall, PepsiCo managers responded harshly and bluntly. Consistent with their reputation for contentiousness (who could forget the cola wars?), PepsiCo took to the media and aggressively denied the possibility of tampering in its production process. Top managers insisted that a national recall of Diet Pepsi cans was unwarranted. The company prepared video footage for news broadcasts to demonstrate the impossibility of inserting a syringe into cans. Craig Weatherup, Pepsi's president of North American operations was selected to make six personal appearances on morning and evening news programs to showcase the company's position: that tampering was impossible—even inconceivable. Despite initial public protest, Pepsi stood its ground.

Days later, the federal commissioner of the Food and Drug Administration—an active partner in presenting Pepsi's case to the public—proved the company right. The complaints of tampering had been entirely fabricated. Some 20 arrests were quickly made. Vindicated by the outcome, Weatherup claimed: "This development reinforces what we've believed all along: that this is not a manufacturing problem and that consumers should not be alarmed about any alleged problems with Pepsi products."[15]

The point is this: Reputation and identity go hand in hand. Pepsi's top brass responded to the crisis in ways that were entirely consistent with its corporate identity. All companies should do the same. For one, it's no good projecting attractive images of yourself that you can't live up to. Sooner or later, someone out there will refuse to judge the book by its cover and will call you on the gap between reality and perception. At the same time, if you've invested in creating and maintaining a successful brand name, why not find ways to capitalize on that name with your company's different constituencies?

NAMES MATTER

As you may recall, the question "What's in a name?" prompted William Shakespeare to reply, "that which we call a rose by any other name would smell as sweet." He was right. A name conveys the essence of a company to observers—its reputation. In turn, the sweet smell of a good reputation is what we associate with its name. As many companies have found, you can easily change your name, but the company's identity, and so its reputation, generally remain.

Names matter because they convey information to people inside and outside of a company. Savvy managers know how to exploit the names of their products and companies to build enduring competitive advantage against rivals. In the final analysis, whether in retail or wholesale, in manufacturing or services, companies earn their reputations because of what they are and how they present themselves—their identity and image.

When asked, most managers acknowledge the importance of a good name. They consider how best to create and maintain favorable assessments of their companies; they want to know how better to exploit these intangible assets. Although the economic benefits of a name are often implicit and difficult to quantify, a good name gives substance to a company's reputation. In turn, a reputation comes to have economic value because its effects are functional. A good reputation generates consistent, shared, and favorable impressions among observers about what a company is, what a company does, what a company stands for. In this way, a company's reputation is itself identity defining. It helps us assess our understandings of the companies with which we do business.

The strength of a man's virtue should not be measured by his special exertions, but by his habitual acts.

—*Blaise Pascal*
Pensées

Enlightened Self-Interest

CORPORATE REPUTATIONS are perceptions held by people inside and outside a company. To acquire a reputation that is positive, enduring, and resilient requires managers to invest heavily in building and maintaining good relationships with their company's constituents. It calls for practices that measure and monitor how the company is doing with its four top constituencies: employees, investors, customers, and communities. Doing so pays off in the long run because favorable reputations produce tangible benefits: premium prices for products, lower costs of capital and labor, improved loyalty from employees, greater latitude in decision making, and a cushion of goodwill when crises hit.[1] Simply put, this chapter suggests that reputation building is a form of *enlightened self-interest*.

THE LONG RUN

In March 1993, business students at New York University's Stern School hosted the tenth annual Graduate Business Conference. The theme? To identify emerging value systems in corporate America. Discussion centered on well-regarded companies that have woven social and environmental concerns into their decision-making practices. The keynote speaker was Anita Roddick, founder of the Body Shop, the 900-store chain of personal-care products with an enviable reputation for being both environmentally conscious and highly profitable. Indeed, at the Body Shop, "No animals are used to test products, bottles are refilled for customers who choose to bring them back, and most of the ingredients are gathered from natural sources. The stores are encouraged to participate in company-backed political programs, like a recent one in the United States to register voters."[2] The Body Shop's profits rose to $34 million on sales of $266 million in 1992, making Roddick one of the wealthiest women in England and amply justifying her contention that "you don't have to lose your soul to succeed in business."

She's right. For many years, business schools have championed the shareholder over the stakeholder, and scorned those concerned with more than the financial implications of corporate decisions. Strengthened by free-market advocates, MBA programs have encouraged narrow-minded, short-run thinking about self-interest that has led to the design of reward systems that support individualism rather than teamwork, fragmentation rather than integration—with the attendant collapse of both ethics and community.

Today we pay the piper as we tally the sorry record of corporate wrongdoings, infractions, and white-collar crimes, all of which can be traced to a diminishing interest in standards, controls, integrity, and that nineteenth-century commodity known as a good reputation. Yet as a society, we define ourselves by the values we choose to emphasize. "Democracy means paying attention," the sociologist Robert Bellah concludes in his insightful book *The Good Society*. In the 1980s, a frenzied quest for efficiency led to the endorsement of individualism over community. The resulting stress on short-term returns encouraged a speculative frenzy in the stock markets and merger mania on Wall Street, variously described as "the casino society"[3] and a "circus of ambition,"[4] attacked in the Oliver Stone film *Wall Street*, and satirized in Tom Wolfe's popular book *The Bonfire of the Vanities*. The reputation of the business community as a whole fell to an all-time low. In the process, companies like E. F. Hutton and Drexel Burnham Lambert lost their good names entirely while others saw their reputations become seriously tarnished. The corporate world squandered much of its reputational capital.

Most managers now deplore the substantial losses occasioned by that short-term outlook. They contemplate how we might better affirm the value of a company's intangible assets, especially its reputation. To focus on a company's reputation is to put the spotlight squarely on the long run; on the ways in which constituents influence its values; on an appraisal of the company not only as an economic engine or money machine but as a social institution.

EMPOWERED CONSTITUENTS

A corporate reputation embodies the general estimation in which a company is held by employees, customers, suppliers, distributors, competitors, and the public. The key point, of course, is that reputation consists of *perceptions*—how others see you. Because a reputation is not directly under anyone's control, it is difficult to manipulate. Try as we might to manage other people's impressions—to put on a good face, as it were—it's not easy to achieve.

Consider some of Lee Iacocca's parting experiences as chairman of Chrysler, the carmaker he saved from bankruptcy in the early 1980s. In 1992, Mr. Iacocca repeatedly took to the airwaves to describe his frustration with Chrysler's reputation. Specifically, he decried his inability to overcome Chrysler's reputation for producing cars of quality inferior to Japanese cars—a reputation that was entirely unjustified. In various television ads and public speeches, the vocal spokesman told the public about survey data the company had gathered that showed how American consumers were more likely to buy a Subaru than a Chrysler even though both cars were in fact identical and were manufactured by joint venture in the same Chrysler plant in the United States. Clearly, the Japanese brand name capitalized on Japan's reputation for manufacturing excellence and quality. It created a perceptual barrier that Chrysler's dealers found difficult to surmount.

Iacocca's experience reminds us that a company's reputation actually derives from several things:

- its ability to directly manage impressions,
- its ability to build strong relationships with key constituents, and
- the indirect rumor mongering engaged in by interested observers, such as analysts and reporters.

Marketers, advertisers, and public relations specialists help to create attractive images of a company.[5] Indeed, many companies rely quite heavily on PR professionals to shape the perceptions of those looking in from outside—principally the customers. But unless those images are anchored in core characteristics of the company and its products or services, they will decay. In general, what companies want and need are reputations that are both enduring and resilient: able to withstand scandal and attack, to overcome crisis and assault. This is not the stuff that traditional public relations is made of. What is needed to sustain reputation is a strong and supportive infrastructure of interwoven managerial practices.

Many companies today are beginning to recognize the difference between image and reputation. They go beyond mere mass marketing and traditional image management by trying to build strong relationships with customers. Motorcycle maker Harley-Davidson is a case in point. The company-run Harley Owners Group (HOG) boasts 200,000 members worldwide. Charging a nominal $35 annual membership, the club provides members with a variety of services that include insurance, travel, and emergency assistance as well as magazines, competitions, and access to 750 local chapters. HOG has been remarkably successful for Harley-Davidson in fostering intense loyalty to the company's products. Its success goes to the heart of Harley-Davidson's identity.

That's fine in terms of marketing. To build an enduring and resilient reputation, however, a company must establish strong relationships not only with customers but with other key constituents. After all, serving the customer goes only so far. A company also has to meet the expectations of its employees, investors, as well as the communities it serves. Although attending to these four key constituencies is work enough, companies cannot afford to ignore certain other specialized and highly influential groups. These specialized groups include government agencies that look at company compliance with regulatory standards, financial-ratings agencies that monitor economic performance, corporate-conscience agencies that evaluate social performance, and consumer agencies that assess product quality. Such groups enjoy lots of analytic resources and often have access to better information than ordinary constituents like you or me. Their opinions significantly affect the way a company is regarded by its less-informed observers. Indeed, a whole performance assessment and reputation-building industry has evolved that scrutinizes, evaluates, and champions companies. (See Figure 3-1.)

Most of these specialized agencies become skilled at articulating and defending the interests of a particular constituency. For instance, government agencies devote public resources to assessing how well companies

Figure 3-1 THE REPUTATION-BUILDING INDUSTRY

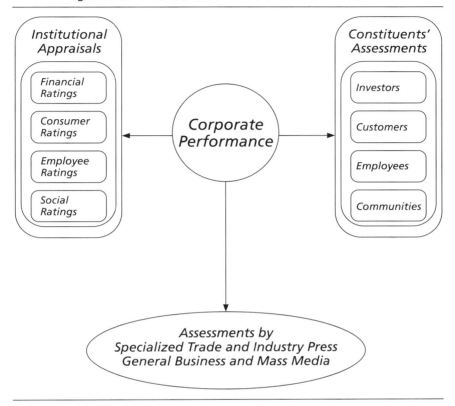

comply with health and environmental standards. A small community of financial analysts including the likes of Moody's Investors Services, Dun & Bradstreet, and Standard & Poor's regularly monitor and assess the performance of companies with publically traded securities. Various consumer advocates collect, summarize, and verify information about the products companies make. In recent years, assorted public-interest monitors have also gained visibility as watchdogs for a company's products and its ethical conduct. The focused ratings that these specialized groups produce draw attention to different aspects of a company's performance and affect its various images and its overall reputation.

Herbert Baum, president of Campbell Soup, keys into the vital importance of constituents to a company's reputation: "What goes into a brand image? A number of things. How the consumer perceives the product, of course. Also the attitudes of the retailers and wholesalers who may buy more of your product because they know it will sell. Then there is the critical corporate image to our shareholders and the financial community. And I would add a fourth element to that, a sense of pride among the people who work here, their understanding that Campbell Soup is a company that makes quality products consistently."[6]

CUSTOMERS EXPECT RELIABILITY

As customers, we want companies to be reliable. We want their claims for their products to prove true. We demand that the products of companies we respect be of better quality and reliability than those of lesser-known competitors, even if sold at the same price. The effects of reputation on customers are arguably strongest in the service sector, where judgments of quality are especially difficult to make. Lacking any objective measure of performance, service providers rely heavily on their reputations to attract clients, and they must deliver the quality they lay claim to if they are to retain those clients.

Consider the plight of Sears Roebuck. In June 1992, serious allegations were made that various Sears Auto Centers in California and New Jersey had sold customers unnecessary parts and services. Aware of the potential damage to the company's strong reputation for service, its managers quickly took action. Exhibit 3-1 reproduces the open letter Sears published in daily newspapers across the country to signal its concern and to outline the aggressive steps being taken to remedy the situation.

Like other service-based businesses, individual lawyers, accountants, consultants, doctors, realtors, insurance agents, and investment counselors survive largely by word-of-mouth advertising—personal referrals that convey trust and credibility. That's also why law firms, auditors, consulting firms, and investment banks struggle to build a reputation for scrupulous honesty and integrity. Once established, these reputations can be relied on to attract other corporate clients. In effect, client companies rent the reputations of their lawyers, accountants, bankers, and consultants as a means of signaling their own credibility and integrity to key constituents.[7]

Most Fortune 500 companies rely heavily on the services of one of the highly regarded Big Six auditors. By renting the potent reputations of Coopers & Lybrand, Ernst & Young, KPMG Peat Marwick, Arthur Andersen, Price Waterhouse, or Deloitte & Touche, they reduce the risk that customers or investors will find fault with their actions; they appear

Exhibit 3-1   SEARS DEFENDS ITSELF

An Open Letter to Sears Customers:

You may have heard recent allegations that some Sears Auto Centers in California and New Jersey have sold customers parts and services they didn't need. We take such charges very seriously, because they strike at the core of our company—our reputation for trust and integrity.

We are confident that our Auto Center customer satisfaction rate is among the highest in the industry. But after an extensive review, we have concluded that our incentive compensation and goal-setting program inadvertently created an environment in which mistakes have occurred. We are moving quickly and aggressively to eliminate that environment.

To guard against such things happening in the future, we're taking significant action:

- We have eliminated incentive compensation and goal-setting systems for automotive service advisors—the folks who diagnose problems and recommend repairs to you. We have replaced these practices with a new non-commission program designed to achieve even higher levels of customer satisfaction. Rewards will now be based on customer satisfaction.

- We're augmenting our own quality control efforts by retaining an independent organization to conduct ongoing, unannounced "shopping audits" of our automotive services to ensure that company policies are being met.

- We have written to all state attorneys general, inviting them to compare our auto repair standards and practices with those of their states in order to determine whether differences exist.

- And we are helping to organize and fund a joint industry-consumer-government effort to review current auto repair practices and recommend uniform industry standards.

We're taking these actions so you'll continue to come to Sears with complete confidence. However, one thing we will never change is our commitment to customer safety. Our policy of preventive

Exhibit 3-1   (continued).

maintenance—recommending replacement of worn parts *before* they fail—has been criticized by the California Bureau of Automotive Repair as constituting unneeded repairs. We don't see it that way. We recommend preventive maintenance because that's what our customers want, and because it makes for safer cars on the road. In fact, 75 percent of the consumers we talked to in a nationwide survey last weekend told us that auto repair centers should recommend replacement parts for preventive maintenance. As always, no work will *ever* be performed without your approval.

We understand that when your car needs service, you look for, above all, someone you can trust. And when trust is at stake, we can't mererly *react,* we must *overreact.*

We at Sears are totally committed to maintaining your confidence. You have my word on it.

Ed Brennan
Chairman and Chief Executive Officer

Reprinted by permission.

more reliable. As the financial deals of the 1980s have unwound, however, accountants themselves have faced a spate of nasty lawsuits that have both eroded their profitability and damaged their perceived reliability, leading some to question the viability of a profession shorn of its principal asset. This state of affairs calls to mind what could be called:

- *The Reliability Principle:* The more reliable a company appears to its key constituents, the better regarded the company will be.

INVESTORS AND SUPPLIERS DEMAND CREDIBILITY

As investors, we expect companies to be credible. We ask that managers live up to the claims and commitments they make in press releases, annual reports, and other communications. Having entrusted them with our hard-earned savings, we demand that they show good faith in their dealings with us. We want them to accurately convey the risks of their strategies, warn us of impending problems, and disclose material facts that might influence our assessment of their performance.

Consider how the financial monitor Moody's Investors Services rates companies. Its ratings depend heavily on how analysts interpret the company's future prospects, the quality of its management, and especially the credibility of its plans:

> *The rating process itself is . . . an opportunity for management to explain its business and its strategies to specialists who are trained to listen and to evaluate critically what they hear. . . . Typically, Moody's asks to meet and spend some time with four to five senior representatives of the company's executive, financial, and operating management. A meeting with the chief executive officer is also desirable. We believe that management is critical to credit quality; therefore, Moody's likes to be briefed on management's philosophy and plans for the future.*[8]

To investors, then, the currency of exchange is credibility. And for companies to project credibility is no easy task. Indeed, companies take great pains to maintain good relationships with financial analysts, especially with those who toil in ratings agencies. They spend considerable sums to promote themselves to those analysts and try hard to build good will.

Few analysts, however, are fooled by glossy PR. Their job is to explore the underpinnings of the company's actions and projections—its credibility. Most will therefore keep detailed records of a company's past claims and make a systematic effort to assess how well managers have lived up to them. Those who do gain credibility; those who don't suffer. I asked a senior analyst at Moody's how the organization rates firms. He put it this way: "We don't rate companies on their morality; we rate them on the credibility of their claims. We have to believe that they will do what they say they're going to do; that they will fulfill their commitments."

Investors are in fact only suppliers of capital. Credibility turns out to be the currency of exchange with parts suppliers as well. Like investors, they ask that companies make credible claims, that they act in good faith when they place orders. The nightmare of suppliers is the cancelled

Why analysts recommend Dial stock.

Leadership products are only part of why many Wall Street analysts are recommending Dial stock. Just listen to what they're saying. **Heather Hay, J.P. Morgan**, says "Dial continues to effect a strategic plan that moves it toward becoming a more understandable, streamlined company. As this plan unfolds, the shares should command a higher multiple valuation. We maintain our BUY on Dial shares."

Jack Kelly of Goldman, Sachs & Co. offers a similar recommendation, noting that his firm is "upgrading our rating on the stock from market performer to trading buy." In the opinion of **Gabe Lowy, Oppenheimer & Co.**, "Dial's consumer businesses have outperformed their branded peers... and are positioned to continue to do so." In addition, **Legg Mason's Jay Leopold** forecasts that "earnings should continue to expand at a healthy clip."

Merrill Lynch's Carol Neves recently counseled investors to buy Dial. Noting performance such as a 32% gain in income from continuing operations for the second quarter of 1994 compared to the same period last year, **Merrill Lynch** headlined a report on Dial "Right on Results."

Jack Modzelewski, PaineWebber, states "We are continuing our buy rating on Dial stock...We believe that Dial will post double-digit EPS gains over the next several years, and...we continue to believe that Dial stock is undervalued relative to its peer consumer products and services companies."

So when you're taking stock of your portfolio, remember what the experts say.

The Dial Corp

Profit Through Leadership

© 1994, The Dial Corp

Dial Corp is the maker of many familiar household products like Purex laundry detergent, Brillo soap pads, Renuzit air freshener, and Dial soap. In this 1995 advertisement, the company tries to capitalize on the favorable assessments of financial analysts to encourage investors to buy its stock. The illustration also reminds customers of the underlying commonality among the company's diverse brands. (Advertisement courtesy of The Dial Corp.)

order. Often it irreparably damages the reputation of the company that placed the order.

Accordingly, a focus on creditors, investors, and other suppliers suggests:

- *The Credibility Principle:* The more credible a company appears to its key constituents, the better regarded the company will be.

EMPLOYEES EXPECT TRUSTWORTHINESS

As employees, we ask that the companies we work for be trustworthy. While we demand that explicit contracts be honored, we also expect implicit contracts to be respected. We count on being treated fairly and honorably in job assignments, salary decisions, and promotions. We ask of companies that they respect our fundamental rights as individuals and as citizens.

These expectations place tremendous pressure on companies to develop policies and programs that support the well-being of all their employees, not just top management. Humane treatment involves not only concerns for health and safety but a growing regard for employees as partners in the work process. In many well-regarded companies, employees are fast becoming part-owners through their pension funds or stock-purchase plans. At a minimum, these employee-owners have earned the right to participate in the strategic decisions of the companies they work for—and are demanding it.

Rapid developments in information technology are also opening up channels of communication and decision making and thereby enhancing employee involvement. Progressive companies are recognizing this opportunity by creating programs that support employee endeavors (see chapter 5). The commitment to the self-realization of all employees, including minorities, the handicapped, and other disenfranchised groups, represents a genuine effort toward relationship-building with employees in better-regarded companies. Well-regarded companies work hard to establish trust with employees, whether those employees are unionized or not. By establishing trust with employees, those companies sustain their reputations.

In many ways, trust is a sign of rising professionalism in the managerial ranks. Traditionally, companies have been managed inside and out by the utilitarian logic embodied in the dictum caveat emptor—buyer beware. For those qualities of life we value highly—such as personal health and freedom—we far and away prefer to deal with so-called professionals like doctors and lawyers whose integrity is (supposedly) ensured by their adherence to sacred oaths and codes of conduct. As employees invest themselves in their companies, they too demand a reciprocating bond of trust from their employers in exchange for their commitment. When they get it, loyalty follows. Which is why I propose:

- *The Trust Principle:* The more trustworthy a company appears to its key constituents, the better regarded the company will be.

COMMUNITIES EXPECT RESPONSIBILITY

Finally, communities ask that companies recognize their responsibility to participate in the social and environmental fabric of their neighborhoods. Most employees live in the communities in which they work. They benefit from the local infrastructure. The popular concept of sustainability proposes that companies should at least put back as much as they take from their social and physical environments. Companies that ignore the well-being of their local communities demonstrate a glaring disregard for its residents.

In the past decade, many companies have stepped in where government has failed: in education, in the inner city, in the environment. Environmentally conscious leaders like U.S. Vice President Al Gore ask that companies incorporate so-called externalities into their strategic decisions—that they internalize the cleanup costs of industrial waste and of air, water, and land pollution. Beyond asking that companies pay economic penalties, however, they voice a clear expectation that companies be responsible citizens of the communities in which they operate. Much as a population of a prey can be wiped out by overconsuming predators, so is the human species threatened, they point out, by irresponsible companies that overconsume our natural and human resources. For these leaders, citizenship means favoring sustainable business activities that take out of society and the environment no more than they put back.

Consider the comments of David Kearns, Xerox's longtime chairman and CEO:

The name Xerox has a very high value, and it is well-earned. In addition to an exciting product and our technological leadership in the early years of the company, the Xerox image was carefully nurtured. The idea of a

Pfizer, Inc. is heavily involved in community development in New York City, its home for over a century. In 1981, the company's then chairman Edmund T. Pratt, Jr., asked his staff how Pfizer could help revitalize the Brooklyn neighborhood where the company has a plant. In 1984, Pfizer and the city jointly proposed a project to build an industrial park and middle-income housing on a site adjacent to the plant. Pictured here in 1991 are Pratt and former New York City Mayor David N. Dinkins (fourth and fifth hard hats from the right) breaking ground for the first set of homes that bear Mr. Pratt's name. (Photo courtesy of Pfizer, Inc.)

socially conscious company didn't just happen. As Xerox began to make money, it put some back into the community. The saying was: You've got to do well to do good. It was part of the corporate strategy and the corporate culture. Support of such things as quality television helped enhance the early image of the company and made it seem bigger than it actually was.[9]

Companies pledged to a mindset that identifies good citizenship as a core value recognize the importance of enabling closer integration of work and leisure, of individual and organization, of individual and community, of company and community. Like Xerox, pharmaceutical giant Johnson & Johnson is well known for its community orientation. As its chairman and CEO Ralph Larsen puts it: "Our image is that of a caring company. It is shaped not by great acts or great decisions, but rather by the sum total of all behavior and actions of the company over a long period of time."[10]

The trend toward company-supported volunteerism, community networking, environmentalism, employee participation, and workplace equity is a practical one that many top companies like Xerox and Johnson & Johnson are joining to reduce employee alienation, to achieve social integration, to improve their reputations, and so to sustain their long-term viability. They go beyond simple philanthropy. Adopt-a-school programs, for instance, are a form of enlightened self-interest. By supporting the local community, these corporate sponsored programs help to upgrade the workforce and to increase a company's competitiveness. It's the challenge of the future.

An awareness of reputational effects encourages us to manage our companies according to:

- *The Responsibility Principle:* The more responsible a company appears to its key constituents, the better regarded the company will be.

UNDER THE MAGNIFYING GLASS

All of a company's actions are not equally visible; nor are they equally appreciated by observers. The business media regularly magnify what some companies do and ignore others. Reporters routinely evaluate the prospects of certain firms and communicate their opinions. In general, studies of the media show that reporters like to highlight the unusual. They are drawn to innovative, unexpected, and deviant practices and products. Larger and better-performing firms also get a disproportionate share of media coverage. It explains why many managers are wary of being scrutinized by the press and often prefer to keep an arm's length relationship with reporters.

Additionally, in every industry the moves that companies make are quickly communicated through a network of friendships and acquaintances, board contacts, and informal social ties among managers. Not all of the information conveyed is accurate. These social networks selectively magnify, interpret, and distort a company's actions. Various studies suggest that managers' actions naturally generate gossip and inuendo that get quickly passed on as more and more people get on the bandwagon.

Because a company's relationships are so diverse, strategic efforts to create attractive images are unlikely to be entirely successful in determining the judgments external groups make of a company's actions. Not only are external groups somewhat remote from the company, they also rely on other sources of information and apply criteria that may be at odds with managers' goals. That's why, for instance, utilities that commit to nuclear power often find themselves the unwitting targets of public-interest groups, media exposés, or community boycotts, no matter how extensively they invest in managing external impressions.

Often a company will develop inconsistent images with different constituent groups—some more favorable, some less so. In the short run, the expectations of some groups can run counter to the expectations of others. For instance, investors tend to prefer high earnings. But consumer demands for quality and service are generally a drain on earnings, as are supplier attempts to get higher prices, employee petitions for higher wages and benefits, and community requests for charitable donations and environmental support.

These seemingly divergent agendas put forward by a company's different constituents actually mask a mutuality of interests. After all, each of a company's constituents has an interest in its long-term viability. A company's survival obviously depends on its ability to generate strong and stable earnings, which it can then

- reinvest in innovative research,

- channel toward quality-improvement programs and supplier relationship building to outperform competitors,

- pay out as dividends to safeguard the returns of investors,

- allocate to internal programs that enhance the well-being of employees, or

- invest in programs that tackle social problems in the local communities in which it operates.

To satisfy all constituents, then, a company must necessarily maintain solid long-term economic performance. On that, we all agree.

Figure 3-2 summarizes the reinforcing network of factors that helps companies build strong and favorable reputations with their principal constituencies: credibility, reliability, trustworthiness, and responsibility; these speak legions about the difference between simply managing a company's tangible assets and safeguarding the long-term well-being of its reputational capital, its intangible wealth.

Figure 3-2 WHAT MAKES A GOOD REPUTATION?

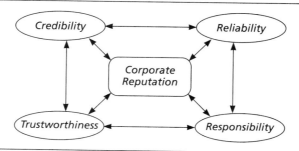

In sum, a reputation comes into being as constituents struggle to make sense of a company's past and present actions. The reputation that constituents ascribe to a company is the aggregate of many personal judgments about the company's credibility, reliability, responsibility, and trustworthiness. It also has the following characteristics:

- A reputation is a cognitive feature of an industry that crystallizes a company's perceived ranking in a field of other rivals.

- A reputation is created from the bottom up as each of us applies our own personal combination of economic and social, selfish and altruistic criteria in judging a company and its future prospects.

- A reputation is a snapshot that reconciles the multiple images of a company held by all of its constituencies. It signals the overall attractiveness of the company to employees, consumers, investors, suppliers, and local communities.

And so I offer the following working definition of a corporate reputation:

- A corporate reputation is a perceptual representation of a company's past actions and future prospects that describes the firm's overall appeal to all of its key constituents when compared with other leading rivals.

WHAT CAPITALIZING ON REPUTATION GETS THE FIRM

If being perceived by constituents as credible, reliable, trustworthy, and responsible is the hallmark of a good reputation, it pays off because well-regarded companies generally:

- command premium prices for their products,

- pay lower prices for purchases,

- entice top recruits to apply for positions,

- experience greater loyalty from consumers and employees,

- have more stable revenues,

- face fewer risks of crisis, and

- are given greater latitude to act by their constituents.

That's why in the long run it's in a company's self-interest to build a strong reputation by serving all of its constituents. As Merrill Lynch's William Schreyer recognizes: "We've put a considerable amount of marketing dollars behind Merrill Lynch's identity and we closely track the impression that our name and our over-all corporate image make with the investing public, with corporations and financial institutions, and with local, national, and international officials. We do that because as a marketing-oriented company we believe that the strength of our corporate identity has a direct effect on how well we can market our products and services to our customer base."[11]

PREMIUM PRICES

Whether for wine, food, or clothing, most of us willingly pay premium prices to buy the products of better-regarded companies. The meals at New York's Lutèce are expensive, but the high-quality ingredients used and the skills of its owner-chef justify the cost. Its reputation promises patrons a high standard of quality and reliability, for which they are prepared to pay. In similar ways, reputable fashion designers promise customers a higher standard of quality, cut, fit, and appearance for which they willingly pay higher prices.[12]

The fashions of French clothing designers Claude Montana and Thierry Mugler are well known. Their reputations create a following among a small coterie of shoppers prepared to pay extravagant sums for their ready-to-wear garments. In similar ways, a performer's fame can translate into high prices at the box office. Concerts by superstar Barbra Streisand come to mind. Throughout 1994, the singer and actress parlayed her fame into concert ticket prices that soared to $1,500 a seat. Indeed, performers like Streisand and other celebrated names routinely attract audiences to events that raise extravagant sums for their pet projects and foundations.

In February 1994, lured by the publicity surrounding the event, I attended the Christie's auction of art and home furnishings owned by Streisand. In the euphoria of the moment, I too bid on some of the 358 items that were put up, thereby marginally contributing to the auction's total sale price of $6.2 million—a 37 percent premium over its expected $4.5 million market value. As Christie's U.S. chairman, Christopher Burge, noted: "An awful lot of the success of the sale had to do with the fact that this was Barbra Streisand's collection. . . . People wanted something from her collection, meaning the smaller lots brought higher prices than we normally see. The celebrity value means less on the more important pieces."[13] In other words, reputation inflates economic value, especially for worthless things. For well-known items, the reputation of the artists who created them supersedes that of the endorser.

In like fashion, companies sometimes use the marquee value of their names for benevolent causes. By sponsoring charitable events, for instance, they not only do good deeds but publicize themselves to some constituents. In the end, the heightened visibility can enable these companies to charge even more for their products than can their rivals. In a way, the premium prices celebrated companies exact for their products are a reimbursement for previous outlays in advertising and promotion that helped them to build their reputations. After all, to acquire a strong reputation requires of both individuals and companies enormous investments in creating public identities and then publicizing them.

Moreover, those reputations are marketable products in and of themselves. The reputations of auditors, lawyers, and investment bankers are often rented at a premium. For instance, a new company ordinarily finds it difficult to raise equity capital. In order to sell an initial offering, it will offer to pay a premium to rent the reputation of an established banker. Investors are more likely to buy a public offering underwritten by a highly regarded bank like Goldman Sachs than one sponsored by an unknown bank, a service for which Goldman Sachs naturally charges a premium price to the company that is going public.[14]

On the other hand, a company with a pristine and well-established reputation can attract investors on its own. So it need not necessarily retain the services of the most highly reputed bankers or lawyers. In a study of investment banks in the United States, I actually found that many prestigious clients preferred to hire less prominent investment banks to do deals. The reputations of the top banks were extremely advantageous, however, in signing up less notable clients.

A reputation effect also explains why many initial public offerings appear to be underpriced after they are issued. Recent examples include the first offerings of bookseller Barnes & Noble and fast-food retailer Boston Chicken. Both companies enjoyed excellent reputations when they went public, which led speculators and investors to bid up the price of their shares well beyond the estimated value of the companies' assets—and even beyond their probable potential.

Consider the Donna Karan Company. In August 1993, the much-celebrated New York–based high-fashion designer Donna Karan announced that her company would soon be going public with an anticipated first offering worth $159 million. The stock issue was among the most eagerly anticipated. Given the company's strong reputation, demand for the limited supply of shares was likely to be high, thereby inflating the selling price. Accordingly, the prospectus showed shares priced at $16, despite an underlying net worth of only $2.70 a share. Since then, however, poor economic conditions have delayed the marketing of the offering at the intended price, and the company has remained privately held.

Companies that are well regarded can benefit from charging premium prices for their products and so reimburse themselves over the long term for the front-end costs of building good reputations. Alternatively, they can also benefit by undercutting rivals. The combination of lower prices and a strong reputation generally attracts the most customers to an offering. Premier banker Goldman Sachs is feared on the street for just this reason. The company occasionally uses its reputation to bid even more aggressively than lesser rivals for a new equity issue, thereby securing its top standing in the industry.

REDUCED COSTS

Having a good reputation can reduce some of a company's operating costs. That's because reputation provides leverage in many negotiations, particularly with suppliers, creditors, and distributors. Suppliers would prefer to negotiate supply contracts with credible companies, companies unlikely to renege on orders. Likewise, before lending money, creditors want to believe that the company is good for it, that their money won't go down the drain. Studies show that a good reputation can reduce a company's cost of capital by improving its ability to raise money in the credit markets.[15]

Wal-Mart is well-known for providing customers with quality goods at discount prices. In part, it keeps prices low by keeping labor costs below the industry average. Because of its good reputation, Wal-Mart jobs—which compensate employees with decidedly inferior wages and benefits—are still prized by the communities in which the company locates its operations. Andersen Consulting has a reputation for paying junior consultants far less than do other firms in the industry. Andersen can get away with it because consultants trained by the firm anticipate capitalizing on the reputational halo of their training later in their careers.

THE PICK OF RECRUITS

In looking for jobs, most studies show that people are not a trusting lot. They prefer an inside view, and so talk to relatives, friends, and acquaintances in an effort to get a sense of the company's "real" identity—its reputation.[16] In choosing between comparable offers, these same job seekers are likely to be swayed heavily by hearsay and rumor—signals that grant one company a better reputation than another. Just as a top school's reputation draws the brightest students, so do esteemed companies more easily recruit the finest candidates for their jobs, those who can pick and choose among multiple offers.[17] As Xerox's Kearns puts it: "A good image helps you recruit good people, especially young people coming out of college who want to join a company they respect."[18]

In every industry, one or a few companies are so well regarded that they serve as a training ground for the rest of the industry. General Electric, for instance, is well known as a breeding ground for top managers throughout American industry. The management consulting firm of McKinsey & Company has many former employees both in the consulting industry itself and throughout American industry as its alumni take jobs with former clients. Chase Manhattan once held that honor in the banking industry, as IBM once did in the computer industry, Sears in retailing, and General Motors in manufacturing. Today, however, the lackluster reputations of these four companies are more likely to detract from their ability to recruit the most talented candidates, forcing them to pay higher entry-level bonuses to outbid rivals.

A company's good reputation attracts consumers to its products because it reduces our insecurity about how well those products will perform. It signals their implicit quality. Despite its high prices, try getting a table for dinner at New York's Lutèce—it takes months. The restaurant's star reputation regularly draws repeat customers who could choose to eat anywhere. Diners keep coming back because they feel sure that they'll get the culinary experience they expect.[19]

Not only does a good reputation attract loyal customers, it also makes for loyal employees: it acts as a morale booster. Who wouldn't feel better about working for a company that's well respected? As Intel's CEO Andrew Grove points out: "The human element of reputation is that it gives people extra energy. It gives you that extra lift to do the tough stuff our life consists of day in and day out."[20]

To salespeople, a company's reputation acts like a calling card. It draws a warm reception and a welcoming nod that often opens doors and grants access to otherwise unreachable people. As a junior professor at the Wharton School in the late 1970s, I can recall many instances in which the school's top-flight reputation opened doors for research in corporate America that I could not have opened alone. In retrospect, Wharton's reputation also provided the faculty with "psychic income," presumably enough to compensate for the dungeon-like offices and primitive classrooms in which we did our work in those days.

A good reputation builds employee loyalty by increasing the willingness of employees to cooperate with unusual requests and by fostering teamwork and a sense of shared destiny. Take the once high-flying People Express. In its glory days, the discount airline enjoyed a glowing reputation as a company on a mission. Its gung-ho employees accepted lower wages to join the family-like environment the company had created. For a time, the combination of cooperative staff, high morale, and low pay enabled People Express to maintain its low-cost strategy—at least until it ran into aggressive competition from larger carriers and its own overly ambitious growth by merger.

Primerica's chairman Sandy Weill puts it this way: "In the service industries, you must not forget that brand reputations are built by people. And so, much of the assets of the brand go down in the elevator every night. It's the job of management to make sure those people are kept to the highest standards and also to make sure that the business is managed so well, that they come back up in the elevator the next day."[21]

INCREASED STABILITY

A good reputation helps to smooth customer demand for a company's products. In a sluggish economy, they are the last purchases we cut. Reputation breeds customer loyalty, repeat business, and so dampens the effects of business downturns. The result is stability: Better rated companies tend to have less volatile stock prices and more stable operations.

Of course, a good reputation is no guarantee against dramatic market changes. So-called blue-chip companies like IBM and General Motors are cases in point. They were once widely recommended by analysts as safe harbors for retirees and pension funds. No more. As both companies have demonstrated, dramatic changes in technology and competitive conditions can destabilize even the best-regarded companies, fostering wild fluctuations in sales revenues and the price at which their shares trade. With their reputations in the gutter, IBM and GM have demonstrated greater sales volatility and instability than ever before, with corresponding fluctuations in investment forecasts, analyst ratings, and shareholder expectations. As graduating MBA students now point out, these are no longer the companies they look to for work.

REDUCED RISK

Companies with strong reputations tend to develop solid internal control systems to monitor their employees and anticipate problems. If being prepared reduces the catastrophic potential of a crisis, it's entirely plausible that better-regarded companies are less risky.

Consider Goldman Sachs. The company is well known for building close relationships with clients. It is also famous for its strong team-based identity and elaborate control systems. It seems unlikely that Goldman Sachs could ever be hit by a scandal like the one faced by rivals Salomon Brothers in 1991 and Kidder Peabody in 1994. At both firms, rogue employees broke rules that seriously jeopardized their banks' reputation and put their survival in doubt. Much of the blame has been placed on the extremely individualistic orientations of Salomon and Kidder, reinforced by weak controls. Since then, both firms have been hard at work rethinking their internal practices in order to safeguard against future infractions. Even Goldman Sachs launched a program to reexamine its own controls and practices after the Kidder Peabody scandal broke in 1994. Increasingly, these firms recognize that their reputations are constantly on the line and are inextricably tied to the ethics of individual traders and bankers. Hence the importance of strong internal cultures that minimize reputational risk.

INCREASED LATITUDE

A good reputation creates a halo around a company; willy-nilly it becomes the standard-bearer of an industry, the one against which rivals benchmark their actions and strategies. Intense scrutiny by rivals and the press creates enormous pressure. Performing in the constant glare of publicity can be inhibiting, which is why so many high-profile companies shy away from the media and maintain an introverted posture (see chapter 6).

At the same time, however, a reputational halo can soften the blow when a crisis or scandal hits. We give the well-regarded company the benefit of the doubt. A case in point is the degree of latitude and forebearance Johnson & Johnson received from consumers and regulators when faced with its second case of product tampering with Tylenol in 1986. The company that regularly neglects constituents won't fare so well. When charges of insider trading were leveled at Drexel in the late 1980s, the company had little reputational credit to draw from in its time of need. Similarly, for years the tobacco industry led by Philip Morris and R. J. Reynolds was extremely successful in using public relations to attract new smokers and maintain their core business. But in the last decade, despite extraordinary efforts to placate constituents with charitable contributions and other promotional strategies, the industry has been losing ground as antismoking groups have grown more vocal. They use aggressive promotional strategies of their own to tarnish the reputations of the tobacco manufacturers. Under the barrage of unfavorable legislative and media attention, managers of tobacco companies may well be at their wits' end in trying to sustain the reputation of their core tobacco business. The reputations of the food subsidiaries of these diversified companies are also beginning to suffer by association.

Reputational factors can also help a company emerge from bad times. A study at Dartmouth's Tuck School of Business shows that among companies facing bankruptcy, creditors are more lenient and flexible with companies that have more prestigious managers at the helm.[22] Put differently, companies with more reputational capital are less likely to go under. Reputation buys a company greater freedom of movement, more time to recover from difficulty.

A GOOD REPUTATION IS A STRATEGIC ASSET

Although the benefits of having a good reputation are many and varied, they come down to one thing: A strong reputation creates a strategic advantage. Since companies are constantly competing for the support of customers, investors, suppliers, employees, and local communities, a good reputation creates an intangible obstacle that lesser rivals will have a tough time overcoming. That competitive advantage alone is enough to guarantee stronger long-run returns to better-regarded companies.[23]

Just as individuals build human capital by investing in their own skills through training and education,[24] so too do companies create value by investing in a wide range of activities that induce constituents to perceive them as reliable, credible, trustworthy, and responsible. In fact, the economic benefits of a good reputation materialize in the excess value investors are willing to pay for the company's shares—that is, its *reputational capital.*

Good *name in man or woman, dear my*
  lord,
Is the immediate jewel of their souls:
Who steals my purse steals trash; 'tis
  something, nothing:
'Twas mine, 'tis his, and has been slave
  to thousands;
But he that filches from me my good
  name
Robs me of that which not enriches him,
And makes me poor indeed.

—*William Shakespeare*
  Othello

Reputational Capital

CORPORATE REPUTATIONS have bottom-line effects. A good reputation enhances profitability because it attracts customers to the company's products, investors to its securities, and employees to its jobs. In turn, esteem inflates the price at which a public company's securities trade. The economic value of a corporate reputation can therefore be gauged by the excess market value of its securities. This chapter explores different ways of quantifying the economic value of corporate reputation and examines more closely a market-based measure of reputational capital.

VALUING IMAGE

When consummate image maker Andy Warhol died in 1987, the value of his estate was estimated at some $700 million. By 1993, that estimate had been revised by Sotheby's to a lowly $220 milion. What happened to the other $480 million between 1987 and 1993? Over the last few years, that exact question has slowly wound its way through the court system. Warhol's former estate lawyers filed suit against the Warhol Foundation, claiming that the higher value was more accurate. To them, of course, this was vitally important; their fee was tied to the "true" value of the estate.

The value of art depends heavily on two familiar factors: demand and supply. A dead artist's work generally increases in value because, while supply remains fixed, demand for the artist's work increases. Demand also depends heavily on the reputation of the artist at the time of death. A strong reputation inflates demand and raises subsequent auction prices for the artist's work. As one art observer put it: "The reputation of the artist and the work reinforce one another: we value more a work done by an artist we respect, just as we respect more an artist whose work we have admired."[1]

In the years since Warhol's death, not only did an economic downturn reduce overall demand for art, but Warhol's reputation itself suffered vilification. Not surprisingly, then, pieces of his art have fetched far lower prices at auction. In itself, this was an ironic outcome, given that few artists since the Dutch painter Rembrandt have proved quite so skillful as Warhol at projecting an image and sustaining a reputation during their lifetime. As one art critic puts it, Rembrandt was an "entrepreneur of the self," someone "who invented the work of art most characteristic of our culture—a commodity distinguished among others by not being factory produced, but produced in limited numbers and creating its market, whose special claim to the aura of individuality and to high market value bind it to basic aspects of an entrepreneurial (capitalist) enterprise."[2]

Like Rembrandt, Warhol deftly manipulated the media in a quest to secure for himself more than the 15 minutes of fame to which he claimed everyone else was entitled. He was an accomplished poseur, endlessly staging himself in a bid for the world's attention. A man of very, very few words, he took to hosting a television talk show. The magazine he edited—*Interview*—published amidst outsized photographs a mere scattering of words, few of them his. The dialogue in the films he directed was entirely improvised. All in all, Warhol probably represents one of our era's most artful social constructions and would be sorely disappointed in the managers of his estate for having so poorly handled the reputation he consigned to them.

In contrast with Warhol's art, Pablo Picasso's paintings have fared rather well at auction. Works that sold for $500,000–$800,000 in the early 1980s fetched $2–$3 million in 1993, despite the recession. Why up for Picasso but down for Warhol? If Picasso's paintings have proved more successful at auction, it's partly because more systematic efforts were made to prop up his reputation. For instance, soon after Sotheby's was retained by a Picasso collector to engineer a sale of 88 pieces, the auction house systematically pursued prospective collectors and dealers around the world. All the pieces were sent on a tour of major art capitals. By the time the auction was held in November 1993, adroit promotion had created pent-up demand. Spirited bidding at the auction racked up a total of $32 million for the collection. Contrast that with a similar auction of 16 Warhol paintings held 6 months earlier at which only 2 pieces were sold.

A recent study by the *Economist* found that prestige products hold their value well over the years. Table 4-1 contrasts the current and

Table 4-1 THE ENDURING VALUE OF A REPUTATION

Company	Product	Original Price	Price in 1992	% Real Annual Price Increase
Jaguar	Top two-seater	$1,085.00 (in 1932)	$73,545.00	3.2
Parker	Duofold fountain pen	$7.30 (in 1927)	$236.00	2.2
Dunhill	Rollagas silver-plated lighter	$19.00 (in 1958)	$205.00	2.4
Louis Vuitton	Suitcase	$29.00 (in 1912)	$1,670.00	1.7
Cartier	Tank watch	$155.75 (in 1921)	$4,180.00	1.7

Source: Adapted from the *Economist*, January 8, 1993, 96.

historical prices of some top products from five high-reputation companies: a top-of-the-line Jaguar two-seater, a Parker Duofold fountain pen, a Dunhill silver-plated "Rollagas" lighter, a Louis Vuitton suitcase, and a Cartier Tank watch. In real terms, the prices of these companies' products have grown systematically over the years, averaging an increase close to 2 percent per year after controlling for inflation, a remarkable rate of growth.

Much as some branded products hold their value well, so have managers begun to recognize that there is enduring economic value in a strong corporate-level reputation. In part, recognition of this fact has come from service providers who are particularly hard put to identify other assets of note in their portfolios. In fact, all companies—whether in services or in manufacturing—rely not only on people and plant and equipment but also on intangible assets such as patents, trademarks, copyrights, brand names, and reputation. Lacking material products, service companies are especially dependent on their reputations to stay in business. In conversation, investment bankers love to remind listeners that their principal assets go down the elevator every night. Don't take that to mean "we care about our people." It simply reflects appreciation for the fact that employees carry with them the capacity to make or break the company's most valuable asset: its reputation. Well-known investor Warren Buffett made a celebrated remark to a group of Salomon Brothers managers in the aftermath of the trading scandal that shook the bank in 1991. "If you lose dollars for the firm by bad decisions, I will be very understanding. If you lose reputation for the firm, I will be ruthless."[3]

The same concern naturally extends to providers of accounting and legal services. In 1992 and 1993, top accountants Arthur Andersen and Ernst & Young agreed to pay $65 million and $128 million, respectively, to settle federal charges that their audits of failed savings and loan banks were negligent or misleading. Joining them with penalties of $41 million, $50 million, and $45 million, respectively, were the blue-chip law firms of Kay Scholer; Jones, Day; and Paul, Weiss. Although assenting to the fines, none of these service firms admitted guilt. Their reasoning: It's cheaper to pay a fine than to risk deflating a firm's economic value in a court battle. Settling avoids protracted litigation and publicity that would only further sully the firm's good name and lower the underlying value of its most prized intangible asset, its reputation.

Despite its obvious worth, the dollar value of a company's reputation proves difficult to quantify. In essence, it derives from the profits a company can expect to generate from its intangible assets, only a small part of which are embodied in patents and other forms of intellectual property. That makes most future revenue streams uncertain. Where patented products are the principal source of value, however, we can estimate the revenue stream that might obtain over the patent's 17-year life, assuming no rival brings out a substitute product to cannibalize sales. Since the costs directly associated with obtaining the patent are easily identified, the task of compiling, capitalizing, and amortizing them on a company's balance sheet is straightforward. So the economic value of a corporate reputation that depends heavily on the patents the firm owns can be calculated in some detail. In essence, the company's reputation merely reflects the value of the firm's intellectual capital.[4]

Not as much can be said for companies with reputations that do not derive from patents. Take companies like 3M or Procter & Gamble, which have a stable full of brand names. If we try to estimate the overall value of these brands using the same logic applied to patents, things get difficult. On the revenue side, although the U.S. Patent Office provides indefinite legal protection for a trademark, who knows how strong a brand will remain, how long it will attract customers, and what future revenues it will earn? Moreover, on the cost side, American accounting rules allow companies to capitalize and depreciate only the administrative costs directly associated with securing a name. They do not allow companies to capitalize the indirect costs associated with building and maintaining a name. In other words, the advertising, service, and support costs that actually create brand equity—the key ingredients of those companies' reputations—never show up on the books.

This is problematic. Although everyone recognizes that the reputation of a company with a stable of brands generates bottom-line returns, no one can agree on how to gauge its worth. Accountants debate how to record goodwill, marketers ponder the hidden equity in the company's brands, financial analysts muse about the strength of the company's franchise. Lacking consensus, the value of the company's reputation goes entirely unrecorded as an asset because, as accountants put it, "Measuring the components of goodwill . . . is simply too complex and associating any costs with future benefits too difficult."[5] Two ongoing controversies reveal how unsystematic our approach is for valuing corporate reputations and what pitfalls we encounter when we do try to quantify them.

GOODWILL: WHAT'S IT WORTH?

Between 1980 and 1990, the total value of intangible assets in the United States increased nearly tenfold from $45 billion to an estimated $400 billion.[6] Conservative U.S. accounting rules prohibit recognizing the value of these hidden assets, and tax authorities prevent a company from capitalizing costs incurred to project an image or to protect a name. This means that advertising as well as research and development costs—outlays that contribute heavily to building a company's reputation—are therefore merely expensed and regularly disappear without a trace.

The consequence of immediately expensing costs that build reputation is that balance sheets routinely undervalue companies. They open to outright conjecture estimates of a company's true worth. Take an independent insurance agency, for instance. Most of its assets are intangible. They consist of customer lists and client contacts—that is, of reputation. On paper, it's worth next to nothing. Nonetheless, such an agency typically sells on the open market for about $200,000. Clearly, its reputation is worth something, and we are left to speculate about its value. Many battles for corporate control in the go-go decade of the 1980s involved just such speculative assessments of the hidden value in a company's balance sheets, what accountants like to call goodwill.

To stay on the safe side, U.S. accountants have agreed to recognize goodwill only when a firm is sold. They measure the value of goodwill as the excess of the company's purchase price over the fair market value of its tangible assets. Goodwill typically incorporates the value of all intangibles, including brand names and reputation. Two questions arise:

1. Should goodwill be capitalized on the balance sheet and depreciated, or immediately charged off against the merged company's retained earnings?

2. In valuing two companies, why deflate the company whose goodwill is generated entirely from within against the company whose goodwill comes from a merger?

In the interests of comparability across companies, industries, and countries, it would seem desirable to maintain a common way of accounting for goodwill. U.S. accounting rules, however, differ from those of other countries, and critics contend that they place American firms at a disadvantage. Here's why.

When a merger takes place in the United States, accountants recognize goodwill as an asset and depreciate it over some arbitrary period, not to exceed 40 years. In turn, the company takes an annual depreciation charge against earnings. On one hand, the company's total assets increase; on the other, so do its expenses. In combination, the net effect is to deflate the merged company's return on assets. Contrast this practice with accounting rules in the United Kingdom, which forcibly write off goodwill against equity. Under these conditions, goodwill has no effect on measures of the company's return ratios. So, in a contest between a British and an American company to buy a third company, the British company's returns invariably look better to investors. When Britain's Grand Metropolitan purchased Pillsbury for $5.7 billion in 1989, for instance, it immediately posted a total of $2 billion in goodwill to equity, with no effect on Grand Met's subsequent earnings. Had an American company bought Pillsbury, it would have been forced to deflate its earnings by about $50 million a year for the next 40 years, an unattractive prospect. Concerned observers contend that foreign purchasers may well be outbidding American companies because of U.S. accounting rules that extort high goodwill charges and penalize a purchaser's stock price.[7]

Discussions about reputation hit center stage in late 1993 as President Bill Clinton presented his economic package to a divided U.S. Congress. Debate raged over forcing a 14-year depreciation schedule on purchased intangibles and over allowing write-offs of those intangibles to only 75 percent of their value. A shorter schedule would mean a company could claim higher annual tax deductions, and so higher short-term profitability. The marginally positive vote in Congress means that the government now recognizes that some intangibles are short-lived. Film companies buy distribution rights to movies whose useful lives are measured in weekends; software companies invest millions in programs that often becomes obsolete in a few years. Unfortunately, recognizing intangibles also reduces the government's tax revenues, something most administrations in Washington are loathe to do.

Whatever the rule, the accounting controversy over intangibles is likely to rage until a reliable and comparative estimate of reputational capital is developed that can be accounted for somewhere in a company's financial statements, if not directly on the balance sheet. As one observer comments in *Financial World* magazine: "Why charge earnings or take a write-off on retained earnings for an asset whose value is generally increasing? Mark brand values to market each year and capitalize advertising expenditures that support it. If the brand declines in value, then advertising expenditures become an expense."[8]

BATTERED BRANDS

In September 1992, Bermuda-based Bacardi agreed to pay $1.4 billion for a 51 percent stake in Martini & Rossi, the European spirits company. That same week, RJR Nabisco put up $100 million to buy the Stella D'Oro Biscuit Company, one of the largest U.S. cookie makers, while it sold off its Shredded Wheat division to General Mills for $450 million. Not to be left behind, Gillette put up $423 million for Britain's Parker Pen Holdings, making Gillette the world's largest producer of pens, with 41 percent of the American market for upscale pens.

These transactions symbolize the enduring value of brands. In most industries, brands are easier to buy than to create because a crowded field of established brands puts up high barriers to entry that prove difficult to overcome. To launch a brand from scratch requires pumping massive amounts of advertising dollars into the media with unpredictable results. Buying a brand, on the other hand, guarantees immediate access to shelf space, to consumers, and so to market share.

On April 2, 1993, name brands came under attack from unexpected quarters. Without warning, cigarette maker Philip Morris announced that it would slash the price of its wildly profitable Marlboro brand by 20 percent. Suddenly, the company that had long ago persuaded smokers not just to remain loyal but to accept average annual price hikes of 10 percent seemed to be capitulating to competition from discount brands. To investors, this was bad news indeed. Individual shares of Philip Morris dropped by some $14.75 on what came to be known as "Marlboro Friday," and the company lost more than $13 billion in market value.

The bad news didn't stop there. Investors interpreted the unexpected vulnerability of perennially profitable Marlboro as a warning bell that all brands were suspicious, their value questionable. A name-brand sell-off began. Within two weeks, other consumer goods companies that had long enjoyed brand-based reputations—companies like Gillette, RJR Nabisco, Coca-Cola, Anheuser Busch, Heinz, and Procter & Gamble—saw their market value fall precipitously by nearly 20 percent.

In fact, Philip Morris's decision to drop its price reflects what critics claim to be a widespread decline of brand loyalty among consumers. In an inclement environment of low growth, persistent unemployment, and increased value shopping, consumers have welcomed lower-priced alternatives to premium products, and sales of private-label merchandise and store-branded products have grown dramatically. Take cigarettes. In 1981, premium brands like Marlboro and Camel accounted for the whole market; by 1992, discount brands had taken over some 30 percent of the $44 billion U.S. market. According to one survey, nearly $26 billion worth of private-label items were sold in supermarkets in 1992, accounting for 18 percent of sales. In categories with traditionally strong brand sales, private-label products have made serious inroads; they now claim 16 percent of the market for bottled water, 7 percent of the market for soft drinks, and 15 percent of the market for disposable diapers.[9] These trends point to the rising quality of private-label goods that has made consumers more confident in discount brands. As savvy buyers, we are not blind to the fact that in many categories it's the same manufacturers of premium-priced products that are making and distributing the value-priced brands. So why pay more?

The turmoil that began on Marlboro Friday appears to be polarizing other industries into high-priced "megabrands" at one extreme and discount brands at the other. A recent decision by Procter & Gamble exemplifies the trend. In May 1993, P&G announced that it would discontinue its number 2 brand of bathroom tissue, White Cloud, to build up its number 1 brand, Charmin. The strategy hints at the likely consolidation of brand names in categories like paper products, soft drinks, cigarettes, and beer in favor of fewer but more visible megabrands that claim larger market shares. When P&G disclosed in July 1993 that it would reduce its 106,000-member workforce by 12 percent over the next four years, the company appeared to explicitly recognize the suddenly depreciated value of all brand names, even dominant ones like Tide detergent, Pampers diapers, and Crest toothpaste.

How valuable, then, is a highly recognizable brand name? Ask Herbert Baum, President of Campbell Soup. "When you look at our balance sheet, you should see right through the cash, accounts receivable, plants and equipment on the asset side, to our brands. Our brands are the real assets we own. Without them, we have nothing."[10] Recently, some companies in the United Kingdom have sought to assign a specific value to their brand names and list them as assets on their balance sheets. Part of their motivation to value intangibles derives from those British accounting rules that compel an acquiring company to write off all goodwill immediately against equity. Because doing so can leave an acquirer with no equity at all, to value acquired brands as assets and place them on the balance' sheet is a tool for restoring equity.[11]

VALUING CORPORATE REPUTATION

Experts in marketing have proposed various methods for assessing the value of a company's brands—its brand equity. None has had universal appeal.[12] One of the more prominent methods for estimating a brand's value involves asking, How much of a royalty on sales would a third party have to pay to obtain the right to use the name?[13] For instance, the ubiquitous Pierre Cardin claims 840 licensees in 98 countries. In 1988, Cardin products grossed some $2 billion, and the House of Cardin collected more than $75 million in royalties—7–10 percent on clothing sales, and 3–5 percent of sales on other consumer goods. It suggests that the Pierre Cardin brand is worth a good deal of money.

Licensing agreements, then, are actually royalty rates for corporate names and so provide a rough ordering of a brand's value. The more a licensee is prepared to pay to rent a name, the greater must be the drawing power of the brand. Every August, the editors of *Financial World* obtain data about corporate royalty rates. They report that fashion companies generally charge higher royalty rates than do consumer goods companies. Topping their list are top-tier houses Chanel and Christian Dior at 12 percent; a second-tier set of companies that includes Yves Saint Laurent, Nike, Reebok, Estee Lauder, Avon, Johnson & Johnson, and Gillette at 6 percent; and a third tier of brand names charging lower rates and including companies like Eastman Kodak, Michelin, Goodyear, Adidas, and Polaroid.[14]

Although licensing arrangements vary wildly, royalty percentages generally range between 1 percent and 10 percent of projected sales. A brand's value could be calculated as the present value of these expected royalty payments over some arbitrary period, say the next 20 years. Such a calculation, however, simply suggests that "bigger is better." Brands with more sales are always more valuable. So the measure does not account for consumers' relative satisfaction with a brand and so does not really gauge its reputation. Most brand assessments rely on just such arbitrary estimates of a brand's "strength."

Financial World uses these royalty rates to estimate and publish the implicit brand value of corporate names each August. To do so, the magazine relies on subjective assessments of the "strength" of a brand prepared by Interbrand, a marketing consulting firm. These assessments incorporate 20 factors, including perceived consumer recognition, line-extension potential, and the name's transferability to other products. Based on an additional estimate of the expected life of the company's trademark, and on various assumptions about sales growth and the discount rate to apply to future revenue streams, *Financial World* arrives at estimates of the brand values of 15 companies.

Take consumer goods giant Gillette, visible most recently for the successful launch of its line of Sensor shaving products. In 1993, the subjective strength score for Gillette calculated by Interbrand (*Fortune*'s list quantifying company intellectual assets) suggested that an 8 percent royalty rate might be expected. Applied to Gillette's $4.7 billion in sales, it meant potential royalty revenues of $375 million in the first year. Assuming sales growth of 5 percent per year over 20 years (the expected minimum life of Gillette's name) and discounting the royalty revenues back to the present at Gillette's own cost of capital of 10.12 percent produced an estimate for Gillette's corporate name of about $4.5 billion.

An alternative approach to estimating a brand's relative value and, by extension, a company's reputation is to assume what finance scholars tell us is the gospel truth: That stock market prices incorporate all known information about a brand and fully reflect a company's future prospects. If we make that assumption, we can define the value of a brand simply as its market value over and above the liquidation value of the net assets involved in producing and selling the brand. A small hitch, here: Accountants normally carry a company's assets at book value. The excess market value therefore incorporates not only the value of the company's reputation but also the market's best guess about the current market value of those historical assets.[15]

One way out of this conundrum is to recognize that, when assessing a company, most investors don't look at its liquidation value. Rather, they probe its ability to generate future profits as a going concern. The market value of a public company should therefore reflect its value as an operating enterprise. It makes the excess market value correspond roughly to the overall regard in which the company is held by its constituents—a gauge of its reputation.[16] Gauging reputational capital provides a simple way of quantifying the dollar value of a company's reputation.

- *What Is Reputational Capital?* A company's reputational capital is the excess market value of its shares—the amount by which the company's market value exceeds the liquidation value of its assets.

Consider five brands that have dominated their product categories since 1923 and proven to be among the most durable of all time: Coca-Cola (soft drinks), Gillette (pens and razors), Kodak (film and cameras), Campbell (soup), and Wrigley (chewing gum).[17] Since these five brand names are the foundations on which their companies' reputations were built, we can calculate a rough dollar estimate of the value of these names by taking the difference between each company's market value and its book value. For Coca-Cola, that number came to about $52 billion in March 1993, placing Coke among the world's most valuable corporate brands. A similar calculation put Gillette's reputation at $12 billion, Eastman Kodak's at $11 billion, Campbell's at $9 billion, Colgate's at $8 billion, and Wrigley's at $4 billion. These numbers provide us with a rough estimate of each company's store of reputational capital.

By extension, we can calculate the reputational capital of all public companies. As before, the additional worth of these companies comes from both undervalued historical assets and from goodwill. Taken together, they add up to investor confidence in a company's future prospects—in its reputation. Much as the value of a Van Gogh painting or a vintage Chateau Margaux fluctuates in auction markets, so too does a company's reputational capital—the value of its brands and other intangible assets—rise and fall in the marketplace. Market prices reflect an instantaneous estimate of market value, a balancing of supply and demand.

Averaged over the longer term, a market-based measure of reputational capital has some merits. For one, it's simple to derive; for another, it enables comparisons of companies across industries and over time; for a third, it recognizes the reputations of companies involved in both the manufacturing and service sectors; and finally, the measure enables comparisons of companies with more than a single product line or business.[18]

LOSING FACE: IT'S COSTLY

Deriving numerical estimates of reputation from the market price of a company's shares also makes it possible to cost out unexpected incidents that damage a company's franchise. When companies face crises, they generally lose market value. To some extent, the loss constitutes the stock market's best guess about the damage done to the company's future profitability—that is, to its credibility and reputation. Exxon and Johnson & Johnson can attest to that.

A few minutes into March 24, 1989, the supertanker Exxon Valdez struck Bligh Reef in Alaska's Prince William Sound, tearing a huge hole in the ship's hull. Within hours, more than 10 million gallons of crude oil had spewn out of the freighter, ravaging 1,200 miles of shoreline and putting Exxon in the way of a media blitz that quickly turned into a public relations nightmare. Besides having to pay an estimated $1.38 billion in cleanup costs, the company was indicted on five criminal counts and faced more than 150 separate civil lawsuits resulting from the spill. Two years later, the courts approved a settlement between Exxon, the federal government, and the state of Alaska to resolve civil and criminal claims, according to which the company would pay $900 million in 11 annual payments. Given the comparatively small fine imposed, the major harm to Exxon from the spill may well have been its loss of reputation.

One way to estimate the reputational loss to Exxon from the accident is to look at the short-term drop in the company's market value, or its loss of reputational capital. The average value of Exxon's shares in the 14 trading days before the spill was $57.64 billion. In the 14 days following the spill, the company's average market value had dropped to $54.64 billion. Investors therefore recognized a loss of reputational capital totaling $3 billion, or 5 percent of Exxon's market value. Figure 4-1 depicts the decline in Exxon's market value—and so in its short-term reputation—during that 28-day window.

A similar analysis can be done for Johnson & Johnson, which faced product tampering with its Tylenol brand in 1982 and 1986. As previously explained, on September 30, 1982, reports of five deaths from cyanide ingestion were traced to a production lot of Tylenol capsules. Worried about losing its reputation for gentleness and safety, J&J's McNeil Consumer Products division promptly pulled all Tylenol capsules from retail shelves. Within days, the company took aggressive action to block reputational loss: (1) All capsules were scrapped and the safe tablet

Figure 4-1   EXXON'S REPUTATIONAL LOSS FOLLOWING THE VALDEZ
OIL SPILL

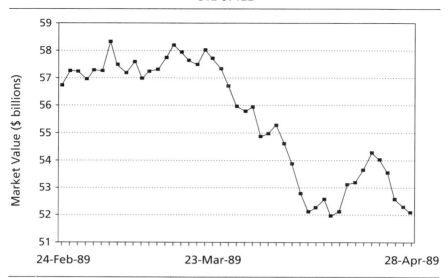

version offered as a replacement; (2) an intensive ad campaign was launched portraying J&J as a victim of sabotage; (3) tamper-resistant packaging was introduced, and more than 80 million new samples were distributed free of charge at a cost to J&J of some $30 million. The actions would prove remarkably effective in rebuilding Tylenol's premier position in the marketplace as well as J&J's long-term stock of reputational capital.

In the short run, however, J&J lost value. Consider the 1982 crisis. In the 14 trading days before the tampering, J&J shares were worth an average $8.262 billion. In the 14 trading days after the incidents, J&J's market value dropped to $7.132 billion for a loss of $1.13 billion, equivalent to a 14 percent drop in the company's reputational capital in 1982. In 1986, J&J's market value fell from its prior 14-day average value of $9.1 billion to $8.1 billion for a loss of $1 billion, equivalent to an 11 percent drop in the value of the company's reputational capital. Figure 4-2 shows J&J's short-term reputational losses during those two crisis periods.

Clearly, accidents and crises can seriously damage a company's franchise and reputation. For public companies, changes in the market value of a firm provide a reasonable estimate of the anticipated losses to a

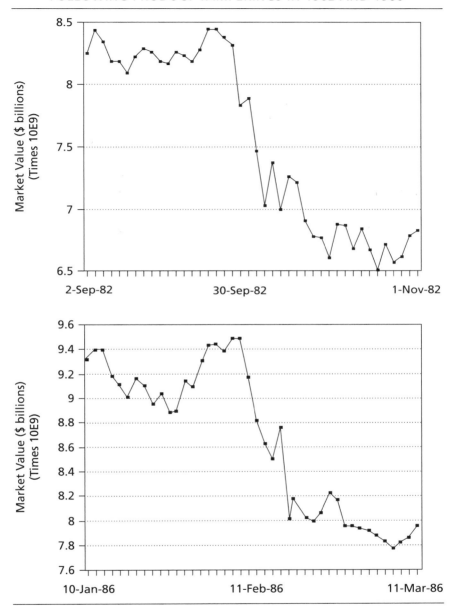

Figure 4-2 JOHNSON & JOHNSON'S REPUTATIONAL LOSS FOLLOWING PRODUCT TAMPERINGS IN 1982 AND 1986

company from attacks on its integrity and credibility; they also provide a gauge of how much of a company's reputational capital is put at risk from such events.

HOT COMPANIES

Table 4-2 sorts American firms into three tiers according to their average stock of reputational capital between 1990 and 1993. While Exxon dominates the list with an estimated $69 billion in reputational capital, other top-10 companies include familiar icons like General Electric, AT&T, Wal-Mart, and Coca-Cola.

A second tier of companies with strong reputations includes pharmaceutical giants Johnson & Johnson and Merck and consumer barons

Table 4-2 THE HIDDEN VALUE OF CORPORATE REPUTATIONS
AMONG SELECTED U.S. COMPANIES

Average Long-Term Reputational Capital (1990–1993)	Companies	
Highest reputational capital (>$30 billion)	Exxon Philip Morris AT&T Merck Bristol-Myers Squibb	General Electric IBM Wal-Mart Coca-Cola Procter & Gamble
High reputational capital (>$15 billion)	Du Pont General Motors GTE 3M Walt Disney Hewlett-Packard	Johnson & Johnson Mobil PepsiCo Ford Pfizer
Good reputational capital (>$5 billion)	Sears McDonald's Kellogg Sara Lee Toys 'R' Us J. P. Morgan	Eastman Kodak Anheuser-Busch American Express BankAmerica Gillette

Procter & Gamble and American Home Products. Many of the second-tier companies actually control individual brands that are better known than their corporate logos. For instance, American Home Products owns Dristan and Anacin, products in nearly every bathroom in America. Minnesota-based 3M is better-known as the maker of Scotch tape and Post-It notes. The total value of their reputations is clearly built up from the sum of their individual brands.

Or take Philip Morris. The company is far more familiar to us as the maker of Marlboro cigarettes, Kraft cheese, and Miller beer. In July 1993, *Financial World* estimated the value of the company's stable of brands using subjective estimates of the "strength" of the company's principal brands. It put individual brand equity at $39.5 billion for Marlboro, $2.3 billion for Kraft, and $1 billion for Miller. Omitting lesser brands, that puts Philip Morris's overall brand value at a total of $42.8 billion.[19] Compare that with our estimated $45.5 billion in reputational capital derived from the company's market value; the two figures are remarkably similar.

Table 4-3 compares in greater detail the brand estimates of *Financial World* derived from royalty rates and the stock market estimates of each company's reputation that we calculated from long-term share prices.

Table 4-3 ESTIMATED VALUE OF SELECTED COMPANIES' REPUTATIONAL CAPITAL IN MID-1993 ($ BILLIONS)

Company	Subjective Estimate[a]	Measured by Short-Term Reputational Capital[b]
Philip Morris	$42.8	$45.5
Coca-Cola	33.5	51.7
Intel	17.8	18.7
Kellogg	9.7	13.9
Anheuser-Busch	8.2	10.2
PepsiCo	7.5	25.0
Gillette	7.2	11.7
Eastman Kodak	4.1	10.7
Goodyear	2.0	2.2

[a]Adapted from Alexandra Ournsoff, "Brands: How We Valued Them," *Financial World,* September 1, 1993.

[b]Calculated as excess of market value over book value on March 3, 1993.

Remarkably comparable numbers obtain for single-product companies like Intel and Goodyear. Discrepancies arise principally because of omitted assets in the estimates made by *Financial World*. For instance, the market valuation of Coca-Cola also includes its distribution arm, something that investors clearly appreciate but that is not included in the magazine's estimate. Similarly, the smaller value for PepsiCo results because the magazine does not include the value of the company's diversified portfolio of food chains (Pizza Hut, Taco Bell, Kentucky Fried Chicken) or of snack-food maker Frito-Lay. Finally, the subjective estimate of the Kodak brand ignores the company's Sterling Drug division. The analysis supports the use of stock market values to make company-wide assessments of reputation. Subjective estimates of brand strength incorporate many "unknowns" and seem to add little to estimates that are more simply derived from market information about a company.

Table 4-4 provides a more complete listing of the leading companies in each of 30 industries. The table contrasts two sets of numbers:

1. *Short-term reputational capital,* a company's reputational capital calculated on the basis of its current market value.

2. *Long-term reputational capital,* a company's reputational capital calculated on the basis of its average market value and book value over many years.

Short-term reputation reflects the current, often temporary regard in which a company is held by investors. It fluctuates with the daily ups and downs in the price of a company's shares. Long-term reputation focuses on the average stock of reputation over a time span—in this case, three years, March 1990 to March 1993. Like any moving average, it discounts short-term changes in a company's fortunes and better represents the company's true standing in the corporate world.

Big companies tend to have better long-term reputations. They're more heavily capitalized, attract more investors, and so tend to be more visible. In the short run, however, size turns out not to be a major predictor of reputation. It's clear, for instance, that many of our largest companies have dramatically lost reputational capital in recent years—companies like IBM in computers, General Motors in motor vehicles, Citicorp in banking, and Sears Roebuck in retail. Investors have recognized the declining values of the historical franchises of these once venerable names and depreciated their stock prices.

Table 4-4 THE HIDDEN VALUE OF CORPORATE REPUTATIONS

Industry	Rank by Size	Company Name	Long-Term Reputational Capital[a] ($ billions)	Short-Term Reputational Capital[b] ($ billions)
Aerospace	1	Boeing	$15.2	$2.6
	2	United Technologies	6.2	2.2
	3	McDonnell Douglas	2.1	−0.9
	4	AlliedSignal	6.4	5.9
	5	Lockheed	1.5	0.4
Airlines	1	AMR	4.3	0.4
	2	UAL	3.2	1.3
	3	Delta	3.2	0.2
	4	Southwest	1.7	2.3
Banking	1	Citicorp	7.0	1.7
	2	BankAmerica	10.1	5.4
	3	Chemical	4.9	2.2
	4	Chase Manhattan	3.3	0.1
	5	Banc One	7.5	7.8
Beverages	1	PepsiCo	24.9	25.0
	2	Coca-Cola	42.1	51.7

Table 4-4 (continued)

Industry	Rank by Size	Company Name	Long-Term Reputational Capital[a] ($ billions)	Short-Term Reputational Capital[b] ($ billions)
	3	Anheuser-Busch	13.5	10.2
Chemicals	1	Du Pont	28.4	14.4
	2	Dow Chemical	15.8	5.8
	3	Occidental	6.2	1.7
	4	Monsanto	7.4	3.4
Computers	1	IBM	54.6	−3.9
	2	Hewlett-Packard	15.2	11.6
	3	Digital	8.2	1.4
	4	Apple	6.6	4.2
	5	Microsoft	15.6	20.4
Control systems	1	Eastman Kodak	14.7	10.7
	2	Xerox	6.4	3.2
	2	Polaroid	1.6	0.5
Financial services	1	American Express	11.6	5.0
	2	Merrill Lynch	4.6	2.7

	3	J. P. Morgan	9.6	5.9
	4	Salomon	3.5	1.2
	5	Morgan Stanley	3.4	1.8
	6	Primerica	3.8	0.5
Food	1	Kellogg	11.7	13.4
	2	Sara Lee	10.5	11.4
	3	General Mills	9.4	10.4
	4	H. J. Heinz	9.5	8.9
	5	Campbell	8.9	9.0
Forest products	1	International Paper	7.3	1.3
	2	Georgia-Pacific	4.8	3.4
	3	Weyerhaeuser	6.5	5.4
	4	Kimberly-Clark	7.3	6.2
Insurance	1	AIG	19.9	13.3
	2	American General	5.6	1.8
	3	Chubb	5.9	4.0
Leisure	1	Loews	5.8	0.7
	2	Walt Disney	19.2	19.2
	3	Paramount	5.4	1.8

Table 4-4 (continued)

Industry	Rank by Size	Company Name	Long-Term Reputational Capital[a] ($ billions)	Short-Term Reputational Capital[b] ($ billions)
Motor vehicles	1	General Motors	25.8	−3.8
	2	Ford	20.1	1.1
	3	Chrysler	6.4	6.4
Oil refining	1	Exxon	69.0	43.9
	2	Mobil	25.7	10.4
	3	Chevron	24.4	10.6
	4	Texaco	15.9	7.6
	5	Amoco	25.8	13.4
	6	Atlantic Richfield	18.7	11.5
Personal care	1	Procter & Gamble	30.8	28.9
	2	Colgate-Palmolive	6.5	8.0
	3	Gillette	9.1	11.7
	4	Avon	3.1	4.3
	5	Clorox	2.4	1.8
Pharmaceuticals	1	Johnson & Johnson	26.9	20.5
	2	Bristol-Myers Squibb	34.8	23.2

3	Merck	42.5	37.5
4	Abbott Labs	20.4	18.0
5	American Home Products	19.2	15.7
6	Pfizer	17.6	13.7
7	Eli Lilly	19.0	10.2
8	Warner-Lambert	8.8	7.5
9	Schering-Plough	11.0	10.2
Publishing			
1	Time Warner	8.7	5.3
2	Dun & Bradstreet	9.2	7.8
3	Gannett	6.7	5.5
4	Readers' Digest	4.5	4.7
5	Knight Ridder	2.9	1.9
Retailing			
1	Wal-Mart	51.0	67.2
2	Sears Roebuck	14.9	5.2

Table 4-4 (continued)

Industry	Rank by Size	Company Name	Long-Term Reputational Capital[a] ($ billions)	Short-Term Reputational Capital[b] ($ billions)
	3	Kmart	8.8	4.0
	4	J. C. Penney	7.9	5.5
	5	May Department Stores	7.3	6.4
	6	Toys 'R' Us	9.3	9.0
	7	Home Depot	10.9	18.9
	8	The Limited	8.9	7.2
Telecom	1	AT&T	51.6	56.8
	2	MCI	9.3	9.3
	3	McCaw Cellular	5.8	5.3
Tobacco	1	Philip Morris	56.2	45.5
	2	RJR Nabisco	7.4	1.4
	3	UST	4.8	5.4

[a]Calculated for the long term, as the excess of a company's market value over its book value during the period March 1990 to March 1993.

[b]Calculated for the short term, as the excess of a company's market value over its book value on March 3, 1993.

Long-term reputations are obviously more stable. Despite its recent troubles, GM continues to enjoy a premiere reputation in the auto industry, as does Sears in retail, despite its poor short-term showing in table 4-4. Among all industrials, IBM still ranks fourth in long-term reputation and tops in the computer industry, despite its dismal performance in the last two years. But IBM's future reputation is in jeopardy. Unless the new management team led by Lou Gerstner regains the investors' confidence, the stock price will continue to drop and do inexorable damage to IBM's long-term reputation.

In the computer industry, while IBM is busy singing the blues, Hewlett-Packard in hardware and Microsoft in software are investors' darling. Du Pont dominates the chemical industry, much as Coca-Cola's reputation dwarfs that of its larger archrival, PepsiCo. In the aftermath of the Cold War, aerospace and defense companies fare poorly, with Boeing the only bright star. In financial services, American Express and J. P. Morgan top the long-term list, and aggressive AIG holds a commanding lead as the only insurance company with lots of reputational capital. In the short term, however, Amex has clearly fallen on hard times, landing just behind first-place Morgan. For pharmaceutical companies, both short-term and long-term reputational capital agree: They all look impressive as they continue to enjoy their bloated prestige among investors, with Merck, the perennial favorite, leading the way. We can expect the ongoing national debate about health care to depreciate the short-term reputational capital of these companies, especially those of prescription drug companies like Merck and Pfizer.

GLITZY INDUSTRIES

At any point in time, some industries enjoy greater popularity than others and so amass more reputational capital; they are the "hot" industries of the day. Biotech is a case in point. Since 1988, investors have sunk more than $4 billion into biotech companies, although few have shown a profit. Clearly, reputation drives biotech research. Much like the motion-picture industry, biotech companies make large, up-front gambles on a product long before they know whether the product can recover its costs; both therefore rely on "blockbusters" to recoup investments lost on hundreds of failures. To fund these gambles, investors bank on the reputations of the players. Movies, for instance, are packaged for investors with known directors and stars. Increasingly, the script derives from a best-selling novel, assuring audience interest. The combination is expected to make for better box-office draw. In similar ways, biotech companies have taken to partnering with reputable drug companies like Merck or Hoffman-La Roche, creating packages of players, products, and marketing rights. As with movie packages, here it's the combined reputations of the companies that attracts investors.

Table 4-5 presents a snapshot of the hot industries in March 1993. Dominating the ranking are the retail, beverage, and telecommunications industries. The pharmaceutical industry is also flying high, despite prospects of regulatory reform of health care that could eat into corporate profits. The global dependence on oil means favorable prospects for the energy industry, and that's reflected in its high stocks of reputational capital.

In contrast, competitive and retrenching industries are faring poorly. U.S. automakers are still struggling to assert themselves against Japanese rivals, and the market still doubts their prospects. Racked by price wars, the airline industry has obviously fallen into disfavor, as has aerospace since the end of the Cold War. Still reeling from the savings and loan crisis, from South American loans gone sour, from insider-trading scandals, and from global rivalry, the banking, insurance, and financial services industries have lost much of the reputational capital they accumulated in the 1980s.

Because some industries claim larger companies than others, the second column in table 4-5 lists reputational capital after controlling for companies' total sales revenues. Given relative industry size, investors are clearly most impressed by the prospects of the computer industry (owing principally to powerhouse software companies like Microsoft and Novell), pharmaceuticals, beverages, and chemicals. The computer industry boasts $5 in reputational capital for every $1 of sales it generates, while the others claim some $2 in reputational capital for $1 of sales they produce—clearly a sign of appreciation. At the opposite end are floundering industries—auto, farm equipment, aerospace, airline—with little reputational capital to back up their sales.

VALUING INTANGIBLES

Sometime in the summer of 1993 I attended a sports auction to benefit AIDS research. Among the items auctioned off to the 1,000

Table 4-5 INDUSTRY REPUTATIONS

Industry	Reputational Capital of the Top Three Companies[a]	Reputational Capital per Dollar of Revenue[b]
Retail	$31.7	1.70
Beverages	28.9	1.99
Pharmaceuticals	27.1	2.46
Electrical	26.8	1.61
Telecommunications	25.1	0.88
Energy	22.9	0.52
Telephone	17.0	1.08
Tobacco	17.4	2.05
Consumer products	16.2	1.45
Computers	13.3	5.03
Food	11.7	1.43
Banking	9.9	1.01
Control	9.3	0.66
Leisure	7.5	1.24
Chemical	6.5	1.80
Insurance	6.4	0.64
Publishing	6.2	1.22
Financial services	5.8	1.40
Transport	5.7	0.88
Forest products	5.0	0.58
Utility	4.8	0.76
Aerospace	3.6	0.23
Rubber	3.0	1.56
Equipment	2.9	0.29
Motor vehicles	2.8	0.12
Metals	2.1	1.12
Airlines	1.4	0.51

[a]Gauged by short-term reputational capital in billions of dollars, March 1993.

[b]Ratio of short-term reputational capital to company's total annual sales, March 1993.

or so participants was a used tennis racquet donated by veteran champion Martina Navratilova. The racquet was a well-worn, ordinary Yonex model, still selling in sporting goods stores around the world for about $250. As I recall, the bidding started at $500. Quickly it went into the thousands. When the gavel finally came down, the second-hand racquet had been auctioned off for the startling sum of $27,000. How valuable is a reputation, you ask? I'll say this much: No one there would have paid much more than $100 for anybody else's marked-up frame.

Even though people who try to evaluate companies invariably disagree on how best to systematically measure the dollar value of a reputation, no matter how we assess it, a reputation is valuable. A strong reputation enhances the value of a company's potential licenses, products, and services, and so raises revenues. In turn, better revenues translate into superior market value over time. As I argue in subsequent chapters, learning to manage that reputational capital is a critical activity that senior managers must call attention to and support.

In fact, the reputational capital that our most celebrated companies have amassed over the years reflects core beliefs that have made their products dear, their capabilities reliable, their actions dependable, their practices distinctive, and their cultures unique. Insofar as these core beliefs reflect a company's identity, they are the bedrock on which every company's reputation sits—a subject to which we now turn.

We are what we repeatedly do. Excellence, then, is not an act, but a habit.

—*Aristotle*
  Niomachen Ethics

Identity Traits

IN 1982, Tom Peters and Robert Waterman, Jr., two consultants from McKinsey & Company, penned a book distilling their experiences and titled it *In Search of Excellence*. The tome became a runaway best-seller, spawning numerous imitators. It would also turn Tom Peters, its lead author, into a new-age management guru, with fame and fortune to rival that of the legendary Peter Drucker.

The message of the "excellence" team was as simple as it was profound: Good companies do everything better. Like Midas, the Phrygian king of Greek mythology, everything they touch turns to gold. They innovate more quickly, make better products, deliver better service, and, naturally, produce better results for investors. Peters and his colleagues praised the dexterity with which prominent companies like Marriott, 3M, and Disney ran their operations; commended the sound visions that corporate founders had instilled in employees; celebrated the care with which their managers engineered products and serviced customers. These companies were excellent, they claimed, because they were exceptionally good at managing the "soft" side of their performance—the values that drive employees and the capabilities that enable them to make the company's products and sell its services.

Reviewers of the new movement were not all kind. Many belittled the methods used to identify the 43 "excellent" companies. Follow-up articles in popular magazines like *Business Week* tracked the economic performance of the companies and jubilantly showed how poorly many of them had fared in the stock market—as if "excellent" companies by definition were always supposed to outperform everyone else. Of course, that's not so. Numerous factors other than a company's managerial skills affect performance, things like new technologies, demographics, changing tastes, business cycles, and competitive conditions. Not everything can be anticipated or controlled. Moreover, even the best companies occasionally hire managers who make mistakes.

In fact, the "excellence" fad hinted not at the ingredients that guarantee peak economic performance but rather at those "identity traits" that combine to build enduring institutions, those attributes that build strong reputations. Although Peters and company rightly called attention to practices embraced by some companies that happened to be financially successful, they failed to recognize the more credible link between those traits and the reputational capital that they nurture over time. They also stopped short of asking probing questions about the internal character and identity of those companies.

NOT EXCELLENCE—IDENTITY!

In May 1983, a team of reporters first published *The 100 Best Companies to Work for in America*.[1] From random interviews obtained by crisscrossing America, the authors generated a list of companies that employees claimed were great to work for. Like *In Search of Excellence, The 100 Best Companies* also became a best-seller and soon sired its own progeny of imitators, each one purporting to identify the companies that were the best run, best to work for, best for women, best for African Americans, best for Hispanics, best for the environment, and so on. Each fulfilled a useful function in calling attention to the particular features that made a company attractive to at least one of its interest groups.

The problem with every one of these books was that a company could very well be good in one area and entirely deficient in another. It might provide employees with a pleasant working environment but not necessarily perform well for its shareholders; it might offer great opportunities to women or minorities and yet pollute the environment. It turned out, for instance, that only 15 of the 43 companies judged excellent by Peters and Waterman were also judged to be good workplaces.

During the 1980s, it became quite evident that managers could easily squander a company's resources to benefit one constituency at another's expense. Among Tom Peters's favorite examples of well-managed companies, one recently joined the list of fallen angels: Stew Leonard's Dairy in Norfolk, Connecticut. In July 1993, the store's founder and three company executives pleaded guilty to skimming more than $17 million from sales in an elaborate tax-fraud scheme. Shortly thereafter, they averred that the store—widely touted by Peters for its entrepreneurial genius—had been practicing short-weighting on its customers. In October 1993, Leonard was sentenced to more than four years in prison and fined $947,000 for his role in the tax fraud. Should the company ever have been thought admirable? The case calls to mind the old dictum, "You can fool some of the people some of the time, but you can't fool all of the people all the time."

To focus on a company's reputation is to determine how it deals with *all* of its constituents; it is to focus on a company's character, or identity. Identity constrains what actions a company takes, how it makes decisions, how it treats its employees, how it reacts to crises. Managers and employees tend to act in ways consistent with the company's identity. Identity is therefore the backbone of reputation. Identity develops from within and limits a company's long-run actions and its performance as benchmarked against rivals'. Identity explains the kinds of relationships companies establish with their four most critical constituencies: employees, consumers, investors, and local communities.[2]

In the past, most companies built their reputations around one dominant trait, be it operational excellence, innovativeness, product quality, financial growth, or customer service.[3] Increasingly, however, companies find themselves being pressured into achieving a more balanced posture. Much as the rising tide lifts all boats, so is competitive pressure forcing companies to achieve excellence in at least one trait while maintaining strong competence across all the others. In the end, I argue, it's the companies with the most widely respected identity traits that will build enduring reputational capital. They'll develop a kind of Midas touch.

GREAT WORKPLACES

What traits build a golden reputation among employees? The authors of *The 100 Best Companies to Work for in America*, now in its third edition, relied heavily on word of mouth to generate a list of companies that are great places to work. After extensive discussions with employees, they concluded, "Despite the diversity, almost every one of the 100 Best has something distinctive to offer its employees." But although "each company is unique . . . there were certain themes we heard over and over again." They then rated each company on five basic features that appeared to build employee satisfaction and morale: relative pay levels, benefits programs, job security, equal opportunity, and "ambience"—the company's elusive work style. If we decant their comments, employees favor companies with three dominant traits:

- They promote trust.

- They empower employees.

- They inspire pride.

TRAIT #1: PROMOTE TRUST

Every good relationship—whether between husband and wife, between friends, or between employer and employee—is built on a foundation of trust. Trust allays our fears of betrayal by people we depend on, whether at home or at work. Odds are we'll be well treated by people we trust. They'll stand up for us if we're under attack and defend our interests if we're not present. As one corporate observer puts it: "Trust does not exist naturally in the workplace. Where it does take root and grow, it is a highly perishable commodity, requiring constant attention and care. Part of the reason for this difficulty in establishing trust is that human beings naturally question the motives and intentions of others. We are all afraid of being taken advantage of. So we are very careful about whom we trust. Managements of good workplaces seem to acknowledge the fact that everyone inevitably has doubts about the company's credibility and reliability."[4]

Well-regarded companies appear to make systematic efforts to demonstrate their trustworthiness by acting evenhandedly toward all employees. They encourage a freer flow of and more equal access to information; often they opt to share broadly the rewards of good work by involving employees in profit-sharing plans or by promoting direct employee ownership of company stock.

Consider W. L. Gore, the company noted for developing Gore-Tex, the synthetic fiber now used to make breathable yet waterproof outerwear, space suits, synthetic arteries, and industrial filters. In the early 1980s, the 3,000-employee Delaware-based outfit was getting a lot of press for its innovative practices. Once I visited there, I quickly saw why: Gore seems to operate with an alarming lack of structure. Plants are kept small in size (to a maximum of 200 people) to enable direct contact among employees, or "associates," as they're called at Gore. To say that people work in a trusting environment would be an understatement. Although they didn't have to, everyone I talked to spoke highly of the company, of founder Bill Gore's open, fair, and forthright policies. The fact that Gore distributes about 15 percent of the company's annual profits to associates doesn't hurt. Nor does the company retirement plan, through which each associate receives the Gore stock equivalent of 15 percent of annual income, which is placed in an ASOP, or Associates' Stock Ownership Plan. It's a lot easier to put your trust in a company that treats you like a family member and a lifelong partner, even if it smacks a little of paternalism.

Also in the early 1980s, another company then being touted as a member of a new breed was Publix Supermarkets in Florida. Curious to know more about them, I visited the company headquarters in Lakeland and spoke with its founder, George Jenkins. Although far more structured than W. L. Gore, Publix conveys a similarly paternalistic attitude. One dominant trait is that the Jenkins family and the supermarket chain's employees are its only shareholders. Publix distributes 20 percent of all annual profits to store employees, and it also funds a profit-sharing plan into which go another 10 percent of profits. As you might expect, everyone I spoke with considered Publix a godsend.

TRAIT #2: EMPOWER EMPLOYEES

It's not only in smaller companies like W. L. Gore or Publix that opportunities for involvement and participation take place. At Avis, employees are not only shareholders but active participants in decision making. Or take giant IBM, long the darling of reputational surveys. In its training manuals, the company speaks of five levels of freedom. At the lowest level is the subservient employee, waiting to be told what to do; at the highest is the "empowered" employee, the one who embraces the highest degree of freedom and autonomy on the job.[5] Since IBM's debacle of the late 1980s, the company has been struggling to push greater levels of autonomy into the corporate structure. Increasingly, managers are being paid on bonus and commission and told to make the sale no matter what it takes. Empowered at last.

In fact, mountains of research confirm that when we are empowered, committed, and involved in making decisions, good things happen. For one, we feel better about our jobs and companies. Feeling good motivates us to work harder and do better. Positive attitudes induce trust, encourage teamwork, and fuel creativity and innovation, all of which can help companies to act more quickly and so to outdistance rivals. Involvement also makes good sense because line employees, being closest to the products, services, and customers of a company, are in a position to assess the wisdom of key decisions.

One way to involve employees is to set up quality circles. Since 1980, interest in quality circles has exploded, demonstrating the bottom-line benefits of empowering employees. More than 2,500 U.S. companies use them to generate participation and capitalize on employees' ideas for improving operations. In the typical quality circle, groups of employees meet one hour a week on company time to discuss ways to improve a department's performance. Westinghouse, for instance, maintains more than 1,600 quality circles in 200 locations, groups that involve both blue-collar and white-collar employees. In all, about 16,000 employees meet regularly in these groups to focus on product improvement ideas.

Quality circles are only the tip of the iceberg. Other attempts to incorporate inherently democratic practices abound. Consider the annual "jobholders' " meetings, at computer maker Pitney Bowes. A direct analog to stockholder meetings, these gatherings provide a forum for substantive dialogue between managers and employees. The question-and-answer sessions are meant to resolve substantive problems in the company that no doubt makes 9 out of 10 postage meters in the United States. But the meetings also signal that managers are accountable to employees as well as stockholders.

To empower is also to reduce status discrepancies among employees. A highly regarded company like Hewlett-Packard maintains an egalitarian environment that enhances morale. In contrast to the hierarchical practices of its far older rival, IBM, there is no established, privileged class of managers at Hewlett-Packard with private parking spaces or corner offices. At specialty steelmaker Nucor, egalitarianism also pervades.

At Avis Inc., our employees* are acting like they own the place.

Recently we, the employees of Avis, Inc., bought the company.

Sure, that's good news for us. But it's even better news for you.

Because we know our success depends on your satisfaction. And we intend to be very successful.

We'll do it by giving you low SuperValue Rates for business and leisure, and fast services like Avis Express.® And Roving Rapid Return, the new Avis Carside Computer℠ that speeds you on your way with a printed receipt in just seconds.†

So the next time you need a car, stop by any Avis corporate rent a car location and shake hands with a new owner.

For information or reservations, call 1-800-331-1212.

Or call your travel consultant.

It'll be the beginning of a great friendship.

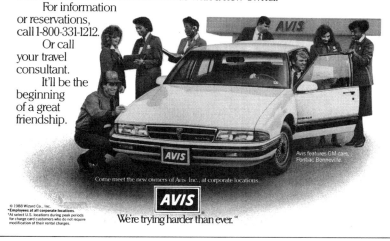

Avis features GM cars. Pontiac Bonneville.

Come meet the new owners of Avis, Inc., at corporate locations.

AVIS

We're trying harder than ever.℠

In September 1987, the 11,500 employees of Avis, Inc. purchased the outstanding shares of the rental car company for $1.75 billion. The employee ownership plan that was created provides employees not only with owner status but also with decision-making involvement. Most significantly, Avis now operates a system of employee participation group meetings to encourage the exchange of information and ideas between local managers and employee-owners. According to company officials, the system has produced many service improvements and could serve as a model for other employee-owned companies. (Courtesy of Avis, Inc.)

Neither Ken Iverson, the company's renowned chairman, nor any of Nucor's other senior managers get perks. They sit in spartan offices, drive their own cars, and fly coach. Just like everybody else.

TRAIT #3: INSPIRE PRIDE

Respected companies elicit from employees a higher degree of emotional involvement with their jobs. When one's work feels meaningless, it's difficult to commit to a job, to a product, or to the company that provides them. When a product is shoddy or otherwise doesn't deliver what customers expect, it's hard to feel good about selling it. When a company scorns job safety, shows favoritism, or mistreats groups of its employees, it's hard to feel loyal, difficult to stick around. Ultimately, then, a good place to work inspires pride in employees: pride in their jobs, pride in the company's products, pride in the way the company operates.

Ask Wal-Mart employees. To work for Wal-Mart is to join a large extended family, an instant community where getting together is fun. Pride in their work in outdoing rival retailers brings them together repeatedly during non-business hours. Every Saturday morning at 7:30 A.M. Wal-Mart managers meet at the general office building in Bentonville to review results and troubleshoot. All employees also participate in a seemingly endless stream of company-sponsored picnics, canoe trips, golf, fishing, tennis, and other shared activities.

Or talk to employees of Apple Computer. With the company flush from a decade of growth that propelled it to prominent status among the Fortune 500, a rah-rah atmosphere is all-pervasive. Apple logos proliferate, as does a relaxed, countercultural, blue-jeans style of dress, a sense of openness, egalitarianism, teamwork, and commitment to hard work. Pride in the product and in the company's democratic mission to bring computer power to the people dominates discussions among employees.[6]

Table 5-1 lists the publically traded companies rated as good workplaces in at least one of the three editions of *The 100 Best Companies to Work for in America*. The table also shows the long-term reputational capital of those companies. It suggests that the average level of reputational capital is higher among companies in which employees consider the work environment to be attractive.

Table 5-1   THE REPUTATIONAL CAPITAL OF TOP-RATED WORKPLACES

Company	Long-Term Reputational Capital[a] ($ billions)
Dana	$0.9
Delta	0.2
Digital Equipment	1.4
Du Pont	14.0
Eastman Kodak	10.7
Hewlett-Packard	11.6
Intel	18.7
IBM	− 3.9
Johnson & Johnson	20.5
Maytag	0.9
3M	16.8
Procter & Gamble	29.0
Raychem	1.1
Wal-Mart	67.2
Average:	$13.5

[a]Calculated over the period 1990–93.

GREAT INVESTMENTS

What traits build reputation among investors? If it's true that employees value trust, empowerment, and pride, investors seldom do. Indeed, most studies show that investors are rather single-minded and look steadfastly to a company's profitability, volatility, and indebtedness to gauge its future prospects and assess its attractiveness. John Whitehead, the former cochairman of Goldman Sachs once put it this way: "What determines which companies sell at six times earnings and which companies sell at sixteen times earnings? It's a complex of factors. But the principal ingredient is the perception of investors as to the quality of management, the quality of the people in the company. That is reflected in the record the company has established over a period of years. It's also reflected in a lot of intangible factors that have to do with . . . the quality of the company's products, and in a general perception of how the company comes across."[7]

TRAIT #4: GENERATE STRONG EARNINGS

What could better predict a company's future than its profitability? Many studies show that habitual investors pick stocks based on the current and historical earnings of companies[8] and favor companies with better and more steady earnings.[9] Following announcements of either strong profits or actions likely to improve future profits, investors generally bid up a company's market value and so increase its reputational capital. Clearly, that's why managers focus so intensely on the bottom line. Falling profits signal declining prospects to investors, lowering the company's market value and its reputational capital.

TRAIT #5: MAINTAIN STABILITY

When we are uncertain about the profitability of a company we invest in, we naturally expect to be rewarded with above-average returns.[10] One way to appraise the riskiness of a company is to look at the volatility of its earnings in past years. The less steady its profits have been, the greater the risk. There has to be a considerable upside to the risk—and that means higher potential profits. Over time, companies that don't deliver what investors expect get downgraded by the market and so sacrifice some of their reputation.

Debt also reduces the residual value of the firm to investors, and it is a good predictor of bankruptcy. That's why companies with comparable total assets but greater debt prove less attractive to investors. Who among us wants to invest in a company that's unlikely to pay us back? All in all, then, earnings and risk are the principal predictors of how both investors and analysts rate companies and their reputations.

TRAIT #6: SHOW GOOD PROSPECTS FOR GROWTH

Ratings agencies like Moody's Investors Services and Standard & Poor's help us to assess the merits of companies as investments. In essence, ratings are judgments about a company's financial and business prospects. Although Moody's acknowledges that there is no fixed formula by which companies get rated, it turns out that its ratings are also most heavily influenced by a company's volatility of earnings and its indebtedness.[11] "In arriving at our conclusion on an issue's rating," states a company brochure, "Moody's adopts a long-term view that extends beyond a brief earnings period. The foundation of Moody's rating methodology rests with one basic question: What is the level of risk associated with receiving timely payment of principal and interest on this specific debt security and how does the level of risk compare with that of all other debt securities?"[12]

At Moody's, a ratings committee reviews the ratings of leading companies. As Harold Goldberg, the chairman of the committee told me: "A rating indicates the degree of comfort we have in a company's ability to deliver expected levels of performance. . . . It's heavily influenced by three factors: the fundamentals of the business, how the company is managed financially, and the credibility of the company's management. . . . We don't rate on the basis of the morality of a company's actions; we rate them based on their prior record of accomplishments, and on our judgment of how likely they are to fulfill their future commitments."

Both Moody's Investors Services and Standard & Poor's devote their resources to assessing the financial strength of public companies. They rate companies on a letter scale akin to classroom report cards, anchored at the top by AAA and at the bottom by C or D. The triple-A grade from either agency is widely regarded as a symbol of gilt-edged credit and indicates a low probability of default under even the worst of circumstances. At the other extreme, a D rating from Moody's or a C from S&P's indicates that the company is probably a bad credit risk.

In Table 5-2, the fourth column from the left lists the May 1993 credit ratings of the highest reputation companies in each industry among the set of industries valued in chapter 4. Table 5-2 shows that companies with higher stocks of reputational capital tend to be assigned better ratings.

Good prospects are hard to figure out. That's why a whole industry of "oracles" has come to the fore on Wall Street, the best of which are canonized annually as the "All America Research Team" by the industry bible, *Institutional Investor.* Since companies know that many investors thrive on the "picks" of these star analysts, many are granted private audiences to discuss a company's strategy with its top brass. Which is probably why those analysts are so highly paid; many earn as much as $1 million a year.

The power that star analysts have to sway investors gives them a lot of influence over a company's reputation, even though most of their

Industry	Leading Company	Reputational Capital[a] ($ billions)	Credit Rating[b]	Price/Earnings Ratio[c]	% Shares Owned by Institutions[c]
Aerospace	AlliedSignal	$5.9	A	17	65%
Airlines	Southwest	2.3	A −	35	62
Apparel/footwear	Nike	3.9	A −	15	51
Beverages	Coca-Cola	51.7	AA	30	53
Chemicals	Du Pont	14.0	AA	33	42
Computer hardware	Hewlett-Packard	11.6	AA+	22	54
Computer software	Microsoft	20.4	n.a.	34	35
Control systems	3M	16.8	AAA	19	67
Electrical	General Electric	50.6	AAA	16	54
Financial	J. P. Morgan	5.9	AAA	9	68
Food	Kellogg	13.4	AAA	23	81

Industry	Company	[a]	[b]		[c]
Forest products	Kimberly-Clark	6.2	A	26	67
Home repair	Home Depot	18.9	A −	58	56
Information	Dun & Bradstreet	7.8	A −	18	76
Insurance	AIG	13.4	AAA	16	51
Leisure	Walt Disney	19.2	AA −	30	40
Petroleum	Exxon	43.4	AAA	17	40
Pharmaceuticals	Merck	37.5	AAA	18	53
Personal care	Procter & Gamble	29.0	AA	20	46
Photographic	Eastman Kodak	10.7	A −	17	58
Retail	Wal-Mart	67.2	AA	38	31
Telecommunications	AT&T	56.8	AA	20	34
Tobacco	Philip Morris	45.5	A	12	60

[a]Long term average over the period 1990–93.
[b]Adapted from *Standard & Poor's Ratings Handbooks*, vol. 2, no. 5, May 1993.
[c]Adapted from *Business Week*, 3 March 1993.

predictions don't pan out. A study of 1,950 predictions performed by Zachs Investment Research showed that only 12 percent came in at exactly the consensus average of analysts' predictions, while 50 percent came in ahead and 38 percent came in behind. In other words, on average, following an analyst's recommendations proves to be no better than tossing a coin.

Another study of 1,221 stocks by Dreman Value Management found a steady erosion of accuracy in analysts' projections between 1973 and 1990. As one observer concludes:

> *When analysts blunder on earnings, it is not just the marginal player at a no-name firm who is off the mark. A surprising number came from the ranks of the "All America Research Team," a list turned out each year by* Institutional Investor *magazine that purports to include only the cream of the analytical crop. Yet those stars made up a disproportionate number of those making the worst estimates. [In part, it's because] too many unpredictable factors enter into a company's earnings . . . making the exercise largely a futile one. And even in those cases where an analyst is an expert with perfect estimates on the company, it doesn't necessarily translate into good stock picks.*[13]

So what real value can we ascribe to analysts if their crystal balls don't work? Those of us who dabble in the stock market would probably argue that, individually, analysts play a symbolic, comforting role that reduces our innate fears of uncertainty. Collectively, however, their effect is far greater. Their recommendations influence the movement of funds into and out of particular stocks, and so affect a company's market value and reputational capital.

A simple estimate of how optimistic investors are about the future prospects of a company is given by the ratio of a company's stock price relative to earnings. Investors generally assign all companies with high price/earnings (p/e) ratios as better prospects than rivals. The fifth column from the left in Table 5-2 lists the p/e ratios for the best-regarded companies. In May 1993, topping the list were Home Depot, Wal-Mart, and Southwest Airlines—consumer-oriented companies with strong franchises in home repair, discount merchandise, and air travel—three of the best-regarded companies in America.

We're also influenced by the moves of pension funds, mutual funds, insurance funds, university endowments, and foundations that invest large sums. These institutions have created large pools of money under the control of professional managers responsible for making portfolio investments. Two observers of the financial markets confirm that "the policy preferences of large institutional holders . . . have become a major force in determining and directing individual corporate policies."[14] Because of their prominence, institutional investors are important to the building of reputation. Fund managers act as brokers of information to smaller investors, who often emulate their moves.

Figure 5-1 indicates how institutions have come to dominate as investors in the shares of major U.S. companies. By 1990, institutional investors accounted for 90 percent of all stock traded on the New York Stock Exchange and some 60 percent of all stocks held. Studies of these institutions find that they emphasize long-term returns more so than do individual investors.

The far right column in Table 5-2 shows that in 1993 large institutions invested more heavily in some high-reputation companies than others, coming to own more than the average 55 percent of companies like Kellogg, Intel, Dun & Bradstreet, and J. P. Morgan. Since many smaller investors stay closely attuned to the expectations of these large investors, they can be expected to invest accordingly. The result is further demand for the shares of the better-regarded companies, which fuels higher market prices and further inflates these companies' reputational capital.

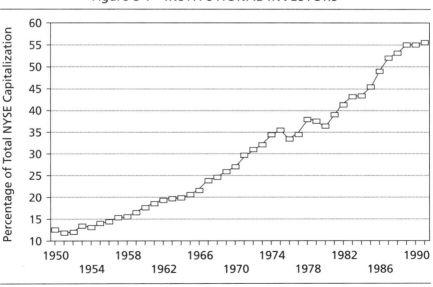

Figure 5-1 INSTITUTIONAL INVESTORS

GREAT PRODUCTS

What companies make the best products? What traits distinguish these companies? These questions dog consumers who want to know what products to buy and puzzle managers who want to know how to make them. Our concerns as consumers are neither those of employees nor those of investors.

A sure measure of a product's popularity is its ability to ring up sales. Products that sell have more customers, and so brand revenues gauge the brand's popularity. Since America was built on cars and oil, topping the list of the U.S. companies with the highest revenues (and the most popular products) are General Motors, Exxon, and Ford. Those companies producing the most popular consumer products are Philip Morris, Procter & Gamble, and 3M. Their revenue base assures them of widespread product visibility; these companies routinely battle for the number 1 position in sales in many product categories.

Among auto producers, consider the rivalry between Honda's Accord and Ford's Taurus. Between 1989 and 1991, the Accord outsold the Taurus. In the last months of 1992, however, the race took on epic proportions as Ford's Taurus closed in. At Ford headquarters in Detroit, sales managers aggressively went after the top spot. And the company did everything to encourage them, including sponsoring various contests. Under the Spin to Win contest, for every Taurus sold a salesperson would dial an 800 number at Ford headquarters to report the sale. An operator would then spin a wheel and award the salesperson a random bonus of $75 to $500 over and above the normal commission.

Clearly, to both companies winning was everything. To get there, each offered deep discounts on their models, scratching and scraping for every customer. As one commentator said, "beyond the question of pride, automakers think the sales leadership that Taurus is seeking can translate into a powerful marketing tool. In advertising and in dealership sales pitches, the 'America's best-selling car' mantra is soothing reassurance for shoppers about to spend up to $20,000."[15]

By January 1993, Ford's Taurus had edged out Honda's Accord for first place. Part of it was the hard push. Analysts estimate that Ford spent more than $50 million on rebates and other incentives to lure customers into its showrooms. But most also concur that Ford's success in getting to the number 1 spot can be traced to a combination of internal traits typical of companies that rate high in sales and customer satisfaction: (1) a commitment to making quality products, and (2) a strong service record. The two go hand-in-hand, as a guide from IBM states: "Quality is real. It is absolute professionalism. It is single-minded attention to customer satisfaction . . . perfection in the eyes of the customer . . . uncompromising dedication to be world-class . . . the sense of urgency to be first, fast, agile and efficient. Or, as they might say in the movies, quality means never having to say you're sorry."[16]

Trait #7: Champion Quality

Probably no one in America has been quite as influential in pushing companies to focus on quality as the late Ed Deming. His "14 points of quality" have become as omnipresent in classrooms and on shop floors as have personal computers in offices. Until his death in 1994, the former professor at New York University essentially preached the gospel that a commitment to quality works to a company's advantage; costs decrease owing to less rework, fewer mistakes and delays, and better use of time and materials. Consumers prefer quality products, so market share increases, and that improves profitability and growth potential.[17]

Persuaded by Deming's logic, Japan took him on after World War II. Lumbering under the low-quality reputation of the Made in Japan label, Japanese companies initiated programs to improve product quality and to rebuild not only their own reputations but Japan's. It worked. And Lee Iacocca's cri du coeur about the relative disadvantage of the Made in America label in the early 1990s symbolizes the remarkable turnabout in Japan's reputation in the last 30 years.

Not until much later did American companies discover the quality movement that Deming initiated. In 1981, it was Donald Peterson of Ford Motor Company—the maker, appropriately enough, of the car that would achieve best-seller status in 1992—who first took him on. As he reached the end of his life, Deming became a virtual guru, drawing standing-room crowds to his business school classes and four-day seminars and influencing thousands of managers at companies like AT&T, P&G, Xerox, and General Motors.

The result? At such companies as Ford, Xerox, and Motorola, management reviews have shifted away from their earlier focus on financial outcomes to discussions of process problems. Motorola's obsession with quality drove its defect rate down from 6,000 defects per 1 million components in 1987 to 40 per million in 1992. Whereas companies like

Ford and GM once picked suppliers for their low-cost bids, since 1980 both have winnowed their base of suppliers and forged closer relationships with those that remain. Much as a family member might, a single supplier more likely identifies with the company. In turn, shared expectations and stable production runs enable both the manufacturer and the supplier to reduce costs by maintaining lower inventories, meeting accurate specifications, and so satisfying customer needs.[18] Once a major manufacturer like Ford, IBM, or Motorola adopts a quality orientation, it tends to demand the same of its suppliers, and that further diffuses quality principles throughout the industry.

The gospel of quality has been actively preached by others, like Philip Crosby and Joseph Juran. Together with Deming, they have pushed companies to develop a quality-based identity: a commitment to reduce defect rates; to continually improve products by empowering employees; and to reduce the cycle time between identification of a deficiency and its resolution, which means listening to the customer more closely than ever.[19]

Xerox's David Kearns puts it this way: "Our basic focus is customer-oriented. Our description of quality at Xerox is meeting the customer's requirements and satisfying them 100 percent of the time. We want our customers to perceive us as providing quality products and services, and the measurement of that is, do we meet their requirements? We believe customer satisfaction will enable us to meet our goals of improved return on assets and increased market share."[20]

TRAIT #8: PUT THE CUSTOMER FIRST

Wordsmiths are likely to remember a company by the name of Wordstar. In the early 1980s, the small company took a solid lead in selling word-processing software for personal computers. Today, few of us rely on Wordstar. That's because throughout the 1980s the company developed a reputation for insensitivity to consumer needs. Its managers communicated poorly with the public, failed to make 800 numbers available for customer service, and routinely put out versions of its own software that were incompatible with previous versions, forcing wholesale retooling by those eager to keep up. Contrast that with the efforts made by rival producer Wordperfect to maintain close contact with its customers. Throughout the 1980s, Wordperfect built a solid reputation for user friendliness. The result? Wordstar, though still in business, squandered its lead and gave up most of the word-processing market to Wordperfect.

Companies with products that rate well with customers rely on a simple and logical strategy: They keep in touch. Toll-free phone lines mean that customer concerns are heard quickly and that problems are resolved on a real-time basis. Regular customer surveys enable companies to analyze sources of dissatisfaction and develop tactical solutions.

Before developing the Taurus in 1985, for instance, Ford spent four years conducting consumer research that identified a wish list of some 1,401 features. Company engineers worked hard to incorporate more than half of them in the design of the Taurus. In the process, benchmarking against leading rivals proved vital. As the author of *Investing for Good* explain, "Ford also listened to drivers and engineers in determining which of its competitors was considered 'best in class' across a range of auto characteristics—seats, dashboard configurations, transmissions, door latches . . . and set out to match or exceed them."[21] The result? The company reduced by more than 50 percent the labor content required to assemble a car relative to domestic rivals. By 1989, Ford's profits dwarfed those of Chrysler and surpassed those of its much larger rival, GM.

The companies consumers respect constantly look out for both positive and negative indicators of their success at meeting needs. On the positive side, they carefully monitor whether they're getting repeat business. They also tally the complimentary letters they receive and the customer referrals they get. On the negative side, they keep a close watch of customer complaints and lost customers. And they reward employees accordingly. IBM Malaysia is one example of a company that awards employees a bonus if the overall customer satisfaction ratings gathered annually improve by at least two percentage points.

GOOD CITIZENS

Finally, what traits build for a company a good reputation in the communities in which it does business? Here again, what's important to the local community will be different from what's important to employees, investors, or consumers. From the public's point of view, doing good is a precursor to doing well.

The laissez-faire decade of the 1980s demonstrated how reckless business interests could be when left to their own devices. Although mergers and leveraged buyouts were widely defended as strategies to enhance corporate efficiency, most proved to be motivated more by exploitative managers and raiders eager to capitalize on market failures, with little concern for the employees that had to be laid off, for the communities that were frequently devastated, or for the companies that were themselves subsequently bankrupted by debt. Many companies and their executives have concluded that we pay a high price for disregarding the social implications of corporate decisions and for endorsing a short-run view of corporate self-interest.

Corporate citizenship is a mindset according to which managers make decisions, design systems, and initiate programs that reflect a commitment to ethical principles and encourage community-wide integration. Consider this statement by journalists Mary Scott and Howard Rothman, authors of *Companies with a Conscience:* "As the '90s wear on, it becomes increasingly apparent that business in general can no longer function, and no longer be judged, solely on the basis of nets and grosses. A positive impact on employees, customers, and the community at large has assumed an equal or even greater significance in the overall picture. Today's bottom line encompasses more than just dollars and cents, and corporations of all sizes and philosophical orientations are beginning to recognize this."[22]

Well-regarded companies make more explicit their commitment to multiple constituents. At J. P. Morgan, chairman Dennis Weatherstone asserts, "If you don't serve your clients well you can't serve your shareholders well; if you don't serve your people well, you can't serve your clients well. To serve your people well means being effective in the community that they work in and that they live in, and it's just reductive and tunnel vision to think of it otherwise. You have to think of the linkages to long-term shareholder value across all your stakeholder communities."

It shows in all well-regarded companies, whether symbolically, as in Johnson & Johnson's credo or in Herman Miller's corporate values booklet; financially, in the contributions they funnel to local communities or through foundations; or personally, in the extensive volunteer programs that these companies conduct. All seem actively, passionately committed to playing a lead role in upholding moral principles and integrating themselves and their employees into the fabric of society. Many support campaigns to enroll voters, others to protect the environment, some to improve schools, others to help the homeless. In a very real way, the reputations of these companies mirror not only their strength of character but also their sense of duty to act as full-fledged citizens and social participants. The British-based Body Shop Company made significant and surprising inroads into the crowded cosmetics industry in the 1980s by redefining the concept of beauty for women—away from makeup to a more natural look. In the process, the Body Shop built a reputation as the West's most caring cosmetics company, less because it produces products much different from those of its rivals than because founder Anita Roddick is aggressive about putting the company's social concerns at the forefront.

In similar ways, Tom's of Maine is a small American company that proudly identifies itself with its natural toothpaste and deodorant products. At a recent gathering of like-minded identity researchers in Utah, I recently had the opportunity to hear founders Tom and Kate Chappell expound on the consistency between their social vision and their market development. As Tom put it: "There's a fundamental unity that I see across all spheres of life. I simply don't think in terms of boundaries. Our customers, investors, and employees are all part of the Tom's of Maine family—we're all members of the same community."

From small to large, companies become well regarded because they increasingly recognize the importance of addressing the interests of all groups affected by a company's actions, decisions, policies, and practices.[23] Since those interests are often incompatible and costly in the short run, these companies obviously take a long-run view of profitability. They recognize that the divergent points of view of employees, consumers, investors, and local communities can and should be accommodated in the long term.[24] Whether from a morally principled point of view or from a more utilitarian logic, they recognize the value of cohering work and play, self, and community.

Listen to Ben Cohen, cofounder of Ben & Jerry's, the Vermont-based ice-cream maker with the pristine reputation. He asks pointedly: "Can a business make a top quality, all-natural product, be a force for progressive change in its community, and be financially successful? Yes. Sure. Why not? We're doing it—and so is a small but growing and (we think) influential group of socially responsible companies. We call our approach Caring Capitalism."[25]

Like Tom's of Maine, Ben & Jerry's, and the Body Shop, some of our larger companies are also answering these questions in the affirmative. They pose moral questions that go beyond the traditional fiduciary role of delivering profits to shareholders. Besides making ritual donations to charity, they willingly take on what they see as a responsibility to sustain the infrastructure of local communities. They encourage volunteerism, adopt troubled schools, and actively search for ways to sustain the fiber of comradeship and social support. Often led by visionaries, these companies increasingly question the viability of an economic system that is not sustainable, that takes more from the environment than it can provide. Despite some press attacks in the fall of 1994 (discussed below), the Body Shop remains one of the most admired companies in the United Kingdom. Anita Roddick puts forth her views passionately, and in somewhat radical terms: "The responsibility of business is not to create profits but to create live, vibrant, honorable organizations with real commitment to the community. . . . I certainly believe that companies should not be evaluated solely on their annual report and accounts. . . . Businesses are the true planetary citizens, they can push frontiers, they can change society. There hasn't been an ethical or philosophical code of behavior for any business body ever, and I think it's going to have to change."

Many of our best-regarded companies now take this message to heart. It's apparent in their efforts to build a stronger, healthier relationship with local communities on one hand and with "spaceship earth" on the other.

Trait #9: Serve the Community

Early in his presidency, Bill Clinton called on Congress to create a National Service program to rebuild the spirit of community, to rekindle patriotism, and to act on the eloquent words of the late U.S. President John F. Kennedy: "Ask not what your country can do for you; ask what you can do for your country." The program was successfully implemented with students benefiting from college funding in return for performing community service after graduation.

A similar appeal to community spreads out from our most respected companies. At ARCO, chairman Lod Cook encourages volunteerism. "I think the CEO has to lead by doing," he says. As a volunteer, he donates a third of his time to supporting education, to countering drug abuse, and to helping local communities. His fund-raising efforts have helped build the Hispanic community center Plaza de La Raza in Los Angeles, the national headquarters for Junior Achievement in Colorado Springs, and the planned U.S. Olympic Training Center in San Diego.[26]

H. B. Atwater is the chairman and CEO of General Mills, an admired company by all accounts. He had this to say: "General Mills has built a reputation as a company that cares about people and about the communities in which we do business. . . . Our contributions include financial support, product donations, and the development of innovative social programs. But the contributions that make us especially proud are those of our employees and retirees who give of themselves in such a variety of ways. Their volunteerism helps make this a great company."[27]

In 1992, the Points of Light Foundation and the Conference Board jointly sponsored a survey of professionals in 1,800 companies. Of the 454 responses received, 50–60 percent believe that company-sponsored volunteer programs help companies to build morale, skills, and loyalty as well as project a favorable image to the community.[28] A set of studies commissioned in 1989 and 1992 by IBM and conducted by UCLA's David Lewin examined 156 companies. The results indicate that employee morale was up to three times higher in companies actively involved in their communities.[29] In my own study of well-respected companies among the Fortune 500, I found the firms most frequently cited were more likely to have created a foundation and to make larger contributions to charitable causes.

A number of esteemed companies go well beyond philanthropy and volunteerism. Take Merck. In 1978, the company developed a drug that successfully combats "river blindness"—so called because it is a disease transmitted by insects that principally affects people who live near rivers, mostly in developing nations. Given the poverty of the affected populations, Merck recognized that the drug was unlikely to be profitable. In an act of benevolence, Merck's CEO Roy Vagelos announced in 1987 that the company would donate its Mectizan drug to all affected populations free of charge for as long as necessary. As Edward Scolnick, head of Merck's research laboratories, puts it: "We should donate Mectizan because we can afford to donate it. We're fortunate." A May 1990 Merck press release reinforced the point: "You cannot let a product like this sit on the shelf. With sales of $6.55 billion and a $750 million budget for research and development last year, Merck can afford to distribute free drugs."[30]

Merck's rival Pfizer stays closer to home. A company founded in Brooklyn in 1849, Pfizer has committed itself to redeveloping the decaying neighborhood in which its plant continues to operate. Through a broad partnership with local nonprofit organizations, community groups, businesses, and city agencies, the company spearheads a $28 million program to create affordable housing, commercial facilities, and jobs in the Williamsburg community of Brooklyn. In 1992, new residents moved into the first middle-income housing units of the project. Soon thereafter, a bilingual school was opened in a building donated by Pfizer, on which the company spent some $500,000 to convert to educational use.

TRAIT #10: GO GREEN

In August 1993, five large companies working with the Environmental Defense Fund formed an alliance to increase their use of recycled paper. The purpose of the alliance is to reduce the burden on landfills and to revitalize the moribund market for recycled paper by creating demand for billions of dollars of secondhand pulp. Only about 6 percent of the 22 million tons of printing and writing paper produced in the United States every year comes from recycled paper. The participating companies are Johnson & Johnson, Time Warner, McDonald's, NationsBank, and Duke University. Clearly, being "green" is in vogue.

Also in August 1993, *Fortune* magazine published a list of 30 prominent companies that they scored for safeguarding the environment. All of the companies going green are among those identified in chapter 4 as having high levels of reputational capital. The environmental ratings provide a broad sense of corporate performance in 20 different environmental categories that range from whether company has reduced emissions of toxic chemicals to whether it has developed comprehensive written policies, goals, and incentives.

Consider these highlights of what took place at AT&T, Apple Computer, and Dow Chemical:

- Between 1988 and 1993, AT&T lowered its air emissions by 81 percent and cut disposal of manufactured waste in half. Between 1986 and 1993, the company cut releases of toxic CFCs by 86 percent. As of 1993 it was recycling 60 percent of its office paper and using 10 percent less of it by making double-sided copies and encouraging electronic memos. AT&T offers financial incentives to employees who come up with ways to improve the company's environmental performance.

- Apple Computer reduced its toxic emissions by 97 percent between 1988 and 1992. The company works with its suppliers to end their use of CFCs. With its Macintosh Color Classic, the company introduced a "sleep" mode that lowers energy consumption by nearly 50 percent.

- At Dow Chemical, toxic releases declined by 32 percent between 1988 and 1991, making the company's total releases among the lowest in the chemical industry. The company is among the first to put its top environmental officer on the board. In 1986, the company launched the WRAP (Waste Emission Always Pays) program. Some 200 teams of workers had by 1993 generated savings of an estimated $700,000 each by increasing efficiency and reducing the waste sent to refills.

Many of these improvements were propelled by government-led programs such as Superfund and the Toxic Release Inventory (TRI). Superfund was written into law by Congress in 1980 following the Love Canal disaster in upstate New York. The 20,000 tons of chemical wastes buried by the Hooker Chemical Company were suspected of causing miscarriages, birth defects, and cancer. Superfund would induce companies to clean up the thousands of toxic waste dumps they had created across America. For all the publicity surrounding the program, most experts consider it to have failed. In 14 years, only 217 of 1,289 seriously toxic sites have been cleaned up, despite $13 billion spent by governments and companies.

TRI has been more successful. Started in 1986 by the Environmental Protection Agency, the TRI program requires that all U.S. plants report annual releases from their facilities into the air, ground, and water of some 317 toxic chemicals. By enforcing tabulation and codification, and by publicizing those numbers widely, TRI provides a highly visible, public benchmark for assessing companies.

The Earth Summit held in Rio de Janeiro in June 1992 also helped. Nearly 180 nations committed themselves to policies that would enable them to develop their economies while preserving the environment and the renewable natural resources on which future prosperity depends— what they termed "sustainable development." They also assembled a broad blueprint for arresting environmental degradation. Subsequently, the United Nations constituted a 53-nation Commission on Sustainable Development to translate the Rio accords into action.

In June 1993, Vice President Al Gore eloquently pledged his support to the group: "If there is any doubt about the support of the United

States for that commitment, let me lay it to rest here and now. This administration not only supports that commitment, we intend to join with all those determined to demonstrate real leadership."[31] Part of that pledge involves reducing emissions of heat trapping gases like carbon dioxide and further stimulating companies to enact environmental programs.

Consumer-goods maker Procter & Gamble recognized the challenge (and opportunities) of environmental protection early on. Since the early 1980s, the company has been actively working to promote environmental quality management in its packaging, marketing, and distribution processes. P&G actively looks for partnerships with local schools, suppliers, and customers to make products safer, to reduce waste, and to replenish the vast forest resources the company saps as one of the world's largest consumers of wood pulp. In 1990, P&G launched the Global Environmental Management Initiative (GEMI), a collaborative effort of 20 leading companies to promote sustainable development. The purpose of the group is to foster environmental responsibility among companies throughout the world by transmitting "best practices." GEMI members now share environmental codes of conduct and coordinate and support research from industry and academia on environmental matters.[32]

The Council on Economic Priorities (CEP) is a not-for-profit group that regularly rates companies on diverse social criteria (see chapter 7). Table 5-3 contrasts two groups of companies to which the CEP has given its highest and lowest environmental ratings. On average, although comparable in size, companies in the highest rated group claim twice as much reputational capital for every dollar of revenue they bring in.

TRAITS THAT BUILD REPUTATION

The best-regarded companies appear to boast a strong sense of identity. Johnson & Johnson is widely known for the conservative but caring convictions that bind its 35,000 employees into a community. Pharmaceutical giant Merck is admired for providing a paternalistic, caring environment for employees, with generous benefits for families. Xerox is lauded for its commitment to innovation, its teamwork, and its high-quality products. Wal-Mart takes center stage as retailing's most folksy, family-oriented, and gung-ho company. And who hasn't heard of Herman Miller's democratic culture, driven by employee ownership, with its stress on trust, morality, and teams? In these companies, a set of core

Table 5-3 ENVIRONMENTAL REPUTATIONS

Highest Rated Companies	Lowest Rated Companies
Abbott Labs	Alcoa
Amdahl	AlliedSignal
Apple	American Cyanamid
AT&T	American Home Products
BankAmerica	Amoco
BellSouth	Archer Daniels Midland
Ben & Jerry's	Ashland Oil
CIGNA	Atlantic Richfield
Clorox	Boeing
Compaq	Borden
Colgate	Browning Ferris
Dayton-Hudson	Burlington
Digital	Chevron
Federated	Chrysler
Gap	Conagra
H&R Block	Du Pont
H. B. Fuller	Emerson Electric
Heinz	Exxon
Helene Curtis	General Electric
Herman Miller	General Motors
Home Depot	Kimberly-Clark
Kellogg	Lockheed
Kroger	Mead
Nalco Chemical	Merck
Nordstrom	Mobil
Pitney Bowes	Monsanto
Scott Paper	Occidental
Tambrands	Pfizer
Tandem	Philip Morris
Timberland	Ralston Purina
Wal-Mart	RJR Nabisco
Wendy's	Rockwell
Xerox	Union Carbide
	USX
	Westinghouse
	Weyerhauser

Source: Compiled by the Council on Economic Priorities, Summer 1993.

and enduring values governs the way employees relate to one another and to the outside world. Not surprisingly, these values influence the way outsiders regard them and shape their lofty reputations.

As employees, consumers, investors, and communities make more visible their demands of companies, they encourage managers to become more responsive. Not long ago, no less a publication than the *Economist* recognized this:

> *In many ways economics seems to be moving in the nice guys' direction. A growing number of consumers now base their buying decisions on 'non-commercial' concerns. Does a product harm the environment? Was it tested on animals? Is it recyclable? Was it made in a Surinam sweatshop? If a firm can answer 'no' to all of the above, it can make an ethical killing. Building a reputation as the West's most caring cosmetics company has helped Britain's Body Shop to out-perform the London share index by a factor of 45 since its flotation in 1984. Yet Body Shop has done nothing especially novel (many of its competitors also shun animal testing); it was simply one of the first firms to realise that wearing its ethics on its sleeve added greatly to the value of its brand.*[33]

Table 5-4 outlines the principal identity traits of companies that have amassed goodwill and a good reputation from pursuing "excellent" prac-

Table 5-4 CORPORATE PRACTICES AND IMAGES

Constituency	Character Traits	Images
Employees	1. Generate Trust 2. Empower 3. Instill Pride	Trustworthiness
Investors	4. Show Profitability 5. Maintain Stability 6. Have Growth Prospects	Credibility
Customers	7. Cultivate Product Quality 8. Provide Customer Service	Reliability
Community	9. Serve the Community 10. Green the Environment	Responsibility

tices in each of four domains: for maintaining good workplaces, producing strong financial results, selling good products, and acting like good citizens. In the final analysis, companies build strong reputations by actively demonstrating excellence in all four domains.

This point was driven home in a scandal-provoking article written about none other than the Body Shop and titled "Shattered Image: Is the Body Shop Too Good to Be True?" The investigative report published in the September–October 1994 issue of *Business Ethics* claimed that the company widely reputed for its progressive humanism and environmentalism did not live up to its claims. According to the reporter, its products were *not* all natural, employee benefits were *not* egalitarian, and little of real value was actually returned to the innovators of Body Shop products from developing nations. In other words, the company's reputation was at odds with the reality.

At this point, the evidence is not all in. Some of the reporter's attacks do not appear justified. Relatively minor infractions may have been blown out of proportion, distorting the record of a company that is, on balance, one with a social record that is far better than average.

The Body Shop example, however, reminds us how difficult it is to develop the Midas touch. After all, most companies are lucky if they achieve top grades in even one of the four domains. The best practices of these model companies, however, can serve as valuable benchmarks for companies concerned about meeting the expectations of all their constituents. To those *internal* practices, however, must also correspond a set of *external* practices designed to convey a set of images coherently outside the company—our next topic.

I read somewhere that everyone on this planet is separated by only six people—six degrees of separation between us and everyone else on this planet, the President of the United States, a gondolier in Venice, just fill in the names.

—John Guare
   Six Degrees of Separation

Shaping Consistent Images

A COMPANY'S identity undergirds the reputation it develops. Ice-cream maker Ben & Jerry's reputation rests not only on the quality of its ice cream but on the credibility of its claims to consumers and employees that it champions a more egalitarian and "caring" form of capitalism. Were Ben Cohen or Jerry Greenfield to adopt lavish lifestyles, to draw exorbitant salaries, or to indulge costly whims, surely the company's reputation would decline. Identity affects not only a company's internal practices but also its external practices. After all, most companies prefer to project their more alluring traits and downplay their less pleasing features. Truth be told, doesn't everyone?

To figure out what a company is up to, we rely heavily on information supplied by the company itself, on data audited by accountants, on the views of investment analysts, on the insights of journalists, and on hearsay from the rumor mill. We count on those auditors, analysts, reporters, friends, and rumor mongers when we make decisions about where to invest our money, what products to buy, and which companies to work for. We use their views to crystallize our own reputational rankings of companies. The questions we explore in this chapter are the following:

How can managers ensure that the judgments we make of their companies are favorable? And how can they ensure that the *aggregate* impressions that form among all constituents remain favorable?

Different constituents look for different things from companies: Investors look for growth; bondholders demand cash flows that are sufficient to meet interest payments and assets that guarantee reimbursement of their loans; employees look for good pay and job security; suppliers want repeat business; customers want reliable products. To assess a company's ability to meet these objectives, we each evaluate signals that are broadcast not only by self-interested managers but also by knowledgeable folks that monitor companies. Since few of us have direct access to companies' inner workings, we often rely on reporters and analysts who act as intermediaries. They screen, spin, and broker information for us; they help us make sense of companies' complex activities—and so affect company reputations.

SPIN DOCTORING

In February 1993, the television news journal *Dateline NBC* aired a dramatic segment that showed a General Motors pickup truck bursting into flames after a collision. The program provoked considerable public outrage. It seemed to prove beyond a shadow of a doubt that GM's trucks were poorly designed and that the automaker was disregarding evidence to the contrary. The program fueled speculation that the lawsuits filed by injured customers—although settled out of court without admission of guilt—were actually wellfounded.

GM's top brass was incensed. Incredibly, it turned out that NBC had tampered with the truck to make sure its gas tank exploded into flames. Not only had the on-camera experiment been rigged, but NBC had abandoned its obligation to inform viewers of as much. Smartly, the automaker pounced. It demanded and obtained from the network an unprecedented on-air public apology. The company also filed a lawsuit against NBC. Within a week, the network agreed to a settlement. To seal the victory, GM proclaimed symbolically that it would pull all of its advertising from NBC news. By now, a disconcerted NBC was cowering in the limelight. Less than a day later, GM rescinded its ban on advertising. As far as GM was concerned, its symbolic purpose had been achieved: Its reputation was restored.[1]

Reputation was again the central issue for GM a month later. When purchasing czar José Ignacio Lopez de Arriortua left GM for a top position with Germany's Volkswagen in March 1993, the executives in GM's front office were fuming. Not only had they just promoted him, but they had loudly touted Lopez to the media as GM's salvation, the masterful cost cutter who would return the company to profitability. Once again, GM was the laughing stock of Wall Street—once too often. With surprising vigor, GM turned the tables on the seemingly victorious Volkswagen by filing charges in both the United States and Germany alleging that Lopez had pilfered confidential GM documents. Taken aback, Volkswagen's top managers fumbled, unable to dispel the charges of industrial espionage. A poll of 1,000 Germans taken in July 1993 indicated that 65 percent believed there was "something" to GM's allegations.[2] In the battle of perceptions that ensued, GM showed aggressiveness, decisiveness, and credibility, whereas Volkswagen appeared defensive and weak, in other words, guilty. The market values of both companies responded accordingly: GM's improved while Volkswagen's tumbled. As with NBC, it seems likely that here, too, GM was most concerned about its image; its aim was to dispel any public perception of having been "taken." In the media brawl over reputation, GM pulled ahead, and that was money in the bank.

Both incidents call to mind a famous essay by media observer Daniel Boorstin, in which he points out that "in the last half century a larger and larger proportion of our experience, of what we read and see and hear, has come to consist of pseudo-events."[3] Although seemingly spontaneous because they are widely reported, "pseudo-events" are actually carefully staged for the express purpose of generating public attention.

GM's efforts to shame both NBC and Volkswagen sound suspiciously like pseudo-events. Embarrassed by the actions of NBC and Volkswagen, GM executives portrayed the company as a victim to elicit sympathy in the court of public opinion. Both companies were bewildered. NBC didn't have a leg to stand on, while Volkswagen sought in vain to establish "the truth" of the allegations. By not realizing that GM was concerned largely with manipulating public perception, Volkswagen executives played right into GM's hands, making of the exchange a bona fide pseudo-event, a "happening" in the international press.

The incidents involving NBC and Volkswagen show GM striving to reinvigorate a once-glorious reputation that had been left in tatters by the press. Indeed, throughout 1993 GM came under heavy fire for inertial management, poor profits, and outsized strategic errors. The NBC and Volkswagen episodes were therefore useful distractions from the day-to-day business of making and selling cars. In Daniel Boorstin's terms: "In competition for prestige it seems only sensible to try to perfect our image rather than ourselves. That seems the most economical, direct way to produce the desired result. Accustomed to live in a world of pseudo-events, celebrities, dissolving forms, and shadowy but overshadowing images, we mistake our shadows for ourselves. To us they seem more real than the reality. Why should they not seem so to others?"[4]

In recent years, pseudo-events have become grist for the mills of the public relations industry. Entire company departments devote their energies to creating, orchestrating, and diffusing pseudo-events, projecting attractive images, and safeguarding the public personas of their companies. In partnership with outside PR firms, often hired on retainer, they play a key role in helping companies to build, maintain, and defend a reputation.

If pseudo-events can fire up attention and generate interest in a company, the flames are stoked by two processes: media mania and the rumor mill. By bearing down on events, crises, decisions, failures, and successes, the media bring a company widespread notice. Paralleling the news media are the informal people-to-people networks that sometimes create and invariably propagate rumors, hearsay, and inuendo. Together, the two often start up a "bandwagon"—a fad-like process, whether in the product market, the job market, or the investment market. It spurs potential employees, customers, and investors to assess an event or a crisis based not on facts but on gossip.

Bandwagon escalations and declines in reputation are fueled partly by speculative frenzies. They are also guided by strategic efforts to project image and construct positive interpretations about corporate prospects. GM's efforts to thwart Volkswagen, its nemesis in Europe, are probably in this vein, as are numerous other pseudo-events that we routinely observe. Ostensibly, these events communicate facts; in truth, their purpose is to disseminate interpretations that safeguard the reputation and prestige of the company in question. In ads, newsletters, and other PR efforts, managers recognize one certainty: Outside observers rely heavily on the reputation of the company and on the reputations of established experts to judge the quality of that company's products, employment practices, and prospects for growth. So it is vital to monitor, to understand, and to shape external perceptions.

BEHIND THE LOOKING GLASS

One of the earliest proponents of public relations, Ivy Lee, recognized that "crowds are led by symbols and phrases. Success in dealing with crowds . . . rests upon the art of getting believed in."[5] He was right. Companies today try hard to manage appearances, to build credibility and reputation, by regularly deploying resources to influence the thinking of key constituents. Especially influential in shaping the ways we come to judge companies are:

- the media organizations through which companies advertise their wares and in which reporters comment on the activities of companies;

- the investment analysts who assess the prospects of companies; and

- the informal person-to-person networks that propagate information, rumors, and inuendo about companies to important constituents and, through them, to the rest of the world.

SWAYED BY THE MEDIA

Direct personal experience with a company's products and initiatives aside, our judgments of it are swayed by how *familiar* it is to us from advertisements and promotions. Both take place through the various ambient media that magnify the actions of companies and disseminate them far and wide.

General business publications like *Business Week, Fortune, Forbes,* the *Wall Street Journal,* and *Financial World,* as well as more specialized industry vehicles like *PC World* in computers, *Women's Wear Daily* and *Gentlemen's Quarterly* in fashion, and *Variety* in entertainment, all help to shape our feelings about the companies they feature. When managers issue press releases and make routine presentations to reporters, it's precisely to influence the "spin" that gets put on published stories.

Reporters also operate in media companies that are political. Despite claims to the contrary, corporate advertisers, media owners, and other interests influence what stories reporters choose to cover. Since advertising budgets represent the lion's share of revenues in most print and television outlets, there is some slight evidence that bigger, more profitable companies that advertise a lot may also get more and better media coverage than rivals, something that can obviously help to enhance their reputations.

This is not to say that reporters are necessarily biased in their reporting; only that they're human. They dwell more heavily on events that they expect to be more "interesting" to the average consumer. Often that simply means reporters prefer to feature attention-getting companies. They favor reporting on companies facing situations that are rare, new, and dramatic—hence their reputation for dwelling on the negative.

Edward Bernays—the widely acknowledged founder of modern public relations—would agree. In 1923, Bernays asked in his pioneering book, *Crystallizing Public Opinion,* how a hotel might increase its prestige and improve its business. Rather than hiring a chef, improving the plumbing, or painting the rooms, he suggested that the hotel stage a celebration of its thirtieth anniversary. A committee was formed that naturally included a prominent banker, a leading society matron, a well-known lawyer, and an influential preacher. The purpose of the celebration was to call attention to the distinguised service the hotel rendered to the community. The event was duly held, photos were taken, and the occasion widely reported by the media, with reputation-enhancing effects and increased business.

The recently deceased Bernays was instrumental in creating opinion-shaping methods that became widely used by companies like Procter & Gamble, Celanese, General Electric, General Motors, Westinghouse, Time, CBS, and NBC. A nephew of Sigmund Freud, Bernays pioneered the prevailing reliance on endorsements from opinion leaders, celebrities, doctors, and experts in ads promoting the arguments of his clients. Among his many campaigns, some have had lasting impact. As the *New York Times* reported on the occasion of his death in spring 1995:

He was instrumental in making it acceptable for women to smoke in public, sponsoring, on behalf of the American Tobacco Company's Lucky Strike cigarettes, demonstrations in which debutantes gathered on street corners to light up. The cigarettes were even called "torches of freedom." On behalf of Lucky Strike, Mr. Bernays also undertook to alter women's fashions. When surveys showed that women objected to Luckies because the green package with its red bull's-eye clashed with the colors of their clothes, he swung into action to make green fashionable. There followed a green fashion luncheon, green balls (at which green gowns were worn), and window displays of green suits and dresses. The campaign was a brilliant success, according to sales figures.[6]

The strategy of self-promotion Bernays originated has since become grist for the mill of the public relations industry. As consultants and advisers to corporate America, PR specialists spearhead the effort by many extroverted companies to project themselves aggressively into the media. Of some 6,644 public relations firms operating in the United States, the top three dominate the industry with a total of more than 6,000 employees: London-based Shandwick and New York–based Hill & Knowlton along with Burson-Marsteller. As with much of the PR industry today, both Hill & Knowlton and Burson-Marsteller are now subsidiaries of advertising agencies, in these cases J. Walter Thompson and Young & Rubicam, respectively.

Take the industry's third largest PR firm, Hill & Knowlton. The company serves more than 1,000 clients worldwide, with 1,281 employees scattered in offices throughout the United States, Canada, Europe, the Pacific Rim, Australia, and Latin America. The company describes its work in this way:

> *How would you teach the cosmopolitan residents of Hong Kong to become do-it-yourselfers? Defeat a planned deregulation of the New Zealand taxi industry? Help thwart the hostile takeover of a major U.S. oil company? Get the media to include your toys among its Christmas toy stories? For Hong Kong, our answer was a careful cultural translation of "do-it-yourself" into an acceptable "proper home and car maintenance" theme. The kicker that carried the day for the taxi association was an imaginative cartoon book that became the talk of Parliament. The key to outwitting the corporate raider lay in mobilizing employees and members of the hometown community in a multitudinous and highly effective cheering section. The hook that woke the toy writers was a survey of toy preferences called the North Pole Poll.[7]*

Identity consultants are a niche business within the larger advertising and public relations industry. In chapter 11, I describe how identity consulting grew out of packaging design and brand marketing. Founded in the postwar era by Lippincott & Margulies, its most visible practitioner, this specialized segment of the broader public relations industry calls attention to how a company is perceived by its different constituents. The brunt of the work done by L&M and its rivals, however, involves instituting coherence in a company's communications with those constituents, with its most visible work coming in the creation of corporate names like NYNEX, Primerica, Hartmarx, Ameritrust, and Amtrak and their attendent logos, symbols, signage, and packaging—their identities.

Some managers entrust PR agents with the task of gathering information with which to market their company. Others prefer less aggressive efforts and choose merely to have PR firms monitor public attitudes and then inform the company of early warning signals about looming social or political threats or of possible opportunities. In both cases, however, the marriage of information with marketing creates diverse images— sometimes of an introvert, sometimes of an extrovert, sometimes aloof, sometimes caring—and builds a reputation for the company with its various constituents. The challenge companies face is to ensure that the multiple images dispersed through the media are consistent. Edward Bernays justified opinion making in this way: "How can you blame the intelligent business who has millions invested in his industry, and thousands dependent on it for jobs, if he attempts by intelligent propaganda to give these shifting tides of taste a direction which he can follow without loss; to control by means of propaganda what otherwise would be controlled disastrously by chance?"[8]

Identifying trends through research has itself become an industry. Among the better-known information-gathering companies today is J. D. Powers, a privately held consulting firm founded in 1968, with revenues of $18 million in 1991. The company built its reputation among analysts with its automobile-owner satisfaction studies. In 1992, however, the firm conducted its first computer end-user satisfaction study. It provides us with one example of how PR joins forces with information research to fuel reputation building. In the computer study, Texas-based Dell Computer turned up as number 1 for PCs in small to medium-sized businesses. Dell's PR agency, Goldberg Moser O'Neill of San Francisco, seized on the ranking to put together a media campaign, creating four print ads and one television spot. According to Mike Massaro, the agency's COO, "One of the things we wanted to do, in a non-disparaging way, was to demonstrate that Dell was number-one, and that a lot of big computer companies were behind it. . . . Over the past year Dell made a lot of gains in stature, and the J. D. Powers survey gave us a reason to catapult Dell against the also-rans by utilizing TV.[9]

Susan Black is a principal at the Dilenschneider Group, a PR firm that specializes in strategic counseling. As she pointed out in a meeting in her office, public relations is a very subtle activity:

In our business, we try to change perceptions and thoughts, and that can be very difficult. You have to go back over and over again. For example, one of our clients, an investment banker, wanted to improve the way they were covered by a specialized trade newspaper. We offered to broker a small private dinner with the publisher. What happened was this: A barrier fell down, they started talking to each other, proposed some ideas for a column in the paper that was subsequently introduced, and information flowed more freely between them, reducing the misperceptions that had been there in the first place.

Over the years, public relations agencies have become masters at brokering situations and creating pseudo-events to project image. Nowhere is it more obvious, perhaps, than in sports marketing, where events are routinely manufactured to promote tie-ins of star athletes like Michael Jordan or Shaquille O'Neal with the companies and products they are paid to endorse.

Mark McCormack is the founder of International Management Group, a global marketing empire for public figures like tennis champions Jim Courier and Monica Seles, football quarterback Joe Montana, classical violinist Itzhak Perlman, and opera diva Kiri Te Kanawa. McCormack is also the author of the 1984 best-seller *What They Don't Teach You at Harvard Business School*. In 1990, *Sports Illustrated* called him the most powerful figure in sports. Supported by a small team of agents and an organization of fewer than 1,600 people spread out in 62 offices across 19 countries, McCormack's IMG generates more than $1 billion in revenues every year. Even so, it faces intense competition. In tennis, for instance, IMG squares off regularly against two key challengers: ProServ and Advantage International. Each of the three management companies boasts its own stable of international stars and regularly tries to lure away talent from its rivals. Each is in business for one reason only: to micromanage the names and enhance the reputations of their superstar clients.

ADVISED BY ANALYSTS

Although PR companies and agents are at the heart of promoting information about their clients, investments analysts are key members of a community of corporate monitors that interpret and distribute information. They, too, contribute heavily to shaping corporate reputations, particularly those of public companies.

Corporate analysts look closely at those regulated disclosures, especially at a company's financial reports. To ensure that we have "good" information on which to judge a company, the Securities and Exchange Commission demands regular reporting of profit-and-loss statements by certified independent accountants. Naturally, in their annual reports, senior executives attempt to influence the way investors will interpret their company's prospects. Hence their increasingly glitzy appearance.

Susan Black of the Dilenschneider Group emphasized the importance of analysts: "We rely heavily on analyst surveys to understand public companies. They are approachable, they have great access to companies, and they act much like the media in shaping the opinions of investors. For instance, when I work on an annual report, I ask them: 'What do you wish you could see in this report?' I also ask them what they wish never to see again."

Analysts recommend stocks based on the past and present accounting performance of firms. Empirical studies show that when companies report their seasonal earnings, investors are quick to react. High profits and low risk generate upturns in the price of a company's shares. Analysts also regularly make recommendations that fuel buying sprees. Take Montgomery Securities. After one of its research analysts recommended the stock of Immune Response in July 1993, shares of the biotech company doubled in price on conjecture about its research into a therapeutic AIDS vaccine. When the company's findings proved disappointing, its stock dropped back to its previous level.

To analysts, high earnings signal that managers are doing things right and that a company's prospects are bright. The logic is simple. A strong earnings report card inclines investors to bid up a company's equity and so increases its reputational capital. Strong earnings also make investors feel more comfortable with a company's ability to service its outstanding debt, and so increase its reputational capital.

Analysts also pay attention to debt ratings by companies like Moody's Investors Services and Standard & Poor's, with the better-rated companies generally having lower leverage and higher profitability.[10] When managers make strategic decisions that decrease debt relative to the amount of equity in the company, they reduce the company's riskiness to investors and so invite an upgrade by ratings agencies. Take Northwestern Mutual Life Insurance. Its financial position is so strong that it has never earned less than top rating from all the ratings agencies. Having such a good rating is a seal of approval that carries enormous weight on Wall Street, enlarging the market for a firm's securities and reducing the rate of interest at which its bonds are sold. The overall effect is to cut the company's interest expense, improving profitability, market value, and reputational capital—attractive outcomes, one and all.

Chrysler's experience is a case in point. In February 1991, after posting a $790 million loss and a blitz of negative assessments by analysts and reporters concerned about the company's declining market share, the company lost its investment-grade rating from Standard & Poor's. Throughout 1992, although Chrysler needed funds to finance new product development, it had trouble selling its low-rated bonds in public markets. In February 1993, buoyed by improved sales and earnings, S&P raised Chrysler's rating to BB +, one notch below investment grade. In June 1993, S&P announced that it was considering a revision of its earlier rating. As an S&P spokesperson told the *New York Times*: "Chrysler's earnings and cash flow are significantly exceeding prior expectations, due largely to overwhelming success with new products and steps to enhance operating efficiency."[11] Chrysler's stock price rose with the announcement, improving the company's reputational capital.

Or consider the plight of commercial banks. In the late 1970s, Citicorp and Chase were both rated triple-A. They were lowered to double-A in the early 1980s as ratings agencies recognized growing competition from financial services firms and foreign banks. By the late 1980s, things had gotten much worse. The credit ratings of Citicorp and Chase Manhattan plummeted after 1986 because of bad loans made to Latin American countries and in real estate.

Low ratings have the predictable effect of raising the cost of borrowing money. For commercial banks, they also restrict activities. Many client companies will not buy risky but profitable services like interest rate swaps from any but the highest-rated banks. That means many banks have lost lucrative business to better-rated rivals like J. P. Morgan.

In 1993, all three banks affirmed their intention to improve their credit ratings. Since its 1991 merger with Manufacturers Hanover, Chemical has claimed to be pursuing a rating hike from triple-B to double-A. At the company's annual meeting in April 1993, Citicorp chairman John Reed indicated that the bank was pursuing a double-A rating. And in early 1993, Chase distributed a four-page pamphlet to its 34,000 employees, proclaiming the bank's mission to become a world-class, balanced, and financially strong institution and to achieve a double-A rating.

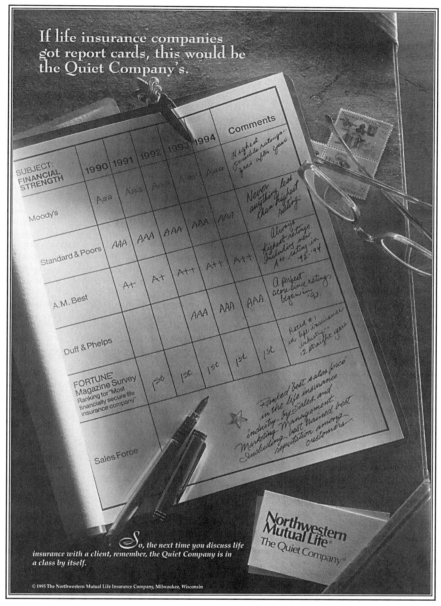

Northwestern Mutual Life Insurance specializes in selling individual coverage. Every year the company is routinely ranked as the most admired of the nation's life insurers in *Fortune* magazine's annual survey. In this 1995 ad, Northwestern Mutual emphasizes how it has never received anything but the highest possible rating from the four major rating agencies, thereby promoting its stability and solvency to prospective policyowners. (Reprinted by permission of the Northwestern Mutual Life Insurance Company.)

When the insurer Travelers was assigned a "weak" rating by specialist insurance-rating agency Weiss Research in the fall of 1991, its executives were horrified. The rating reflected the company's portfolio of troubled real estate loans. According to the *New York Times*, it touched off a wave of telephone calls to the company from jittery policyholders and agents, which quickly got management's attention: "In September [1991], a team of Travelers executives boarded the company's private jet and flew to Weiss Research's headquarters . . . in an attempt to get the rating changed. . . . The executives tried to persuade Weiss analysts that Travelers had ample capital to weather its difficulties. But despite two hours of tense negotiations, the analysts, who use an A-to-F grading system, agreed only to raise their rating to C−, from D+."[12]

Companies aren't the only ones to experience the negative reputational effects of credit ratings. In November 1992, Moody's downgraded the debt of the city of Detroit to just barely investment grade, with potentially damaging consequences for the city's ability to finance its debt. One observer noted the subjective but highly influential process involved: "The downgrading of Detroit sheds vivid light on the polite, behind-the-scenes pas de deux that is the ratings process. . . . In one sense, there is no disagreement between the rater and the rated. A city proposes, Moody's disposes. There is no appeals court or court of last ratings resort. Complaints are considered bad form and quite possibly not in the rated's best interests. 'Who is going to brawl with the ratings agencies?' "[13] A lowered credit rating discouraged private-sector investment in the city. It damaged Detroit's reputation, with potentially dire implications for attracting business, tourism, and growth.

I asked Harold Goldberg, chairman of Moody's Corporate Ratings Committee, to explain the visible role that financial ratings agencies play. He put it this way: "We're viewed by many people on the street as a vehicle to communicate with the investment community. That makes us careful about what we say and who we talk to. For instance, it would be unthinkable for us to discuss our rating with another agency like Standard & Poor's. Our ratings are independent. At the same time, we sometimes talk to investment bankers as extensions of clients. Some of them have close relationships with client companies and can speak as corporate insiders."

Examples like these remind us that sustaining a reputation requires skillful self-promotion with financial monitors like S&P's and Moody's. It also calls for establishing and maintaining favorable relations with the professional community of analysts and regulators working at the stock exchanges and in investment banks like Goldman Sachs, Morgan Stanley, or Salomon Brothers, as well as in increasingly influential social conscience monitors like the Council on Economic Priorities; social investors like Kinder, Lydenberg and Domini; and public interest groups like the Business Enterprise Trust. Each of these groups itself struggles to establish and protect its reputation and participates actively in efforts to shape its image in the press, with corporate observers, and with one another.

GRIST FOR THE RUMOR MILL

Legend has it that most business deals get done after hours, on the golf course. As the saying goes, "It's not what you know, but who you know." If so, then social networks should constitute an important vehicle for building reputation. High-powered networks can quickly convey early signals about a company's potential, getting favorable word of mouth out into the wider business community.

Companies live in tightly connected worlds. Managers, investors, and customers constantly participate in ascribing features to a company on the basis of rumor, inuendo, hearsay, and word of mouth. Tales and anecdotes circulate throughout an industry as employees come and go, and as they interact with suppliers, distributors, customers, analysts, and reporters who listen to them recounting their personal experiences with a company.

Investors listen, too. Although experienced analysts routinely caution neophyte investors to be wary of rumors, few of us follow their advice. We routinely ascribe to rumors greater status than they warrant, letting them fuel us with hope or terror. Indeed, for all their savvy, even investment professionals themselves often act more on the basis of rumor than analysis, and so encourage faddish speculation.

In fact, both individual and institutional investors rely heavily on information supplied by personal contacts when they make stock purchases. Studies of how Wall Street operates show that an elite group of 10 investment banks—led by Goldman Sachs, Morgan Stanley, and Salomon Brothers—has a finger on the pulse of most financial transactions. These banks shape the deals negotiated by our best-regarded companies and thereby exert influence on the prestige and reputations of these companies. In turn, the reputations of client companies cast a favorable glow on the reputations of the investment banks. A mutuality of interest is obvious that understandably encourages corporate managers and bankers to strengthen their relationships.[14] Appropriately, bankers use the expression "relationship banking" to characterize the strong ties that typically develop between an investment bank and its key clients.

In some industries, specialized bankers directly assess the creditworthiness of customers. In the apparel industry, for instance, bankers are known as factors. They buy a manufacturer's receivables at a discount and collect directly from the retailer. Factors are in sync with the industry. They know which retailers are in good shape and which ones are in trouble. By denying or approving a particular retailer's sales order, they essentially signal to the rest of the industry the credibility of the retailer. As one industry observer says: "Not only do factors traffic in valuable industry information, they are also invaluable sources of news about weddings, bar mitzvahs, golf scores, illnesses and fashion trends."[15]

They play a key role in containing, creating, and influencing the spread of information, rumor, and inuendo, and so directly influence a company's reputation. According to a senior executive at Heller Financial, a leading factor in the industry: "This is a relationship kind of business. . . . We've been with some of our clients since they started their business, with some through several different businesses and in some cases, with their children as they took over the family business. It's a longstanding kind of thing."[16]

In August 1993, the *New York Times* published an article on the annual summer conference hosted by investment banker Herbert Allen of Allen & Company in Sun Valley, Idaho. The gathering, part conference and part summer camp, the reporter noted, was oddly reminiscent of the annual High Yield Bond Conference that Michael Milken presided over in the heady days of Drexel, Burnham, Lambert. The lineup of guests at the Idaho conference read like a roster of prominent corporate chieftains: "Among them were Sumner Redstone and Frank Biondi of Viacom International, H. Wayne Huizenga of Blockbuster Entertainment, Michael Ovitz of Creative Artists Agency, Tom Pollock of Universal Pictures, Jeffrey Katzenberg of Disney, Robert Wright of NBC, John Malone of Tele-Communications, Barry Diller of QVC and Warren Buffett of Berkshire Hathaway—not to mention brass from giants like Coca-Cola, McDonald's, Fidelity Investments and J. P. Morgan."[17]

Clearly, the informal network cements social ties among executives of leading companies, propagating information about who's in and who's out, what's hot and what's not, and where the action is. Insofar as the corporate chieftains and bankers relay some of that hearsay, rumor, and inuendo through other informal ties, they surely influence the choices investors make as to what companies to put their money in, and so contribute to building or damaging company reputations. It's interesting to note that within two months of the Allen conference, Viacom, QVC, Tele-Communications, and Blockbuster found themselves on opposite sides of the bitter struggle over the purchase of Paramount, the giant entertainment company. In this particular bidding war, QVC's investment advisor was none other than Herbert Allen.

My point is this: Like all human groups, the corporate world is a social community constructed from interactions between many different participants. Those at its core and its periphery convert information into rumors and hearsay that help to shape how we, as investors, perceive a company's prospects. That's why so many Wall Street investors try to get "inside" information by hanging out in business bars like Harry's. Some investors *do* trade on hearsay. If enough of them do, it's bound to affect the market value of the company's equity, and so its reputational capital.

In a sense, then, a company's reputation builds, grows, and changes with the flow of information that runs across informal networks of personal contacts.[18] Managing the spread of rumor and inuendo through these networks is the heart and soul of the practice of public relations.[19] Indeed, by multiplying the indirect interactions between people, electronic networks like the Internet play an increasingly central role in propagating rumors. As discussed in the final chapter, the rising importance of these electronic networks is evident in the debacle that ensued in late 1994 following allegations of defects in Intel's highly touted Pentium chip.

In *Six Degrees of Separation,* playwright John Guare reminds us how small the world really is. It only takes six people to reach any person on the planet. A series of well-known experiments in social psychology actually demonstrates that fact. Imagine being asked to hand-deliver a package to someone living in a small town, somewhere far away. Odds are you won't know that person or anyone else in that town. Nonetheless, it turns out that if you give the package to someone you know who lives closer, and that person gives it to someone else, and so on, the package will soon reach someone who can hand-deliver it to the addressee; in fact, it will take an average of only six people to get that package delivered. But as a character in Guare's play muses, "I find it like Chinese water torture that we're so close because you have to find the right six people to make the connection."

Some managers use the small world in which we live to help them manage the reputations of their companies. Bryan Thomlison, director of public affairs for Church & Dwight (maker of Arm & Hammer products) is among them. He recognizes the critical role a network of contacts can play in helping his company address strategic issues. A piece of the process he and his department follow involves (1) identifying and maintaining a list of a few hundred key influentials around the world in specific issue areas and (2) regularly calling on these influentials to get factual information and support or to disseminate information or defend against a rumor. As Thomlison recognizes, "You can get in touch with the whole world by talking to only a few people. Armed with phone and fax, I make it a point to be able to reach quickly just about anyone I need to in order to make appropriate information available or take action against a rumor about our company. These people are great in providing early reconnaissance about problems. They're also the most efficient way to get the word out that I know." In chapter 12, I describe at greater length Church & Dwight's network-oriented approach to building, sustaining, and defending a company's reputation.

RUMORS AND THEIR SIDE EFFECTS

In struggling to manage the complex social process through which favorable corporate reputations develop, it's important to realize that rumors often take on a life of their own, with occasionally favorable and frequently devastating consequences for a company's reputation. In the mid-1800s, Charles MacKay documented some remarkable episodes of mass mania. His *Memoirs of Extraordinary Popular Delusions* describes 16 cases of seemingly irrational speculation by investors. All were fueled by rumors and inuendo that played into the latent dreams and fears of hopeful investors. Noted economist John Kenneth Galbraith recently picked up the theme in a short treatise on financial euphoria. It typically starts when something that looks new causes a stir in financial circles. People who have a stake in it become "blockheads"—they refuse to acknowledge that anything odd is going on. Those who point out that prices are out of line get shunned. Sooner or later, a time comes when, suddenly, prices fall—at which point insiders rush to be the first to sell, fueling a rapid downward spiral.[20]

Consider the bizarre episode in the tulip trade in the early seventeenth century, as described by MacKay:

> *The first roots planted in England were brought from Vienna in 1600. Until the year 1634 the tulip annually increased in reputation, until it was deemed a proof of bad taste in any man of fortune to be without a collection of them. . . . The rage of possessing them soon caught the middle classes of society, and merchants and shopkeepers, even of moderate means, began to vie with each other in the rarity of these flowers and the preposterous prices they paid for them. A trader at Harlaem was known to pay one-half of his fortune for a single root, not with the design of selling it again at a profit, but to keep in his own conservatory for the admiration of his acquaintance.*[21]

By 1636, the demand for tulips had increased so much that they were traded throughout Holland at ever more extravagant prices. Fortunes rose and fell with the price of tulips, as even the richest no longer bought the flowers to keep them in their gardens but to resell them at a profit. At some point, enough people began to think that this was sufficiently preposterous that they stopped buying. With belief in the value of the tulip destroyed, prices quickly fell to distressingly low levels. "Substantial merchants were reduced almost to beggary," reports MacKay, "and many a representative of a noble line saw the fortunes of his house ruined beyond redemption."[22]

Economist John Maynard Keynes recognized the potential for similar folly in the stock market. He once wrote that the market was much like a newspaper contest in which readers are asked to select the six prettiest women from pictures of 100 candidates. The winning entry, he argued, is the one that most closely matches the "favorites." To win, you shouldn't choose the ones you think are the best looking. Instead, you should pick those that you expect the public to put forward as the prettiest—the ones likely to garner the most votes.

The same holds not only for corporate stock but also in the markets for art, wine, and all goods sold at auction. Winning investors should not select their personal favorites; rather, they should pick the artist, vintage, or stock that they expect everyone else to favor. These artists, wines, or companies may or may not be any good. What counts is that they have that intangible "something" that draws others to them.

Some time back, the *New York Times* reported on an apparent speculative frenzy behind family-run Andrea Electronics Corporation. In the eight months between November 1992 and July 1993, the stock of the communications company grew to 37 times its original value. Andrea's sudden popularity with investors began when the small company announced that it had developed a product to filter out all the undesirable background street noise from public pay phones. Of the relatively few investors in Andrea's stock, a sufficient number were optimistic enough about the potentially large market that they drove up the price fourfold. At this point, however, Andrea had yet to show off the device. Nor had the sleepy, 60-year-old company made even one sale to a telephone company. Alerted by the pronounced rise in price and volume, other investors quickly joined in. Pretty soon, speculation on the company's future encouraged a feeding frenzy. When the dust settled, the communications company had seen its stock price zoom from $7 to $265 a share. Although in 1992 Andrea had lost $691,000 on sales of $3.4 million, in mid-1993 investors were valuing the company at a staggering $186 million.[23]

Rumors are not always to a company's benefit; they can drain away valuable reputational capital. In 1990, a rumor spread that Equitable, the nation's third largest insurer, was going bankrupt. By damaging public confidence, the rumor threatened to send the company on a downward spiral. Since the company was not public, Equitable's policyholders would have rushed to surrender policies and annuities had panic spread, causing a cash crunch similar to a run on a bank. Lacking the ability to pay, Equitable would have faced bankruptcy. Fortunately for the company, the rumor was false.

Students of rumor mongering indicate that rumors typically spread in three stages:

1. *Simplification:* The story shortens and loses detail.

2. *Exaggeration:* Some details become sharper, and the story increases in dramatic content.

3. *Interpretation:* People reinterpret the rumor in terms of stereotypes that reflect their worldview.[24]

As a rumor gets simplified, exaggerated, and reinterpreted, it comes to resemble an opportunistic virus, thriving because of its ability to create fear and anxiety. People are more likely to pass on rumors that they believe, rumors that make them anxious.

A company's reputation can be seriously damaged by the persuasive power of innuendo. In the early 1980s, Procter & Gamble was rumored to be giving part of its profits to Satanists. As evidence, gossip mongers claimed the company's logo—which showed the moon with a face in it and 13 stars—was a demonic symbol. More recently, rumor had it that apparel giant Liz Claiborne was in cahoots with the Church of Satan. In most cases, rumors like these lead to product boycotts that can seriously damage the company's market value and reputation.

The best defense against rumors is (1) to take a rumor seriously, (2) to deny its veracity vigorously and quickly, (3) to muster concrete evidence that disproves it, and (4) to present that evidence convincingly to all constituents. Equitable's reaction is a case in point. The company's executives responded aggressively by writing memos to employees, sending letters to customers, and holding press conferences. They also enlisted the New York State Insurance Department to certify that all was well. Their astute actions averted panic. Similarly, in 1991, when it was rumored that Entenmann's Bakery was owned by the Reverend Sun Myung Moon of the Unification Church, the company held a news conference at which Robert Entenmann, the chairman, reviewed the history of the family-owned business and declared that the rumor was untrue. Within 24 hours, the rumor was dead.[25] While P&G did hire private detectives to track down the origins of the rumor of profit sharing with Satanists and also sent editorials to news dailies and threatened lawsuits, its responses were sporadic and effective only in quieting the rumor for a time; it continues to surface every now and again.

In 1992, soft-drink maker Snapple also dealt poorly with a particularly ugly rumor. Word spread in the San Francisco Bay area that the company was surreptitiously supporting the Ku Klux Klan and the antiabortion group Operation Rescue. Snapple executives admit that they were far too slow to react. As the company's president, Leonard Marsh, stated, the rumors were "so ridiculous we thought they would go away, but they didn't. It reached the point it was getting out of hand and we had to address it." After a year in which it was even said that the small letter *k* on Snapple labels—short for kosher—actually stood for the KKK, the company finally launched an advertising campaign in September 1993. It declared, "We are not involved in any way whatsoever with the KKK, Operation Rescue or any other type of pressure group or organizations, period."[26] It is not known how many sales or how much reputational capital the rumor actually cost the then privately held company in the meantime.

PUBLIC FACADES: PROS AND CONS

Most companies tend to limit access and to withhold information. Often managers are frightened by the glare of publicity and opt to minimize disclosure. It reflects the deep-seated and widely held belief that openness and disclosure hinder flexibility and destroy advantage. To seal off boundaries is to retain an edge.

That's not always true. In fact, there are two main strategies that companies adopt and that shape the perceptions of constituents: strategies of extroversion and of introversion. Which strategy a company follows depends on its clients. A company that sells at retail tends to benefit from broad-based familiarity with the public and is likely to adopt an extroverted posture; a company with a bottom line that depends on fewer transactions, carried out at wholesale, tends to favor a more introverted posture. Each presents a distinct facade to the outside world.

THE EXTROVERT FACADE

When sales depend on brand recognition, companies regularly promote themselves to their mass audience of customers. Managers advertise to signal constituents about important features of their companies' products. They aggressively advertise themselves to build visibility and lure customers and investors. Advertising also helps to stabilize sales. It creates a niche that competitors find difficult to overcome.

Naturally, companies with portfolios of consumer products spend a good deal on advertising. Following is a list from *Advertising Age* of the top 10 categories of products advertised across all media in 1991:

1. Cars

2. Food

3. Restaurants

4. Nonfood retail products

5. Entertainment and media

6. Beverages

7. Toiletries

8. Telephone service

9. Beer

10. Airlines

Topping the list of big media spenders are the Big Three automakers, GM, Ford, and Chrysler; tobacco company Philip Morris through its food subsidiaries General Foods and Kraft; consumer-goods giants Procter & Gamble and Unilever; soft-drink maker PepsiCo; and retailer Sears. Their constant exposure through advertising has made them accustomed to public scrutiny and has encouraged them to develop more extroverted facades.

The pervasive link between apparel, perfume, and other consumer items invites fashion-based companies to erect extroverted facades. The highly public persona of a couturier or designer is often the centerpiece of a fashion house's marketing strategy, of the image it projects to consumers. Think back to the success stories of Halston, Anne Klein, and Calvin Klein. Their products are difficult to untangle from the personal sagas of the designers who launched these companies. Liz Claiborne was the entrepreneurial success story of the early 1980s. She built a fashion empire on the premise of selling designer-label clothing at a moderate price. Donna Karan conquered the world of high fashion for the working woman. Like most of fashion's high-profile designers, Donna Karan's product is very much herself. She projects her temperament into the products she designs and then heavily, aggressively, and personally markets them.

In the 1980s, many companies made similar efforts to reach out to consumers by harnessing the personalities of their CEOs. Victor Kiam's ads for Remington come readily to mind, as do Lee Iacocca's ads for Chrysler. Though quite different in size, both companies were facing turnarounds and sought to personalize their relationships with consumers and to signal an intimate familiarity with their company's efforts and prospects. They reinforced the extroverted postures of their companies through aggressive advertising and public relations. Iacocca became omnipresent in a blitz of direct mail, media interviews, industry roundtables, and public functions. As one analyst said, "Even though he wore a flashy pinky ring and shiny alligator shoes, Iacocca came off in those ads as a man traditionalists could trust; he seemed to be one of them—honest, dependable, the salt of the earth. When he walked through the Chrysler factory in each 30-second pitch, down the assembly line and past the bodyworks, he projected total command of automobile production. Viewers believed that they would never get a lemon from Lee, because he seemed to be on top of things—helping his guys put each and every vehicle together."[27]

Companies with extroverted facades tend to spend a lot of money on public causes. They "do good" by actively contributing to charities, creating foundations, placing women and minorities on boards, showing concern for the environment, or proclaiming their acceptance of industry codes of conduct. Although some companies (like Anita Roddick's Body Shop, perhaps) do it because of deeply held core beliefs—an identity trait—most are also aware that corporate citizenship actions increase public visibility and can improve long-run returns. For extroverts, "doing good" and "going green" are a form of corporate "advertising," an opportunity to project favorable images in the media and to garner the marketing benefits of a good reputation.

Of course, there are also those companies that are extroverts by necessity. Companies with a core business in tobacco, oil, or chemicals are cases in point. Recurring attacks on their leading products have forced these companies into a defensive posture. Rather than retreat entirely into introversion, however, they seek out opportunities to aggressively link up with consumers by promoting cultural and sporting events. Tobacco companies like Philip Morris (forbidden by law to advertise their tobacco products directly) have found other means of gaining exposure. Philip Morris is a longtime sponsor of tennis, both of the men's tour (renamed for Kraft/General Foods) and the women's Virginia Slims events. Notorious polluters like Mobil and Exxon favor public television, while chemical maker Du Pont actively supports environmental causes. Their extroverted facades are clearly in the service of self-defense.

THE INTROVERTED FACADE

A number of companies opt to minimize their public profile. They shy away from activities that attract attention, seemingly in the belief that all press is bad press. Managers whose companies adopt introverted facades take it as gospel that the best way to protect their company's reputational capital is to avoid publicity at all cost.

In fact, their concerns are not unfounded. In a study of the reputational ratings that *Fortune* presents every January to its readers, a colleague and I found a strong negative association between press visibility and reputation. At best, favorable media coverage did nothing for a company's reputation; at worse, high visibility actually depressed a company's rating. The study seemingly justifies the introverted postures some public companies favor.

Investment banks like to maintain introverted facades. They cherish their privacy and prefer to limit their public exposure. As a leading banker reminded me, until the 1980s most leading securities firms did no PR whatsoever. For one thing, very few people really cared what investment bankers did. Before merger-and-acquisition mania set in, bankers were considered stuffy white shirts toiling in near obscurity. For another, the introverted posture of many leading investment banks reflects their clientele. Premier firms like Morgan Stanley and Goldman Sachs market their services mostly to large corporations. As wholesale businesses, investment banks are unlikely to see any direct bottom-line return from broad-based celebrity. Their reputations derive from building strong person-to-person networks and from developing close relationships with current and potential corporate clients; with important institutional allies like their regulators (the Federal Reserve, the U.S. Treasury); with investment service companies like Moody's and Standard & Poor's that rate their clients; and with the leading MBA schools from which they hire employees. Moreover, many firms like Goldman Sachs operate as partnerships, and so don't even have to reveal information about their internal operations to public shareholders.

Introversion is a feature investment banks share with other professional service companies. Law firms, accounting firms, and consulting firms do not need retail visibility to attract clients. Naturally, then, they do their utmost to minimize activities that might attract the attention of the press and invite outside scrutiny. By keeping an arm's length relationship with outsiders, they discourage the potential for negative assessments that visibility can attract. You'll see very few lawyers, accountants, or consultants interviewed in the press. When they are being talked about, rest assured that it's under duress. Either they're speaking out in defense of a client or they're facing a crisis of their own.

In introverted companies, donations and other forms of doing good are not matters of corporate policy; they are a "sacred," personal matter for each employee. Many of the senior partners at Goldman Sachs donate considerable sums of money to charitable organizations and cultural institutions. They do so individually, however, and nowhere does the Goldman Sachs name appear as a donor.

There is some evidence that companies with fewer external controls favor introversion. For instance, privately held firms, as well as public firms whose boards are dominated by inside directors, tend to more actively present false images of themselves. Introverts can do this because they are less subject to the close monitoring of independent directors or investors.[28]

An ironic side effect of all this is that the introverted facade may actually prove even more vulnerable to rumors. As writer Thomas Mann once pointed out, "Speech is civilization itself. The word, even the most contradictory word, preserves contact—it is silence which isolates." In private companies and partnerships, rumors take hold more easily because constituents operate behind a wall of silence, encouraging speculation. In contrast, companies that maintain open lines of communication with constituents are better able to control the spread of rumors. A noted consultant on corporate identity recognized the significant risk of adopting an introverted facade: "Although many companies assume that the safest course is to keep a low profile, this may in fact be a dangerous tack. If some inadvertent disclosure brings high visibility or even incidental exposure, an unknown company maintains little credibility as it moves to counter public criticism. . . . When people first get acquainted with a company through an unfortunate disclosure, they often distort what little they know and make generalizations about missing information. The less filled out a company's image is, the more subject that image is to wild distortions."[29]

PROS AND CONS

In a rapidly changing environment, not only are the opaque boundaries of introverted companies difficult to maintain, they are obstacles to overcome. I once studied a slow-moving New York publisher with a long tradition of making closed-door decisions. Its managers found it difficult to keep up with changes taking place in the rapidly converging worlds of publishing and telecommunications. Faced with declining profits and a plummeting reputation, the company was forced to rethink its paternalistic practices and open itself to an influx of ideas, personnel, and technologies at all levels.[30]

In contrast, openness creates trust and increases managerial options. At ice-cream maker Ben & Jerry's, boundaries are so permeable they are difficult to identify. The company projects itself outward, not only through its products but through its visible campaigns in support of the environment, the homeless, and the Third World. The egalitarian philosophy of founders Ben Cohen and Jerry Greenfield is apparent in the company's compressed pay scales, which it broadcasts to one and all through brochures and press releases. Consider this: How many companies conduct public tours of at least a part of their offices and plants? Ben & Jerry's does. As does the New York Stock Exchange. Much as these organizations offer visitors an observation gallery, so do esteemed companies increasingly welcome closer personal contact with their local communities.

Permeability, of course, extends far beyond physical access by outsiders. Companies that develop strong linkages with suppliers, distributors, wholesalers, and retailers up and down the value chain improve their ability to gather information about market and technological trends. Having their ear to the ground enables them to more quickly anticipate and act on developing threats and capitalize on opportunities.

Table 6-1 contrasts the assumptions outside observers tend to make of companies with extroverted and introverted facades. Lacking information about introverts, outside constituents are likely to ascribe arrogance and elitism to them. The result may be an inclination to resent the arm's length relationship and to deplore the impermeability of the introverted

Table 6-1 ASSUMPTIONS ABOUT CORPORATE FACADES

Area Being Judged	Extroverted Facade	Introverted Facade
Activities	Above board	Suspect
Attitudes	Personable	Arrogant
Values	Egalitarian	Elitist
Relationships	Familial	Impersonal
Boundaries	Transparent	Opaque
Posture	Nothing to hide	Something to hide

company's activities. A possible conclusion is that the introverted company and its managers have something to hide.

In contrast, observers of extroverted companies are more likely to see the company as trustworthy and above board, democratic and egalitarian. That's because extroverts bombard observers with self-serving information, forcing us to applaud the apparent transparency of their operations. For extroverts, familiarity seems to breed not contempt but respect.

A STRANGER IN THE MIRROR?

Most managers want their companies to maintain favorable images among constituents. Projecting those images means paying close attention to the company's relationships with consumers, investors, analysts, and the media. Unfortunately, images are difficult to control. Information competes with rumor, hearsay, and inuendo to create impressions that influence a company's net reputation. Efforts to shape reputation can end in a backlash.

Consider this description of how professional image makers around the president of the United States try to manipulate the "pack" of reporters monitoring the White House . . . and how their efforts can backfire:

> Obsessed with the appearances of things, the pack is perpetually susceptible to the machinations of the image-makers. It rewards, with glowing praise, triumphs of form over content: medium-well-turned phrases, smart photo ops, effective PR stunts. But it is also unhappily aware of its vulnerability, and exacts a perverse revenge by seizing on the slightest misstep, the smallest deviation from the perfect image . . . a metaphoric event that presumes to cut through the theater to show the true man. A single such event—Clinton and the haircut, Quayle and the potato(e), Bush at the checkout counter—its significance heightened with every retelling, can permanently scar a public figure, and several in a row can be fatal.[31]

It's much the same in corporate life. Public relations machinery can miscarry and actually damage the reputation and prestige of a CEO or company. Ultimately, we do well to remember that the word *prestige* itself shares a common root with the English verb *prestidigitate*, a skill most closely identified with magicians. Both words come from the Latin *praestigium*, which means "illusion" or "delusion." The etymology of these words suggests how a reputation can be fool's gold when we assess a company only on the basis of the external images it seeks to project and not on its inner character. Sooner or later, a discrepancy between a company's reputation and its identity will discredit the company and stigmatize it for a long time to come.[32]

To become well regarded, companies must deserve it. They must develop coherent images and a consistency of posture internally and externally. And that's true whether they present themselves to the world as reclusive introverts or as outgoing extroverts. Identity and self-presentation beget reputation. As often as not, a coherent reputation also generates external recognition in the form of ratings and rankings, prizes and awards—the subject of our next chapter.

I don't care what people think of my poetry so long as they award it prizes.

—*Robert Frost*

Of Pageants and Horse Races

COMPANIES REGULARLY participate in contests of one kind or another. Often it's a company's products that compete for favor in a local or regional forum. When products get top ratings in these competitions, they are generally awarded a prize or award that confirms the company's reputation. Prizes can then be used to expose a brand to a wider audience, and that can mean money in the bank. Winners get more favorable mentions in the press, increasing their visibility and, indirectly, their ratings by constituents. The popularity of *Fortune*'s annual rankings of admired companies and *Business Week*'s rankings of the best business schools confirms that reputational standings are of widespread interest to corporate observers. This chapter examines the different kinds of contests in which companies participate and the ways in which the outcomes of these contests influence corporate reputation.

COMPETING FOR AWARDS

One of the favorite pastimes of American homemakers is to submit their choice recipes to county and state fairs. Panels of judges sample and rate all kinds of food products, awarding prizes to the best of everything from pies to chili. Art Bousel is a Chicago-based licensing attorney. Over the last few years, he has compiled an interesting database. It consists of some 5,000 recipes for a wide range of products like brownies, jams, and salsa that have won awards in local contests around the country. In January 1993, he formed a joint venture with a manufacturer to market a new supermarket line of products based on these recipes. Promoted under the label Award-Winning Foods, the packaging cleverly highlights the contest that the original recipe won. For instance, one of the products on the market is a macaroni-and-cheese dish that won the Best Cheese Award at the U.S. Cheese Championship in Madison, Wisconsin. The 200-item line aims to capitalize on a food award's implicit guarantee of quality to attract consumers. Reputation buys valuable shelf space and a chance to compete against established brand names.

Sometimes it's the company itself that gets rated by a panel of judges. Take the ongoing rivalry between the Whirlpool Corporation and Frigidaire Refrigerator Products. Both recently turned up as finalists in a contest known in the appliance industry as the Golden Carrot, an award made by 24 utilities to the company with the best design for a refrigerator that both saves energy and uses a refrigerant that is gentler on the earth's protective ozone layer than the once widely used Freon. On June 30, 1993, when the winner was finally announced, Whirlpool took first prize—along with the whopping $30 million dollar grant that it came with.

In fact, companies participate in many such contests. The prizes and awards they win help to build up their names and crystallize their reputations. Individuals, foundations, and organizations establish awards to promote causes, to encourage leadership and creativity, or to memorialize individuals. Sometimes attractive monetary prizes are attached to awards—the Golden Carrot being a case in point. Most of the time, however, awards are merely symbolic. They confirm achievements that might not otherwise get widespread notice in the marketplace. By drawing attention to these accomplishments, sponsors hope to inspire imitators. Awards thus help to create standards against which other contenders can be measured.[1]

Contests and awards are news in and of themselves and tend to generate lots of publicity. Since the publicity that surrounds an award is created by the awarding organization—and so comes from a third party—it often appears more credible than a company's self-serving promotions. That's why most companies welcome awards given by credible judges.

There is also competition for the honor of hosting competitions. Cities, for instance, regularly compete for the honor of hosting the Olympics. They do so because they recognize the future gains in tourist and investment income that their association with the Olympics will provide. In the music industry, New York City and Los Angeles have a long-standing rivalry to host the annual Grammy Awards. In 1993, the ceremony returned to Los Angeles after two years in the Big Apple—but New York still hopes to win it back.[2] In the end, awards cast a reputational halo over both prizewinners and sponsoring organizations, which are themselves competing for status.

As gastronomes know, every year the *Michelin Guide* pronounces what's hot and what's not among the more than 10,000 restaurants, bistros, and hotels of France. Receiving a coveted third star from the Guide is not only a heady experience for the chef but a virtual guarantee of patronage for the restaurant. Of the 4,000 restaurants cited in 1991, a mere 19 carried the treasured three-star rating, while just 90 were awarded two stars.

The honorary degrees granted by universities ostensibly recognize the achievements of people the university finds deserving of attention. Most awards, however, typically applaud the achievements of already quite prominent citizens. The principal function of these awards, I suggest, is to annex an individual's established reputation to that of the university. When the next graduation season rolls around, note the mad scrambling that goes on as prominent universities compete to attract high-profile award recipients to their commencement ceremonies and then bask in the reflected glory.

CORPORATE CONTESTS

These days corporate awards seem to be handed out in almost every industry and by every possible constituency. There are industry-specific supplier awards, distributor awards, client awards, environmental awards, government awards, and community awards. Indeed, some 16,000 such awards are given annually to individuals and organizations by more than 6,000 different donors throughout North America.[3] They highlight the tangential competitions in which companies regularly face off. The more prominent the award, the more likely it is to beef up a company's reputation and so improve its standing in other competitions. In turn, the awards magnify selected aspects of a company's identity and can reinforce employees' sense of self. Four major types of contests and awards contribute to building corporate reputation:

- product awards,
- process awards,
- social performance awards,
- environmental awards, and
- leadership awards.

Product Awards

Most companies like to participate in product competitions because they look forward to the free publicity an award will generate. Product awards tend to be industry-specific competitions that force judges to make comparisons between companies that make similar products.

The best-known product awards are probably those given by the publishing and entertainment industries. Mention the Pulitzer Prize, the Academy Award, or the Grammy Award and most people know what you're talking about. Consider the Pulitzer. This prestigious award is given annually to journalists, novelists, poets, and editors and their publishers. Winners invariably enjoy enhanced clout among their peers. Reporters at smaller newspapers suddenly find themselves being recruited by more prestigious newspapers and offered book contracts; authors and playwrights find the marketability of their subsequent works dramatically improved.

The Pulitzer Prize also confers reputational advantages to the sponsoring organization. Significant prestige accrues to the companies that publish a winner's work. As Douglas Bates, author of *The Pulitzer Prize*, points out: "In newspaper journalism, the prize works a form of magic that defies logic or easy explanation. . . . Winning it is useful in boosting a newspaper's circulation and promoting a positive image among readers. The prize also enhances a paper's relationship with stockholders and directors. And it polishes a company's industry-wide reputation, enabling the paper to lure more top-drawer talent to its newsroom."[4] Book publishers often find the sales and associated shelf life of their books increased.

Columbia University manages and hosts the award. The university and its journalism school benefit greatly from the publicity that surrounds the Pulitzer. In its promotional literature, the university likes to boast of the number of Pulitzers and Nobel Prizes that its faculty and graduates have received. In some of its 1994 annual reports, Columbia lays claim to its position as "U.S. Leader in Nobel Prizes," with 34 Nobelists having graduated from its various schools.

Every year book publishers submit a selection of their authors' work for consideration. Of the 590 titles presented for the 1990 competition, publisher Alfred A. Knopf entered 58, continuing an aggressive strategy that has paid off handsomely for the company. During the 1980s, Knopf's books were awarded 11 Pulitzers—more than any other publishing house—a result that has helped to crystallize its reputation as a stable for high-quality authors.

If we look not only at the Pulitzer but at the 290 other awards given out to newspaper publishers, studies show that prize-winning newspapers owe their reputations to some key traits. A survey of 125 of the nation's most consistent award-winning weeklies found that they tend to show greater respect for their readers, to pay more attention to cultivating staff loyalty, and to put more emphasis on telling interesting stories.[5] They support the view that there is a link between internal practices and success in producing award-winning products.

The competition for reputation-building prizes in the movie industry is intense. Film buffs can't fail to have noticed the growing rivalry between the film awards themselves. Every year, the Academy Awards now competes with the French Césars and a growing number of smaller competitions at festivals to identify the crop of best films, best peformers, and best directors. The film critics' awards (Golden Globes) have become increasingly prestigious, as have the awards handed out at the Sundance Film Festival and at the festivals in Telluride, New York, Toronto, and Sydney. These awards draw public attention to the merits of particular films, actors, and directors, and so enhance their individual reputations; they also inflate the reputations of the studios that financed the films. If you doubt the reputational capital hidden in an award-winning library of films, look at the battle for Paramount Pictures that pitted Barry Diller's QVC against Sumner Redstone's Viacom in early 1994. By the time Viacom won the rights to merge with Paramount, the price had escalated by $2 billion. Presumably, it was for Paramount's unrecorded intangibles (among which is its film library) that Mr. Redstone was prepared to pay so dearly.

Not coincidentally, awards boost film returns. It's estimated that an Academy Award for best picture is worth an additional $20 million to $35 million at the box office.[6] It helps explain why movie studios, directors, and stars will go to great lengths to influence the judges' vote. In 1992, after the film *Scent of a Woman* starring Al Pacino was awarded a Golden Globe for best picture, questions were raised about the validity of the award. It was widely rumored that members of the foreign press had been illegally flown to New York to meet with Pacino before casting their ballots.[7]

Even nominations generate publicity. When the Oscar nominees for the sixty-sixth annual awards were announced in February 1994, the reaction was immediate. The most nominated film, Steven Spielberg's *Schindler's List,* was quickly made the subject of a television and newspaper campaign by Universal Studios. In one week, the film went from being shown in 350 theaters nationwide to 750. As Tom Pollock, chairman of MCA's Motion Picture Group (and the parent of Universal Studios), put it: "Certainly what these nominations do is give . . . our pictures a lot more visibility and validation in the marketplace."[8] Even films that initially fared poorly at the box office are now getting re-released when they receive an Oscar nomination.

What the Pulitzer does for publishers and the Academy Award does for movie makers, the Grammy Award does for music producers and the Emmy Award for television producers. These contests crystallize the reputations of various companies and their products and solidify their market visibility and profitability. Before singer Bonnie Raitt's album *Nick of Time* was awarded the Grammy in 1989, only 650,000 had been sold; less than two weeks after the award, sales were up by another 1.1 million copies.

In recent years, and in varying degrees, most industries have developed product awards of this sort. Consider the advertising industry. For a time, the Clio Awards dominated the annual advertising sweepstakes. Conflict and dissent within the sponsoring group led to the decline of the Clios in 1992, however, and they have been in turmoil ever since.[9] In the meantime, other competitions have gained visibility. In February 1993, the Leo Burnett Company swept the twenty-second annual Mobius

Advertising Awards. Later in the month and for the second time in a row, Ogilvy & Mather took top honors from judges at the fifteenth John Caples International Awards for Direct Marketing.[10]

Even industry segments have their own awards and every year annoint their stars. The Council of Fashion Designers of America presents awards to designers and other industry players who made fashion news during the year.[11] Cable programmers have their CableAce Awards. In 1993, Time-Warner's HBO programs won 32 CableAce Awards from the National Academy of Cable Programming, more than four times those given to its closest competitor, the Disney Channel.[12] Makers of audio equipment—receivers, CD players, speakers—covet the Grand Prix for outstanding design awarded annually by an independent jury convened under the auspices of *Audio-Video International,* a leading trade journal.

Indeed, most trade magazines give out annual product awards. Auto industry experts pay close attention to the awards presented by *Popular Mechanics* and *Motor Trend.* In 1993, Mazda's RX-7 won the coveted Popular Mechanics 1993 Design and Engineering Award, while Ford's Probe GT was named Motor Trend Car of the Year.[13] Awards from the music magazine *Billboard* are said to pack a significant sales punch for retailers, according to buyers for several leading chains.[14] In 1993, *R&D Magazine* presented 100 awards to companies making technologically significant products. Award-winning designs ranged from the holographs used on credit cards to the photon tunneling microscope. *Inc.* magazine presents annual design awards to companies putting out innovative products. In 1993, the media gave so much free publicity to award winner OXO International for its ergonomically designed kitchen utensil handles that the company got away with an advertising budget of virtually zero.[15] Every year *Business Week* sponsors and features the Industrial Design Excellence Awards (IDEA) for best product designs. The 1993 gold-medal winners were a familiar cast of high-reputation companies that included Apple, Hewlett-Packard, Boeing, General Motors, and IBM. The top gold and silver IDEA award-winning companies between 1980 and 1993 are tabulated in Table 7-1, which shows the remarkable consistency of automakers GM and Chrysler and computer companies IBM, NCR, and Apple.

Clearly, these kinds of product awards raise the public profiles of the companies that win them, which is why award contests are growing ever more popular inside and outside the corporate sector. Service organizations like schools and government agencies that lack concrete measures

Table 7-1 TOP IDEA AWARD WINNERS, 1990–93

Company	Number of Awards
General Motors	18
NCR	15
IBM	14
Apple	13
Steelcase	10
Chrysler	9
Herman Miller	8
Fisher-Price	6
Texas Instruments	6

Source: Adapted from "Winners: The Best Product Designs of the Year," *Business Week,* June 7, 1993, 59.

of performance see tremendous motivational benefits from awards that recognize employee efforts to deliver better service. In 1993, for instance, Pearls Elementary School 32 in Yonkers, New York, was named one of the country's elite Blue Ribbon Schools of Excellence—a significant symbolic reward for its underpaid staff.[16]

PROCESS AWARDS

Occasionally an award is developed that recognizes a company for its inner workings—its human and organizational processes. The most prestigious is probably the Malcolm Baldrige Award. Established by Congress in 1987, the contest is sponsored twice a year by the U.S. Department of Commerce and the National Institute of Standards and Technology. It is loosely modeled after Japan's competition for the Deming Award, a prize given annually since 1951 to companies such as Ricoh, the maker of copiers and fax machines, that regularly improve the quality of their products. The Japanese award was named for quality guru W. Edwards Deming, whose ideas were largely disregarded in the United States but acclaimed by companies in postwar Japan. In recent years, a number of cities throughout the United States have also presented quality-improvement awards to local companies. The Austin Quality Award, for instance, was initiated by the Texan city's local government as a means of attracting new business and stimulating economic growth.[17]

FEW CORPORATIONS HAVE EVER WON A DEMING MEDAL

RICOH HAS TWO OF THEM

It is among the world's highest awards for quality. Many pursue it. Less than 100 companies have ever won it.

Ricoh was the first office equipment manufacturer to win the Deming Medal. And today, Ricoh is the only such company to have won two.

It is our company-wide obsession with quality control that earned us these two Medals. And it is this obsession that makes our high tech copiers and facsimiles some of the most reliable office machines in the world. *Official Copier and Fax*

So you see, we don't just have a reputation for quality. We have proof.

THE NAME TO KNOW

RICOH®

1 - 8 0 0 - 6 3 - R I C O H

USA Volleyball Team

© 1994 Ricoh Corporation

Ricoh is the American subsidiary of a leading Japanese manufacturer of copiers, fax machines, cameras, and measuring instruments. The company had sales of $9 billion in 1994. In this ad, the company conveys its pride in earning two Deming medals for the quality of its highly-rated office equipment. (Deming ad courtesy of Ricoh Corporation.)

Quality awards like the Baldrige invite companies to compete in two areas: customer satisfaction and product quality. Applications are reviewed by an independent board of 16 examiners that screens each company's detailed responses to 33 questions. The process requires judges to evaluate the company's internal operations, information systems, and human-resource practices and to assess its success in sustaining a focus on quality.

Baldrige awards are given in three categories: manufacturing companies, service companies, and small businesses with fewer than 500 employees. So far, recipients have included GM's Cadillac division, IBM's Rochester division, air courier Federal Express, and Xerox's business products and systems unit. Winning has not been without costs: Xerox admitted to sinking some $800,000 and 14,000 labor hours into the process of completing applications and preparing employees for site visits by examiners. Winners contend that the awards pay off in increased employee motivation and productivity. After all, who isn't proud of working for an award-winning company? According to John Grettenberger, general manager of GM's Baldrige-winning Cadillac division, "The great benefit is to the corporation itself. When you go around the offices and plants you see people smiling again."[18]

Various business magazines have also created awards that recognize companies for internal practices. In December 1992, *Fortune* magazine teamed up with the American Center for Design to announce the Beacon Awards competition for companies that demonstrate strong, focused, integrated corporate communications. Thirty-one companies entered. After extensive deliberation, a group of independent judges finally settled on four winners: furniture maker Herman Miller, footwear giant Nike, newcomer Starbucks Coffee Company, and Crown Equipment.

Personnel Journal gives its Optimas Awards to companies for their innovative human-resource management programs. In 1993, Hewlett-Packard was among 10 award winners that included such prestigious companies as Gillette, Textron's Bell Helicopters, and Steelcase. Hewlett-Packard was cited for its exemplary restructuring of the company's human-resource management systems. Gillette won for the quality of its international graduate trainee program. In the case of Bell Helicopter, judges noted the valuable role that staffing and training programs had played in easing the company's move to a Canadian facility. Steelcase won for designing an innovative return-to-work program that reduced worker's compensation costs by nearly $4 million.[19]

Finally, many companies are participating in award programs designed to applaud the achievements of public service organizations like schools, police departments, and government agencies. In a recent program of this sort, Motorola joined forces with the International Association of Chiefs of Police to create the Webber Seavey Quality in Law Enforcement Award.[20] Aside from monetary inducements, the awards confer prestige on winning groups that can help boost employees' pride and motivate them to improve the quality of the products and services they provide. Awards are a form of recognition, something industrial psychologists often contend is a more motivating influence than money.

SOCIAL PERFORMANCE AWARDS

A number of awards are given to companies for their so-called social achievements. Magazines like *Business Ethics* and *Black Enterprise* as well as various foundations regularly announce awards to companies deemed noteworthy for their progressive treatment of minorities or for community support. One of these is the Corporate Conscience Award, presented annually by the Council on Economic Priorities.

The CEP is one of a growing number of social monitors that assess companies' social records. It is a not-for-profit group that was founded in 1969 to explore the role companies play in resolving some of society's most pressing concerns. In 1987, the CEP's book *Rating America's Conscience* was published to wide acclaim. The volume rated 130 consumer-product companies on such criteria as their hiring records, charitable contributions, involvement in South Africa, and defense contracts. The success of the book led to two further publications. One was the pocket-sized guide *Shopping for a Better World,* which rated 168 companies and more than 1,800 products. The other was *The Better World Investment Guide,* an investor's guide to large and small companies (and fund portfolios) reputed for their socially responsible postures. These books provide consumers and investors with detailed information about the social practices of various companies. In particular, they call attention to what many large and small companies are doing to promote employee well-being, to reach out to local communities, and to protect the environment.[21]

To be eligible, for the CEP's Corporate Conscience Award, which was established in 1988, a company cannot be a weapons manufacturer and must demonstrate a credible commitment to community outreach, responsiveness to employees, charitable giving, equal employment opportunity, and environmental preservation.

Awards are given to both small and large companies. Previous award winners include cereal giants General Mills and Kellogg, computer maker Pitney Bowes, Xerox, and Herman Miller. Of the smaller companies, Aveda, Tom's of Maine, and South Shore Bank of Chicago are among those who have received awards. Aveda is recognized for its organic line of beauty products and for its environment-friendly practices in packaging and recycling. Tom's of Maine, a maker of natural health-care products, is well known for its active involvement in community outreach, charitable giving, and equal employment opportunity. South Shore Bank of Chicago has the distinction of being the country's first community development bank with more than $230 million in assets. The bank is well regarded for its visionary lending practices in disadvantaged communities.

In December 1993, I joined a panel of 10 judges at the CEP's headquarters in Manhattan to decide the 1994 Corporate Conscience Awards. After reviewing company-submitted materials, CEP ratings, and background research and after undertaking exhaustive debate, we solidified our nominations for CEP's Silver Anniversary Awards as well as for the annual awards to be made in each of six principal categories. Nominees and winners were subsequently announced to the media and awards presented at New York's Waldorf-Astoria Hotel. The well-attended event drew a prominent group of senior executives from the winning companies and significant attention from the media. The commonly expressed hope was that these awards would also interest consumers, investors, and competitors in the merits of the chosen companies' social practices and so encourage imitation.

ENVIRONMENTAL AWARDS

Although they constitute a subset of many social performance screens, environmental awards have become so popular that they merit special attention. The sponsors of these awards want both to honor companies that have made an outstanding effort to promote energy efficiency and minimize pollution and to encourage others to do the same. Some awards are backed by government agencies, some by watchdog groups; others are sponsored by companies themselves. The most prestigious are the Gold Medal for International Corporate Achievement and the Global 500 Roll of Honor for Environmental Achievement.

The Gold Medal honors industrial companies that have shown outstanding, sustained, and well-implemented environmental management policies in their international operations. The award was singled out by then President George Bush as an exemplary and worthwhile competition. The Global 500 is sponsored by the UN environmental program. Nominations are made by third parties and awards are given in 27 areas of environmental accomplishment. The awards identify companies that have demonstrated sustainable development practices; that have mobilized public attention and support or taken action toward solving an environmental protection issue; or that have contributed significantly to intellectual, scientific, or theoretical approaches to environmental concerns.

Of the growing number of other environmental awards, five are among the more visible:

1. The Du Pont/Conoco Environmental Leadership Award relies on nominations from customers of Du Pont or Conoco Mining Services. It recognizes mining operations in North America for success in reclaiming mines, protecting land use and water quality, and demonstrating local environmental leadership.

2. The Edison Award for Environmental Achievement is sponsored by the American Marketing Association. It champions American companies making commercial products that contribute significantly to source reduction.

3. The Environmental Achievement Award goes to companies that exceed regulatory requirements on environmental projects and that develop creative and innovative solutions with proven economic and environmental benefits. The award is sponsored by the National Wildlife Federation's Corporate Conservation Council.

4. The Safety Award for Excellence (SAFE) targets oil companies and applauds those that achieve the highest levels of safety and environmental compliance in U.S. offshore drilling operations. Nominees are selected from inspection reports, and the award is sponsored by the Minerals Management Service of the U.S. Department of the Interior.

5. The Searching for Success National Environmental Achievement Award is sponsored by the not-for-profit group RENEW America. Awards are made in 20 environmental categories to individuals, community groups, schools, companies, and government agencies with outstanding environmental programs.

LEADERSHIP AWARDS

Various awards highlight the role that top business leaders play as architects and champions of programs that improve a company's economic and social performance. By far the most visible award is induction into the National Business Hall of Fame. In 1993, honorees included Chrysler's former chief Lee Iacocca, the *Washington Post's* Katharine Graham, S. C. Johnson's founder Samuel Johnson, retailer L. L. Bean's founder Leon Bean, and publisher Amory Houghton of Houghton Mifflin.[22]

In 1989, leading representatives of American business, academia, labor, and the media founded the Business Enterprise Trust, a national organization seeking to shine a spotlight on acts of courage, integrity, and social vision in business. The trust presents five annual awards to individuals and companies in recognition of exemplary acts of business responsibility. Prudential was among the 1992 recipients, lauded for designing innovative policies that give terminally ill patients early access to their insurance savings.

RISING IN THE RANKINGS

Talk to any manager about how his or her company ranks against rivals in the industry and I guarantee you a strong, almost visceral reaction: piqued interest if the ranking is good, defensiveness if it's bad. Managers are attentive to such ratings because they know that a company's reputation matters. They know that a pristine reputation is like a magnet—for employees, customers, investors, and local observers—whereas a bad one sends them running to rivals.

In December 1993, for instance, *Fortune* magazine asked senior executives to cast their votes in a popularity contest for the most innovative companies in U.S. industry. Following are the top 10 innovators nominated:

1. Microsoft
2. General Electric

3. 3M

4. AT&T

5. Motorola

6. Apple Computer

7. Intel

8. Merck

9. Wal-Mart

10. Chrysler[23]

The executives rated software giant Microsoft far and away the most innovative of all companies—no doubt to the considerable satisfaction of Microsoft's managers.

Less specific but equally meaningful to managers are the many rankings of companies put out by monitoring agencies. Consider the airline statistics that are regularly gathered and published by the Civil Aeronautics Board. One is a record of on-time service. Northwest Airlines, rated number 1 in on-time service in 1993, quickly took out an ad in the *New York Times* to publicize its ranking.

Most companies look hard to find a statistic—any statistic—that provides them with a number 1 ranking to use for self-promotion. For instance, the trade journal *Institutional Investor* regularly ranks investment banks by the total assets they manage, the volume of underwriting they do, and the quality of advice they give. Banks that come out on top in any of these categories are generally quick to take out ads in the business media to convey their prominence and remind existing and potential clients about their relative standing.

The recent proliferation of both general and specialized rankings attests to the growing popularity of corporate pageants and horse races. In just about every industry possible, we now have lists of "the top 10," "the best managed," "the most socially responsible," "the greenest," or "the most admired" companies. Magazines expend considerable energy assessing business schools, hospitals, small businesses, cities, states, and regions. Every year, for instance, the National Education Standards agency sponsors *The Gourman Report*, a ranking of the undergraduate programs of leading business schools. The business magazine *U.S. News & World Reports*, like *Business Week*, regularly reports rankings of the country's graduate management programs.

Not only do these published lists help to create best-selling books and special issues of trade journals and general business magazines like *Institutional Investor, Fortune, Forbes, Inc.,* and *Business Week*, but they also stimulate frenetic activity on the part of the managers and institutions being appraised. More favorably rated institutions bask in the reflected glory of their rankings, while lesser-rated institutions engage in vigorous soul-searching and rethink their resource deployments. By crystallizing the relative standings of business schools, the ratings by *U.S. News & World Reports* and *Business Week* were instrumental in launching a virtual revolution in management education that has only gathered steam since 1988.

PERCEPTUAL RATINGS

Perceptual ratings establish the relative value of one firm's intangible assets against another's. Just as beauty pageants reduce the complex construct of "beauty" to a single superficial dimension, so do reputational ratings simplify the many complex dimensions of a company's "performance." They supplement familiar financial statements by telling us how well a company is doing in other than purely economic terms. By forcing us to juxtapose rivals on a single dimension, these reputational rankings help us make decisions about which firm's products to buy, which firm's stock to invest in, or which firm to work for.

In part, perceptual ratings have grown popular because most companies prefer to avoid the limelight. Which is why we search for information. Annual statements provide us only with past information about how a company did financially; they tell us little about how clients like the company's products, how skillfully its employees perform their jobs, how much damage the company's plants inflict on the environment, or how well the company supports the local community. They tell us little about the company's intangibles.

In an attempt to make such information more public, a number of coalitions have formed over the years to disseminate ratings of social and ecological performance. The oldest is perhaps the Motion Picture Association of America's ratings of adult content in commercial films. Efforts to extend these ratings to the music and television industries have been fraught with dissent. In January 1994, however, the U.S. cable industry endorsed a plan to create a new rating system for television programming. The plan approves the hiring of an outside monitoring agency to produce regular report cards on cable companies. Product ratings of this sort are disturbing to broadcasters. They stand to significantly influence not only viewership but advertisers, and so are likely to alter programming decisions.

The ratings controversy is being extended to many other industries. The burgeoning field of so-called ethical investing encourages reliance on social ratings, such as those of the Council on Economic Priorities, when picking stocks or mutual funds. Ethical funds act somewhat like monitoring agencies. They include in their portfolios only those companies which have passed screens for product quality, customer service, environmental performance, employee relations, and corporate citizenship.

Some 290 investment funds now offer social screens of this sort. One such fund brings together a portfolio of 400 companies. The resulting Domini 400 Social Index, its founders report, performed at least as well as the S&P 500 between 1988 and 1992. It provides not only investors but managers with a potentially powerful benchmark for targeting activities that might improve their companies' reputations.[24] Social activists estimate that assets with a collective value of more than $625 billion are currently screened for ethical considerations through such investment funds. Although a small pool compared with the totality of all financial investments, these social funds represent a rapidly growing source of influence on companies' activities, not least of which for the media attention that they attract.

Various books rank noneconomic corporate achievements. They include *The 100 Best Companies to Work for in America* and *The Best Companies for Women* as well as trade magazines and surveys that document discriminatory practices, investments in South Africa, pollution levels, and involvement in military expenditures, tobacco, alcohol, or gambling.[25] These reputational rankings make internal operations more transparent to outside observers and help to crystallize and validate a company's reputation.

FORTUNE'S ALL-STARS

Among the more visible perceptual rankings of large American companies is the one *Fortune* has published in its January/February issue since 1984. Every fall the popular business magazine asks an independent research firm to develop a ranking of companies based on a poll of

6,000–8,000 knowledgeable executives, directors, and analysts. Operationally, the survey gets respondents to nominate leading companies in an economic sector and to evaluate each company on eight dimensions:

1. the quality of the company's management;

2. the quality of its products and services;

3. its long-term investment value;

4. its innovativeness;

5. its financial soundness;

6. its ability to attract, develop, and keep talented people;

7. its acknowledgment of community and environmental responsibility; and

8. its use of corporate assets.

Table 7-2 summarizes the top 10 firms rated in these surveys from 1983 to 1995. The turnover in the survey is considerable. Only three companies can be said to have owned the number 1 slot: IBM, Merck, and Rubbermaid. Even their reigns have been periodically challenged by veteran performers like P&G, Coca-Cola, J. P. Morgan, and 3M, while potent newcomers with strong growth spurts—like Liz Claiborne in apparel, Wal-Mart and Home Depot in retailing, Intel and Microsoft in computers—are making strong showings. The timeline presents a bird's-eye view of the changing landscape of corporate America over the last decade.

A recurrent theme in discussions of corporate reputation is one that *Fortune*'s researchers themselves express: "How much of a company's reputation can be traced to the tangible numbers of the balance sheet, the income statement, and stock performance?" Their brief and largely anecdotal conclusion is simply this: "A lot . . . but far from all."[26]

To explore this question in detail, Mark Shanley and I conducted a detailed study of *Fortune*'s rankings.[27] What kinds of information, we wondered, do these ratings embody? To what extent do *Fortune*'s reputational rankings simply reflect the prior profitability of rated firms? Or might they also account for aspects of the social records of these companies? After much statistical analysis, we were able to show that two sets of factors predicted why some companies were better regarded than others; one is a company's performance history—its economic record—

Table 7-2 FORTUNE'S MOST ADMIRED COMPANIES, 1983–95

Rank	1983	1984	1985	1986	1987	1988	1989	1990	1991	1992	1993	1994	1995
1	IBM	IBM	IBM	IBM	Merck	Merck	Merck	Merck	Merck	Merck	Merck	Rubbermaid	Rubbermaid
2	HP	Dow Jones	Coca-Cola	3M	Liz Claiborne	Rubbermaid	Rubbermaid	Philip Morris	Rubbermaid	Rubbermaid	Rubbermaid	Home Depot	Microsoft
3	J&J	HP	Dow Jones	Dow Jones	Boeing	Dow Jones	3M	Rubbermaid	Procter & Gamble	Wal-Mart	Wal-Mart	Coca-Cola	Coca-Cola
4	Kodak	Merck	3M	Coca-Cola	J. P. Morgan	Procter & Gamble	Philip Morris	Procter & Gamble	Wal-Mart	Liz Claiborne	3M	Microsoft	Motorola
5	Merck	J&J	HP	Merck	Rubbermaid	Liz Claiborne	Wal-Mart	3M	Pepsi-Co	Levi Strauss	Coca-Cola	3M	Home Depot
6	AT&T	Time	Anheuser-Busch	Boeing	Shell Oil	3M	Exxon	Pepsi-Co	Coca-Cola	J&J	Procter & Gamble	Walt Disney	Intel
7	Digital	GE	Boeing	Rubbermaid	IBM	Philip Morris	Pepsi-Co	Wal-Mart	3M	Coca-Cola	Levi Strauss	Motorola	Procter & Gamble
8	Smith-Kline Beecham	Anheuser-Busch	GE	Procter & Gamble	J&J	J. P. Morgan	Boeing	Coca-Cola	J&J	3M	Liz Claiborne	J. P. Morgan	3M
9	GE	Coca-Cola	Kodak Eastman	Exxon	Dow Jones	RJR Nabisco	Herman Miller	Anheuser-Busch	Boeing	PepsiCo	J. P. Morgan	Procter & Gamble	UPS
10	General Mills	Boeing	Merck	J. P. Morgan	Herman Miller	Wal-Mart	Procter & Gamble	Du Pont	Eli Lilly	Procter & Gamble	Boeing	UPS	HP

Source: Adapted from various issues of *Fortune*, 1983–95.

TIME TO SELL YOUR MUTUAL FUND?

MARCH 6, 1995

$4.50

FORTUNE

AMERICA'S MOST ADMIRED CORPORATIONS

The Envelope, Please...

In January 1983, *Fortune* magazine first published a survey of senior executives that asked them to rate companies on various dimensions. The issue was a sell-out and has since become an annual, highly-anticipated event. Pictured here is the cover of the magazine for March 6, 1995. (*Fortune* is a registered trademark of Time Inc. All rights reserved.)

the other, the company's commitment to projecting an attractive image to employees and the local community—its institutional record.

Figure 7-1 depicts the main predictors of a company's reputation. It suggests that some companies owe most of their reputational standing

Figure 7-1 WHAT PREDICTS CORPORATE REPUTATION?

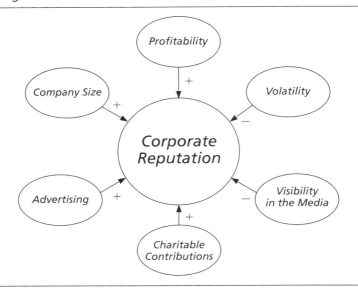

to dazzling economic performance, while others owe their reputations primarily to the strength of their outreach practices and policies. The most highly rated companies in *Fortune*'s annual survey, however, turn out to be those companies that achieve both—not only do they demonstrate the kind of solid economic performance that pleases investors but they also look to the interests of employees, customers, and communities.

THE ECONOMIC RECORD

Everybody loves a winner. In business, nothing impresses us more than a company with a strong record of profits. To investors, past profits not only constitute necessary short-run returns on investments but a strong signal that the company is well positioned for the long haul. To employees, profits are the source of generous bonuses and perks. Since products often develop problems, customers are more likely to buy the products of more profitable companies, if only because they want them to be around when something goes wrong. Finally, the local community welcomes the stability of operations, tax revenues, jobs, and other contributions that profits make possible. Nothing makes everyone more edgy and skeptical about a company than volatile earnings: one year good, one year bad; one year up, one year down. Companies earn better reputations with their constituents when they show steady, positive economic returns. Not surprisingly, return on equity for the 10 companies that were most highly regarded in early 1993 averaged a sterling 25 percent in the prior year. It's a result that holds over the long term: Better-rated companies have higher 10-year returns than their lesser-rated rivals.

THE SOCIAL RECORD

Our study demonstrates that three social factors affect a company's reputation in the *Fortune* survey: (1) advertising, (2) community involvement, and (3) visibility in the media.

Companies that advertise more heavily than their rivals benefit from the marginally greater exposure. However allocated, those advertising dollars appear to raise the status of rated companies.

Like advertising, involvement in community-based initiatives is good. It tends to heighten a company's public profile and enhance its reputation. Companies supporting foundations or donating more to charities enjoy better reputations than their principal rivals. Casual inspection against the roster of stocks in the DSI 400 portfolio confirms this: The 20 largest companies included in the index claim a much higher than average reputational rating on *Fortune*'s scale.

Visibility in the media, however, is all too often bad visibility: It heightens public attention, raises eyebrows, and reduces the latitude managers have in making strategic decisions without interference. In other words, the results show that investigative reports and newspaper write-ups—whether positive or negative—do little to help a company's reputation. The lower a company's visibility in the media, the better its reputation.

When companies make the news for their involvement in social causes, however, it helps their reputations. For instance, reporters like to write about Sara Lee's outstanding record of social involvement: its charitable giving, its active foundation, its commitment to women, and its volunteerism. Procter & Gamble is frequently applauded for its efforts to rethink manufacturing processes, to conserve energy, or to design environmentally friendly consumer products. Rubbermaid routinely passes ethical screens for its conscientious efforts to make household products that are safe, durable, and carefully designed; for its support of recycling; and for its positive labor relations.

On the face of it, then, *Fortune*'s rankings are valid. The 1993 rankings justifiably deflated companies that were facing bankruptcy (Wang Labs, Continental Airlines). They also marked down companies with prospects for profitability that were low because of intense rivalry (McDonnell Douglas in aerospace) or overextension (Sears, Roebuck in retail, Citicorp in financial services). And they applauded innovators in retailing (Wal-Mart), in reliable package delivery (UPS), in global competition (Coca-Cola, General Mills, Boeing, Deere), and in conservative growth (J. P. Morgan).

Table 7-3 compares companies that were ranked at the top and bottom of their industries in the fall of 1993. Again, the winners make sense. Within industries, the top companies confirm most expectations: Merck in pharmaceuticals, Boeing in aerospace; J. P. Morgan in banking, Wal-Mart in retail. Overall, the top 10 for the year turn out to be Rubbermaid, Home Depot, Coca-Cola, Microsoft, 3M, Walt Disney, Motorola, J. P. Morgan, and UPS—a familiar cast of characters, each one highly regarded for a consistent record of both economic and social performance, for sensitivity, to customers, employees, and communities as well as to investors. The only surprise is that long-time favorite Merck dropped from the top spot, doubtless reflecting the financial community's concern over the loss of revenue that could result from the company's merger with mail-order drug distributor Medco and the possible changes in the health-care system nationwide.

At this point, *Fortune*'s survey is probably the most visible of all the perceptual rankings of companies now published. It seems to be reasonably constructed and produces an interesting summary ranking of rival companies. What's more, these rankings also provide unique information of value to investors. In the statistical study I conducted with Mark Shanley, the stocks of better-rated companies showed a small but marginally positive return in the two-day period after *Fortune*'s survey issue appeared on newsstands. It's not much, but as these things go, perhaps it's something to trade on.[28]

Despite its popularity, the *Fortune* survey suffers from some serious limitations. For one, it reflects the assessment of only a single constituency: senior executives, directors, and analysts. As such, the ratings do not incorporate the independent and possibly divergent judgments of employees, customers, or local communities. Although our empirical

Table 7-3 FORTUNE'S RANKING OF INDUSTRIES AND COMPANIES

Highest Ranked Industry		Highest Ranked Company (1994)	Lowest Ranked Company (1994)
1	Oil refining	Shell Oil	Coastal
2	Rubber and plastics	Rubbermaid	Insilco
3	Pharmaceuticals	Merck	Warner-Lambert
4	Banking	J. P. Morgan	Chase Manhattan
5	Telecom	AT&T	Sprint
6	Entertainment	Walt Disney	Bally
7	Construction	Fluor	Ryland Group
8	Publishing	Berkshire Hathaway	Times Mirror
9	Pipelines	Enron	BP Pipelines
10	Merchandise	Wal-Mart	R. H. Macy
...			
33	Aerospace	Boeing	McDonnell-Douglas
34	Airline	Southwest	TWA
35	Specialty retail	Home Depot	Woolworth
36	Tobacco	American Brands	Brooke Group
37	Apparel	Levi Strauss	Leslie Fay
38	Forest products	Kimberly-Clark	Stone Container
39	Textiles	Shaw Industries	Amoskeag
40	Building materials	Corning	Lafarge
41	Computers/Office	Hewlett-Packard	Amdahl
42	Metals	Alcoa	LTV

Lowest Ranked Industry

Source: Adapted from *Fortune*'s annual survey of more than 8,000 analysts, executives, and directors. The data were gathered in the fall of 1993 and published on February 7, 1994, 58ff.

study shows that raters unconsciously managed to factor into their assessments some of the concerns of these other constituencies, a more representative sampling of all corporate constituents would surely improve the validity of the rankings as comprehensive measures of reputation.

A similar problem confounds the rival rankings of business schools presented in the popular press. As I discuss at length in chapter 10, these ratings are based on a sample of different groups of raters and so reflect the disparate criteria that these groups apply. For instance, the ratings of MBA programs published by *Business Week* reflect a sampling of recruiters and alumni but completely exclude faculty, students, donors, and the local communities in which these institutions operate. For its part, *U.S. News & World Reports* surveys business school deans, but no one else. The final ranking incorporates a wide range of archival measures that may or may not reflect the judgments of other groups. The net effect of these disparate criteria is to make the surveys inconsistent and difficult to compare. How then can they be used to evaluate the schools?

To develop more systematic reputational profiles of companies, business schools, and other institutions, it would make sense to pick a representative sample across all major constituent groups. The resulting rankings would better capture the multidimensional functions that these institutions try to fulfill. Drawing on the sampling techniques of political pollsters would surely make feasible a more balanced assessment of constituents, and so a more accurate depiction of corporate reputations.

RATED TO DEATH

It has become commonplace in literary circles to bemoan the proliferation of prizes and awards given to articles, books, and authors. A recent *Vanity Fair* article laments the fact that literary prizes have become "a dime a dozen." The apparent concern is that prizes and award ceremonies seem to exist only as a way to reward sponsors, to pacify egos, and to generate sales. The article goes on to deplore what appears to be a distinctly American phenomenon: our embarassing thirst for prizes and trophies.[29]

A similar phenomenon characterizes the corporate realm. Ratings and rankings, prizes and awards are now proliferating. I disagree with the literary pundits, however. In my view, in the corporate realm, ratings and awards are to the good. The widespread interest in these contests demonstrates our increasing discomfort with relegating assessments of a company's merits to a small coterie of self-styled "experts," most of whom are largely and solely financially oriented. By soliciting and combining many individual judgments on many criteria, by forcing us to make comparisons between companies, ratings help us to judge the overall quality of a company. Just as literary prizes guide us to worthwhile readings, so do corporate prizes suggest what companies we might prefer to work for, to invest our money in, or to buy our products from. If well-conducted, these corporate competitions can provide us with valuable information about the overall economic and social performance of our companies—a worthwhile objective in itself. At a minimum, they force us to examine more closely the images and identities of our favorite companies.

The meaning of a message is the change
which it produces in the image.

—*Kenneth Boulding*
  The Image

The Reputational Audit

SOME TIME ago, I read a brief op-ed piece written by a public relations consultant. The author deplored the industry's lack of strategic insight, its failure to understand that the purpose of public relations is to help a company to exploit and defend its reputation. He also proposed that companies appoint a chief reputation officer to do the job.[1] Eager to know if he had been heeded by his peers, I met the author, Alan Towers, at his midtown office in Manhattan, only to hear him describe his continuing frustration with PR professionals who were concerned more about quick "deliverables" than about fundamental questions of strategic merit. As he put it: "PR practitioners are insecure. They worry about one thing: quick results. They recognize that reputations are important, but it's hard for them to see any immediate payoff from working on the reputation level. Getting stories into the press—now that has clear returns. Reputation tends to only count after the fact, when a crisis has already hit. Then they want you for damage control."

His speech sounded strangely familiar. I had witnessed a similar problem in discussions with human-resource professionals in the early 1980s. In a book edited with my colleagues Noel Tichy and Mary Anne Devanna, we challenged the traditional operational view personnel managers take of their role. Instead, we proposed that a well-structured personnel department had a strategic role to play as a caretaker of the company's human capital and corporate culture.[2] It took time for the idea to gel. Today, forward-thinking managers take it for granted. They rely heavily on their human-resource departments not only for the traditional operational duties of employee recruitment, training, and compensation but for the more strategic tasks of controlling and shaping the internal climate and culture of their companies—their identities.

Much the same could happen to departments of public relations and investor relations if these professionals would recognize their roles as caretakers of their companies' reputational capital. As noted public relations expert James Grunig commented recently: "For public relations to be valued by the organizations it serves, practitioners must be able to demonstrate that their efforts contribute to the goals of these organizations by building long-term behavioral relationships with strategic publics—those that affect the ability of the organization to accomplish its mission."[3] It's also the case for investor relations, as noted in a recent article in the *New York Times*: "At some companies . . . many consider investor relations nothing more than a public relations function, where there is only coincidental concern for stockholders or the availability of meaningful information. . . . But many companies are getting wiser. They realize that institutional investors prefer to put money into companies that provide lots of information and that good investor relations can help their stock price."[4]

Increasingly, companies are recognizing that relationship building must take place not only with employees and the general public but also with customers, investors, the local community, and the media. In a world where intangibles like reputation matter at least as much as tangible assets like plant and equipment, competitiveness demands strong relationships with all constituents. Indeed, some analysts estimate that the stock price—and so the reputational capital—of many diversified companies would probably be at least 20 percent higher if those companies helped investors make better sense out of the diversity in their portfolios.[5]

Unfortunately, most companies deal with their publics in a fragmented manner. For the most part, they relegate them to distinct functional silos—finance, marketing, human resources—with minimal opportunity for contact or coordination.[6] Doing so reflects a poor understanding of the determinants of corporate reputation. It also imperceptibly damages a company's competitiveness and profitability while increasing its riskiness and vulnerability to crisis. I suggest here that to exploit reputational capital and build more resilient companies, we will have to institute new roles and structures in our companies, as well as better, more creative scripts for the managers who run them. The reputational audit is a systematic effort designed to help managers assess the practices that undergird a company's reputation with its constituents.

MANAGING RELATIONSHIPS

In practice, a company's reputation derives from the more or less healthy relationships it establishes with seven audiences:

- customers,
- investors,
- employees,
- competitors,
- the local community,
- government, and,
- the public at large.[7]

The quality of each relationship shapes the particular image the company develops with that constituent. Whether consistent or inconsistent, these images combine to create a company's reputational halo.

The form each relationship takes depends greatly on the way information flows between the company and the constituent, the frequency of their contact, and the level of trust between them.[8] Distinct image projection strategies may be required to reach a constituency effectively. Self-presentations run the gamut from corporate advertising, identity systems, and financial reports to press releases, charitable contributions, and pro bono work. Seldom are they fused into a coherent whole.

Traditionally, a company has indicated the seriousness of its commitment to a particular constituency by staffing an internal department exclusively devoted to it and giving that department a discretionary budget. There are six key departments of this kind:

1. *Customer-service relations:* This department tries to shape customer perception of the company. Key strategies include product

and image advertising, the creation of customer-service centers, the provision of warranties, and investments in building brand equity to market the company's goods and services. Managers also try to get the nod from clients—and repeat business—by meeting their expectations for quality and service.[9]

2. *Investor relations:* The historical function of investor relations is to maintain investor confidence in the company's prospects. Key strategies include hiring credible auditors, issuing optimistic financial statements, and making assertive presentations to investment analysts and institutional shareholders. This department's mission is to generate favorable judgments from these opinion leaders by signaling a genuine commitment to strong economic performance.[10]

3. *Employee relations:* This department is principally concerned with the design of human-resource practices for recruitment, compensation, and development that show commitment to and concern for employees. When recruiting, human-resource practitioners often try to convey to prospective hires the nonfinancial benefits of working for the company to elicit positive feelings.[11]

4. *Community relations:* The purpose of the typical community relations department is to convey a company's benevolence, corporate citizenship, and social responsiveness. Key strategies range from pro bono activities and charitable contributions to relationship building with artistic, educational, and cultural institutions. In this way, companies integrate themselves into their local communities and surround their activities with a positive halo of goodwill.[12]

5. *Government relations:* These departments developed in the 1960s and 1970s as companies struggled to find ways of maintaining positive relationships with regulators. Key strategies for doing so include distributing position papers, testifying before committees, lobbying regulators, and supporting the political campaigns of elected officials. By forming close ties with legislators and regulators, managers try to ingratiate themselves with powerful monitors and participate in shaping more favorable environments for their activities.[13]

6. *Public relations:* A company's PR staff is responsible for influencing broad questions of public opinion. Expert communicators

are assigned to manage relationships with the media and to help a company create identity programs, construct corporate advertising campaigns, issue press releases, and, broadly speaking, develop the set of strategic issues and frames of reference that govern the conversations of outside audiences.[14]

Missing from this list is a seventh department of "competitor relations." I know of no company that has one. It may help explain why companies never address the structure and form of their relationships with competitors consistently. Doubtless the omission is a legacy of antitrust legislation that has long prohibited close ties between rivals. As alliances proliferate in the globalized world economy, however, companies are increasingly participating in constellations of supplier deals, joint ventures, and consortia. Corporate reputations are therefore increasingly tied to those of their alliance partners, and visionary companies may want to consolidate oversight of these competitor relationships into one department.[15]

Analytically, the above relationships describe the strategic efforts a company's managers can make to shape coherent images for constituents and to build reputation. The research record suggests that companies committed to sustaining their reputational capital are likely to budget more funds, pursue closer social ties, and disseminate more extensive imformation targeted to each of the company's principal audiences: customers, investors, employees, competitors, government, local communities, and the public at large.[16] That task is increasingly likely to require its own administrative unit.

CREATING A NEW EXECUTIVE ROLE

In any company, power and influence derive from position in a corporate structure. Where should these six staff groups—each of which worries about a particular constituent—be positioned? To whom should they report? If we examine existing practice, in most companies the activities of these six groups are typically isolated within business units, with disparate reporting lines and involvement in corporate-level decision making. What this says is that in terms of reputation management, no one is really minding the shop.

Much as companies appoint a chief financial officer to safeguard financial capital, a chief operating officer to monitor operations, and a chief information officer to control and manipulate corporate databases, so might they benefit from appointing a chief reputation officer (CRO) to watch over the company's intangible assets. As PR consultant Alan Towers suggests: "The CRO's tactical responsibilities would include oversight of pricing, advertising, quality, environmental compliance, investor relations, public affairs, corporate contributions, and employee, customer and media relations. Rather than literally do each of these jobs, the CRO would act as a corporate guide, working with specialists in each area to help them see the reputation consequences of their decisions. If necessary, the CRO could impose an opinion . . ."[17]

With or without the title, such a position would help to signal the importance and make explicit the hidden value of the company's reputation. It would also encourage other managers to more systematically relate knowledge drawn from brand marketing, public relations, organization theory, and strategic management. Figure 8-1 shows how the CRO could be made to join the executive suite as a full partner, complementing the more traditional chief executive, financial, operating, and information roles. The CRO would recognize the different tasks that a

Figure 8-1 THE CHIEF REPUTATION OFFICER

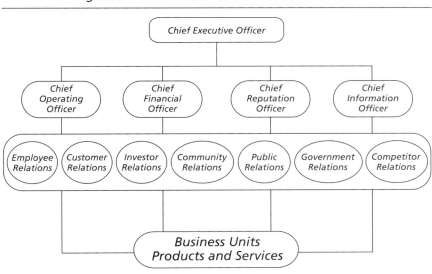

company must undertake to build, sustain, and defend its reputational capital. In all aspects, however, it's a role that emphasizes close coordination—a matrix arrangement—with the traditional functions of marketing, finance, human resources, and operations.

The downside to appointing CROs in our corporate structures may lie in the ease with which they can be made scapegoats for events beyond their control. In the United States, however, CEOs have not always shouldered the blame for reputational losses, despite being the first to lay claim to reputational gains. In this they differ from Japanese CEOs, who are expected to shoulder full responsibility for reputational losses as well as gains. By comparison with Japan, it's apparent that senior executives in the United States have been artificially sheltered from concerns about corporate reputational matters. Formalizing the position of CRO would arguably return accountability where it belongs—to the top team.

BUILDING REPUTATION

New companies are well aware of how difficult it is to launch a business without a track record. As every salesperson will tell you, it's not easy to get the ear of an established buyer when you're trying to sell them an untested product. Conversely, that same salesperson will readily attest to the value of having a highly regarded corporate name to get you in the door.

Start-up companies are not the only ones to face the challenge of having to build reputation. Large companies launching new divisions as well as older companies changing their names face similar issues. Take the largest company of them all, AT&T. In 1984, under the terms of an antitrust settlement, the courts presided over the breakup of the telephone colossus. Seven regional companies were spun off with responsibility for providing regulated telephone service, but they would be allowed to participate in unregulated businesses as well. Rising from the ashes of the old monopolist was a new entity, divorced from local phone service but with the freedom to roam unfettered into the brave new world of telecommunications products and services. No longer would the benevolent reputation of "Ma Bell" hover over these companies. Each would face an uphill battle in the ensuing years to crystallize new identities and build reputational capital.

In 1983, the corporate identity consultants Lippincott & Margulies were called in to advise the largest of the spin-offs, the company that would cover New York and New England. L&M's task was to develop a new identity for the nameless entity that would draw its employees and culture from AT&T but that would also soon be entering the foreign terrain of unregulated business. L&M recommended the NYNEX name and designed its communications program. As Clive Chajet, L&M's current chairman, recalls:

> The new company needed identity practices to differentiate its regulated businesses from its unregulated ones, and to establish separate yet linked identities for an entire range of the unregulated ones. We recommended retaining the names of NYNEX's regulated subsidiaries New York Telephone and New England Telephone, and making sure that subscribers directed all their attention, payments, and service needs to those entities. . . . On the other side, we recommended that the whole line of NYNEX unregulated businesses be positioned so that they all primarily made use of the NYNEX name—NYNEX Enterprises, NYNEX Information Resources, and NYNEX Mobile Communications. . . . Lippincott & Margulies produced a series of a dozen manuals on how to use the new NYNEX identity on everything from vehicles to signage to advertising . . . and so some of these manuals that we wrote were actually codes of conduct for the employees, teaching them the manner in which NYNEX wanted them to do business.[18]

In 1994, NYNEX unveiled the latest phase in its reputation-building effort. With a series of upbeat print and television ads, the company announced that it was adopting the NYNEX name for all of its subsidiaries, including its telephone operations. Clearly, this development culminated the company's efforts to cohere disparate images.

When Japanese manufacturer Nissan decided to enter the luxury car market in the late 1980s, it too approached L&M for assistance. Concerned about Nissan's established reputation as a low-price producer, the consultants encouraged Nissan to completely separate its luxury car from its other products. Nissan's top managers agreed and devoted millions of dollars up front to building reputation. They focused on three areas: (1) developing the new division's name, logo, and identity, (2) persuading and assisting the company's dealers to construct the separate showrooms the new car would require, and (3) targeting creative ads to consumers that portrayed the car's distinctive image. All this well before the prototype of the car—the Infiniti—had even been created.

It would prove to be a successful campaign. As Chajet recalls:

Infiniti was introduced during the fall of 1989, and its initial awareness level was at an unprecedented high. . . . Everything that surrounded it was distinctively Japanese, from bamboo frames for the background to the foliage used in the foreground. This too was a reinforcement of the message Nissan wanted to convey. . . . Since we hadn't seen the actual car when we'd made the logo, we were now pleased to see that it stood the test of good badges, that it could be applied in both expected and unexpected ways to various parts of the car from the hubcap to the dashboard, and still maintain its integrity. . . . As a measure of the detail to which Nissan committed itself to the positioning and design theme, by way of greeting and thanks, Nissan sent to dealers a distinctive and expensively original origami Infiniti Christmas card, the final touch in a fully integrated identity and image management program.[19]

The efforts of both NYNEX and Nissan illustrate the critical decisions managers face as they try to define a company's principal character traits. In chapter 11, I describe in depth how these identity programs can help a company to build reputational capital. They force a company to explore the merits of establishing closer relationships with key constituents and add another dimension to the debate about the linkages that should exist between a company's old and new businesses.

The questions listed below should provoke extensive debate about a company's competitive strategy and corporate culture. They place discussion about reputational matters where they belong—as a centerpiece in the formulation and implementation of business and corporate strategy.

- What kind of company do we want to be? What are our defining traits?

- How do those internal features correspond to current perceptions of our company by our different audiences?

- How can our internal features build competitive advantage against rivals?

- How distinctive is our reputation from the rest of the industry's reputation?

- How accurate and consistent are the images that we project to our different audiences?

- How can we strengthen our relationship with our key audiences?

SUSTAINING REPUTATION

Identity programs also have a great deal to do with sustaining reputation. Coherent self-presentation and consistent projection of reinforcing images help to build and maintain favorable appraisals by constituents. More central to the task of maintaining reputation, however, are two sets of programs: (1) internal monitoring programs that secure compliance to a set of principles and (2) external relations programs that manage the interface with key constituents.

Internal monitoring programs address two areas that have enormous potential impact on a company's reputation: product quality and organizational integrity. As discussed in chapter 5, to manage product quality well is to signal to employees the importance the company places on meeting its implicit contracts. All employees must believe that a company is serious about its product claims. They must recognize that if the company's reputation is to act as a credible warranty in a transaction with a customer, the product must regularly live up to its quality claims. Of course, that's long been a strength of the Japanese and German programs of quality management. As many management gurus have pointed out, German and Japanese employees take inordinate pride in the products their companies make. Their companies support well-crafted programs that train and socialize employees to help make this possible. It hasn't always been true of U.S. companies.

Numerous programs are put in place to help companies address external constituencies. Environmental programs convey concern about a company's effects on the planet; community programs signal an interest in helping to solve the problems of the town or region in which the company operates; investor relations programs try to satisfy the needs of the company's major fiduciaries; government relations programs examine the interface of the company's interests with regulatory bodies; media relations programs deal with the informational needs of the press; and public relations coordinates them all.

When well executed, these internal and external programs can help a company to elicit positive feelings from constituents and sustain its reputation. As I pointed out in chapter 6, the difficult challenge is to coordinate the multiple messages that are broadcast by the various and sundry professionals involved in managing these different programs. By being structurally empowered, a chief reputational officer could perhaps ensure that the dialogue between functions is institutionalized.

In order to focus attention on sustaining reputation, an empowered CRO would ensure that the following questions are addressed systematically:

- What are we doing to maintain healthy relationships with all of our constituents?
- How well do we monitor our images with each of our different audiences?
- Could we improve our reputation by developing better, more consistent images?
- What kinds of activities should we engage in to sustain our reputation?
- Do our employees understand and appreciate the importance of our reputation? Do our customers, suppliers, and rivals? The local government and community? The public at large?
- How much money should we give to charity? Through a foundation or direct giving? How much publicity do we want from corporate giving?
- How can we obtain favorable reviews and ratings in the media?
- How can we generate more favorable appraisals by financial analysts?
- How can we improve our relationships with those organizations which monitor social responsiveness?

DEFENDING REPUTATION

In the late 1980s, perhaps egged on by a rising stock market, many investment banks fell victim to a rash of scandals. With the conviction of junk-bond king Michael Milken and the collapse of the investment bank Drexel Burnham Lambert that he had helped raise to the top ranks of the industry, many expected these scandals to subside. As chapter 12 describes, that has not been the case. In 1994, General Electric's Kidder Peabody subsidiary came under fire for reporting false profits and disguising more than $300 million in losses. The scandal has meant considerable bad press not just for Kidder but also for GE, tarnishing somewhat the company's reputation for savvy management. It cost Kidder's chairman his job and led to a court case against the rogue banker in charge of the bank's government-bond-trading unit. In 1995, the British investment bank Barings PLC was driven into bankruptcy by its investments in financially risky "derivatives"; Bankers Trust saw a dramatic drop in its reputational capital as lawsuits brought by customers produced costly government sanctions, layoffs, and mounting losses. In all of these cases, lax controls made it possible for enterprising employees to circumvent internal programs that were intended to secure adherence to common standards of reporting and to monitor compliance. Clearly, these companies have not done a good job of protecting their valuable reputations.

All too often companies become aware of such reputational issues only when it's too late—when a scandal looms or a crisis has already hit. Generally, the problem is allowed to develop because top managers are leary of taking valuable time away from operating duties to postulate unlikely contingencies. After all, it's difficult to anticipate the future, and everyone agrees that the future never conforms to expectations. The result? Very few effective crisis preparedness programs. There's a tendency to either completely avoid the issue or to prepare weighty manuals detailing how to respond to a crisis—manuals that are easily set aside and seldom, if ever, consulted.

That's bad news. As Chajet, points out:

Since it's virtually impossible to imagine in detail every potential nightmare, the real requirement is to have an overall plan for dealing with crises, to establish the context in which your later actions may be judged. This, in turn, mandates an attitude that both in good time and in bad, image matters. A contingency plan to clean up the spill, as well as to handle public reaction, certainly would have helped Exxon, and a similar plan did help Johnson & Johnson—but Johnson & Johnson's evaluation of the significance of image, its willingness to invest in its nourishment, and its commitment to making the necessary resources available to do the job were the true differentiators. Having managed its image extremely well for many years, the company was able to deal with its crisis from a position of true strength. Its positive, honest, forthcoming image allowed the employees and divisions to rally to the company's side, furthered communications with the press, and afforded the company time to make the necessary adjustments in the product packaging without losing too much ground.[20]

The good practices of Johnson & Johnson have since been imitated by many others. Source Perrier is a case in point. When some Perrier bottles were found to be tainted with benzene in February 1990, the company quickly recalled all of its outstanding stock of 160 million bottles from shelves around the world. Some thought Perrier had over-reacted. But as Gustave Leven, Perrier's 75-year-old chief, put it: "We don't want the slightest doubt to weigh on Perrier." From a reputational standpoint, he was dead right. Total recall was necessary to safeguard—and actually reinforce—the image of purity on which Perrier's sales are based, which is why the brand quickly returned to its original market share after it was reintroduced a few weeks later. The cost? A mere $30 million after taxes—not much considering the company's $500 million in annual sales of sparkling water.

Union Carbide has also been commended for its handling of an accidental lethal gas leak from its pesticide plant in Bhopal, India, in December 1984 that killed more than 2,000 people and injured some 10,000 other local residents. Had the crisis been poorly managed, it could have wiped out the company entirely. Instead, most experts acknowledge that the company's reaction to the disaster was a textbook example of good management *and* good reputation management. Union Carbide's chairman Warren Anderson immediately visited the site, pledged to correct the source of the problems, launched independent investigations, and quickly offered financial compensation to the victims and their survivors. The negative impact of the tragedy was softened by the company's well-executed campaign in crisis management, vis-à-vis its public relations, media relations, customer relations, and investor relations.

In chapter 15, I describe the crisis faced in 1991 by the investment bank Salomon Brothers. Its successful handling of that situation illustrates how skillful self-defense can help overcome disastrous circumstances after the fact.

Public relations firms maintain specialized units to advise companies facing such crisis situations. At Hill & Knowlton, a team of experts called the special situations team provides planning, counsel, and logistical support in crisis communications and risk management: "The team has a worldwide reputation earned through its work in labor disputes, takeover contexts, industrial accidents, financial irregularities, product tampering and recalls, bankruptcies, controversial legislation, natural disasters and other major client problems. . . . Special Situations helps ensure that the client communicates its position to all concerned audiences as effectively and clearly as possible."[21]

Depending on the crisis situation and a client's particular needs, a PR firm can help a company in the following ways:

- Draft an issues-response advertisement.
- Set up a company crisis committee.
- Prepare materials—releases, statements, Q&As, position papers, backgrounders, third-party testimony.
- Secure interviews and handle media calls.
- Monitor and analyze media coverage, and correct mistakes.
- Retain third-party influencers as spokespersons.
- Serve as liaison with governmental groups.
- Set up and staff hot lines.
- Conduct overnight polls and public attitude assessments.
- Arrange for press conferences, media tours, satellite feeds, teleconferences.
- Develop employee communications materials.
- Work with outside groups—lawyers, investigators, or insurance firms.

Successful programs appear to share the following characteristics:

- Involve top management early on.
- Build third-party support for the company's position.
- Establish an on-site presence if the crisis is not centered at headquarters.
- Centralize all crisis-related communications.
- Cooperate actively with the press.
- Keep employees informed.
- Keep the crisis in perspective and within context.
- Position the company for the postcrisis future.

- Continually monitor and evaluate progress in handling the crisis.[22]

In matters of reputation, however, it remains true that the best kind of self-defense is—as the saying goes—a good offense. Much as physicians distinguish between acute care—emergency situations that require immediate attention—and primary care—the everyday practice of health maintenance that helps prevent illness—so should managers participate in actions designed to avoid damaging a company's health. To safeguard a hard-earned reputation, a company must take preventive action long before a crisis occurs. It means empowering the company as a whole, and someone in particular—perhaps a chief reputation officer?—to act as the primary care physician, to ask probing questions that link managerial initiatives to their effects on the health of a company's identity and reputation.

To help a company defend its reputation, a vigilant CRO should routinely call attention to the following questions:

- What could go wrong in our business?
- How good are we at anticipating rogue behavior, unethical acts, scandals, and other forms of crisis that might threaten our reputation?
- How prepared are we to react to unanticipated events?
- What kinds of behavioral controls and monitoring systems have we put in place to prevent a crisis from occurring?
- What kinds of compliance programs do we have in place to safeguard the integrity of our actions? To deal with unusual events? Who's in charge of these programs?

MANAGING REPUTATION

To successfully manage reputation, a company must establish the programs necessary for actively relating to constituents. In turn, the company must regularly audit its reputational profile—its position against rivals. Figure 8-2 presents the three principal components of a fully executed reputational audit:

- *Stage 1:* A diagnostic review of the company's current identity, images, and reputation.

Figure 8-2 THE REPUTATIONAL AUDIT

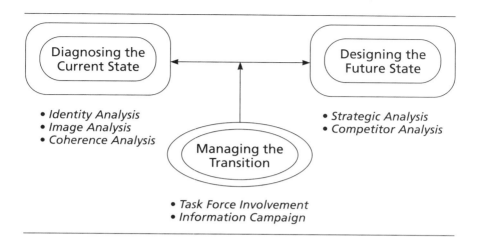

- *Stage 2:* A strategic analysis of trends, plans, and competitive positioning that defines the company's desired future state.

- *Stage 3:* A review of the company's plans for managing the transition toward the future state.[23]

STAGE 1: DIAGNOSING THE CURRENT STATE

The first step in conducting a reputational audit is to accurately assess a company's identity, the images it projects, and the reputation it enjoys.

Identity Analysis. Here, all of a company's communications with its different audiences—customers, employees, shareholders, suppliers, distributors, regulators, reporters, analysts, and the public at large—are reviewed. That generally means putting together advertisements, brochures, manuals, posters, correspondence, logos, and signage. Communications experts assess the company's graphic support systems and naming practices for products and businesses. Ethnographic experts interview *representative groups of employees* to identify their personal understanding of the company, their sense of what it stands for, its strengths and weaknesses. The purpose of the analysis is to explore whether the company's identity systems convey a set of impressions that are more or less consistent with the company's self-concept. The identity analysis also explores the myriad ways in which the company presents itself to constituents, whether by phone, through a visit to the company's facilities, or in correspondence with corporate representatives. At the conclusion of the process, the identity portion of the audit should provide an accurate rendering of how a company sees and presents itself, both to its employees and to the outside world.

Image Analysis. Having established how the company projects itself outwards, the reputational audit can assess current perceptions of how well those projections are communicated. How do constituents rate the company's performance on key financial and nonfinancial dimensions? To what rivals do constituents compare the company? On what dimensions? What businesses draw most of their attention? Which businesses rate more highly than others?

Probably the most critical decision in the constituent survey involves identifying those individuals who should be surveyed. The process begins by developing as accurate a map as possible of the company's principal constituencies. Within each constituency, key influentials should be identified and interviewed along with a representative sampling of other constituents in the group. To develop an accurate reputational profile, a well-balanced sampling of all influential constituents is essential. Polling methods are highly appropriate to use in developing a valid sample, especially for companies that have large groups of customers and shareholders. For instance, relatively small samples of 500–1,000 people are found to represent national public opinion with a margin of error of 3–5 percent at a 95 percent confidence level. In addition to conducting face-to-face interviews, telephone polls and mail surveys can be used to provide more valid depictions of a company's images and reputation profile.

Coherence Analysis. The final step in diagnosing the company's current state is to explore the coherence of the different images obtained from the constituent surveys. Where do images converge, and where do they diverge? On what dimensions? How well do the images represent the company's sense of its identity? How much of the company's identity is reflected in its self-presentations? How accurately are these presentations perceived by constituents? As indicated in chapter 3, a company's reputational profile is the overall halo that emerges from all the images held by constituents in different groupings.

STAGE 2: DESIGNING THE FUTURE STATE

A clear understanding of the company's strategic intentions and competitive circumstances is necessary before a desired state can be formulated.

Classic discussions of a company's strategic position in the industry through scenario planning, trends analysis, and competitive analysis should be paralleled by a discussion of rival companies' relative reputational standings and self-presentations. Which companies have a higher status in the industry, and why? What kinds of strategies are they pursuing to maintain their reputational positions?

From these discussions a feasibility analysis can emerge, and the stage is set for developing a consensus opinion from top managers that elaborates where they would like their company to be positioned given its strategic direction and resource constraints. The key point to remember at this stage is that identity projections are not one-shot deals; to have any effect, they require nontrivial commitments of money, time, and energy.

STAGE 3: MANAGING THE TRANSITION

The gap between current and desired states raises significant questions about transition management. The close involvement of a representative cross section of employees is necessary to ensure the success of any intervention. As with all programs for change, lack of information generates rumors that can sabotage the intervention. In this case—and unlike discussions of key corporate strategies—secrecy is not essential, and the company should probably encourage broad discussion of its efforts to convey identity and reputation to its audiences. Not only are representative multi-function and multi-level teams appropriate as testing grounds for ideas, they are also vital to disseminating information inside and outside the company. The more positive the signals that emanate from these teams, the more likely the intervention is to be well received by constituents.

As an identity program crystallizes internally, parallel systems must be installed to train employees in the use of common graphics, the procedures for dealing with constituencies, and mechanisms to monitor compliance. Although it often seems simple to generate such programs, it actually proves ever more difficult to secure general adherence by employees, especially in the pursuit of a monolithic identity across divisions of a diversified company.

In part two we explore many of the issues raised in a reputational audit through case studies of particular companies and industries. We focus in particular on how organizations as diverse as fashion businesses, consumer product makers, business schools, and investment banks build, sustain, and defend their reputational capital.

THE UPS
AND
DOWNS OF
REPUTATION

. . . the fashion wears out more apparel than the man.

—*William Shakespeare*
  Much Ado About Nothing

Fashion's Ins and Outs

PERHAPS NOWHERE is reputation more of an obsession than in the world of fashion. In newspapers and magazines—and now even on CNN's regular news broadcasts—fashion designers flaunt their seasonal flights of whimsy to mesmerized observers the world over. The fanfare and publicity they generate for their high-priced and frequently unsalable clothing lines place reputational halos around their names, halos that support numerous and highly profitable subsidiary businesses such as perfumes, personal care products, and home furnishings. This chapter explores the peculiar rhythms of fashion businesses: how they invest in building high-profile labels; how the prestige of a label sustains a pyramid of derivative licenses; how those licenses generate extraordinary wealth and reputation for the designer at its core; how the reputation of a label can be tarnished; and how that tarnished reputation might be restored. Reputation building in the fashion business is a collective affair. A designer's ability to sustain visibility requires active cooperation by a large and diverse coterie of constituents, all of which are intimately involved in the creation of images.

FASHION'S EMPIRES

Every season, the world's great fashion centers—Paris, Milan, London, and New York—are set abuzz as designers whip the industry into a frenzy of creativity. Their purpose: to invent next year's look—the shape of the clothes to come. The profits of a staggering $2 trillion dollar community depend on the ability of designers to anticipate tastes, capture trends, and at the same time create uniqueness.

Contrary to the romantic image, the establishment of a style involves far more than the creative output of a lone designer working in blissful isolation. To create a look requires the active cooperation of players up and down the industry's value chain: the upstream textile mills that produce sample yardage of exciting fabrics; the forecasting services that predict the shapes, lengths, and color trends of the next season; the cottage trade that makes complementary trim, lace, buttons, and hats; the buying offices, department stores, and retailers who will later order the fashions; and the fashion press, whose critical eye will either praise and popularize or disparage and discourage purchases. Although creating a signature look would seem to be an artistic pursuit carried out in solitude within the great fashion houses of the world, its actual production is, in fact, a collective effort of coordination among a diverse community of designers, manufacturers, wholesalers, promoters, retailers, and reporters. Success comes to those designers more skillfull than the rest at weaving a web of linkages among specialized players in the industry. Good relationships get press; press generates celebrity; celebrity fuels sales.

The fame that attaches today to the Parisian fashion houses of Chanel, Christian Dior, or Yves Saint Laurent, to the Italian design companies of Gianni Versace or Giorgio Armani, or to America's Donna Karan, Bill Blass, or Calvin Klein derives in large part from the success each has had in planting a unique set of expectations in the minds of consumers. Each has established a reputation that reduces our uncertainty as to what its clothing will be like—the fit, the durability, the overall look.

We also rent the reputational halos of fashionable designers to draw status, image, and success to ourselves. As historian Daniel Boorstin reminds us, we buy products emblazoned with prestigious names because they provide us with "a feeling of shared well-being, shared risks, common interests, and common concerns that come from consuming the same kinds of objects. . . . A designer label is a community of consumers on whom some of the celebrity of the name rubs off."[1] That's why, once in place, the reputations of top fashion companies are worth a lot of money.

Take Donna Karan. As mentioned in chapter 3, in August 1993 the New York designer announced that her company would be going public with the sale of 11 million shares worth an anticipated $159 million in a first offering. Although economic circumstances conspired to delay the sale, it is instructive to look at the logic that propelled the initial announcement. According to the *New York Times:* "Most, if not all, of the shares of the fashion company, which tapped into the psyche and physique of American career women with easy-to-wear clothing cut for a real woman's figure, are almost certain to be spoken for by the time the offering hits the market. The offering, which was rumored for months . . . is one of the most eagerly anticipated of the year, and even the skeptics are angling to buy shares."[2]

By improving demand for the limited supply of shares, the designer's established reputation obviously inflates the prospective selling price. Individual shares are expected to sell at $16 according to the prospectus, despite an underlying net worth estimated at less than $2.70 a share.

Whether for wine, food, or clothing, many of us willingly pay premium prices to buy the products of high-profile fashion companies. The stratospheric prices of Donna Karan's ready-to-wear clothes—and of the company's shares—are justified by the company's reputation for making high-quality products, a reputation based on the designer's success at providing her customers with a unique look, a signature.

To acquire such a reputation requires enormous up-front publicity. Fashion companies exact premium prices from customers in order to reimburse themselves for heavy initial outlays in advertising and promotion. Donna Karan's highly visible billboards in the late 1980s used the busy New York skyline to showcase the company's secondary label, DKNY, targeted to the career woman. In the mid-1980s, Calvin Klein's provocative ads featured a sultry Brooke Shields whispering seductively, "nothing comes between me and my Calvins." The campaign was designed to draw young customers to newly introduced product lines that included, in quick succession, jeans, underwear, active wear, and the wildly successful Obsession fragrance. In the early 1990s, Calvin Klein's print ads featured rap singer Marky Mark, scantily clad, in sexually suggestive poses. Again the campaign captured widespread attention, reaffirming the company's controversial image. It also helped to boost the market value of the business. In January 1994, retailer Warnaco paid $64 million to buy Calvin Klein's lucrative underwear franchise.

Once established, a designer's reputation acts like a bond. It guarantees potential customers that the fashion enterprise will deliver on both old and new products whatever its reputation claims: a classic fit, an innovative cut, an avant-garde look—not to mention the status that comes with it.

Table 9-1 lists the design empires that dominate the fashion world. Each company contributes not only to the sale of high-priced clothes but to the selling through licensees of a wide range of consumer products that bear its name. In essence, they sell us status; they sell their reputations.

Table 9-1 THE WORLD'S TOP FASHION EMPIRES

Country	Fashion Label	Estimated Sales ($ millions)
United States	Ralph Lauren	$2,500
	Calvin Klein	2,500
	Liz Claiborne	2,200
	Oscar de la Renta	500
	Bill Blass	500
France	Pierre Cardin	2,000
	Yves Saint Laurent	2,500
	Emmanual Ungaro	675
	Pierre Balmain	30
	Chanel	750
	Christian Dior	4,200
	Thiery Mugler	90
Italy	Giorgio Armani	3,000
	Gianfranco Ferre	500
	Gianni Versace	700
	Gucci	250
	Valentino	1,500

BUILDING A LABEL

Every year, a coterie of ambitious juveniles, middle-aged dropouts, and newly minted graduates of fashion academies sets out to conquer the world. Their dream? What else—to become a household name. Their strategy? Launch a fashion label.

I met many such upstarts between 1985 and 1991 as I closely followed the progress of one beginning designer and documented his efforts to make a name for himself in Manhattan's dynamic fashion industry. Some of those I met at trade shows and conventions specialized in shirts, others in scarves; some made hats, others made coats; many made full collections. As their experiences showed me, the industry has peculiar rhythms that outsiders have difficulty identifying. To build a label from scratch requires a good understanding of those rhythms, as well as exquisite timing. I break down the experience into three stages, each with its distinct challenges.

STAGE 1: DEVELOPING UNIQUENESS

The upstart designer breaks into the fashion business by creating difference. Before a garment can reach the customer, it gets screened by an established group of store buyers who act as gatekeepers of the industry. All buyers are looking for one thing: uniqueness. They want to know what's new about the coats, pants, shirts, jackets, dresses, scarves, gloves, bags, or earrings the newcomer is trying to sell. The search for just the right degree of uniqueness dominates the early efforts of most of the small companies I observed. Some never achieve it; lacking uniqueness, they eventually go out of business.

Each newcomer picks a spot on a continuum from contemporary to avant-garde. Collectively, they present to store buyers varying degrees of fashion-forward cuts, styles, fabrics, and colorations. It remains for those seasoned buyers to intuit the future and anticipate what consumers will clamor for some six months hence when the garments actually reach the stores. Of all the clothing on display, what will be eye-catching? What will stand out just enough to attract customers but not too much to alienate them? What garments, fabrics, and colors better reflect the "times"? And, more important, what will sell? These are the questions that dominate the concerns of specialty and department store buyers, the questions that make or break the newcomer.

Most of today's established designers are remembered for designing a unique product. In the 1920s, Coco Chanel revolutionized women's wear with simple, elegant dressing. The "little black dress" and the two-piece suit with gold buttons and braid trim anchor the Chanel collections to this day. Pierre Cardin brought us space-age designs in the 1950s. André Courreges flashed into the 1960s with his cookie-cutter dresses and little white boots. Laura Ashley put her trademark prints on frumpy little dresses and made them the rage of the late 1970s. French designer Azzedine Alaia created the slinky skintight look of the 1980s. In the mid-1980s, Donna Karan centered her first solo collection for executive women on the body suit. In the late 1980s, Christian Lacroix brought back the ill-fitting (and highly inconvenient) "pouf" silhouette in his introductory collection, to the considerable dismay of women and men the world over—but oh, the publicity!

For most designers, early visibility comes from proposing to the fashion world a uniquely different look, one that often becomes the kernel around which their reputations are built and that remains with them for life. Who can imagine Calvin Klein or Giorgio Armani offering anything but soft, simple, contemporary clothing? Their established reputations create expectations among clients, store buyers, and media critics that heavily constrain the look of the clothes they continue to create.

By far the most important link a newcomer in the fashion industry must forge is with the store buyer. Gaining access to store buyers is no mean feat. Hounded by would-be designers, buyers naturally try to distance themselves from every Tom, Dick, and Harry that comes along. At the same time, they recognize the importance of remaining sufficiently accessible to appreciate what's out there, to feel the pulse of the times. In the mid-1980s, the buyers of two prominent Manhattan retailers, Bergdorf Goodman and Henri Bendel, initiated open houses to which newcomers flocked with samples. Although most hopefuls were eventually turned away, everyone I spoke with claimed to know of at least one fashion designer whose beginnings could be traced to a small initial order by a prominent retailer. The most frequently mentioned stories were Ralph Lauren's career-launching sale of a small collection of ties to a specialty retailer and Calvin Klein's first $50,000 dress order from the tony retailer Bonwit Teller. Word of mouth obviously keeps fashion's hopefuls lining up at every such open house. Not coincidentally, being in touch with the market and on the cutting edge enhances the reputations of the retailers.

More significant are the sales reps and trade shows through which retailers come to know designers and their offerings. There are two types of sales reps: in-house reps and outside agents. In-house reps work for a single designer—often it's a job start-up designers do themselves. They spend their days contacting and courting stores in an effort to attract the buyer to the designer's showroom. Lacking clout, most newcomers spin their wheels in a vacuum. Few succeed in getting top retailers to review their collections. This drives many start-up operations to call on outside agents, who represent multiple designers. Outside agents contact stores directly and sell on commission. They rely on their own network of contacts and personal reputations to attract store buyers. The better regarded the set of collections an outside agent represents, the more inclined are prestigious buyers to patronize the agent.

Most designers also take advantage of the industry's seasonal trade shows to make direct contact with retailers. At trade shows, newcomers join forces with more established companies and so stand to benefit from being "accidentally" discovered as top buyers stroll by their booths. Participation in a trade show also legitimizes newcomers. They benefit from the reputational halo that the show enjoys. Each segment of the fashion industry supports various trade shows around the world, and each show has developed a distinct reputation for attracting different types of retailers. A show's status derives from the reputations of both its exhibitors and its clients.

In the New York menswear market, for instance, I saw firsthand how the Designer's Collective (DC) built a distinctive image as the leading trade show in the pricier segment of the American market between 1984 and 1990. Although periodically challenged by gate-crashers like the International Design Group, the DC was able to assert itself in the field by carefully cultivating an elite image. Founding members elected a board that was charged with screening trade show applicants to ensure high quality; selecting a first-class site for the show (a luxury hotel rather than typical trade show venues); and publicizing it widely through ads in trade papers and close contact with the fashion press. Consistent with the image the show sought to project, exhibitor fees were far higher than those of rival shows. Not only did it help to demarcate the show, but it created a significant barrier to underfunded entrants. The results were astounding. Thanks to strong attendance and extensive favorable press coverage, within a few seasons the trade show had established itself as a leading purveyor of U.S.-based, designer-quality menswear. By 1989, the DC relied on its established reputation as a purveyor of prestigious trade shows to spawn its own progeny. The organization launched a similar show to feature American designers of women's fashions—the Fashion Coterie.

STAGE 2: PROJECTING IMAGE

Getting press—any kind of recognition—is central to the success of every fashion start-up. Here, too, uniqueness is important. Reporters like to feature novelty, and so are more likely to review the work of fashion's more distinctive and forward-looking newcomers. In the United States, the fashion press is dominated by the editors and writers of a small group of daily and weekly newspapers and magazines, none more visible than *Women's Wear Daily (WWD)* and *Vogue*. Designers who manage to catch the eye of these veteran journalists get free publicity and instant legitimacy from favorable reviews. Publicity opens many doors, most critically, those of the industry's top retailers.

Fashion shows are by far the most important means of showcasing a designer's uniqueness and projecting the company's image. By displaying garments on attractive models in an ambience of the designer's choosing, runway shows more clearly convey the designer's intent than can the showroom. Fashion shows are also theatrical events. Buyers far prefer a fashion show's aura of glamour and excitement to the stark anonymity of a giant trade show or the pressured environment of a designer's showroom.

Fashion shows are also an extremely expensive means of promoting a line of clothes. Few things are more depressing than to attend a newcomer's show that the fashion establishment snubs. That's why most designers who present runway shows are already established. They can count on the media to publicize the event and so can justify the show as a promotion expense.

The fashion cycle is regularly punctuated by the runway shows of the world's most prominent designers, with Paris and Milan at the pinnacle, London and New York a notch below. Every January and July, the top designers in the world's four centers of high fashion show their ready-to-wear collections with great fanfare. Everyone awaits with baited

American designer Oscar de la Renta amid thunderous applause after the finale that showcased his 1993 collection. In February 1993, the Paris-based House of Balmain confirmed Mr. de la Renta's reputation by hiring him to design its couture collections. (Courtesy of Oscar de la Renta.)

breath the designs that will come walking down the runways. Buyers pay caution fees that can amount to thousands of dollars for the right to attend these shows. Large retailers like Bloomingdale's and Saks Fifth Avenue rely on the shows to plot the direction of their private labels. Indeed, a whole industry of illustrators, photographers, and trim and accessory manufacturers depends on the couture showings to develop the knockoff designs that will be mass-marketed throughout the world for the year to come. If imitation is truly the sincerest form of flattery, then the fashion industry clearly adulates its star couturiers.

Fashion companies spend a great deal to convey an image to customers. Gucci invests $10 million a year in print advertising alone, while arch rival Louis Vuitton lays out more than $30 million. Calvin Klein is probably better known for his controverial ads than for his clothes. The early Calvin Klein ads that featured Brooke Shields cost the company $16 million in 1979. Not only did the campaign help build the moribund jeans business, but it helped to solidify Calvin Klein's reputation in youth-dominated urban markets. In 1990, Ralph Lauren's new fragrance Safari was launched with an advertising budget of $23 million and was boosted again in 1993 with another $20 million campaign. In 1992,

Italian designer Giorgio Armani launched his new perfume Gio with a marketing budget estimated at some $20 million. In 1993, the marketing campaign for Calvin Klein's Escape fragrance was gauged at $30 million. Generating visibility and maintaining reputation are costly propositions.

Since generating press is the sine qua non of reputation building in the industry, designers often try to gain media attention "by association." Designer Halston's popularity grew exponentially when First Lady Jackie Kennedy wore his trademark pillbox hat on national television in the early 1960s. British designer Vivienne Westwood gained notoriety by outfitting the punk group Sex Pistols. In the 1980s, designer Stephen Sprouse got publicity for designing the clothes of Deborah Harry, lead singer for the new wave group Blondie.

In fact, designers routinely lend out their clothes to celebrities. Association with a prominent, visible, or admired personality works like an endorsement. It conveys to potential customers an implicit guarantee of prestige and quality; it also assures store buyers that an order will have a good sell-through at retail.

Given the importance of getting press, the relationship between fashion designers and reporters is fraught with tension. Today's media darling could be tomorrow's fashion outcast. Listen to how the notorious editor of *Women's Wear Daily*, John Fairchild, viewed his reporter's role in the flagship newspaper of Fairchild Publications, his family's business: "I had learned early on that the world of fashion was a gossipy, theatrical, unscrupulous, dogmatic, and opinionated business, and that to succeed, *WWD* had better be alive in this alive business, controversial in this controversial business, smart and snobby in this smart and snobby business. As a result, it approached its world like a tiger and not like a cat."[3]

Over the years, many designers have felt the tiger's claws, among them Yves Saint Laurent. For years the fashion press lauded the talented French designer, until one day a critique by Fairchild provoked Saint Laurent to ban the reporter from his subsequent fashion shows. As a result, Saint Laurent's work languished for a time in the fashion press.

A similar story is told of a feud between New York designer Geoffrey Beene and Fairchild that has unquestionably diminished Beene's public profile. Since 1983, *WWD* has shunned the designer's fashion shows, in return for which Mr. Beene has studiously avoided advertising in the trade paper. In his book on the fashion industry, Fairchild gives Beene only passing and unflattering reference. In my own search, I could find only limited coverage of Beene in the fashion press, far less so than his stature as a leading American couturier warrants. Clearly, to build reputation in the fashion world involves maintaining close interpersonal ties not only with store buyers but with celebrated reporters.

Fashion companies also build reputation indirectly through philanthropic acts. Liz Claiborne's $2 billion fashion empire routinely supports community arts projects and makes charitable contributions. In 1991, the company donated $10 million to Columbia University's Graduate School of Business. Calvin Klein sponsored an extravagant showing of his collections in Los Angeles in 1993. The $600,000 raised was targeted for scientific research on AIDS. The event brought considerable publicity to the name. Bill Blass's $10 million donation to the New York Public Library in January 1994, put his name in gilt over the entrance to its public catalogue room. Philanthropy begets visibility.

Ultimately, a designer's reputation reflects acquired status in fashion's pecking order of celebrity customers, store buyers, and media reporters. Until the late 1970s, winning the prestigious Coty American Fashion Critics' Award for fashion designer of the year was considered a great honor. Since its inception in 1943, the contest had been sponsored by the cosmetics and fragrance division of the giant pharmaceutical company Pfizer in obvious recognition of the symbiotic link between fashion and perfume.

When the Coty began to lose prestige in the late 1970s, the Council of Fashion Designers of America (CFDA) instituted its own annual award. Like the Coty it replaced, the CFDA helped to crystallize a designer's emerging reputation. Past winners include the full roster of today's top names (Calvin Klein, Anne Klein, Bill Blass, Oscar de la Renta), most of whom won Coty awards in the 1970s and were repeatedly recognized with CFDA awards throughout the 1980s. If form holds, the most recent award winners of the 1990s should be the next decade's top fashion names. At the 1993 CFDA awards, Italian designer Giorgio Armani was on hand to present Donna Karan with the menswear award. Gianni Versace also came to accept the international designer award from another celebrity, pop singer Elton John. Besides Donna Karan, recent award winners whose names will likely stand for fashion empires in the coming years are those of Isaac Mizrahi and Joseph Abboud.

Table 9-2 crystallizes the reputations of fashion's leading empires in terms of the industry's two main considerations: styling and price.

Table 9-2 A REPUTATIONAL MAP OF FASHION COMPANIES

Price	Style		
	Forward	Contemporary	Classic
High	Gianni Versace Gianfranco Ferre Claude Montana	Chanel Christian Dior Yves Saint Laurent Pierre Balmain	Bill Blass Oscar de la Renta Gucci Valentino
Medium	Donna Karan Yamamoto Kenzo	Calvin Klein Perry Ellis Anne Klein	Ralph Lauren Laura Ashley
Low	Girbaud Byblos	Liz Claiborne Pierre Cardin Benetton	L.L. Bean The Gap

STAGE 3: CAPITALIZING ON REPUTATION

Once established, a designer's reputation quickly acquires value. It's evident in the number of licensing offers designers receive. Fashion companies appear to charge higher royalty rates than most consumer goods companies. For simply putting its name on items like ties or sunglasses, a fashion company earns from 5 percent to 12 percent of sales in royalty income. Top-tier houses like Chanel and Christian Dior are known to charge 12 percent. Designer names with less drawing power at retail charge less. This means that licenses net some $50 million to $100 million annually for the billion dollar businesses of megadesigners like Calvin Klein and Ralph Lauren. Christian Dior's licensed products posted a wholesale volume of $1.1 billion in 1992; royalties to Dior from those sales totaled some $65 million. All licensed apparel products accounted for a staggering $20 billion in retail sales in the United States alone in 1990.

Older fashion houses tend to grant more licenses. Yves Saint Laurent has 211 licenses, Christian Dior 280. In contrast, Ralph Lauren has only 16 licenses and Calvin Klein 12; Italian designer Gianfranco Ferre limits its licensees to 18. By far the most promiscuous of all designers is Pierre Cardin. His name appears on more than 840 products (from alarm clocks and telephones to scuba suits and skis) sold in more than 100 countries. In 1992, worldwide retail sales of Cardin's licensed products amounted to some $2 billion, and the House of Cardin collected more than $75 million in royalties—7 percent to 10 percent on clothing sales, and 3 percent to 5 percent on sales of other consumer goods.[4]

The most lucrative of all licenses are perfumes. The U.S. market for perfumes is estimated at close to $1 billion. Ever since Coco Chanel introduced her now classic Chanel No. 5 in 1921, fashion designers have sought to capitalize on the link between clothing and fragrances. In 1991, Chanel brought out its popular Egoiste fragrance. Calvin Klein's Obsession, introduced in the late 1980s, is now the company's most profitable product. Oscar de la Renta has Parfums Stern. In 1990, Pierre Cardin launched its most recent perfume, Rose Cardin. In 1993, Donna Karan added scents to her rapidly growing empire, improving the company's profitability and so the marketability of its future public offering of shares.

Perhaps the most recent licensing trend is for designers to put their names on residential buildings. In a novel partnership with local real estate developers, French designers like Paco Rabanne, Ted Lapidus, Guy Larroche, and André Courreges have created signature buildings in Brazil. Construction is now under way for Maison Paco Rabanne, a cluster of designer condos in Florida's trendy Miami Beach. Can Maison Pierre Cardin be far behind?

Many fashion companies also try to capitalize on their reputations and improve their profitability by opening up their own retail shops in direct competition with their wholesale customers. For instance, Yves Saint Laurent has built a network of about 150 boutiques around the world. Christian Dior operates 35, Chanel 41. In the early 1990s, Giorgio Armani entered retail in force, opening a string of Emporio Armani and A/X Armani Exchange shops in major U.S. cities in one fell swoop.

Designers see many advantages to retailing their own products. Direct interaction with consumers provides rapid feedback about styles that sell; it also facilitates risk taking, since designers can always place their excess inventories in their own stores. More important, the fashion company generally favors retailing because it reduces dependence on whimsical store buyers. Ralph Lauren opened his flagship store in New York's trendy Upper East Side in the late 1980s. In 1993, a new store opened nearby under the Polo Sport banner to capitalize on that label's younger image.

A number of prominent designers, such as Calvin Klein, opt to negotiate with prestige retailers like Bloomingdale's and Bergdorf's to maintain free-standing boutiques within those stores. The self-contained boutiques increase a designer's sense of control. They ensure the integrity of the clothing presentation and so protect the company's image and reputation. Many leading designers go so far as to hire, train, and pay the sales staff in their boutiques, much as they might if the boutiques were independent entities. In 1995, however, the reputational gains and other benefits expected from direct marketing through company-owned stores led rival labels Calvin Klein, Anne Klein, and Liz Claiborne to open flagship stores within blocks of each other on New York's Madison Avenue.

Of the 30 or so start-up companies that I became familiar with over five years, only a handful survive to this day. Of those, only two have identified a viable niche, one in the design and production of knit sweaters, the other in lower-priced menswear. Despite continued growth over the years, both are still struggling to get past stage 1, and have yet to capitalize on their budding reputations with licenses.

When designers make it, however, the results are certainly impressive. Although estimates of the personal fortunes of successful designers are difficult to obtain and unreliable at best (most are privately held or dispersed in interlocking corporations), what seems clear is that celebrity status brings considerable income and wealth. Ralph Lauren, arguably the most successful designer in America in terms of earnings, has built a personal fortune that was estimated at more than $700 million in 1993. The prolific Karl Lagerfeld designs for many collections, most notably for the Chanel and Fendi labels. Each collection he designs reputedly pays him more than $1 million a year—a total of $4 million from Chanel alone. In 1989, the Christian Dior label hired Gianfranco Ferre to design its couture collection, for which he is reportedly paid $2 million a year. Minor arithmetic leads most analysts to "guestimate" the personal incomes of top-ranked designers at anywhere from $5 million to $100 million a year. Not a bad return on reputation.

THE DIFFICULTIES OF MAINTAINING
A LABEL'S REPUTATION

If establishing a label is difficult, maintaining it—which comes down to maintaining its reputation—can be even harder. Designer label companies are regularly plagued by problems of growth and succession. Transitions from one stage of development to another often more closely resemble revolutions than expansions. Diversification from menswear to women's wear, from a U.S. market to an international market, or from clothing to accessories often tax a company's ability to adapt. Following are some of the problems a company may face in the fickle and volatile world of fashion.

CHANGE OF OWNERSHIP

Of all the top fashion companies listed in Table 9-1, all but two are still run by their founders. Insofar as the reputations of most such companies rest squarely on the shoulders of their individual creators, constituents find it difficult to accept replacements. Those who are brought in fail to convince former customers to remain loyal, and as the vision that animated the early years dissipates, the business loses a sense of identity.

Take Liz Claiborne, one of the most successful fashion empires created since the 1970s. The company went public in 1986 and built a billion-dollar franchise in no time. Despite the company's strong management structure, however, succession proved difficult to implement when founder Liz Claiborne and her husband elected to retire in the early 1990s. The company's direction has been somewhat uncertain since then, and its reputational capital has eroded significantly.

All too often it is death that proves insurmountable. Most top companies take out "key man insurance" on their designers. While that can buy some time, it seldom proves sufficient. When American menswear designer Perry Ellis died in 1986, the company collected a $5 million benefit; it had not identified a successor. The company struggled for a time under the leadership of Ellis's business partner. When he too died a year later, a succession of designers stepped in, until the company hired newcomer Mark Jacobs. Despite the initial success of the Jacobs collection, however, it proved difficult to sustain momentum; the company's design business is now entirely run by committee, and its reputation has suffered.

Throughout the 1980s, newcomer Willi Smith built a successful fashion business based on affordable but innovative styling, carefully targeted to urban youth. When the designer died in the late 1980s, the company floundered despite solid financial backing from prestigious retailers like Barney's in New York. Today, little is left of the Willi Smith label, and the likelihood of its return declines daily as its once valuable reputational capital evaporates.

The death in September 1990 of Halston, who had been wildly successful in the 1970s, proved to be the final blow in a series that severely
damaged the reputation of the label, as will be explained later in the
chapter.

Competition from Knockoffs and Counterfeits

If the engine of fashion is uniqueness and innovation, the fuel that propels
the industry along is imitation. Every season, it's the job of the top designers
in the fashion capitals to interpret fashion's trends; everyone else's job is
to follow. That's why an underground community of fashion "spies" scours
designers' backrooms, chasing down leads that they might sell to faraway
manufacturers eager to get an early start on next season's styles.

To protect themselves, designers operate guardedly and under a veil
of secrecy. Models and photographers with early access to next season's
designs swear their undying allegiance and, fearful of reprisal, keep their
word. Attendance at the top fashion shows is by invitation only. Rival
designers and copycat manufacturers are not welcome.

After the shows, once a designer's new collection has garnered the
free worldwide publicity necessary to secure next season's orders from
retailers, it's a free-for-all. Sketches and photographs are faxed to copy-
ists, who quickly translate the trends defined by the major fashion houses
into affordable imitations that will be sold around the world. Fashion's
brightest stars propel industry-wide knockoffs.

The knockoff is an understood and, in fact, expected phenomenon.
Imitation serves to strengthen the reputation of the fashion centers.
Unfortunately, in recent years, along with knockoffs have come more
threatening counterfeits. Sold at far lower prices, these imitations appropriate not only the styles but also the labels and logos of the originals.
In the early 1980s, leather-goods maker Louis Vuitton lost much of its
once exclusive cachet because of widespread copying of the company's
logo all around the world. A few years ago, I watched street vendors
aggressively hawk counterfeit Gucci watches and accessories right outside the company's Fifth Avenue store. Though superficially similar,
counterfeits are generally of far lesser quality than the company's branded
goods. When consumers mistake them for originals, they seriously depreciate the reputational capital of fashion's biggest names. To the dismay
of fashion's movers and shakers, piracy has proven resilient.

Designers strive to produce unique looks. That's why they are extremely sensitive to the threat of imitation, particularly from major rivals. A major brouhaha ensued in 1994 when French couturier Yves Saint Laurent charged none other than Ralph Lauren with knocking-off the tuxedo dress from his couture collection that is pictured here. In May 1994, Ralph Lauren was fined £250,000 for infringing the YSL trademark. (Yves Saint Laurent Haute Couture Collection Fall/Winter 1992–1993.)

In the early 1980s, British designer Katherine Hamnett created a line of slogan T-shirts. The popularity of the T-shirts and the ease with which they could be copied led to worldwide piracy of her designs. More than 30 unlicensed manufacturers from Brazil to Hong Kong turned out counterfeits of her line. They proved difficult to prosecute, however, because of U.S. laws of public domain that do not protect goods and ideas that have entered the public consciousness. To prosecute successfully, the designer must prove direct copying of dimensions and proportions from an actual sample, not just from a photograph—a difficult prospect at best.[5]

LOSS OF CONTROL

A name loses its sparkle when the products that bear it are either sold in the "wrong" retail outlets or made too widely available. Both signal a loss of prestige and reputation for the designer name. The company has lost control.

Perhaps the most devastating loss of control in the recent history of the industry befell Halston, whose reputation suffered from being licensed to an incompatible distribution outlet.

In the early 1970s, the American designer was fashion's brightest star. The darling of the press, he surrounded himself with an entourage of celebrities that included choreographer Martha Graham, entertainer Liza Minelli, and actresses Candice Bergen and Raquel Welch. In the mid-1970s, to capitalize on his snob appeal and enter larger markets, Halston sold the rights to his name to the Norton Simon Industries in exchange for a lucrative employment contract and guaranteed royalties. By the early 1980s, Halston products generated some $90 million a year, $75 million of which was from fragrances.

In 1983, interested in further expanding the Halston business, Norton Simon persuaded Halston to go along with licensing his name to mass retailer J. C. Penney. The deal was attractive. Spanning women's sportswear, menswear, home furnishings, and children's wear, the six-year plan projected sales at a staggering $1 billion, with a guarantee of an estimated $16 million to Halston Enterprises, on top of which Halston himself would be paid a $1.25 million annual salary, with increasing royalties.[6] The deal went through.

The backlash was terrible. No sooner did prestige retailer Bergdorf Goodman hear of the Penney deal than it dropped Halston's clothing line and fragrance completely. Others quickly followed suit. By the time the Halston III line was released in June 1983 throughout the Penney empire, the designer was widely considered to have sold out.

Tremendous success greeted the mass-market-priced line. Nonetheless, Halston's prestige would drop another notch when in September 1983 Norton Simon Industries—Halston's parent company—was bought by the $6 billion conglomerate Esmark. Without warning, Halston Enterprises found itself fused with two other Norton Simon units—Max Factor and McCall's Patterns—into Esmark's International Playtex division. In terms of prestige, that was the ultimate blow. As Halston's biographer put it, "Suddenly Halston had become part of a bra and girdle company."[7]

For Halston, things would never be the same. Playtex executives were horrified at the casual and informal character of Halston Enterprises. They struggled to impose corporate controls but succeeded only in alienating the designer. By 1984, Halston had seemingly lost all interest in his operation, and the Penney line began to falter at retail.

It would get worse. This was the era of the corporate takeover, and in 1984, Esmark and its Playtex unit were themselves bought by food conglomerate Beatrice. Halston Enterprises was now an inconsequential part of a huge empire; the company's identity was threatened, its reputation in tatters. The unit would be sold again, this time to the cosmetics giant Revlon. Following the designer's death in 1990, Revlon shut down his famous offices in New York's prestigious Olympic Tower. Halston's reputation has drifted into corporate oblivion.

The reputations of other fashion houses have also faltered owing to placement in unlikely outlets. In the 1970s and 1980s, France's House of Chanel lost its clout from seeing its licensed products turn up in discount outlets. Or consider prominent licensee Cosmair, the maker of fragrances under the names of Ralph Lauren, Giorgio Armani, Lancôme, and L'Oréal, among others. In 1993, Cosmair launched an aggressive effort to keep its well-known brand names from getting diverted to mass retailers. A key problem fashion companies face is the difficulty of tracking down distributors who sell their products to unauthorized, less prestigious outlets.

Many prominent fashion labels lose reputation from overexposure. In the late 1980s, Gucci had either scrawled its name or put its well-known logo on more than 22,000 items. In 1989, overexposure had so tarnished the Gucci name that the company's U.S. sales fell by 25 percent to $120 million. It didn't help the company that its owners were embroiled in highly public disputes for control, as well as facing charges of tax evasion by the IRS that led to heavy fines. The combination of excessive licensing, counterfeits, and overexposure seriously depreciated the Gucci name.

Then there's French designer Pierre Cardin, with his 840 licenses and $1.2 billion in retail sales a year. As one observer wrily observed: "His current reputation rests more on the variety of his endeavors: on the theatrical, musical, and artistic events he sponsors at his theatre L'Espace Cardin, as well as on his undaunted efforts to dress (or somehow affect) every human being in the world. One wonders what the space-age couturier will do when other planets are made accessible to him."[8] By putting his name on everything in sight, the designer's reputation has undoubtedly suffered, forcing him into businesses ever more remote from the heart of fashion. Having lost significant credibility as a leading designer, Cardin's attempts to return to fashion in the last few years have proven difficult.

Some companies are too quick to lose control of their name entirely by selling it to another. This holds for Halston as well as for Christian Dior. Dior's fragrances are wholly owned by the French luxury goods conglomerate LVMH (Louis Vuitton-Moet Hennessy), from which Dior collects no royalties and, more important, over which it has no control. Regaining control is key, as Gianni Versace showed when in 1988 he paid $12 million to buy back the rights to a fragrance that bore his name.

To avoid depreciating a fashion company's reputational capital, its managers must retain control of the name. It proves vital to limit the number of licensees, to exert strict supervision over the products that carry the name, and to pursue counterfeits agressively. Internally, it requires building a credible process of leadership succession that shores up the viability of the name and secures the company's reputation with its outside publics.

THE COMEBACK TRAIL

Although names can be tarnished, they can also be brought back. A surprising number of fashion companies have demonstrated the resilience of their names in recent years, none more so than Chanel.

The House of Chanel is one of France's oldest and most prestigious fashion houses. Begun in 1914 by Gabrielle "Coco" Chanel, the couture operation built a reputation for emancipating women and dressing the well-to-do. In 1921, Chanel pioneered the link between fashion and cosmetics by launching Chanel No.5, the perfume that became synonymous with glamor and that remains an enduring best-seller. Despite the charges of German collaboration that were leveled at the designer and her company during World War II, consumers continued to snap up Chanel products, and its reputation soared.

Following Ms. Chanel's death in 1971, however, creative control of the house passed to lesser-known designers, and its reputation went into a tailspin. Despite efforts to expand through product-line extensions in both cosmetics and ready-to-wear, Chanel lost its avant-garde reputation and became widely known for producing dowdy clothing for society matrons. Sales languished. By the late 1970s, Chanel products had become widely available in discount outlets. Counterfeit products proliferated and served to diminish the exclusivity of the company's imprint.

In the early 1980s, the Swiss family Wertheimer, the inheritors of the Chanel name, plotted a course to revive the house's reputation. They recognized that Chanel, like all fashion companies, relies on its name to sell a large number of products at retail. Under Alain Wertheimer's leadership, Chanel executives opted for an aggressive reputation-building strategy. They decided to cut the number of distribution outlets, raise prices, and open more company-owned stores. At the same time, the company initiated aggressive litigation against low-priced knockoffs and hired a legion of lobbyists, lawyers, and detectives to protect it against counterfeiting. The company also launched an intensive advertising and public relations campaign. Top models were retained to represent and promote the company's cosmetics, and the high-profile designer Karl Lagerfeld was hired to revitalize the clothing collections.

By 1986, the House of Chanel had once again become the darling of the fashion press and returned to widespread popularity and profitability. With its reputation resuscitated, the company saw a phenomenal increase in sales not only of clothing and cosmetics but of related categories like leather goods and accessories.

A number of other flagging fashion reputations have been revived in recent years. The strategies these companies pursued to rebuild their eroded franchises suggest some revealing lessons.

RENTING REPUTATION

To offset the loss of a founder from either disinterest or death, many fashion houses turn to other established designers and "rent" their reputations. Just as Chanel brought in Karl Lagerfeld in 1983 to revive its fashion appeal, so did the Dior empire call on Italy's highly regarded Gianfranco Ferre in 1989 to design its couture collection and bring out its first ready-to-wear line. The relationship worked. Ferre added luster to Dior's faded label, and critics and customers once again flocked to the company's products. The revival enabled Dior to go public in 1991, capitalized at some $2.33 billion.

The languishing Lanvin label tried the same strategy by hiring avant-garde designer Claude Montana to revive its fashion-appeal. As one reporter put it: "Its banker/chairman, Leon Bressler, bet big—some say bet the company—on Claude Montana's ability to deliver a riveting couture performance that would win the house the attention and excitement it needed to galvanize a new image and a new future."[9] Unfortunately, it didn't work. Lacking a coherent strategy to rebuild—not only couture but the all-important licensing and ready-to-wear businesses—Lanvin's fortunes continued to sag despite Montana's involvement. So much so that in 1990 Bressler sold Lanvin to a joint venture of the Vuitton family and the L'Oréal Group for $90 million. Their notion? To rebuild Lanvin as the flagship of a new luxury empire.

In 1990, the design house of Pierre Balmain was also in serious trouble. Lacking cash, the company tried to lower costs by pulling out of couture entirely. Instead, it invested heavily in advertising its fragrances and refurbishing its flagship store. The strategy failed. Faced with declining sales and a faltering image, in early 1991 the company reversed itself and announced its return to couture. Within months, a change of ownership was in the works as banks called in their loans against the company.

Under new leadership, Balmain is now the latest couture house to try to rent an established designer name. In February 1993, the company hired U.S. designer Oscar de la Renta to revitalize its business. As Mr. de la Renta put it, "couture is still the best way to create and sustain an image"[10]—and the best way to invigorate the money-making machine of ready-to-wear clothing and the licenses that come from it.

REVIVING IMAGE

Advertising can help to polish up a tarnished reputation: Christian Dior boosted advertising in 1992 to $20 million, and Balmain did much the same by throwing some $7 million at the marketplace.

Like Balmain and Dior, Gucci's heavily tarnished reputation in the late 1980s was cause for alarm. Gucci's ad campaign of $10 million a year couldn't seem to overcome the company's declining panache. Gucci's chairman Maurizio Guzzi realized that it would require more than advertising to stop the slide and reverse track. Unlike Balmain, Lanvin, and Dior, Gucci elected to bring in not a well-known designer but a top merchandiser. In 1989 the company chartered Dawn Mello, the former president of top retailer Bergdorf Goodman, to restore the Gucci name to the prestigious position it had occupied from 1950 to 1980.

The Gucci strategy was straightforward:

- redesign the product line;

- pick a new logo;

- slash the number of items carrying the label;

- buy back licenses, including perfumes, watches, and eyewear; and

- cut back points of sale.

In 1989, the number of Gucci products dropped from 10,000 to 5,000. In 1990, the old double *G* logo that had appeared on thousands of counterfeit products was dropped in favor of a new logo, a blazing sun. In 1991, the company launched its first-ever catalog in the United States and Italy.

A key component of any attempt to revise image is generating favorable press. Gucci got it in spades. Since 1991, the fashion world has been busily proclaiming Gucci's rebirth.[11] Besides receiving positive press from reporters, designers like Donna Karan, Christian Lacroix, and Gianni Versace are frequently seen sporting Gucci products, as are celebrity entertainers like Warren Beatty, Candice Bergen, and Sigourney Weaver. Gucci became "hip" again, and its reputation and fortunes are rising.

LIMITING DISTRIBUTION

One vital component of Gucci's strategy was reducing distribution. Whereas in 1985 Gucci products were available in more than 2,500 retail outlets, by 1991 the company had pulled back to 300, of which 150 were company-owned stores and franchises. A cornerpiece of Chanel's rebirth was its decision to showcase the company's products only in its 41 Chanel boutiques around the world. Christian Dior similarly reduced its licenses from 250 to 200 to improve quality and consistency. (In 1990, Dior also opened its first two boutiques in the United States, one in Beverly Hills and one in New York.)

Lanvin appears headed in the same direction. Backed by two owners with deep pockets, L'Oréal and Louis Vuitton, Lanvin is pursuing a long-term strategy of reclaiming control over distribution and manufacturing to improve quality. Since 1990, it has bought back or terminated all of its former licenses outside of Japan at a cost of over $54 million. The company has also closed its two costly New York stores. As one former Lanvin executive put it: "Lanvin's policy is to create a vertically integrated company, controlling the design, manufacture, distribution, and retailing through fully owned stores or franchises. Everyone dreams of doing that, but only Lanvin has that sort of money."[12] Lanvin is taking the long way, recognizing that it takes time to restore a faded reputation.

FASHION'S VICTIMS

Joanna Mastroianni designs evening wear on Manhattan's prestigious Seventh Avenue. She started out with $100,000 in 1990, determined to work only with expensive fabrics to create the most elegant dresses she could conceive. At the beginning, she recalls, "I used to call store buyers 20 and 30 times, and they'd never call back." A little luck got her high-priced clothes first into Bergdorf Goodman and then into prominent specialty retailer Martha's International. She never looked back. By 1993, sales had topped $1 million and she had parlayed her first sales into a network of some 40 other exclusive stores nationwide. Company buyers and private customers now regularly come to her—she's one of the lucky ones.

In contrast, consider the more common experience of newcomer Sarah Philips. At Bill Clinton's inaugural ball in 1992, First Lady Hilary Clinton wore a dress created by the unknown New York designer. The press had a field day interviewing Philips, heralding the rise of a new fashion star. Despite television interviews and considerable media hoopla, however, Philips has since struggled to finance and produce her subsequent collections and has largely disappeared from view—another of fashion's victims.

To outsiders, fashion is at its best a world of beauty and fantasy, chock full of fun, fame, and fortune; at its worst it's a frivolous enterprise, replete with scheming, artifice, and mendacity. To fashion's insiders, it's both. Success requires more than a combination of skill and hoopla—it requires luck. Enduring reputations are conferred on only a few designer names. The winners are those savvy enough to have both identifed and exploited a unique look and wise enough to have judiciously managed the name associated with that look. To them go the spoils of victory—fame and fortune.

C H A P T E R   T E N

We know what we are, but know not what we may be.

—*William Shakespeare*
  Hamlet

The MBA Academies under Siege

APPAREL MAKERS are not the only ones to depend heavily on their reputations to compete for customers. In the service sector, intangibles like reputation are even larger contributors to a company's economic performance. Businesses that rely on people skills, information, know-how, and other "credence goods"—companies involved in consulting, advertising, law, software development, and accounting—depend heavily on their reputations to attract customers and investors.

It's also true of colleges and universities, a fact that has perhaps nowhere become more apparent than in the scrambling for reputational standing among the MBA academies over the last decade or so. This chapter describes the sudden turmoil that beset leading centers for management training in the United States following the publication of reputational rankings by the popular magazines *Business Week* and *U.S. News & World Report* in the late 1980s. Similar reactions can be anticipated from companies in any industry where performance is measured principally in reputational terms.

NAME THAT BUILDING

On an overcast Friday in April 1993, a group of New York City dignitaries gathered on Gould Plaza, in the heart of New York University's campus on Washington Square. Their purpose? To join in dedicating the university's latest addition to Manhattan real estate: the Stern School's Management Education Center. Named for the business school's newest benefactor—entrepreneur Leonard N. Stern, chairman of the Hartz Group—the building capped a massive campaign to secure a place for the Stern School among America's top business schools. The state-of-the-art building aptly symbolizes the reputation-building efforts of business schools now under way on college campuses across the country.

The 1960s, 1970s, and early 1980s were heady years for U.S. business schools. Bullish deans invested heavily in attracting cutting-edge faculty to boost the academic reputations of their programs within the university and to convince corporations of their legitimacy as training centers for managers. Flush with rapid postwar growth, large companies turned en masse to business schools for skilled personnel with which to staff their expanding empires. In short order, the master of business administration grew from its humble origins as a variety of vocational training to undisputed status as a passport to career success in corporate America. Students enrolled in droves, abandoning liberal arts and engineering programs for the more lucrative opportunities an MBA could provide. And the MBA academies grew—not only in their fund-raising muscle and public profile but also in their power and status on the university campus, quickly gaining ground on the older professional schools of law and medicine.

In the mid-1980s, the tide turned. A surge of rivalry from Japan caught American companies by surprise, driving down profitability rates. Graduates with hard-earned MBAs found themselves blamed for the downfall of American business. Critics blamed the declining competitiveness of U.S. companies in global markets on the short-run thinking of corporate managers, on their rash avoidance of long-term investments in technological innovation, product development, and human capital. It was not long before the short-run orientation of companies was traced to inadequate management education and ascribed to the narrow training provided by the MBA academies—the very same schools that had enthusiastically claimed responsibility for credentialing those arrogant managers. By decade's end, many were those who questioned the merits of

Built in 1992, the Stern School's Management Education Center at New York University consolidates its undergraduate and graduate programs in a state-of-the-art facility. It anchors the school's bid for a place among the nation's top 10 business schools. (Courtesy of NYU.)

pursuing an MBA, swayed as they were by critics who argued persuasively that the degree was both too narrow in focus and too distant from operations.

Demographics didn't help matters any. By the late 1980s and early 1990s, business schools found themselves threatened by a shrinking pool of applicants for MBA training. The shrinking numbers had been predicted for some time. They reflected the bulge of the baby boom that had caused a boom-bust cycle in every sector of society as it pushed its way through elementary school, high school, and college from the 1950s to the 1980s. As boomers moved into middle age, they left a vacuum that spelled declining enrollments and increasing competition among schools for students.

If dissatisfaction with the MBA was growing rampant in companies and among alumni, it did not immediately command the attention of most business schools. After all, educational institutions are notorious for insulating themselves. For years administrators and faculty asserted the greater wisdom of a research-based view of reputation building in business schools. It took unexpected scrutiny by the business media in the late 1980s to bring the issues to the forefront, and the coup de grâce was probably delivered by *Business Week* in its cover story of November 1988. In that issue, the magazine reported on a detailed survey that sought to rate the MBA academies. The results took everyone by surprise. In the minds of the two key constituencies surveyed—recent graduates and corporate recruiters—Harvard was unexpectedly rated not first but second, and the Midwest's Northwestern claimed the top spot. Championed by vocal and loyal alumni, tiny Dartmouth came in a resounding third, while—surprise—the perenially prominent Wharton and Chicago both rated far lower.

The rankings fell on the MBA schools like a ton of bricks. As it turned out, this was the first time anyone had bothered to ask the schools' clients what they thought of their educational experience. Prior efforts at assessing business school programs had always relied either on the opinions of the deans that ran the programs or on measures of the prestige of the school's faculty. Not surprisingly, those ratings had invariably weighted the academic quality of the school rather than its teaching, its curriculum, or the value of its graduates to the school's clients in the corporate sector.

Nothing might have happened had not *Business Week*'s reputational rankings proved so enormously informative to the public. Not only did the magazine itself sell out, but other newspapers and periodicals around the world reported the findings. Widespread dissemination of the rankings had direct economic implications. They influenced the following year's applicants to MBA programs. And the once genteel world of graduate education was suddenly thrown in disarray. Like American industry in general, the MBA academies suddenly felt pressured to answer to the demands of their clients, and top schools, historically committed to the "publish or perish" mindset that championed research over teaching, began to recognize that clients must come first. Those who enroll in

MBA programs select a school not merely on the quality of its faculty's research but on the school's overall reputational standing—a far more complex halo that incorporates teaching quality along with other measures of the school's value.

The call to action resonated through the corridors of the MBA academies. Attracting applicants to costly MBA programs would require meeting the criticisms head on, and so throughout the 1980s leading U.S. business schools launched parallel strategic programs designed to enhance their reputations. Addressing corporate and alumni concerns required a radical attack on the core character of the business school: Deans were goaded not only to invest in new facilities, in fund-raising, and in public relations but also to initiate radical internal changes in course content, teaching style, faculty reward systems, and promotion processes. A revolution was under way—one characterized by more balanced attention to both research and teaching; growing dependence on external fund-raising and image management; and more intense competition among schools for status and reputation.

THE MBA ACADEMIES

In 1994, some 680 American institutions offered MBA degrees, up from 389 in 1974. Of these, fewer than a third met the minimum standards set by the American Assembly of Collegiate Schools of Business. The vast majority of students were enrolled in the 220 or so accredited schools.

Throughout the 1960s and 1970s, management education was a growth industry for colleges and universities that rushed to capitalize on the rich harvest of MBA tuition dollars. Today, more than 220,000 students are enrolled in MBA programs. About 75,000 students are awarded MBAs annually, a 30 percent jump from 1980, a threefold rise from 1970, and a fifteenfold increase from 1960, when only 4,800 got the degree. Since 1950, more than 500,000 students have earned an MBA.

Although a quintessentially American industry, management education has developed an international presence as well. For many years, the only MBA programs offered abroad were direct clones exported by Harvard's Business School to institutes like INSEAD in Fontainebleau, France, and IMEDE in Lausanne, Switzerland. They have since spread to the four corners of the globe, with MBAs being offered in Japan,

Singapore, South Korea, Costa Rica, Brazil, Argentina, and the Philippines. Most recently, Europe's finest private universities have recognized the potential gold mine from management education, and prestigious names like the London School of Economics, Oxford, and Cambridge have thrown their reputations at marketing MBA programs. For simplicity's sake, I focus here only on the U.S. programs, although many of the ideas we discuss are relevant to the international schools as well.

Table 10-1 lists the largest private business schools in the United States and their MBA enrollments.[1] The heavy hitters in management education

Table 10-1   THE LARGEST U.S. BUSINESS SCHOOLS

School	MBA Enrollment[a]
Harvard	1,592
Pennsylvania (Wharton)	1,575
Texas-Austin	1,212
Columbia	1,191
NYU (Stern)	1,173
Chicago	1,011
UCLA	969
Northwestern (Kellogg)	930
Michigan	800
University of Southern California	659
Stanford	654
Indiana	593
Duke (Fuqua)	530
Wisconsin-Madison	525
Virginia (Darden)	476
UC-Berkeley	459
Cornell (Johnson)	420
Carnegie-Mellon	399
MIT (Sloan)	391
Washington (Olin)	376
Yale	370
Dartmouth (Tuck)	343
Rochester (Simon)	330
Purdue (Krannert)	285

[a]Number of full-time students in 1993.

are clearly the schools affiliated with the nation's oldest universities, with institutions like Harvard, Wharton (Penn), Columbia, Chicago, and NYU accounting for 22 percent of all MBAs. Business schools obviously benefit from the visibility that a university affiliation provides. Besides the MBA, many of the schools also offer undergraduate degrees in business.

In the mid-1970s, Northwestern and Duke chose to abandon their fledgling undergraduate business programs to concentrate on the more lucrative MBA market. The decision proved salutary. Both schools rode the MBA boom to prominence in the 1980s. In fact, of the schools listed in table 10-1, only two have stuck with their university's core base of undergraduates—Wharton and NYU. In both schools, the undergraduate programs are the lifeblood of the institution. They justify a much larger faculty body and so increase the school's public visibility. Since most of the other top schools specialize exclusively in graduate education, they tend to boast far smaller faculties, a factor that has a significant influence on their identities.

We can identify two contrasting models of business education: a scholastic model and a practitioner model. The two models anchor opposite ends of a continuum, and all of the MBA academies have traditionally leaned more heavily to one extreme or the other. More scholarly programs emphasize the intellectual grounding of their instruction, while practitioner-sensitive programs place higher value on the pragmatic "relevance" of their curriculum.

A school's relative position on the educational continuum affects its activities in three principal areas: (1) the types of faculty hired and promoted, (2) the composition of the curriculum and teaching pedagogy that the faculty rely on, and (3) the kinds of relationships the school maintains with practitioners. Eventually, the model of choice determines the principal character traits of the school that faculty and students come to experience. It also shapes the reputation that schools develop with their key constituencies—especially corporate recruiters and alumni. Figure 10-1 summarizes the typical features of the two opposing models.

THE SCHOLASTIC MODEL

MBA academies that lean more heavily toward the scholastic model favor research-oriented faculty, social scientists whose primary identification is with developing knowledge rather than imparting it. By recruiting social

Figure 10-1 APPROACHES TO MANAGEMENT EDUCATION

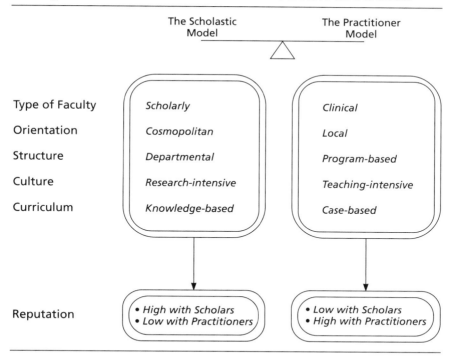

scientists versed in cutting-edge analytical techniques, these schools develop an internal culture dominated by the publish-or-perish mindset typical of mainstream university departments. Not coincidentally, these professionally oriented, cosmopolitan faculty members identify more closely with peers at other institutions than with the cultures of their own schools. They participate with greater interest in a school's doctoral program since that's where they get to discuss scientific ideas and find junior assistants with whom to draft research articles. The result? More limited contact with MBA students and practitioners, whose presence newly recruited faculty generally regard as, at best, incidental to their core scientific pursuits. The business schools of the University of Chicago and Stanford, for instance, owe their reputations principally to the academic content of their programs and the kind of school culture that it implies.

THE PRACTITIONER MODEL

At the opposite end of the continuum from the scholastic model stands the practitioner model, with its main focus on the flagship MBA program.

More practitioner-styled schools hire and promote faculty who show skill and interest in creating and conveying usable knowledge to students. Given their pragmatic interests, faculty often build strong advisory and research ties to the corporate sector and identify in more limited ways with the scientific concerns of more academic programs. The business schools of Harvard and the University of Virginia have both built strong reputations in the corporate world for their leading-edge, practitioner-oriented programs—their proven ability to prepare general managers. In turn, however, both schools have suffered from a lower standing in the academic community. By most measures, their faculties produce less research and have less impact on the development of knowledge about business than their more scholarly counterparts.

FROM PRACTICE TO SCHOLARSHIP

From the founding of the nation's first business school, the Wharton School, in 1881 and lasting well into the 1950s, U.S. business schools were run pretty much on the practitioner model of established professional schools. Just as on university campuses the faculties of the law and medical schools prepared students to practice law and medicine, so were business school faculties expected to train people to manage businesses. Throughout the early years, much of the instruction was vocational and descriptive rather than analytical, aimed at preparing students for industry jobs rather than general management.

As corporations expanded throughout the 1950s to take advantage of the postwar surge in economic growth, critics called for business schools to create and disseminate more scientifically grounded knowledge about corporate life. Reports sponsored by the Carnegie and Ford Foundations recommended improving the quality of business education by building stronger links to academic disciplines like economics, mathematics, and behavioral science. Rather than simply convey information to students, the faculty should extend knowledge through active research and publication and engage students in a process of analytic reflection and problem solving that would stimulate lifelong learning about the world of business.

The reports were highly influential. Spurred by Ford and Carnegie Foundation grants, the major business schools sought to build credibility throughout the 1960s and 1970s by recruiting ever more highly credentialed faculty members from mainstream university departments such as economics, psychology, and sociology. In doing so, business schools departed radically from the models pioneered by the law schools and medical schools, which had built prestige on the practitioner model. The MBA academies sought to model themselves after traditional academic departments, embracing the scholastic, scientific model that favored research over teaching, the ivory tower over the factory floor.

BUILDING ACADEMIC REPUTATION

To develop credibility as scientific research institutions, throughout the 1970s business school deans hired legions of younger faculty that were skilled at carrying out methodologically sophisticated research programs. Working under the publish-or-perish mandate, these academics released their often ponderous research studies to small-circulation, peer-read, peer-reviewed journals and encountered little pressure to interpret their findings for the seemingly forgotten practitioner.

The character of the leading MBA academies was heavily shaped by that total commitment to research. Departments sought to buffer junior faculty from institutional pressures that could divert attention from scientific study and analysis. For promotion purposes—and especially for the all-important tenure decision that young professors normally face by their sixth year in residence—teaching had to be adequate, but merely that. Published journal articles were expected to demonstrate the candidate's facility in carrying out complex research. Everyone assumed that success in publishing obscure academic notes would have greater impact on the reputation of the school than publishing practitioner-styled articles.

To build scholarly credentials, most business schools funded costly doctoral programs that were intended to serve as incubators of ideas. From a managerial standpoint, however, there can be little doubt that doctoral students are costly perks that principally benefit research faculty. Unlike MBA students, who pay (or whose companies pay) their way, most of the top schools write off tuition fees and disburse living expenses for their highly touted doctoral students. Under the scholastic model, however, doctoral programs were considered investments in knowledge creation. Among top 20 schools, only Dartmouth's Tuck School did not offer a Ph.D., for which it was initially castigated. Much later, critics would point approvingly to Tuck for its generalist orientation and chastise deans for not recognizing that doctoral programs are a diversion of both money and faculty time from practitioners' concern with "relevance."

In those heady days of the scholastic model, schools measured faculty performance by adding up the numbers: How many conference presentations had been led? How many books had been written? How many doctoral dissertations had been sponsored? How many awards did faculty research bring in? How many funded grants did the faculty hold? And, bottom line, how many prestigious journal articles had the faculty published? Numbers like these enabled comparisons of schools and departments according to faculty prominence: their productivity, visibility, and stature, in other words, their academic reputations.

One study of the research productivity of the MBA academies counted the number of articles published by faculty members between 1979 and 1985 in the top 18 academic journals devoted to business topics. A total of 125 different schools contributed articles to these journals. Fewer than 20 schools, however, supplied the bulk of those articles. Table 10-2 lists the most prominent schools and the rankings obtained from counting either the total number of articles published by their faculty or the total number of published pages of research. The two rankings differ, largely because the faculty in those schools published articles of differing length. For instance, although NYU's business school published more articles than either Wharton or Chicago's business school, the articles written by NYU's faculty tended to be shorter. Note how highly rated NYU's business school is on this particular measure. I'll come back to this point later.

Another measure of research excellence that had its fans in the late 1980s was derived from looking not at the quantity of articles published by faculty members, but at their impact on the research ideas of other scholars in the field. In recognition of Einstein's dictum that we stand on the shoulders of giants, authors of academic articles always make explicit reference to the papers of scientists who influenced them. By compiling these "citations," it occurred to many researchers that one could assess the influence a particular individual had on a field and, by extension, the contribution that any faculty group had made to knowledge.[2]

At one point, I gathered data on the number of citations received between 1966 and 1990 by a subset of the international community of faculty members who study problems in the management of organizations. Figure 10-2 presents a graph of some of those data. It demonstrates

Table 10-2 THE SCHOLARLY REPUTATIONS OF LEADING MBA SCHOOLS

School	Articles Published[a]	Rank	Pages Published[b]	Rank
NYU (Stern)	203	1	3,997	3
Columbia	195	2	3,512	7
Pennsylvania (Wharton)	185	3	4,890	1
Illinois	175	4	3,277	9
Stanford	173	5	3,899	4
Chicago	164	6	4,210	2
Indiana	152	7	3,597	6
Northwestern (Kellogg)	146	8	3,457	8
Ohio State	144	9	2,855	11
MIT (Sloan)	135	10	2,541	15
UC-Berkeley (Haas)	135	11	2,969	10
Texas-Austin	133	12	2,626	13
UCLA	133	13	2,561	14
Michigan	129	14	1,892	23
Purdue (Krannert)	120	15	2,763	12
Wisconsin	119	16	3,660	5
Washington (Olin)	110	17	2,118	20
Cornell (Johnson)	109	18	1,761	26
North Carolina (Kenan-Flagler)	107	19	1,737	27
Florida	101	20	2,381	17

[a]Based on number of publications in 18 academic journals from 1979 to 1984. See W. W. Williams, "Institutional Propensities to Publish in Academic Journals of Business Administration: 1979–1984," *Quarterly Review of Economics and Business* 27 (1987): 77–94.
   [b]Based on the number of pages published in 14 academic journals between 1975 and 1985. Adapted from A. W. Niemi, Jr., "Research Productivity of American Business Schools, 1975–85," *Review of Business and Economic Research* 23 (1988): 1–17.

the typically skewed shape of the reputational plot that results: Whether artists, musicians, or opera singers, very few people always attract the bulk of the attention—they are the superstars. And so it is in scholarly research. Few business school faculty members achieve celebrity status; most toil for a lifetime only to remain in relative obscurity.[3]

Because extraordinary scholarly success is so rare, business schools tend to build reputation in one of two principal ways: (1) by investing in junior faculty in the hope of producing a "star" (*star making*) or by waiting patiently for researchers at other schools to become "stars" and

Figure 10-2 THE VISIBILITY OF FACULTY IN MANAGEMENT RESEARCH

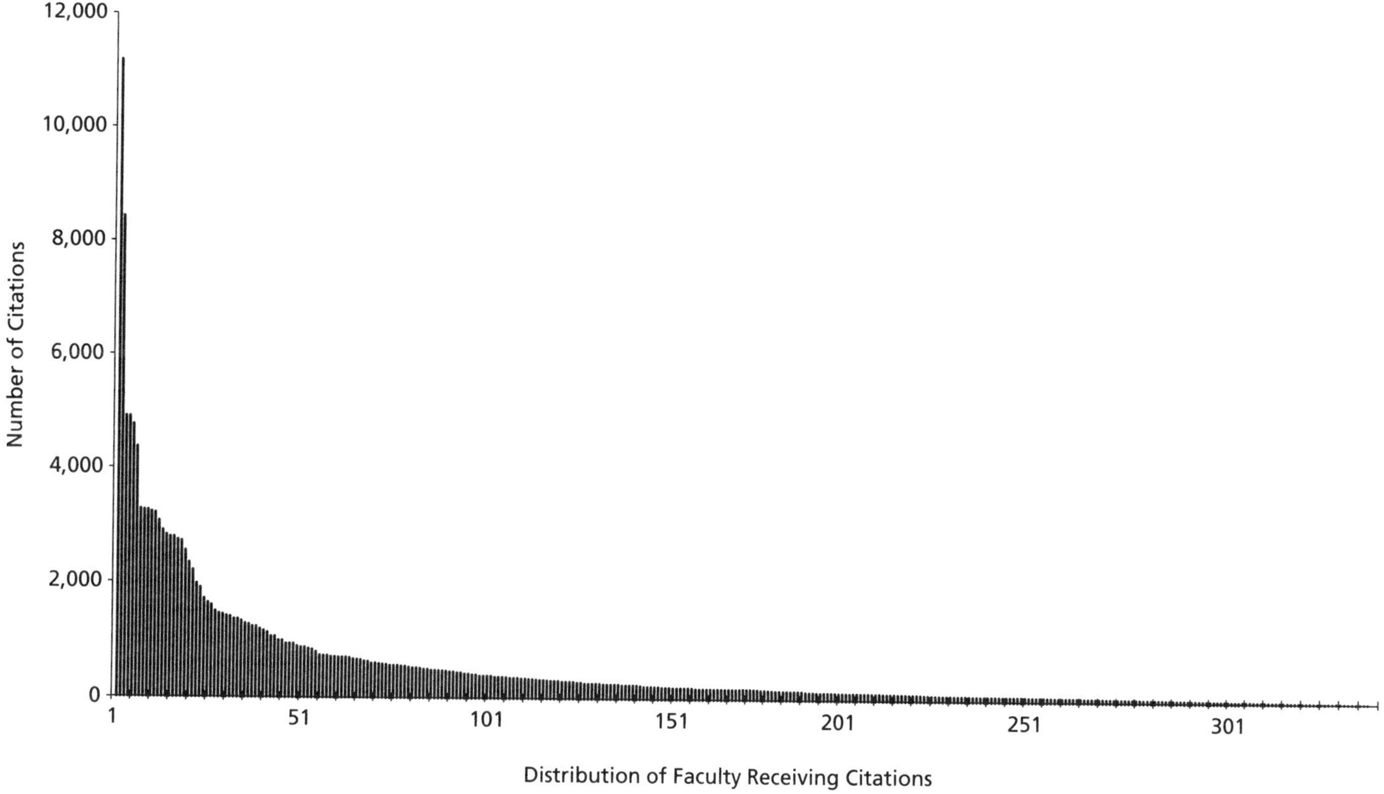

Distribution of Faculty Receiving Citations

Source: Compiled from the Social Sciences Citation Index, 1945–90 (Philadelphia: Institute for Scientific Information).

then recruiting them (*star buying*). Throughout the 1980s, debate raged among faculties and deans about the relative merits of star making and star buying. Some favored the far less certain but seemingly more supportive and humane path of internal development and promotion; others endorsed the safer strategy of building reputation by buying established stars.

By the late 1980s, it wouldn't matter much. The scholastic model was unravelling as nagging questions of relevance were posed ever more insistently by students, alumni, and recruiters. The pendulum had come full swing. As they had been in the early 1950s, the citadels of management education were again under siege—this time by the all-important but forgotten pratitioner.

BUSINESS SCHOOLS BESIEGED

The challenge to which the MBA academies are still actively responding probably originated with a *Harvard Business Review* article of 1980 entitled "Managing Our Way to Economic Decline" (not coincidentally, penned by two Harvard professors). In it, the authors ascribed the rapidly declining competitiveness of American companies against Japanese and German rivals to the preference our managers displayed: "for (1) analytic detachment rather than the insight that comes from 'hands-on' experience and (2) short-term cost reduction rather than long-term development of technological competitiveness."[4]

In those transitional years for the U.S. economy, their comments found a receptive audience. Orders for reprints of the article set a record at the review, lending credence to the authors' conclusions. So much so that, according to Earl Cheit, then dean of Berkeley's well-regarded business school, "within a year, there was widespread support for the conclusion that the nation's competitive problems were in large part attributable to managerial problems, which could in turn be traced to business education."[5] The criticisms boiled down to this: that business schools had become too academic and removed from the day-to-day problems of practitioners, had retreated too far into the ivory tower to be relevant to the concerns of the factory floor. The pendulum had gone full swing since the pre-1960s era when B-schools had been accused of being too vocationally oriented and unscientific in their teachings.

Despite these grumblings, however, few business schools felt any real sense of urgency in the early 1980s. After all, the economy was booming,

graduate salaries were higher than they had ever been, and MBA enrollments were up. Why rock the boat? In fact, not until November 1988
did deans feel their blood pressure rise. That's when *Business Week*
published its first ranking of business schools based on actual surveys
of some 3,000 alumni and 265 corporate recruiters.

The results startled the MBA academies. It wasn't just that the practitioners' rankings did not match the now standard rankings by academic
reputation, it was that practitioner feedback was raising a whole new
set of concerns that business schools had long ignored. By juxtaposing
schools starkly on the basis of client assessments, the rankings forced
faculty and administrators to realize that, unlike most other academic
departments, B-schools would henceforth be competing not for legitimacy in academic circles but for the approval of students and executives.

Table 10-3 summarizes the rankings of the top 20 business schools first
published by *Business Week* in 1988 and then enlarged and replicated in
1990, 1992, and 1994. Most surprising in these rankings was the strong
showing of midwestern schools over traditional bastions of excellence
from both East and West. In an impressive show of reputation building,
Northwestern had seemingly come out of nowhere to overtake the
acclaimed Harvard Business School. In the 1992 rankings, Chicago had
risen to number 2, while Michigan eclipsed top Ivy League contenders
like Stanford and Columbia. By 1994, Wharton was claiming the top
spot, unseating Northwestern and eclipsing Harvard.

Naturally, criticisms of the *Business Week* rankings abounded. After
all, some observers pointed out, business schools have many constituents,
and a business school should not be ranked exclusively on the basis
of what practitioners think. Scholarship and research are also a core
responsibility of the faculty. And there are other constituents to please.
Why should business schools attend only to the concerns of recruiters
and alumni?

Eager to tap into the enormous publicity generated by the *Business
Week* rankings, the competing magazine *U.S. News & World Report*
proposed a rival measure of reputation that sought to balance the perceptions of both academics and practitioners, gauging schools on both
dimensions. The overall measure of excellence also incorporated information about the selectivity of MBA programs, the quality of their
students (as measured by scores on application tests), and the placement
success of the schools. Table 10-4 summarizes the rankings obtained by
the news magazine between 1990 and 1993.

Table 10-3 THE PRACTITIONER REPUTATIONS OF
LEADING MBA ACADEMIES

Rank	1988	1990	1992	1994
1	Northwestern	Northwestern	Northwestern	Pennsylvania
2	Harvard	Pennsylvania	Chicago	Northwestern
3	Dartmouth	Harvard	Harvard	Chicago
4	Pennsylvania	Chicago	Pennsylvania	Stanford
5	Cornell	Stanford	Michigan	Harvard
6	Michigan	Dartmouth	Dartmouth	Michigan
7	Virginia	Michigan	Stanford	Indiana
8	North Carolina	Columbia	Indiana	Columbia
9	Stanford	Carnegie-Mellon	Columbia	UCLA
10	Duke	UCLA	North Carolina	MIT
11	Chicago	MIT	Virginia	Duke
12	Indiana	North Carolina	Duke	Virginia
13	Carnegie-Mellon	Duke	MIT	Dartmouth
14	Columbia	Virginia	Cornell	Carnegie-Mellon
15	MIT	Indiana	NYU	Cornell
16	UCLA	Cornell	UCLA	NYU
17	UC-Berkeley	NYU	Carnegie-Mellon	Texas-Austin
18	NYU	Texas-Austin	UC-Berkeley	North Carolina
19	Yale	UC-Berkeley	Vanderbilt	UC-Berkeley
20	Rochester	Rochester	Washington	Purdue

Source: Rankings are from issues of *Business Week* dated November 28, 1988; October 29, 1990; October 26, 1992; and October 24, 1994.

Clearly, the new measure was more robust. In contrast to the *Business Week* measures, which reflected solely practitioner views, the better balanced ratings of *U.S. News & World Report* produced more stable rankings from year to year. It didn't hurt that the traditionally dominant schools (Harvard, Stanford, and Wharton) came out on top year after year. The new rankings did, however, confirm Northwestern's newfound prominence. Some schools showed marked improvement over the years—Michigan, in particular. Others declined, most notably Indiana and Illinois.

A side effect of the reputational maelstrom started by the two magazines was that it goaded most of the lower-ranked schools into action. Following the widespread distribution of the conflicting rankings, many deans could be heard to proclaim a renewed sense

Table 10-4 OVERALL RANKING OF BUSINESS SCHOOLS

Rank	1990	1991	1992	1993
1	Stanford	Harvard	Stanford	Harvard
2	Harvard	Stanford	Harvard	Stanford
3	Pennsylvania	Pennsylvania	Pennsylvania	Pennsylvania
4	Northwestern	Northwestern	Northwestern	Northwestern
5	MIT	MIT	MIT	Michigan
6	Dartmouth	Chicago	Chicago	MIT
7	Michigan	Duke	Michigan	Duke
8	Chicago	Dartmouth	Columbia	Dartmouth
9	Duke	Virginia	Duke	Chicago
10	Columbia	Michigan	Dartmouth	Columbia
11	Virginia	Columbia	Virginia	Virginia
12	Cornell	Cornell	Cornell	Cornell
13	Berkeley	Carnegie-Mellon	Berkeley	Carnegie-Mellon
14	Carnegie-Mellon	North Carolina	UCLA	Berkeley
15	UCLA	Berkeley	Carnegie-Mellon	UCLA
16	Indiana	UCLA	Yale	NYU
17	North Carolina	Texas-Austin	North Carolina	Yale
18	NYU	Indiana	NYU	Texas-Austin
19	Purdue	NYU	Indiana	North Carolina
20	Penn State	Purdue	Texas-Austin	Indiana
21	Illinois	USC	USC	USC
22	Wisconsin	Pittsburgh	Rochester	Georgetown
23	Rochester	Georgetown	Purdue	Purdue
24	Texas-Austin	Maryland	Pittsburgh	Rochester
25	Ohio State	Rochester	Vanderbilt	Vanderbilt

Source: Rankings are from issues of *U.S. News & World Report* dated March 19, 1990; April 29, 1991; March 23, 1992; March 22, 1993. Based on surveys of business school deans and composite scores on various measures of school selectivity.

of vision, with the specific intent of serving constituents more convincingly. Their comments indicated growing awareness that in an era of declining enrollments and reduced job opportunities, the MBA academies were going to have to compete. They would be doing so based not only on their academic strengths but on their overall reputations with their constituents—with students, alumni, faculty, and practitioners.

THE RACE TO NUMBER 1

The Wharton School has long been celebrated as the oldest center of management education in the United States. As a junior professor there in 1979, I was surprised at how far the school's reputation outdistanced its resources. Until 1984, Wharton's facilities were among the most antiquated of all leading business schools. Classrooms were of the old-fashioned sort, with antiquated furnishings and scratchy blackboard and chalk, and there was an absence of modern technologies like video or overhead projectors. Most of the faculty toiled in small, dungeon-like cells, many of them like mine, physically underground, and students could be seen shuffling down dimly lit corridors to meet with them. If facilities reflect in part the character of any organization, Wharton's identity seemed incongruous with the school's external reputation.

Over the years, Wharton's character would reveal itself more clearly to me. Junior faculty were treated as expendable resources, meant largely for rapid consumption rather than development. As I discovered, the school was principally committed to the "star-buying" model; successful researchers were brought in to fill a growing number of high-status endowed chairs. In the management department, it had been more than 17 years since a faculty member had actually been promoted to tenure.

In 1983, Russ Palmer was appointed dean at Wharton. I attended numerous meetings as a junior professor at which I recall how the former managing director of the accounting firm Touche Ross International (since then absorbed into Deloitte & Touche) conjured up for the faculty a vision of "Wharton #1." His intent was clear: to mobilize support for a campaign that would put Wharton's reputation ahead of those of its leading rivals, crystallized in everyone's mind principally as Harvard and Stanford. To faculty members like me, the campaign rested on two pillars:

- *External image:* The need to increase fund-raising and marketing; to enhance physical facilities.
- *Internal character:* The need to recruit faculty "stars"; to tie rewards to both scholarship and teaching; to make the curriculum more relevant; to produce integrative learning experiences rather than specialist training.

In fact, Wharton was just a small half-step behind Kellogg, the business school at Northwestern that had begun making waves in the late 1970s under its aggressive dean Don Jacobs. The early initiatives of Kellogg and Wharton would soon be imitated around the country, as comparable efforts at reputation building took hold in most of the MBA academies during the 1980s and 1990s.

NEW DIGS, NEW MARKETS

In the mid-1980s, it seemed like every top MBA academy was involved in a major capital project: building new facilities. A deteriorating physical plant at many of the top schools was thought to deter students from enrolling and to reduce the quality of their educational experience. At the same time, B-schools saw an opportunity to capitalize on a booming market for executive education that required state-of-the-art facilities.

If nothing else, the challenge was to keep up with the acknowledged sovereign in business education: the resource-rich Harvard B-School. After all, Harvard boasted the largest endowment by far, estimated at some $350 million in 1992. As a result, the school maintained modern facilities, with tiered classrooms, audiovisual equipment, and a fitness center (including whirlpool) for students. How much ground could lesser schools keep giving up while still charging comparable tuition?

In 1982 Wharton enclosed its antiquated Dietrich Hall in a new building with sponsorship from its high-profile benefactor, Reliance chairman Saul Steinberg. At about the same time, Columbia Business School launched a major extension and renovation of its facilities. Michigan embarked on construction of a seven-building complex that would triple the size of its business school, also adding a computer center and library. Duke's Business School broke the ground for a sparkling new concrete and glass building.

With the booming 1980s, deans also recognized the lucrative opportunities for executive education. The B-schools of Columbia and Harvard already boasted well-established and highly profitable executive programs. Earlier in 1979, Northwestern's school had opened the James L. Allen Executive Center to wide acclaim. Surprisingly quickly, Northwestern's reputation had soared as the school demonstrated its relevance to the 3,000 or so executives it hosted annually. Its midwestern neighbor Michigan quickly decided to follow suit. By 1992, Northwestern and Michigan proved that their efforts had been worth it: The two schools ranked third and fourth behind Harvard and Stanford in surveys of executive programs.

In an all-out effort to capitalize on its name recognition with senior managers, Wharton jumped into the executive education market in 1985. A state-of-the-art center was built that would make money and at the same time exploit the school's high-profile faculty and strengthen the school's links to practitioners. The executive training center might also present other advantages. By supplementing faculty incomes, it would fuse faculty self-interest to the pragmatic interests of companies, encouraging research that was more relevant and credible to executives. From 1986 to 1992, Wharton's revenues from executive education more than tripled, and its program had come to be ranked sixth behind the older ones of Harvard, Stanford, Northwestern, Michigan, and MIT.[6]

The early 1990s marked a second wave of capability-altering efforts by business schools struggling to catch up to their front-running rivals. In 1993, the University of Maryland completed its new building, as did UC-Berkeley and New York University. All three schools abandoned crowded facilities and consolidated their operations on the university's main campus. For NYU's business school, the building was, in fact, the centerpiece of a strategy designed to shake the school's vocational image, born of a large part-time program and the school's roots as a night school to which Wall Street managers once walked from work.

Investments of this magnitude are impossible without major funding. To carry them out, the MBA academies ran major fund-raising campaigns throughout the 1980s. Solicitations to alumni multiplied as schools tested the loyalty of their graduates. Centers for research and chaired professorships proliferated as donors dedicated their gifts to pet uses, particularly to programs in international business, information systems, and entrepreneurial studies. At Northwestern, Kellogg gathered more than $40 million between 1986 and 1989. Between 1988 and 1993, Columbia's business school increased the value of its endowment from $6 million to $35 million. From 1983 to 1990, Wharton tripled its endowment to $90 million.

Newly established outreach staffs pushed business schools to realize the value that high-profile business leaders place on lasting association with a top school. A number of them pursued "naming gifts." Northwestern's business school was named for cereal king J. L. Kellogg. In 1979, it opened its $15 million James L. Allen Center, named for the founding partner of consulting giant Booz Allen & Hamilton. In 1980, for $20 million, Duke's business school was reborn as the Fuqua School in honor of industrialist J. B. Fuqua. Others quickly followed suit. In the late

1980s, Cornell's business school became the Johnson Graduate School of Management in memory of Samuel Johnson of Johnson's Wax fame. Berkeley named its business school in honor of former Levi Strauss chairman Walter A. Haas. NYU's business school was named for its $30 million benefactor Leonard N. Stern, chairman of the Hartz Group.

A school like Wharton, which was among the earliest named schools of a university, obviously could not change monikers. To acknowledge Saul Steinberg, its most recent donor, the school grafted his name onto the new building. In 1982, the ponderously titled Dietrich Hall–Steinberg Hall was born, immortalizing hefty gifts, past and present. By the early 1990s, the leading troika of Stanford, Harvard, and Chicago were among the few to remain "nameless." In 1993, of the top 25 MBA academies, 15 prominently proclaimed their association with a corporate donor. The funds raised through these naming gifts would help both to finance new facilities and to provide discretionary funds with which to make significant changes in the internal identities of the schools.

RESHAPING SCHOOL IDENTITY

Naming gifts, glitzy PR, fund-raising, and new facilities enhance the external image of any organization. They do not alter its identity. Prompted by the inimical environment for management education in the late 1980s, deans initiated internal changes that were designed to alter the core character traits of the MBA academies and to swing the pendulum away from the scholastic model and toward the practitioner model. Table 10-5 describes the fundamental changes that are under way in the capabilities, controls, and cultures of business schools.

At NYU, Stern's vocal dean Richard West conveyed the changes in this way:

The real challenge for business schools after all is not to tear down the research traditions and disciplinary strengths that have developed over the past three decades. Rather, it is to give teaching and education a more equal place in the life of the institution and to avoid the overemphasis on disciplinary purity at the expense of more applied concerns. The objective, in short, should be to have a professoriate whose members are highly adept both as teachers and scholars and whose interests bridge theory and practice.[7]

To achieve that objective, the MBA academies began slowly altering the reward systems that encouraged faculty to dedicate themselves almost

Table 10-5 BUILDING REPUTATION IN THE MBA ACADEMIES

	Change in Capabilities	Change in Control	Change in Culture
FROM:	"Star" research faculty	Promotion based on articles and citations	Scholarship
	Crowded and antiquated facilities	Low communication across departments	Fragmented curriculum
	Low concern for students	Low contact hours with students or practitioners	Fortress mentality
TO:	Faculty good at both teaching and research	Promotion based on both teaching and scholarship	Relevance
	State-of-the-art facilities	Closer interdepartmental relationships	Integrative curriculum
	High concern for students	High contact hours; emphasis on placement	Boundary-spanning orientation

exclusively to publishing in arcane, peer-reviewed journals at the expense of applied research and high-quality teaching. No reward is more visible than tenure in academe. In May 1990, NYU's business faculty voted in a policy that placed equal importance on teaching and research in tenure decisions. It promised to shift priorities in how up-and-coming professors would allocate their time.

With the quality of education now being pushed toward center stage, the MBA academies encouraged closer inspection of the formal instructor ratings gathered after every course, what business enterprises would refer to as customer feedback. Vigorous debate about the composition, validity, and reliability of those ratings animated many discussions throughout the 1980s. Most schools coalesced around summary ratings of the educational experience, and these ratings—already widely publicized among students—became increasingly scrutinized by faculty and administration. To reward teaching excellence, opinion polls were taken; monetary and symbolic prizes were awarded to the most popular members of the faculty.

Little by little, the center of gravity at MBA academies was shifting toward the practitioners. Nowhere was this more apparent than in the metamorphosis of the business school curriculum. By the late 1980s, most schools had created advisory committees composed of faculty, alumni, and corporate advisers. After much analysis, they all made similar recommendations in favor of:

- increased contact between faculty members and student,
- stronger integration across courses and among faculty, and
- redesign of the curriculum to reflect business practice.

In content, the message was also clear: New courses were needed that would explore the "softer" skills of leadership and teamwork rather than finance; that would place more emphasis on quality rather than quantity and cost; that would focus more on technology, change, and cooperation than on economics. It meant that faculty should strive to teach future managers not about narrow specialty areas but about the world of business, one that practitioners saw as an intertwined whole.

To faculty and administrators, conveying holism and complexity intimated a radical change from the specialist orientation of the scholastic era. Organizationally, it signaled a shift toward *integration*—the breaking down of the many walls that the traditional departments of marketing, finance, management, and accounting had erected to protect their specialties. These internal barriers had discouraged joint research on business problems, confused students, and alienated practitioners. It suddenly seemed vital to foster more dialogue across departmental lines and to explore the creation of partnerships with companies. Under the scholastic model, those faculty members who consulted had been widely disparaged as money-grubbers. Under the practitioner model, consulting suddenly appeared immensely attractive as schools saw benefit in encouraging their faculties to build ties to elite consulting firms that might help promote applied research and better prepare students for jobs in that small but highly visible market.

Since taking over the Wharton deanship in 1990, Thomas Gerrity, a former head of the Index Group (now the CSC Consulting Group), has been busy "reengineering" the school, breaking down barriers across departments and encouraging teamwork:

The changes . . . have taken many forms. In the classroom, old semester structures have been flung aside; flexible mini-courses have been introduced;

cross-functional areas of study have been fused together; and leadership, teamwork, innovation and globalization have emerged as recurrent themes in most courses. Outside class, Wharton's 1,550 MBA students and 2,340 full-time undergraduates have been organized into teams to work on academic and field projects.[8]

At Northwestern, Kellogg insisted on building a group culture that rewards teamwork and leadership. Chicago's Business School launched a leadership program with companies like Exxon, Bankers Trust, and Pfizer designed to foster interaction between students and practitioners. Michigan introduced a six-week apprenticeship program that would immerse students in corporate problem solving. Wharton inaugurated week-long integrative learning experiences designed to encourage systemic analysis of complex problems. Virginia's Darden School mustered support from leading companies for an apprenticeship program that involved students closely in corporate projects. All of these pedagogical innovations were designed to tie academe more closely to the world of practice.

Behind the scenes, faculty were also taking part in integrative experiences of their own. Perhaps nowhere more so than at NYU's Stern School, where a radical change in both the curriculum and the culture was launched in the fall of 1993 with elements not unlike those introduced earlier by Wharton, Columbia, and Michigan. The new program had students moving through their coursework in "blocks" of 65. Students within blocks worked together intensively, as did the faculty who taught those blocks. In a sense, it was much like creating smaller, more tightly knit "family groups" or primary units within the school. It served to heighten interaction, in the hope of generating a more intense learning environment and sense of shared experience. On the faculty side, it meant far greater communication across traditionally isolated departments as the school encouraged integrative experience: studying common cases, sequencing assignments, and cross-fertilizing class work. A lot more work for everyone, all around.

A parallel effort was under way on the academic front. During the summer of 1993, for instance, I participated in a retreat that the 27-member faculty of the management department initiated as part of the school's efforts to shift its center of gravity closer to the practitioner model. As these things go, we naturally began by venting our mixed emotions about the radical changes we were experiencing. Anxieties aside, we then turned to building a roadmap for the future. The process looked like this:

- First we identified our key constituents as students, companies, other departments, peers in other schools, and the media.

- Next, we discussed the kinds of resources, relationships, and information linkages we might want to establish to project to constituents a better image of ourselves as a department.

- Finally, we assigned responsibility to individual faculty members for each set of activities.

Ultimately, we committed ourselves to some short-run, incremental actions that might help build up the department's self-image and project it outward. Figure 10-3 summarizes the matrix of initiatives that we felt would accomplish greater integration of the department with the rest of the Stern School and with its key constituents.

Implementation of departmental plans began during the fall of 1993, as we moved into the Stern School's new Management Education Center in New York's Greenwich Village. The faculty had picked a new dean—George Daly, formerly dean at the University of Iowa's business school—to lead the school into the next phase of its reputation-building efforts. When Dean Daly came on board, he articulated his personal commitment to two strategic themes with familiar overtones:

1. *The need for integration:* This was articulated as the need to increase coherence across traditional departmental boundaries—the need to emphasize school-wide, mutually supportive activities that combine rather than dissipate the school's diverse strengths. As Daly told the faculty, one of the Stern School's most fundamental weaknesses is "anti-synergy"—the whole was somehow less than the sum of its parts. "How can we have top departments in finance and international business—the two most popular majors nationwide—yet not be in the top five overall?" he asked. "Somehow these diverse parts of the school have not come together to add up to more than their sum."

2. *The importance of boundary spanning:* This was expressed as the need to link up more closely with the university and with the school's other constituents—the need to transmit a concise, meaningful image of the school, its qualities and its mission.

Figure 10-3 ENHANCING THE REPUTATION OF A DEPARTMENT

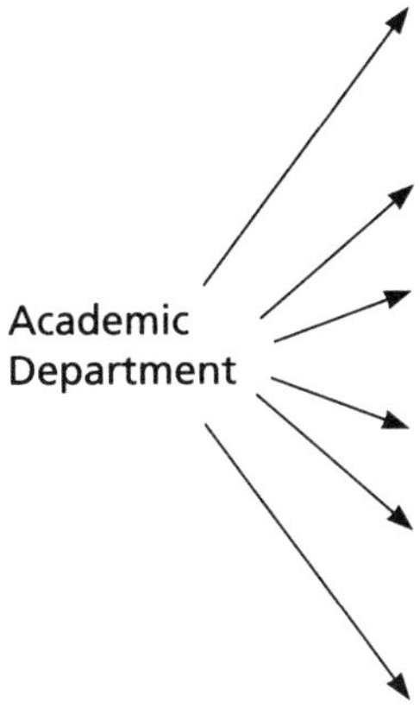

	Resources	Activities	Information
Student Relations	Provide workspace	Create student clubs	Hold seminars Give advice
Corporate Relations	Get research access	Form advisory board	Make corporate presentations
Alumni Relations	Make contact	Create newsletter	Track students' careers
Media Relations	Get access to reporters	Develop PR campaign	Distribute informative brochures
School Relations	Exchange ideas	Hold seminars	Increase familiarity
Academic Relations	Share work-in-progress	Sponsor conferences	Distribute working papers

Academic Department

In February 1994, the Stern School engaged an outside public relations firm—the Dilenschneider Group—to help sharpen its messages and images. Among the first tasks that the Dilenschneider Group undertook was to survey some of the school's constituencies—in essence, perform a reputational audit. The results presented to the faculty in May 1994 suggested that Stern had unclear and inconsistent images among key constituencies. As Dean Daly put it: "To some, it is an incoherent image; to others, because Stern is a new name, it is an unknown image. . . . We have not projected a consistent and meaningful image." Whereas the names Wharton, Kellogg, and Tuck convey strong images to constituents, the name Stern does not.

Time will tell whether the dual objectives of integration and boundary spanning will succeed at bringing coherence to Stern's multiple images and will help to enhance its overall reputation. Looking at it in mid-1995, and from my vantage point in the academy, the strategy seems to be working; external perceptions may be catching up to the reality as we creep up, ever so slowly, in external rankings like those of *Business Week*.

OUTSIDE THE SCHOOL'S GATES

As we head into a new millenium, the leading MBA academies appear to have recognized and addressed head on the challenges posed to them by their critics of the early 1980s. Spurred by competition for status in popular rankings, aggressive deans are hard at work propelling reputation-building efforts and shifting the center of gravity back to the familiar practitioner model of professional schools like law and medicine. Challenges remain, however. They include:

- firmly anchoring a "local" teaching and service orientation in faculty recruited and raised in an era dominated by the more "cosmopolitan" scholastic model;

- building lifelong faculty-student relationships that promote alumni giving and involvement;

- staying adaptable to changing environmental trends that are likely to induce the further rebalancing of the demands from different constituents; and

- ensuring that realistic student expectations are set and met, both during their stay on campus and in subsequent job placements.

So far, luck has been on the side of the business schools. Ominous warnings of declining enrollments have not panned out. Despite the smaller size of the baby-bust generation, MBA applications have continued to increase. The startling surge is somewhat perverse. Although poor economic conditions fostered massive layoffs and decreased job prospects, applicants to graduate programs have actually increased as managers seek ways to improve their future employability. If you combine that with the popularity of the MBA academies among international applicants, you have an offsetting trend: By 1993, foreign students accounted for more than 30 percent of MBA student population.

If a decade ago the Harvard Business School was the tantalizing object of every dean's daydreams, by the early 1990s it was no longer as attractive. In part, it's because throughout the greed decade resource-rich Harvard changed its internal character very little. *Business Week* launched a frontal attack on its MBA program in mid-1993, lambasting the institution for its dinosaur-like slowness to change; its excessive emphasis on competition rather than cooperation; and its failure to integrate international issues into the curriculum. In other words, the business school with the world's largest endowmnent was assailed for resting on its laurels while others had moved aggressively ahead.[9] Harvard's sagging reputation was concretized in *Business Week*'s 1994 survey: The school had plummetted to fifth place.

The assault on the Harvard Business School is likely to carry over to other MBA academies as their parent universities struggle to respond to a real decline in enrollments and to resource tightening. Since 1991, for instance, Harvard's president Neil Rudenstine has tried to unite the university's 11 disparate schools—including the law school, the business school, and the medical school—into a more coherent whole. As he put it, "What we need to do is to figure out how to get more out of what we've got, to coalesce more, rather than to add."[10]

A similar call for greater integration of the business school into the university was made by Columbia's newly appointed president, George Rupp, at his open-air inauguration in the fall of 1993. Rupp told his 2,300-member audience that the challenge for major universities heading into the next century would be to desegregate schools to make better use of the university's limited resources:

There's a real danger that different parts of the institution grow independently. By my count, we have 123 separate centers and laboratories. There simply must be a great deal of overlap. In some areas, there are huge amounts of money involved. We have to learn to get more out of the same investment. We will be pulling people together. . . . The business school will work with the economics department rather than replicate its offerings. The school of public health will not duplicate the investment of arts and sciences in statistics.[11]

Doubtless the next challenge for the MBA academies will be to respond to the pressure for increased integration with their parent universities. For some schools, it could prove debilitating as universities rashly give in to the temptation to plunder the lucrative niches of their professional schools. For others, however, their high-profile progenitors could turn into a rich source of competitive advantage capable of differentiating them more strongly from rival programs. In March 1995, an article in the *New York Times* suggested the progress NYU had made in entering the top tier of universities in the United States. The paper traced the reputational gains of NYU to extensive fund-raising and investments in upgrading facilities, hiring world-class faculty, and raising entrance standards for students.

Ten years ago, New York University was what college-bound students from New York regarded as a safety school, fourth or fifth on their application lists. If you didn't get into Cornell or Brandeis or Brown University, you could always commute to NYU. . . . But the administration, doing some long-range planning, decided that being the safety school was not good enough. So in 1984, it began a brash campaign aimed at moving the school into the nation's top tier of universities. And according to academics around the country who have looked on with envy, the strategy worked. In what was a remarkable fund drive at the time, the university set out to raise $1 billion. But unlike most institutions which plow such sums into their endowments and then live off the interest, NYU spent nearly all of it to rebuild the university.[12]

For the first time in its history, then, NYU's university-wide reputation casts a favorable halo over its member schools. For the Stern School, capitalizing on that halo may be a sound strategy for the future. The best-regarded MBA academies of the future could well be those that succeed in blurring the boundaries that now separate business schools from neighboring professional schools like law, medicine, and engineering. As Columbia's Business School dean, Meyer Feldberg, points out, it is likely that in the continuing contest for reputation, "the strong schools will get stronger and the weak will get wiped out."[13]

In the next chapter, we explore how the identity-shaping programs that business schools are putting in place to build reputation are actually created. To do so, we examine in detail the consulting practice of Lippincott & Margulies, the acknowledged founders of the industry.

In order to create loyalties, the organization has to manufacture the symbols of loyalty: the flags, the rituals, the names. Affirmation of faith must be followed by constant re-affirmation.

—*Wally Olins*
    Corporate Identity

So You Want a New Identity . . .

A COMPANY'S reputation sits on the bedrock of its identity—the core values that shape its communications, its culture, and its decisions. To help companies conceive, develop, and manage their identities, a small group of consulting firms has developed a niche within the larger public relations industry. These advisors help clients develop effective naming practices and counsel them on related reputational matters. This chapter describes identity consulting in general and focuses in particular on the contributions of Lippincott & Margulies, the firm largely credited with initiating the practice. Its work shows how companies benefit from systematic practices that support identity and reputation.

THE IDENTITY MAKERS

Throughout the 1980s, General Cinema Corporation was known as a highly diversified conglomerate with interests in publishing, retailing, entertainment, and financial services. After acquiring publisher Harcourt Brace in the late 1980s, however, General Cinema elected to pursue a more focused strategy, with publishing at its core. In 1992, the company crystallized its reorientation by taking on a new name: Harcourt General. To Wall Street observers, the christening signaled a welcome commitment both to exploit Harcourt's established reputation in publishing and to capitalize on the conglomerate's financial strength.

Not long after Harcourt's rebirth, Korea's largest company—the Samsung Group—celebrated the fifty-fifth anniversary of its founding by unveiling a new identity system to 10,000 of its employees at Seoul's Olympic Park Gymnasium. As Samsung's chairman, Lee Kun-Hee, indicated, henceforth the corporate name would appear in English typeface on all of its operations throughout the world. The clear message was that Samsung intended to unify the disparate identities of its many subsidiaries. A singular corporate philosophy would now apply to all of the company's internal and external activities.

Now consider the Gillette Company. In the early 1990s, the well-known maker of branded products like Sensor razors, Paper Mate and Waterman pens, Braun appliances, and Oral B toothbrushes sensed that its broad portfolio of products was undervalued: "Management felt that the financial community underappreciated the full value of all of the company's consumer brand franchises; the trade underperceived the company's capacity to meet its diverse merchandising needs; and employees and potential employees frequently had too narrow a view of the career opportunities available within the company."[1] Much as Harcourt and Samsung were doing, Gillette embarked on a campaign to strengthen and more systematically project its corporate identity. By May 1993, the company had introduced a new corporate logo (the dynamic G), an identity statement (World-Class Brands, Products, People) that would appear in all of its media advertising, and had adopted a visual design to unify all of its corporate communications.

Finally, take TW Holdings, the company that owns fast-food chains like Denny's, Quincy's, and El Pollo Loco and is also the largest operator of Hardee's franchises in the United States. On June 15, 1993, the company held a ceremony attended by some 1,000 corporate staff and coordinated via satellite with its 119,000 other employees around the country. The purpose? To announce the company's rebirth as Flagstar. Along with the company's new name, chairman Jerry Richardson pointed to a new logo, visual design, and communications plan as key elements that would help to integrate the different subcultures of its subsidiaries. As he put it: "Showing our employees that our future success depends on unity and a single vision for our entire company is a high priority.

Using a new corporate identity to get this message across has proved to be a great way of getting this important job done."[2]

What do Flagstar, Gillette, Samsung, and Harcourt General have in common? All of them benefited from the creative advice of Lippincott & Margulies. Since its founding in 1945, L&M has helped numerous Fortune 500 companies—well-known companies like Coca-Cola, Chrysler, and Nissan's Infiniti division—to crystallize and project their public personas. Common to all the identity programs they create is a three-phase process through which they

1. examine how a company is perceived by its different publics,

2. compare that perception to management's desired perception, and

3. develop a coherent set of identity tools—name, design style, and nomenclature systems that help achieve the desired image while reinforcing the company's corporate strategy.

As environments have changed, as companies have globalized their operations and consolidated their product lines, questions of self-presentation have gained increased attention in the executive suite. By itself, globalization compels a careful analysis of diversity. How do a company's products, brands, factories, advertising, and strategies cohere across regions and countries? To expand more quickly, companies often grow by acquisition—a strategy that multiplies their identities and inevitably raises questions about the values, commitments, and actions of the merged entity. The result: widespread interest in communicating a company's uniqueness through the use of clearly identifiable and consistent names and symbols, in projecting an overall "look" that crystallizes a company's singular identity.

Just as some of our largest companies are growing more aware of the hidden value of establishing and reinforcing their identities, so too are small start-up companies showing a more sophisticated understanding of the images that they project. Lacking the capital to hire full-time staffs and support heavy overhead, many entrepreneurial ventures turn to franchises like Mail Boxes Etc. and HQ Business Centers for help. From them, a start-up can purchase a "business identity package" that provides part-time office space and support services as well as an "image package" that offers professionally designed stationary and business cards. Positioned at the low end of the market, these standardized services enable entrepreneurs to convey an attractive image to prospective clients, to sound big when in fact they are quite small. What these packaged services do for small firms, identity consultants do with far greater sophistication for large firms. They help a company to construct a customized architecture for naming its products and communicating its merits to the outside world.

LIPPINCOTT & MARGULIES, BROKERS OF PERCEPTION

Identity consulting is a lucrative niche that lies at the intersection of advertising and public relations. It typically helps a company in three ways: (1) to assess its external images, (2) to establish the key character traits that top managers want the company to be known for, and (3) to develop a graphical and verbal infrastructure that conveys those characteristics to the company's different audiences.

Most advertisers focus narrowly on creating media messages that will sell a company's products. At the other extreme, public relations deals with the broader strategy of persuading key influentials about a company's merits. Identity consultants dwell on a company's visible symbols and its means of routinely broadcasting its actions, especially at the corporate level. That means developing a coherent package of names, logos, symbols, graphics, and supportive practices to convey the company's sense of self, unique features, and character traits—its identity. This identity appears ubiquitously and without any incremental costs to the company.

Four companies control most of the corporate identity work done in the United States: Lippincott & Margulies; Anspach, Grossman & Portugal; Landor Associates; and Segal & Gale. Of the four, L&M—and particularly its founder Walter Margulies—is widely credited with having invented the expression "corporate identity" and made it a profitable business. Today, the identity business remains distinctly American in flavor, the only other notable outfit being the United Kingdom's Wolf Olins/Hall, a company similar in style and product to L&M.

L&M's early thrust was in industrial design and product packaging. In various meetings during June and July 1994 in his office, Clive Chajet, L&M's current chairman, recalled how Gordon Lippincott, a professor of design, and Walter Margulies, an architect, joined forces:

They got their start in the design business after World War II, when a lot of the hotels that had been requisitioned by the army as facilities for soldiers were returning to commercial use and needed to develop a more attractive image. Gordon and Walter were also involved in the early days of industrial design and product design. According to Walter Margulies, he and Gordon went over to MOMA [New York City's Museum of Modern Art] in the early 1950s and looked at the products that were on display. They were all beautiful, but most of them had been commercial failures. Now Walter Margulies was a business man heart and soul. Why can't industrial design, he wondered, produce not just esthetic success but also commercial success? And so they went to work on products. The Tucker automobile, the subject of the Hollywood film Tucker, *was among the early products that were "styled" by Gordon Lippincott.*

In the 1950s, the rapid growth of mass marketing throughout the United States created enormous interest in packaging. L&M and its key rivals grew the business accordingly, abandoning much of their earlier commitment to industrial design. The rise of supermarkets and department stores called for a substitute voice for the salesperson who used to stand behind the counter. Packaging design fulfilled that role, and what was once a sideline that printers had dreamed up to sell boxes and containers quickly became a full-fledged business. As Chajet recalls:

Walter Margulies was among the first to recognize that packaging design was an enormously important component of business and to argue that we should get good money for it. He founded the Package Designers Council (PDC) as a way to make it a profession—we don't give our stuff away. After all, if accountants, lawyers, and architects can have professional associations, so should package designers. Packaging design became the thrust of the business at L&M, and in the 1960s we were undoubtedly the premiere packaging design company in the world. Just imagine, we did all the packaging design for the world's most famous brand, Coca-Cola. At one point, we had 150 people working for us.

As the art and technology of packaging design grew familiar to corporate America, however, CEOs increasingly delegated the work to product managers and marketing directors. And when packaging turned into a cost item on the profit-and-loss statements of staff instead of management, it meant tighter budgets and less lucrative design opportunities. Consulting companies like L&M sought to diversify away from strict design work. Full-fledged identity consulting came into being when one of L&M's packaging clients, the furniture wax maker Johnson's Wax, came looking for advice. In the 1960s, Johnson's Wax started to diversify away from the furniture wax business. It had bought a company called Metrecal, an extremely successful diet-food product—the Slimfast or Weight Watcher's of its day. According to Chajet:

It occurred to the Johnson's Wax people that their image was not exactly compatible with a health-food product. They are purported to have said among themsleves: "We ought to repackage our corporation. Well, who would you go to for help if not to a packaging company, and to who else but L&M?" So Gordon went out to the magnificent Frank Lloyd Wright headquarters of Johnson's Wax in the Midwest to help them repackage their image. According to Gordon, that was how corporate identity programs began. L&M invented the term and the discipline at that time.

Because identity consulting had the ear of top management, it quickly proved more lucrative than packaging design. CEOs recognized in the concept of "identity" a valuable way to imprint their companies, and so they stayed closely involved with the programs. Naturally, L&M cut back on packaging design, moved aggressively into the identity business, and established a more consultative relationship with clients. At that time, says Chajet, L&M relied heavily on Walter Margulies's strengths in networking with prominent corporate chieftains.

In his heyday, Walter could call the chairman of the board of General Motors and get through. He was very sosphisticated, distinguished; not a salesman type. There wasn't a major corporate identity program that L& M didn't do. We had no rivals in those days. It was a design-driven business. If somebody asked what corporate identity was in those days, it was described in design terms: the logo and how to use it.

From logos and visuals, L&M soon got involved in nomenclature. A name is an important symbol for communicating a company's core values and character traits. According to Chajet, this was a public relations bonanza for L&M:

For some reason, whenever a company changes names, it gets a lot of press. Everybody's got an opinion when you change your name. So L&M became even more famous. We got double favors because we created some of the most famous names in American industry. Throughout the 70s, naming and design dominated the practice of corporate identity. Rivals sprang up. It was a good business, profitable and interesting. Unfortunately, Walter was not inclined to share ownership of the business and held on to it 100 percent, so that many entrepreneurial people left to work for themselves. That's how Anspach Grossman & Portugal started. They graduated from L&M. Many of those rivals did better than L&M. They were more aggressive, more sharing, and more motivating to their key people. By the late 1970s, L&M was at a standstill and had begun to decline as a force in the business. Mind you, it was still considered the Tiffany of the business, but it simply wasn't growing.

By the early 1980s, Margulies's health was failing. With no family members interested in the business, he sold it to Chajet, who until then had been an independent package designer with his own company, Chajet Design Group. As Chajet recalls:

Negotiations were conducted in total secrecy. The deal was to merge Chajet Design Group with L&M. When I finally got into L&M, however, I found only 5 people on staff and about 8 clients, some of which were in litigation with L&M. I went home, thinking to myself: What have I done! I'm in debt up to my ears. . . . The reality, of course, was that Clive Chajet had bought an image. I didn't know it then, but that's the truth: I had bought nothing more than an image. I quickly saw in the first 90 days that it was crazy to have a staff of 20 people to do packaging design, when L&M with only five people was making more money than Chajet Design Group. So I made the difficult decision to get out of the packaging design business entirely. I also recognized that the Chajet name brought nothing to the party, so over my wife's and my mother's objections, I dropped it entirely, kept the valuable L&M name, and got to work matching L&M's reality to its fantastic image.

The 1980s surge in mergers and acquisitions created strong demand for creating new identities and reconciling the new names with existing brands, subsidiaries, and entire companies. For L&M, it meant big-time identity consulting work. None was bigger than the court-ordered breakup of AT&T, the world's largest telephone company in 1983. It created seven new companies, each of which needed to develop and project a unique identity. Chajet recalls how it was a lucky break for L&M:

Walter Margulies was determined that the business would outlive him, that it would be his monument. So he was unstinting in supporting me. In particular, he was very well connected. A couple of months after I bought L&M, the telephone rang for Walter. It was a friend of his on the board of the New York Telephone Company. He tells us that one of the companies to emerge from the breakup of AT&T would be a merger between New York and New England telephone companies, that it would need a new name, and that he'd told them to use L&M. That was the power of Walter Margulies. We got the job without competition. Subsequently, we created the NYNEX identity and its communication strategy—it was the first big break that I got. It also coincided with a great increase in the incidence of mergers, acquisitions, and divestitures. And all of a sudden, those of us doing corporate identity work were in a boom.

By the end of the 1980s, the industry was scrambling for position. While L&M held a premiere position in identity consulting, it faced growing rivalry from its three principal competitors as well as from PR firms and ad agencies interested in doing identity work at the margin. They turned out to be so interested, in fact, that L&M's three rivals were bought by leading advertising agencies: Landor Associates is now owned by Young & Rubicam (Y&R), Anspach Grossman & Portugal by WPP Group, and Segal & Gale by Saatchi & Saatchi. For its part, L&M resisted offers from ad agencies, at least in part to avoid potential conflicts of interest that might develop from doing both identity research and advertising campaigns. As Chajet puts it:

In the late 1980s, service companies become fashionable. The idea came from Saatchi & Saatchi in England, who decided that they would buy ad agencies, consultancies—any service company—for very fancy prices. The fad quickly spread to others like WPP and Y&R. Y&R came up with the "whole egg" idea, which meant that we at Y&R will take on every one of your image needs, whether it be identity, advertising, sales promotion, or you name it.

Friends in advertising also approached us. I thought, however, that L&M would not achieve its potential as a partner with an ad agency. Compared to advertising budgets, ours is a small business and we will never be financially significant. If an ad agency bought us, it would be merely to have us introduce them to the chairmen of our clients. They'd want our contacts. But I never wanted to be a shill for an ad agency. Anyhow, an ad agency would definitely think it understood our business, would want to run it, and I'd hate that.

Instead of lining up with either an advertising agency or a public relations firm, in 1987 Chajet sold L&M to Marsh & McLennan, the diversified professional services company that owns Mercer Management Consulting. Chajet believed the financial resources of Marsh & McLennan would help to forge a link between identity consulting and management consulting:

I liked the concept of Marsh & McLennan. They bought service companies for their own sake, for their inherent value, not for the synergistic benefits they could bring to a portfolio. They also had no interest in running the business, and had a history of leaving their acquirees alone. Six months ago, we merged L&M with the marketing consulting practice of Mercer Management Consulting. I realized that we were playing in a very big league and that, as a standalone, L&M [didn't] have the financial resources to compete on a global scale. By combining with a world-class consulting outfit with offices all around the world, however, with access to talent that we [wouldn't] have to pay for on a day-to-day basis, I felt we would be a strengthened company. What Mercer and L&M together provide is a unique combination of skills. Part of what Mercer does is to create a corporate strategy. There comes a point when corporate strategy needs visual and verbal expression, and that's where L&M comes in.

L&M's link to Mercer Management Consulting also gives it a competitive advantage over its key rivals, which have chosen to partner with ad agencies:

We now have access to the kinds of professionals that ad agencies don't have accesss to. An ad agency's discipline is to solve communications problems through a creative communications response. If a management consultant is faced with a business problem, he creates a business solution to the problem. If an ad agency is faced with a similar business problem, however, it creates a communications solution. When you're dealing with a corporate image, where the reality must match the image, you've got to understand that reality, and only a broad, business-based approach can grasp the reality of the company and its future. An ad agency by definition thinks in terms of short-lived campaigns. Corporate strategies, however, are not short-lived. And corporate identities must not be short-lived. So we've become consultants. What we offer over and beyond management consulting is a creative component to carry out some of the implementation.

Over the years, L&M has worked with more than 2,500 companies on corporate identity programs and has developed hundreds of corporate and product names. Owing to its early start in the business and to prolific output, the company has spawned numerous start-ups and many of its own rivals.

THE ART OF LOOKING GOOD

Professionals in the industry often use the words *identity* and *image* interchangeably, a fact that contributes in no small way to some of the confusion and perhaps skepticism that surrounds corporate identity programs. As the prominent British consultant Wally Olins points out:

> There is no consensus among organizations that purport to practice corporate identity on what it is precisely that they do. The difference between what the various companies in the field offer is startling. So is the difference in their fees. Many of them prefer to emphasize their graphic design role; they offer corporate identity as part of a wide range of services. Others have a more specialized approach to the business and have nondesign consultants on their payroll or available on a part-time basis. What they deliver also differs.[3]

In fact, the term *identity* is probably best used to describe the self-concept of the company's internal constituents—its managers and employees. It summarizes how the company thinks of itself, how it would like to be seen on the outside. Identity is therefore closely aligned with notions of corporate character, personality, and culture. According to Kate Moran, a long-time identity consultant with L&M: "Identity consists of the building blocks of communication, the visual wardrobe. Corporate advertising elaborates on those building blocks, while product advertising uses them to talk about how valuable the company's offerings are to the planet and how they enhance our lives."

On the other hand, *image* is the word used at L&M to describe how a company is actually perceived on the outside. A company may have more than one image (as shown in Chapter 2), and its many images may not be consistent—in which case its reputation suffers. Those images themselves may or may not correspond to the company's self-concept or accurately describe the company's key character traits. The purpose of most identity programs is therefore to influence the coherence of the images that the company projects. Ultimately, identity programs are self-presentations designed to achieve a closer match between a company's inner reality and constituents' perceptions of that reality.

Which is not to say that an identity program is merely a facade, that it can portray false characteristics. As audiences have grown more sophisticated, they have become adept at separating the wheat from the chaff, the real from the imaginary. Which is why a good identity program tries to reflect the reality of the company, not its self-delusions. As Kate Moran says: "We have a savvy, almost cynical audience out there. You need both good performance and good communications. The standards of what the marketplace is looking for are very high, and amateurism doesn't fly anymore."

Despite the apparent diversity of corporate identity programs, most share some basic commonalities. In part, it's because the companies in this business are driven by common pressures: mergers and acquisitions, organizational change, morale issues, market pressure, poor internal relations, recruitment problems, and lack of internal cohesion.[4] In fact, the factors within companies that create perceptions—the building blocks of identity, as it were—are threefold: (1) the constituent relationships of the company, (2) its naming practices, and (3) its visual designs. Jointly, they project the company's persona to outside audiences and create a more or less coherent set of images in the minds of observers.

Figure 11-1 depicts these three drivers of perception. At L&M, for instance, they are in evidence in the official breakdown of the company into three main departments: analysis and planning, naming, and design. Though assigned to different departments, in practice professionals from all three areas work jointly on overlapping project teams, and the company operates more like a loose federation of client-centered projects.

CONSTITUENT RELATIONS

Generally, identity programs are initiated by CEOs who are unhappy about the way their companies are perceived by some key audiences. As an L&M publication describes it: "Perhaps these publics still see the company as it was, and fail to perceive its present performance and future potential. Or they mistake a part of the company for the whole. Or in other crucial ways they misread or misunderstand the company. The concerns of the CEO about the identity his company is projecting and about how the company is perceived are, in many cases, warranted."[5]

To gauge external perceptions, identity consultants conduct a broad range of interviews with a company's key audiences. The interviewers seek to paint as accurate a picture as possible of how constituents perceive

Figure 11-1 APPROACHES TO MANAGEMENT EDUCATION

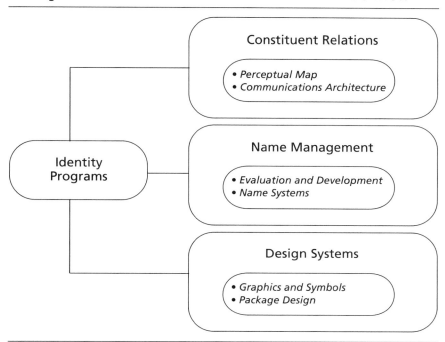

the company, its businesses, its products, and its prospects. A leading consultant describes it this way:

> *The intention behind the interviews is to find out how the organization is perceived by the different groups of people with whom it has relationships. . . . The organization's own employees at various levels of seniority, in varying geographic locations and in different divisions, are selected largely on the basis of the "diagonal slice," topped up with a number of special cases who for one reason or another have to be on the list. In addition, representatives of various outside groups must be interviewed: shareholders and others with a financial stake or interest in the organization, business journalists, financial institutions, customers, suppliers, competitors, collaborators, trade unions, national and local government. Consultants in public affairs, advertising, management, organization, personnel and finance are all appropriate interviews.[6]*

Exhibit 11-1 summarizes key areas that interviewers routinely probe. Most of the time, the data that come out of these sessions are qualitative;

Exhibit 11-1

Questions for Internal Constituents

- *What are the company's key cultural features?*
- *What are its main structural and behavioral attributes?*
- *What is the corporate mission?*
- *What strategy is the company pursuing?*
- *What are the company's key strengths and weaknesses?*

Questions for External Constituents

- *What is the company's reputation in the industry?*
- *Which is better known, the company or its brands?*
- *What are the company's most visible character traits?*
- *How do constituents see the company's prospects?*
- *Are constituents satisfied with the company's performance?*

sometimes they can be quantified. The purpose of the analysis is to examine the diversity of viewpoints put forward. The job of the identity consultant is to cull the data for areas of consistency and areas of difference. Points of convergence and divergence are the backbone of all subsequent discussions surrounding the company's image. "When suppliers, competitors, customers, consultants and financial analysts speak about an organization and its separate parts, different perspectives inevitably emerge. The same story keeps being told, but always from a different point of view. Each version underlines and confirms the others, and gradually the reputation of the whole, and of its individual parts, emerges."[7]

To many at L&M, this is the backbone of the identity business: offering consulting services to companies that are grounded in an analysis of constituents' perceptions; helping clients to better position themselves against rivals in their industry; facilitating the implementation of strategies that require stakeholder support. The newly created link with Mercer Management Consulting is widely expected to enhance L&M's ability to deliver a more broadly based strategic service.

NAME MANAGEMENT

Often a client's changing circumstances require expertise in naming or renaming a product, a brand, a division, or the company as a whole. Some 400 to 800 companies make a name change every year. L&M's naming department provides research and analysis around naming systems. In many cases, a company's products and brands may have proliferated, and it lacks a coherent strategy for tying together its operations. The critical concern is to maximize the value and equity inherent in a brand name and a corporate reputation. That may mean streamlining existing managerial practices and altering the decentralized decision-making process that created so many names in the first place.

Name development takes place in three stages:

1. *Analysis* involves exploring the image and functional requirements of the name, how it should relate to business objectives, and what the sensitivities of key audiences might be.

2. *Creative development* uses individual and group brainstorming to identify a broad range of naming alternatives. Should the name capitalize on existing familiarity? How close should it be to the old name? How much of a bridge should there be to past, present, and future? How suitable is the name to the global marketplace?

3. *Decision making* involves name evaluation based on legal screening, linguistic analysis, and market research. What does the name connote? Is it available? Can it be trademarked?

L&M has been a major force in creating many famous corporate names and logos in the United States. Infiniti, Duracell, and Amtrak are among some of the better known. As mentioned earlier in the book, one of its most successful identity programs was put into place at NYNEX, the $17 billion company that came into being following the breakup of AT&T in January 1984. The fusion of New York Telephone Company and New England Telephone and Telegraph raised serious considerations about the choice of name and the way it would be communicated to its 3 million shareholders, a group accustomed to predictability from years of investment in AT&T. While still regulated in its telephone operations, the new company would be free to expand far beyond its roots as a utility and move into the emerging telecommunications marketplace.

Lippincott & Margulies is widely credited with founding the identity segment of the consulting industry. Illustrated here are some of the now familiar logos that the firm has designed for its clients over the years. (Courtesy of Lippincott & Margulies.)

L&M began by conducting an in-depth study of the landmark AT&T antitrust settlement and its impact on the spun-off operating companies that would keep their individual names. Consultants interviewed telephone company executives and board members as well as members of the financial community. They also studied the company's confidential goals and strategies.

Several management concerns were defined in those interviews. One was to establish a public perception of a reliable telecommunications company. Another was to help the new company's employees understand and appreciate the competitive, market-driven business they were now in. A third was to focus the attention of external audiences on the company's technological leadership in advanced telecommunications. It was also critically important that the new company be favorably positioned in the eyes of the financial community in order to raise capital in the years ahead. That meant earning a high price/earnings ratio on Wall Street. Continued perception as purely a telephone company instead of as a sophisticated, broad-based technological company would place it at an immediate competitive disadvantage.

Discussions with management and analysis of external perceptions led L&M to formulate a list of criteria for the generation of a new name. For one, the name should easily interrelate the two operating companies (New York Telephone and New England Telephone) as well as its service subsidiaries and products. The name should also recognize that the company:

- is a major corporate organization,
- is highly experienced and well managed,
- embraces telecommunications,
- is technologically driven,
- serves the sophisticated Northeast, and
- and has a strong link to its history.

A company report described some of the issues raised during the reputational audit in the following way:

In selecting a name that would meet the particular criteria agreed upon for the company, and that would be distinctive, non-limiting, brief, phonetic, and appropriate—literally hundreds of alternatives were considered. Inclu-

sion of "Bell" in the new name was ruled out. It would have created problems of limitation, suggesting too restrictive a link to telephones and regulated utilities, AT&T, and dated technology. Also it would not distinguish this baby bell sufficiently from the other newly formed regional holding companies who would probably choose to use Bell in their name. NYNEX, the new name created for the holding company, is derived from the initials and geographic designation of the two principal subsidiaries, linking their traditions of quality and dependability to the "new" company. It is non-limiting in the descriptive sense, embracing the spectrum of present and future telecommunications services and activities. And it is a distinctive name in the field of high technology where the coproration's operations are rooted. Appropriately the name ends with an "X," the mathematical symbol for an unknown quantity: the future. The forward thrust of the new company is reinforced by the visual presentation of its new name. The logotype was designed especially to support the marketing and communications strategy developed for NYNEX.[8]

Today, the NYNEX name is used to relate the service and product subsidiaries to the parent company, including NYNEX Mobile Communications and NYNEX Information Resources. Until the NYNEX name was both well established and well regarded, the company chose to retain the names of its well-known phone subsidiaries for local phone service. In January 1994, NYNEX executives finally announced that the company would no longer be using *New York Telephone* and *New England Telephone* as identifiers and would henceforth be known simply as NYNEX in all of its businesses. The identity program was truly complete.

DESIGN SYSTEMS

Along with compiling the perceptions that constituents have of a company, British consultants Wolff Olins/Hall conduct three complementary audits to determine why outsiders have the perceptions that they do:

The communication audit examines how the organization talks and listens, and to whom. The design audit looks at how the different parts of the organization present themselves and how all that relates—if it does—to the presentation of the whole. The behavioral audit examines what it is like to deal with the organization, to come into contact with it in any way. Listening, looking, and feeling audits, you could call them.[9]

Expert communicators examine how the company speaks with its customers, investors, the media, regulators, and lawmakers. They get involved with designers early on by accumulating all of a client's existing communications in print, video, and electronic forms and displaying them on the walls of a large room. As Connie Birdsall, L&M's design director, describes it:

> In a typical project, we'll gather boxes and boxes of materials, a room full of stuff. We'll pin it up on the walls and then analyze the overall effect of the ads, brochures, letterheads, logos, and signage. What kind of images do they project? How consistent or contradictory are the messages and use of identity elements? We'll spend a lot of time studying and reacting to these signals before we actually start doing anything.

Finally, a behavioral audit complements the communications and design audits by looking at how the company deals with different constituents: how it interfaces with potential recruits, addresses customer complaints, responds to services inquiries, and answers phones. Advisors might also investigate, as anthropologists would, the myriad small signals the company broadcasts about itself. At Wolff Olins:

> Michael Wolff, the eminent designer, speaks of a journey through the company starting with an exchange of letters and culminating in visits, in which the consultant monitors everything around him, including the physical state of the reception area, the date and condition of the reading matter provided and the manner in which refreshment, such as coffee or tea, is offered—and carrying on from there.[10]

Throughout the program, designers work closely on project teams with the different kinds of expert consultants needed to conduct these audits. Together they explore ways to visually express a company's main character traits in different media, including print, signage, video, and electronic. They assess alternative forms of expression appropriate to global markets and look for ways to create a cumulative image—a reputation—that reinforces the strengths of the company and helps to correct any unwanted distortions. Throughout the process, the key concern is with improving the reputational profile of the company vis-à-vis its principal rivals, especially in the global marketplace.

WHAT DRIVES CORPORATE IDENTITY?

As even a casual appraisal suggests, companies demonstrate widespread diversity in the identities they develop. Some companies seem weak and fragmented, while others boast a strong and monolithic presence. Some seem downright open, candid, and extroverted, while others appear more guarded and introverted.

In fact, Figure 11-2 shows that corporate identities range along a continuum from monolithic to fragmented. Exxon, IBM, McDonald's, and Coca-Cola are examples of companies with seemingly monolithic identities. Their names immediately convey the essence of their corporate character to uninformed observers and proclaim key character traits for all to see. At the opposite extreme, few of us would immediately associate much of anything with corporate names like Grand Metropolitan, Procter & Gamble, or Church & Dwight. Grand Met is better known for its Pillsbury brands, Procter & Gamble for its stable of branded products like Ivory soap, and Church & Dwight for its popular Arm & Hammer brands of baking soda, toothpaste, and detergent. Their identities are more fragmented than unitary.

Closer examination suggests that three main factors account for the different types of identities that we observe in most companies:

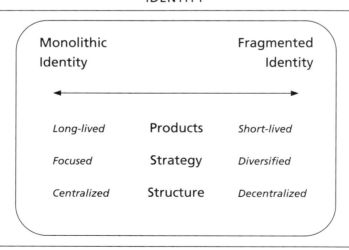

Figure 11-2 TYPES OF CORPORATE
IDENTITY

Monolithic Identity		Fragmented Identity
Long-lived	**Products**	Short-lived
Focused	**Strategy**	Diversified
Centralized	**Structure**	Decentralized

- Product characteristics.
- Corporate strategy.
- Administrative structure.

HOW PRODUCTS AFFECT IDENTITY

Short-lived products benefit more from brand-level marketing than from corporate-level endorsement. That's because they require frequent replenishing. Customers make many small purchases, and product sales depend heavily on advertising and promotion to maintain visibility and encourage impulse buying. Companies in industries that sell soft drinks, fast foods, and other short-lived products—companies like PepsiCo and Procter & Gamble—emphasize their branded labels and evolve a bottom-up identity. According to D. Wayne Calloway, PepsiCo's chairman and CEO:

> We focus on our strong brand names. Names such as Pepsi-Cola in soft drinks; Frito-Lay and its line of snack foods; and Kentucky Fried Chicken, Pizza Hut and Taco Bell in quick service restaurants. We believe that concentrating on promoting our brand names is our best investment. We market Pepsi with a youthful, feisty, aggressive advertising campaign, and we don't mind that kind of image as a company. So instead of a corporate image working its way down, in this case the brand image works its way up. I don't think that telling people that PepsiCo is a wonderful corporation that also owns a lot of other wonderful companies would help us sell any more Diet Pepsi or Mountain Dew or Doritos.[11]

Procter & Gamble is another company that has traditionally emphasized its brand identities. Like PepsiCo, P&G specializes in consumer products with short shelf lives, where the key is to generate many repeat purchases. In recent years, the company has placed growing emphasis on developing its corporate identity. This reflects a recognition of the possible value of generating additional equity from corporate-level familiarity and recognition by consumers, investors, and analysts. According to Edwin Artzt, P&G's longtime chairman and CEO:

> Our traditional approach is changing. Procter & Gamble as a company is fast becoming one of our most important brands. The integrity of the company and its policies and practices concerning the environment, nutrition, the safety of our raw materials and our social consciousness all can

have an important bearing on how the consumer feels about our brands. It is still our policy that our brands must stand on their own feet. But today the image and reputation of Procter & Gamble visibly stand behind them as well.[12]

In companies selling long-lived products, a monolithic identity is more likely to build reputational capital. For large-ticket items such as cars and refrigerators, in which consumers make big investments that they expect will last for years, the GM, GE, or Sony standing behind them creates trust and credibility.

HOW STRATEGY AFFECTS IDENTITY

Reputations and identities reflect observers' interpretations of a company's activities. Companies that operate in multiple, unrelated businesses—conglomerates, for instance—have difficulty establishing a corporate-level, top-down identity. In part, this is because the individual businesses in the corporate portfolio are often older than the parent organization that owns them. The conglomerate Gulf & Western, for instance, struggled for years to establish name recognition on Wall Street. In the end, it failed, and Gulf & Western sold off many of its businesses. By the late 1980s, the company had consolidated its remaining operations to such an extent that it made sense for the company to take on the name and identity of its best-known subsidiary, Paramount Pictures, and emerge from the doldrums as simply Paramount.

Companies pursuing strategies of related diversification—especially those that grow from within rather than through takeover—benefit most from developing top-down identities. They capitalize on the top-down identity and enhance their reputational capital by imprinting each new product line and business with the corporate identity.

AT&T is a case in point. After the breakup of the telephone monopoly in 1984, AT&T lost the use of its trademarked Bell logo and name to its former operating companies. The company worked hard to establish a new identity for itself by imposing the new AT&T name and logo on all of its businesses. Throughout the 1980s and 1990s, as the company extended itself into telecommunications, computers, and financial services, it systematically leveraged its top-down identity. We were introduced one after the other to AT&T Long Distance, the AT&T Personal Computer, and the AT&T Universal Credit Card. In other words, individual brands endorsed by a corporate parent. As Robert Allen, AT&T's chairman and CEO, pointed out in 1990:

> *We changed the structure of our business a year and a half ago so that we now have many smaller business units that are more or less self-contained and focused on specific customers and markets. In making that change, we stressed the importance of the AT&T image and how it could be advantageous to the new units. These strategic business units have a good deal of autonomy, but at the corporate-level we maintain a substantial measure of control over how the brand and the image are portrayed, so that nobody damages them to the detriment of everyone else. . . . I don't think we could sell an AT&T car or potato chips. We should use that name in connection with what we know best and do best. An AT&T Universal Card is an extension of that because we have the Calling Card. As we add products to that card in the future, they should be related to technology and information services. I wouldn't want to use the AT&T name for products and services that don't fit our heritage and tradition and don't normally fall into the concept of what the brand means.*[13]

Like their AT&T parent, most of the former Bell operating companies have also tried to establish monolithic corporate identities. Like Bell-South, Ameritech, and Bell Atlantic, NYNEX identifies all of its subsidiaries with the corporate emblem. This reflect efforts by NYNEX to enhance its reputational capital as it diversifies into technologically related businesses in telecommunications.

How Structure Affects Identity

Top-down identities are more difficult to create and manage in companies with decentralized administrative structures. If most key decisions are made at the level of the subsidiary, the corporate-level controls are necessarily weak and compliance with an identity program is difficult to enforce. In other words, companies that develop monolithic identities tend also to develop more centralized administrative structures.

Some companies have tried to mix the monolithic and the fragmented identity models. General Motors and United Technologies, for instance, tried for many years to capitalize on the benefits of both. Between 1920 and 1980, GM used its corporate-level umbrella identity to endorse five major car divisions: Chevrolet, Pontiac, Oldsmobile, Buick, and Cadillac. At the same time, each car division differentiated itself in the marketplace in both price and quality, supported by an elaborate identity system. In similar ways, United Technologies developed a corporate-level identity in the 1980s (with the help of identity consultants Lippincott & Margulies) that would take advantage of synergistic relationships among the related businesses in its portfolio. At the same time, it promoted the distinct identities of its decentralized subsidiaries with customers: Otis Elevators and Carrier Corporation's air conditioners are among its better-known brands. As one commentator says:

> General Motors and . . . United Technologies reorganized their huge structures, with their multiplicity of names and identities, in such a way as to achieve coherence. Where the group strength was required—in purchasing, senior recruitment, research and development, government relations or relationships with the financial community—they presented the whole; but when individual companies needed to express their own identities—in relation to their customers, their collaborators, the local community—they could do that too.[14]

Results are mixed for these endorsed models. Over the years, it has proven difficult to maintain a balance between monolithic and fragmented identity systems. At GM, for instance, the purchase of EDS and the launch of its Saturn small-car division has fostered a more fragmented identity system than ever before, one that has undermined the company's reputational capital.

IN SEARCH OF IDENTITY

Identity systems are important tools for a company to use in developing a coherent sense of self and communicating it to the world. If properly developed, they put forth the company's most attractive character traits and improve our ability as outsiders to understand what the company is up to. By helping us to pierce the barrier behind which most companies hide, they reduce skepticism about a company's operations, intentions, and performance.

At the same time, identity systems are an important set of controls that can help a company to build shared values, mobilize employees around a common vision, and hence mitigate the kinds of crises that arise from rogue behavior. As Gordon Lippincott, one half of the founding team at Lippincott & Margulies, observes:

> Unless a company manages its image as professionally and systematically as it manages any other valuable business asset—with standards of account-

ability across all business lines, in all areas of operations, throughout the organizational ranks—the value of that asset will depreciate, along with the company's ability to achieve its business objectives. . . . Image management programs cannot make weak companies strong, mask unethical practices or actually prevent management from making stupid decisions. What they can do is help prevent decisions that appear harmless when made but that can, years later, generate image-damaging headlines around the world.[15]

That's the kind of work L&M continues to do for prominent companies around the world. It's at the heart of managing reputation in companies as diverse as consumer-goods makers Church & Dwight and Procter & Gamble and premier service firms like Goldman Sachs, J. P. Morgan, and McKinsey & Company.

Remember that green is magic . . . and the color of your money is green. Use your green magic as if the fate of our planet depends on the decisions you make every day. It does.

—*Senator John Heinz (R-Pa.)*

Pitching Arm & Hammer

MAKERS OF consumer products like Procter & Gamble and Unilever have extensive experience in managing brands. Success with branded products, they insist, depends on persistent and savvy marketing, advertising, and promotion. The fervent belief in the merits of advertising explains why every year companies spend over $200 billion in promoting their products through the media.

To Church & Dwight, the makers of Arm & Hammer baking soda, advertising goes only so far. Rather than merely advertise, at Church & Dwight some forward-thinking managers advocate growing involvement in direct relationship building with the company's key constituents as an effective tool for promoting the brand. They argue that forming win-win partnerships with key constituents creates and disseminates positive images of the company that translate more effectively into sales than diffused advertising.

Partnering with constituents also helps to strengthen the brand. In recent years, Church & Dwight has effectively capitalized on its famous Arm & Hammer brand of baking soda to diversify into other product categories. This chapter examines the innovative alliances created by

Church & Dwight, particularly those that helped tie the Arm & Hammer brand to the environmental movement. Their success provides valuable insight into alternative means for creating economic value through systematic reputation management.

AWAKENINGS

In the late 1960s, the Church & Dwight Company was a small and sleepy family-run business with about $15 million in revenues. A single product accounted for most of the company's sales: baking soda, sold then as now in the small yellow boxes with the red, white, and yellow Arm & Hammer logo. Today, less than 25 years later, Church & Dwight racks up an impressive $500 million a year in sales of products as diverse as toothpaste, laundry detergent, and industrial cleansers. To what can we ascribe its startling growth?

From all accounts, Church & Dwight's success results from equal parts strategy, luck, and consistency. Since 1969, the company has benefited from the leadership of Dwight Minton, a direct descendant of the company's original founders. When he assumed the presidency in the late 1960s, he helped to articulate a growth strategy that was designed to leverage the Arm & Hammer brand name. Over the years, Church & Dwight would diversify more or less consistently into areas that capitalized on its identity as "the baking soda company." Rather than scatter the company's limited resources, as so many others did during the conglomeration and deal-crazed decades of the 1970s and 1980s, Church & Dwight diversified into products and markets that were more directly related to its core competence in sodium bicarbonate.

Over the years, the company also benefited from good old-fashioned luck when it stumbled into various related markets for baking soda and washing soda, used along with soap in doing laundry before the development of modern detergents. Probably none proved more productive than the niche created by mounting social concern about the environment. No one had predicted it, no one had anticipated it. Yet, as many consumers grew increasingly concerned about the nefarious effects of chemical additives in commercial detergents and household products, they turned to the mild and relatively harmless alternatives of washing soda and baking soda.

For Church & Dwight, it was a lucky stroke. As consumers flocked to the company's benign products, they encouraged its senior managers to recognize the environment as a social issue, and to shape a strategy and image that would address it. The result? In a relatively short time, Church & Dwight built a corporate reputation centered around the environmentally friendly features of its versatile core product—baking soda. These features now anchor public perception about Church & Dwight's products among employees, consumers, regulators, and investors. And more than any other single factor, the company's environmental reputation now takes center stage in animating, motivating, and guiding strategic decisions. As Bryan Thomlison, Church & Dwight's director of public affairs, points out: "Our corporate reputation has become a competitive advantage for us in the marketplace. For instance, few people realize that we compete head on against Unilever and Procter & Gamble, each of which is 50 to 70 times larger than we are. Yet we've repeatedly made inroads against these giants because we've been able to build trust in our products and capitalize on our reputation with the right consumers."

The role Thomlison plays at Church & Dwight is far broader than that of a traditional director of public affairs. Not only is he responsible for corporate philanthropy and environmental management, but he also oversees employee communications, government relations, media relations, and public relations. His role in the company therefore closely resembles that of chief reputation officer, as discussed in chapter 8.

To help Church & Dwight manage its reputation as an environmentally responsible company, public affairs relies on a "stakeholder-relations" model that is entirely consistent with the reputation-management models discussed throughout the book. It involves:

- identifying groups with a vested, often ideological, interest in seeing Church & Dwight outperform its rivals,

- exchanging information with key influentials who shape informed opinion on environmental issues,

- forming partnerships with stakeholder groups to achieve mutual goals and, ultimately, generate positive word of mouth, and

- coordinating internal efforts and expenditures to produce consistent images of Church & Dwight on the outside.

Although Church & Dwight now strategically links its products to environmental issues, the company could just as well have identified itself with some other critical social concerns. In the rest of the chapter, I examine the company's general approach to creating reputation and economic value. Its experiences should prove valuable to managers interested in helping their own companies derive value from building relationships with key constituents and tying their reputations to a strategic issue.

THE GREENING OF BAKING SODA

In 1846, Dr. Austin Church developed a method to convert soda ash into bicarbonate of soda and, with his brother-in-law John Dwight, founded a company to make and sell the now familiar baking soda. In the early years, the compound was used primarily as a leavening agent in baked goods. Over time, however, it would prove to have an ever-widening array of uses in food products, in personal care, and in household and industrial cleaning. The highly recognizable red, white, and blue Arm & Hammer logo was first developed in 1867. Today it is a key identity element and appears on virtually all of the company's products.

When Dwight Minton, a fifth-generation descendant of Austin Church, took over as chairman of Church & Dwight in 1969, he set the company off on a growth strategy that would essentially build on the environmentally oriented tradition of his predecessors. As he points out, however, using "the environment" was not planned a priori. Rather, it resulted from opportunistic reaction to an emerging social issue:

> The "greening" of Church & Dwight first crystallized in 1970. We had already started long-range planning, but our plans made no mention of the environment. A young and inexperienced maangement team thought our then-existing business to be at the end of its life-cycle. Innovative new products and acquisitions were the way to go. . . . Operating earnings in the late 1960s came from baking soda and an old-fashioned product called washing soda. In its heyday, washing soda had been a normal companion to laundry soap. This was the way washing was done before phosphate-built synthetic detergents were developed.
>
> Much to our surprise, washing soda sales reversed a long decline and started to grow rapidly. We hadn't a clue as to why, but were smart enough to go ask our customers. Concern that excessive phosphorus was damaging our lakes and streams had started a movement back to traditional soap and soda. At the rate Arm & Hammer Super Washing Soda was growing,

*we could project that it would soon overtake Arm & Hammer Baking
Soda! We enjoyed the current earnings effect, but quickly concluded that
consumers would not long tolerate the inferior washing results achieved
with soap and soda. Our next thought was therefore opportunistic. Let's
make a nonphosphate detergent to meet this demand. We and several score
other companies had the same brilliant idea. We are the survivor.*"[1]

The opportunistic reaction to growing concerns being expressed about
the environment proved fortunate. Church & Dwight entered the nonphosphate laundry detergent market in 1970. Despite fierce rivalry from
Procter & Gamble and Unilever over the years, by 1993 Arm & Hammer
could lay claim to more than $200 million in annual sales of laundry
detergent—having displaced Colgate as the #3 "soaper."

The result was impressive, if only because Church & Dwight achieved
it with far less marketing spending than its rivals. Table 12-1 reports a
comparative study of advertising expenditures per market share point
gained and shows how much Church & Dwight was able to capitalize
on its brand-equity and environmental reputation to drive sales of its
laundry detergent.[2]

Church & Dwight would subsequently repeat that strategy in other
related markets. In 1988, the company introduced a toothpaste with
60% baking soda. Here, too, the Arm & Hammer brand name and
trusted reputation enabled rapid market penetration with far less advertising expenditure than rivals were forced to make (Table 12-2). Indeed,
consumer tracking data showed that in less than five years, the Arm &

Table 12-1 REPUTATION AND DETERGENT SALES

Company (Brand)	Millions $ Spent in Ads per Market Share Point
Church & Dwight (Arm & Hammer)	$0.09
Dial (Purex)	0.80
Procter & Gamble (Tide)	1.60
Colgate-Palmolive (Fab)	1.80
Unilever (Surf)	2.20

Data compiled by the public affairs department of Church & Dwight. Based on
information from *LNA, Advertising Age,* and *IRI.* Data for the detergent category
are averages of 1991 and 1992.

Table 12-2 REPUTATION AND TOOTHPASTE SALES

Company (Brand)	Millions $ Spent in Ads per Market Share Point
Church & Dwight (Arm & Hammer)	$1.20
Colgate-Palmolive (Colgate)	2.60
Procter & Gamble (Crest)	4.70
Chesebrough-Pond's (Mentadent)	15.30

Data on toothpaste reflect average annual advertising expenditures for 1989–1992 for each 1993 market share. All data for P&G are for 1993 only.

Hammer name had captured an estimated 10 percent of the U.S. market against fierce competition.

Besides diversifying into new consumer product areas, Church & Dwight has also moved aggressively into industrial products. Among the many uses to which bicarbonate could be put, four key product areas have been uncovered: animal feed; industrial cleansers; agricultural fungicides; and pollution prevention and environmental remediation. For many years, Church & Dwight has supplied sodium bicarbonate to the animal feed market. It is given to dairy cattle, for instance, to improve digestion of higher-energy foods and to increase milk production. This has been the largest use for baking soda. The company's expansion to industrial cleansers is more recent and involves product extensions into more than 300 markets.

Church & Dwight's Armex, for instance, uses a water-sodium solution that is blasted onto various surfaces—much like low-pressure sandblasting—to remove paint and corrosion without damaging underlying materials. Armex was originally developed to remove layers of tar and paint from the Statue of Liberty during restoration before its 100th anniversary. The development of another cleanser, Armakleen, was inspired by a dinner conversation with members of an environmental group in late 1990. One of Thomlison's guests made the suggestion that Church & Dwight produce a cleanser to substitute for CFCs and other environmentally harmful solvents used to clean electronic circuit boards. As Bryan Thomlison recalls:

We took this idea generated by one of our stakeholders back to our scientists. Within 18 months we introduced a proprietary technology covered by several patents. Of course, our environmental friends received a substantial fee. But the real point here is that we came up with a product that we simply would never have created if we hadn't been out of our offices talking to people with a different perspective on life. Product innovation is just one of the many benefits of stakeholder sharing.

Most recently, Church & Dwight has been finding new uses for bicarbonates as alternatives to traditional pesticides in organic and commercial agriculture. And the company has put bicarbonates to use in various technologies that remove lead and other metals from drinking water and replace solvents used in cleaning precious metals. Bicarbonates have even been used to neutralize a lake that had been damaged by acid rain.

Jointly, these product applications move Church & Dwight more forcefully into the environmental arena. Not coincidentally, it's estimated that 95 percent of all Americans now have at least one Arm & Hammer product in their homes. Consumer surveys also show that the Arm & Hammer name and logo have a 92 percent recognition factor, making it one of the strongest and most enduring franchises in the United States. We now examine more closely how Church & Dwight has managed the Arm & Hammer name in recent years.

NETWORKING ON ISSUES

Key to coherently managing a company's reputation is a centralized corporate role vested with broad responsibility for relating to the company's diverse constituents. As previously mentioned, Church & Dwight created just such an innovative position under the title director of public affairs. Since 1991, Bryan Thomlison has been the company's point man on reputational matters. As director of public affairs, Thomlison is fully responsible for all constituent relations, including pollution prevention, environmental outreach, corporate philanthropy, employee communications, community relations, government relations, and PR. He reports directly to chairman and CEO Dwight Minton as well as to the presidents of Church & Dwight's two main divisions: Arm & Hammer, which sells consumer products, and specialty products, which develops and markets the company's industrial products.

At Church & Dwight, it is difficult to untangle the person from the role. Indeed, it would not be wholly inaccurate to say that Bryan Thomlison *is* public affairs—the head of a lean operation with a total annual budget of less than $2 million for managing all constituent relations. Among the more attractive features of Thomlison's background is his extensive experience in sales and marketing. Having worked at both Procter & Gamble and Unilever, he understands firsthand the aggressive but more traditional marketing approach of Church & Dwight's two chief rivals in consumer products. He can therefore speak the language of marketing and counterpose it to the potential benefits of alternative strategies for reaching consumers and other constituents.

A critical problem facing a reputation manager, however, is the lack of a clear bottom line. Unless the building of constituent relationships is measured on the same yardstick as other forms of promotion, it will not have access to sizable budgets. As Thomlison points out:

> *Constituent relations is generally considered "do good" work. For example, in the United States, the total funds allocated to corporate philanthropy is only $6 billion—a drop in the bucket when you contrast it with the $200 billion that corporate America spends on product advertising and promotion. . . . What we've shown—and what we're trying hard to continually verify at Church & Dwight—is that for every dollar we spend in constituent relations, we generate $10 in sales. This ROI changes the stature of our programs in the eyes of our top management. We now have access to a larger pool of resources. Imagine if others followed our lead; corporate philanthropy managers would be more likely to tap into the $200 billion and would no longer have to settle for the crumbs.*

To Thomlison, then, networking with key influentials is a far more cost-effective strategy for reaching consumers than is direct advertising when the objective is to build corporate reputation. At one of our meetings, he recalled how in 1989, as marketing director for Church & Dwight in Canada, he had successfully driven Arm & Hammer Super Washing Soda into a market leadership position, usurping the dominance of Bristol-Myers's number-one-ranked product. As Thomlison argues, he achieved the win not through traditional advertising but by developing a third-party endorsement campaign, hand-in-hand with a network of environmental stakeholders:

> *At the beginning of 1989, Arm & Hammer's Super Washing Soda was the number 2 brand behind Bristol-Myers's Bleach for the Unbleachables, a brand that held a 40 percent share in Canada. By mid-1990, Arm & Hammer became number 1 in the segment while Javex dropped to less than a 30 percent share. The interesting thing was this: In 1989, I pulled all the advertising dollars away from our brand and put it all into a third-*

party endorsement campaign involving a multitude of stakeholder organiza-
tions and influentials. They helped us to promote baking soda and washing
soda as alternatives to the other household cleaners.

For instance, we ran a free-standing insert on washing soda, one corner
of which we donated to an environmental group. They used that space to
promote their own book, one which had many references to the benefits
of baking soda and washing soda. Now our ad copy had nothing to do
with the environmental organization, but the juxtaposition of the two told
an environmental story.

We also worked closely with authors and broadcasters, helping them
verify information about baking soda and giving them access to our
R&D staff. We got a lot of extra media attention because of that. It gave
us free exposure and was far more effective in driving the brand than any
direct advertising would have been on its own.

That early success in Canada with both baking soda and washing soda
was instrumental in getting me brought down to our headquarters in
Princeton [New Jersey] and in making the environment a driver for our
products.

As pointed out in chapter 6, researchers confirm that networking with
key influentials can be an efficient strategy for reaching consumers.
That's because research shows that people form their own opinions
about products and companies through a trickle-down process in which
respected leaders help to shape the ideas conveyed to wider audiences.[2]
As numerous studies have confirmed, few people in a country set policy;
most people simply follow. Moreover, within a particular issue area, an
even smaller clique of primary gatekeepers shapes the opinions of others.
Thomlison recognizes that simple fact, and tries to use it:

Take the issue of household hazardous waste. There are probably only a
few hundred people around the country who are gatekeepers on this issue.
They're the ones who are influencing and formulating policy in Washington
and in the different states around the issue. If we want to affect public
opinion on the issue, they're the ones we need to reach. Having close contact
with thought leaders enables us to do that. They help us fan out into an
issue-related community and discover its key concerns as well as explore
ways for addressing them.

With these ends in mind, public affairs at Church & Dwight maintains
an active database of some 3,000 key influentials—writers, legislators,
educators, scientists, advocates, and other opinion leaders—in various

issue areas, but especially in environmental issues. The network helps the public affairs staff to assess the impact of a possible corporate initiative, to mobilize supporters for a cause that's of mutual interest, or react to threats from rivals that encroach on Church & Dwight's business. For instance, when the company's marketing staff recently proposed substituting a certain low-cost but more harmful chemical to one of Arm & Hammer's laundry detergents, public affairs opposed the recommendation based on a poll of key influentials who uniformly opposed the additive on health grounds. Rather than betray the accumulated trust between Church & Dwight and its stakeholders, the company opted against the additive.

In and of itself, the company's database of key influentials constitutes a prime market for Church & Dwight's products. Research by Cone Communications indicates that key influentials generally tend to be:

- "greener" than most other consumers,
- more active in their communities,
- early adopters of products,
- more likely to recycle,
- more active participants in more environmental issues, and
- opinion leaders—they whisper to others what to do.

Not only are these opinion leaders key consumers of the company's environmentally oriented products, but they also provide an early warning system for understanding consumer preferences, trends, and other signals from the marketplace. Calling on them before making a strategic decision can help prevent a company from making strategic mistakes.

A case in point concerns the poor results the company experienced in 1994. Much of the downturn can be traced to the public beating Church & Dwight took in the market for liquid laundry detergent when it opted to move to a more concentrated product in a smaller bottle. Archrival Procter & Gamble did not follow suit, and the Tide brand products P&G sold in larger containers drew market share away from Church & Dwight. Consumers mistook Church & Dwight's smaller size for fewer "uses," failing to recognize the environmental benefits of the smaller containers. To Bryan Thomlison, the strategic mistake was one of failed communication. He suggests that if management was determined to lead P&G into the more concentrated product market,

Church & Dwight should have called on its network partners earlier for support in launching the new product. This might have increased the likelihood of success. At this point, he sees the role of public affairs as that of mobilizing support for the concentrated form, especially from

In an effort to capitalize on the environmentally friendly attributes of its products, Church & Dwight reaches out to consumers and investors through a variety of stakeholder programs. Pictured here is a display that the company prepared to showcase the positive environmental properties of its products for Earth Day. (Courtesy of Church & Dwight.)

environmental and consumer groups, which are more likely to recognize its ecological value at smaller size in terms of conservation of natural resources and reduction of waste.

REACHING OUT TO STAKEHOLDERS

Who are Church & Dwight's stakeholders? Who should the company contact to promote its products? They are of two sorts: *internal stakeholders*—the company's shareholders and employees—and *external stakeholders*—customers, vendors, and regulators, educators, environmental and other advocacy organizations, industry associations, media, and community groups. As Thomlison recalls, he initially worked on building a supportive internal constituency for his public affairs department; then he tackled a variety of external considerations:

> *When I came on board, I did a series of things; First, I interviewed all the vice presidents, directors, and managers throughout the company. From those interviews, I lined up the key internal stakeholders—the folks from R&D, purchasing, manufacturing, marketing, etc., whose support would be critical to moving ahead in linking product development with the environment. Second, I hired a PR firm that could put a green team in place. Since I was coming from Canada, I knew I needed the resources of a large firm that could get me assimilated into the U.S. context quickly. Burson-Marsteller stood out from the others who pitched us because they put together a core "green" team headed by a former Jesuit priest. Third, I asked Burson-Marsteller to prepare an environmental binder for the executive committee of Church & Dwight that would bring them up to speed on the importance of the environment—the key issues and players involved in household cleaners, household hazardous waste management, and other environmental concerns. It had to be informative, yet readable in two hours.*
>
> *We then worked with our sales management to coordinate "top-to-top" meetings with leading U.S. retailers. Our seven-member executive committee fanned out across the nation and met with the most senior executives of our customers, inviting a partnership with Church & Dwight around the issue of environment. On a parallel track, we met with leading environmental advocates, regulators, and educators to gain an understanding of issues, opportunities, and mutual goals. Within six months we crafted our communications strategy around the theme "multistakeholder partnerships for environmental education." We kicked it off on two fronts: internally, we infused the environmental ethic into our quality management process; externally, we ran a retail merchandising program and a consumer commu-*

nications campaign that were integrated with the resources of participating retailers, environmental groups, and the print and broadcast media. Just as we were introducing the program to the trade, Ad Week's Marketing Week *magazine, I recall, ran a cover article describing the program. On the basis of that article and prior to a call from our sales reps, in January 1991 Kmart phoned in the single largest order in our company's 149-year history. It was so large, we had to scale it back by 50 percent because we simply did not have the stock on hand in the time required.*

Contacts beget other contacts. As a result of those early efforts to mobilize support internally and meet with key stakeholders externally, Thomlison was invited to join the planning committee for the U.S. Environmental Protection Agency's annual conference on household hazardous waste management. The purpose of the committee was to set the agenda for the conference. Committee members represented trade associations, regulators, companies, and advocacy groups involved in disseminating information on issues related to household hazardous waste. As he recalls, being a member of the committee was invaluable: "Membership really brought me up the learning curve quickly about these issues in the U.S. It also connected me with a lot of key influentials. From then on, my personal stature, knowledge, and involvement mushroomed. Church & Dwight became a visible player in the whole arena of household hazardous waste and the setting of public policy around the issue."

Spurred by its entrepreneurial public affairs group, Church & Dwight now actively targets each of its key constituencies in an effort to create win-win relationships. Figure 12-1 presents some of Church & Dwight's key reputation management programs and their activities in 1994.

- *Pollution prevention:* Identified ongoing opportunities and disseminated information in partnership with the engineering, law, and facilities management departments.

- *Employee communications:* Produced "Hammerings" (the company-wide newsletter), "Environmental Solutions" (the annual employee update on their pollution prevention and waste-management initiatives), and various publications designed to reinforce the environmental ethic.

- *Public relations:* Coordinated an information "news bureau" campaign through several outside agencies, each with particular

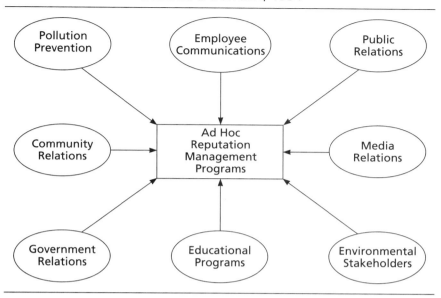

Figure 12-1 REPUTATION MANAGEMENT PROGRAMS AT
CHURCH & DWIGHT, 1994

strengths in different sectors—consumer press, industrial press, knowledge of the communities in which they operate, and state and federal government relations.

- *Media relations:* Worked with journalists, book authors, TV producers, movie producers, and conference organizers toward estab-

The Department of Public Affairs at Church & Dwight handles both external relations and internal communications. Pictured here is the masthead of the company's monthly newsletter entitled "Hammerings." It bears the familiar red & yellow Arm & Hammer logo that appears on all Church & Dwight products and communications.

lishing multistakeholder partnerships for environmental education.

- *Environmental stakeholders:* Built bridges between opposing forces in the environmental arena and sponsored the environmental education programs of many national, state, and local environmental organizations. One such program was a 65-part radio series coproduced with three national environmental organizations and offered at no cost to radio stations.

- *Educational programs:* Coproduced an Audubon television special, "This Island Earth"; codeveloped an educational curriculum, "Give Water a Hand"; and cosponsored a program of the Management Institute for Environment in Business for including the environmental ethic in the curricula of graduate schools of business.

- *Government relations:* Created awareness among legislators and regulators of pollution prevention and remediation products and technologies. By 1995, this effort had led to the adoption by the White House of Thomlinson's idea of creating a President's Environmental Technology Leadership Challenge, a program that brings together developers and potential users of environmental technologies.

- *Community relations:* Cofunded the Washington-based "Environmentors" project, a large-scale community relations program designed to add value to students, educators, and existing service organizations in the communities in which it operates.

In addition to running these company-wide programs, Church & Dwight invests in projects designed to help market the products of its consumer and industrial divisions. I highlight below two interesting programs, one at the corporate level, one at the divisional level. Each addresses an important social issue but is also intended to benefit Church & Dwight by bringing about more favorable attitudes toward the company's products and increasing sales. In the language of game theory, both are win-win projects, one short term, the other long term.

"EN-GRAFFITI"

In 1994, Church & Dwight formed a coalition with four other groups to address a crucial urban social issue: homelessness.[3] The other partners were the Office of the President of the Borough of Queens in New York City, the Queens County Overall Economic Development Corporation, a Salvation Army homeless veterans' center, and the public interest group We Care about New York. The coalition targeted a group of prescreened homeless veterans motivated to become entrepreneurs and establish their own graffiti removal businesses.

Church & Dwight's interest in the coalition was twofold. It would help address an important social issue, and it would promote the use of one of its proprietary technologies for graffiti removal—a machine that uses sodium bicarbonate and pressurized water to clean buildings without damaging their surface. The Borough of Queens, blemished by old and new graffiti, stood to benefit from improving its appearance. The Queens Overall Economic Development Corporation identified graffiti vandalism as a deterrent to local economic development. And the Salvation Army's Borden Avenue Veterans' Residence housed 400 homeless veterans known to be responsible, motivated, and sufficiently skilled to work.

Since every participating member of the project stood to benefit directly, it created a win-win situation. Moreover, besides the obvious perceived benefits to the coalition partners, the community as a whole would gain indirectly from an employed labor force. It would also gain from Church & Dwight's environmentally friendly bicarbonate technology. Because of the system's reliance on baking soda, runoff would not further burden the borough's sewage system and water supply with toxic chemicals, as would other commercial cleansing systems.

For this program, public sector organizations contributed funds for training the homeless veterans; borough president Claire Shulman's office provided meeting space and vehicles; and Church & Dwight put up the seed capital, the baking soda, and the graffiti removal equipment. By August 1994, a group of some 14 homeless veterans had graduated from the program and were ready to start work in the hope of eventually owning their own businesses.

After the program was tested, refined, and proven successful, a press conference was held to announce it formally. The press conference included a demonstration of the technology by the formerly homeless veterans as well as speakers, among them Bryan Thomlison, Mayor Giuliani, Claire Shulman, city council members, a congressman, and coalition members. The Arm & Hammer brand had a prominent presence, and Thomlison recalled that "the amount of broadcast and print media pickup was absolutely stupendous." Thomlison argued that a project such as this gains far more access to influential people than high-priced lobbyists can achieve, making this stakeholder approach analogous to his environment technologies: better, cheaper, faster, safer (entailing less risk).

"GIVE WATER A HAND"

Since the late 1980s, a variety of public and private organizations has produced curricula to promote environmental education in schools. Many of the materials developed on water conservation have tended to reflect the biases of their developers, thereby increasing the level of confusion around it. According to Walter Coddington, an environmental consultant and project facilitator, "While successful at conveying basic water science and education about specific water concerns such as wetlands and water conservation, as a rule water curricula fail to help youth to integrate information about water topics or to provide youth with practical, local, community-oriented activities."

To address the issue, on September 18, 1993, Bryan Thomlison convened representatives of the National Fish and Wildlife Foundation, the U.S. EPA, the U.S. Department of Agriculture Extension Service, and the National 4-H Council. The purpose of the meeting was to form a coalition with the purpose of developing and promoting a curriculum on water preservation. Each partner would agree to leverage its network and available resources to ensure maximum distribution of the curriculum. As the partners concluded: "It is the belief of the members of this Multistakeholder Partnership for Water Education that a multiparty, multidisciplinary approach to water curricula development will deliver an objective, action-oriented, and widely distributed water education curriculum. This effort is in support of the goals of 'Water Quality 2000,' a cooperative effort of over 80 public, private, and nonprofit organizations."[4]

By April 1995 the completed curriculum had been distributed to more than 35,000 environmental educators. Table 12-3 lists the composition of the partnership. The core partners of the program, titled Give Water a Hand, defined their objectives as follows:

- National 4-H Council/USDA Extension Service: To support youth development with environmental education and stewardship pro-

Table 12-3 GIVE WATER A HAND

Core Partners	Supporting Partners	Participating Partners
Church & Dwight	EPA, Office of Water	Izaak Walton League
USDA Extension Service	U.S. Fish and	Water Environment
National 4-H Council	Wildlife	Federation
University of Wisconsin	USDA, Forest Service	Western Regional
National Fish and Wildlife	USDA, Soil	Environmental
National Drinking Water	Conservation	Education Council
Alliance	U.S. Geological	Project Wet
	Survey	Earth Force
	Tennessee Valley	Groundwater
	Authority	Foundation
	American Water	Trout Unlimited
	Works Association	National Association
	America's Clean	of Conservation
	Water Foundation	Districts
	Baltimore National	American Forests
	Aquarium	
	Project Green	

gramming; to promote the use of research-based information about natural resource topics and environmental education techniques; and to secure funding from public and private sources to help develop environmental programming.

- National Fish and Wildlife Foundation: To promote water-related conservation and protection education; to support experts in the development of an educational currriculum.

- National Drinking Water Alliance: To develop public awareness of the hydrology of sources of water supply and of threats to water quality integrity; to stimulate public appreciation of the science and technology of water treatment and supply; to encourage public understanding of the importance of water quality to public health; to increase public involvement in the water supply and use decision-making process.

- Church & Dwight: To educate youths and adults on water issues and the science of sodium bicarbonate; to work with environmental advocacy and conservation organizations and government agencies to develop an environmental education curriculum; to promote, by example, the merits of multistakeholder alliances for environmental education.

The program is designed to involve youths between the ages of 6 and 18. Target groups for the curriculum include schools, 4-H clubs, Girl Scouts, Boy Scouts, Junior Achievement clubs, YMCAs, YWCAs, Campfire Girls, Future Farmers of America, and other formal youth environmental groups. If successful, the program should increase youth awareness of home and community water management issues and provide young people with experience in community action, practice in life skills, and a sense of empowerment in knowing that they can make a difference in their community.

Church & Dwight's role was to sow the seeds of the new curriculum. Ultimately, public and private sector teams representing multiple constituencies actually articulated the full curriculum. The final output incorporated insight about water-related ecosystems, everyday life needs, water testing, and home water treatment. It also invites students to contemplate careers in water management.

Church & Dwight's Multistakeholder Model

Both of these projects illustrate the stakeholder-relations model that Bryan Thomlison advocates for managing a company's reputation. The graffiti removal project offers obvious short-term benefits to Church & Dwight. On one hand, it disseminates the company's proprietary technology into local communities, increasing its visibility and potentially enlarging the market. On the other hand, by addressing a pressing social issue, it generates favorable word of mouth about the company and its products. In contrast, Give Water a Hand is a long-term program with mostly indirect benefits. By including discussions of the benefits of baking soda in educational materials, Church & Dwight stands to benefit from widespread exposure to millions of children—the future consumers of its products.

Developing strategic alliances with diverse nonindustry groups requires the ongoing nurturing of mutual trust. In general, the multistakeholder model employed by Church & Dwight operates as follows:

- Define the social issue that fits best with your core competences and business objectives.

- Gain the CEO's clear, unequivocal, long-term commitment to the "cause."

- Map out all the constituencies affected by the cause and your possible role with them.

- Identify and contact key influentials in those constituencies.

- With both internal and external constituents, define mutual needs and objectives; then rank the potential partners for strategic fit.

- Forge alliances and engage the new stakeholders in issues, opportunities, and projects of mutual benefit.

- Bring your trusted constituents into every stage of your projects, allowing you to both develop opportunities with the input of a diverse array of stakeholders and revamp inappropriate concepts or programs.

- Work with the constituents to determine how your goods, services, and operations can be modified to reflect your commitment to the cause. This is what differentiates your company from your competition and separates the committed from the opportunists.

- Understand that you must deserve the reputation you are trying to create, and ensure that everyone in the organization is continually energized and empowered toward that end.

Alliances can be both internal and external. Internal alliances are designed to encourage employee involvement in environmental issues. They also help to mobilize employee stakeholders around a common strategic orientation. Among the many programs managed by public affairs, for instance, the publishing of the company-wide newsletter gives the office a direct reading of employee viewpoints. As Bryan Thomlison points out:

The philosophy was that if I am going to be the key influencer on environmental issues, then employee communications was vital. So I changed the newsletter and introduced other forms of employee communications on environmental matters. I also changed how we handled our community relations program. Instead of simply attending Chamber of Commerce meetings and funding any old philanthropic project that came along, I decided to create a short list of action plans. If something doesn't tie in directly to building business for the company, then it doesn't make it onto the short list. For the most part, we try to orient everything we do now, all outreach programs, to building business.

Church & Dwight's data suggest that the core consumers brought into the franchise with the multistakeholder model are its most profitable consumers. Unlike brand-switchers or price-buyers, they are more likely to buy the brand repeatedly, and those who identify with the cause are more likely to switch from another brand to Arm & Hammer. Compared with the national average, these consumers are almost twice as likely to buy based on trust, rather than on advertising. And they are more likely to be among the 10 percent of Americans whom the Roper organization calls "influentials," those most likely to influence the purchases of others. Thomlison claims that his database provides almost instant access to the most powerful environmental influentials in the country and, through them, to the homes of millions of environmentally oriented consumers.

By generating and nurturing mutual trust and credibility within a network of key constituents, stakeholder alliances help companies to create reputational capital. In turn, alliances prove invaluable, both in helping the company to make key strategic decisions and to react more quickly to attacks on the company and its products. As the relationships mature, the allies become frontline "eyes and ears" for each other, readily communicating nonconfidential issues, opportunities, trends, and even competitive reconnaissance.

CAPITALIZING ON REPUTATION

Has Church & Dwight been successful in managing its reputation? Although cause-and-effect relationships are always difficult to establish, there is some evidence that the company is benefiting from identifying the environment as a strategic issue and from owning a reputation as an environmentally friendly company. Besides spurring the design of many new products in the last decade, Church & Dwight has enjoyed faster growth and higher profitability than its rivals over the past 25 years. The record suggests that the company's success may result from a combination of two factors: (1) its ability to attract a large proportion of so-called green consumers to its products and (2) its ability to earn widespread support from the institutions that influence those green consumers. In recent years, the company has received a number of awards that confirm its harmonious relationship with influential institutions.

GREEN CONSUMERS

Opinion surveys conducted in 1993 suggest that Arm & Hammer customers are greener than those of rival companies. In responding to the question, "How concerned are you about the environment?" some 84 percent of Arm & Hammer customers indicated high concern, compared with only 64 percent, 65 percent, and 70 percent, respectively, for each of the company's three leading rivals. In this, Arm & Hammer customers appear to more closely resemble the "evergreen" group defined by the opinion research firm of Yankelovich, Skudder, et al. Moreover, Arm & Hammer appears to have increased its penetration into the green market. In a comparable survey conducted in 1990, only 77 percent of its customers had indicated high concern for the environment.

In another comparative survey of consumers by Environmental Research Associates in 1993, some 9 percent of respondents claim to purchase Arm & Hammer products because of the company's reputation for environmental concern compared to 1 percent for Procter & Gamble, Clorox, Colgate-Palmolive, Dow Chemical, and Du Pont.

Several corroborating studies lead Church & Dwight to estimate that a significantly higher proportion of its customers are green than the national average of 16.5 percent. Of its $200 million in laundry detergent sales, the company ascribes some $43 million to the green segment—$10 million more than the company would expect to get on average. Across its consumer product categories, the company estimates increased product sales of about $17 million—$10 million in laundry detergent, $1 million in baking soda, and $6 million in toothpaste. Stakeholder-generated product innovations, incremental business attributable to access to new customers, and reduced manufacturing costs due to pollution prevention and waste management efforts jointly create several million dollars in additional benefits.

With an annual budget of less than $2 million, Bryan Thomlison's public affairs department takes responsibility for generating an incremental $20–25 million in revenues as a result of the company's strategic focus on the environment. Table 12-4 shows the comparative leverage

Table 12-4 RELATIVE EFFECTIVENESS

	Stakeholder Programs	Marketing Programs
1. Incremental Sales	$17.0 million	$508 million
2. Marketing Expenditures	1.9 million	116 million
1./2. Program Productivity	9	4

of his stakeholder-based programs against Church & Dwight's more traditional marketing programs.

HONORS AND AWARDS

Between 1990 and 1994, Church & Dwight was the recipient of a variety of awards. In 1992, the company was nominated by the well-regarded Council on Economic Priorities (of which I am a board member) for one of its prestigious America's Corporate Conscience Awards for Environmental Stewardship. In 1993, the United Nations Environment Program named Church & Dwight the recipient of a Corporate Achievement Award for Environmental Responsibility. Also in 1993, Dwight Minton, the company's CEO, was singled out by the American Marketing Association for its Edison Achievement Award. Distributor Ace Hardware made Church & Dwight the winner of its Ace Environmental Award for environmental stewardship and marketing innovation, while Meijer made it the recipient of its Meijer Environmental Award. In 1994, Connecticut College picked Church & Dwight for its Inherit the Earth Award. The company was also made the recipient of an Earth Day Award from *Imagine Magazine* and Earth Day USA. Most recently, American Rivers selected Church & Dwight for its Corporate Citizenship Award. In 1995, Bryan Thomlison was recognized by Claes Nobel with a United Earth award for personal environmental achievements.

Together, these awards demonstrate growing recognition by important stakeholder groups that Church & Dwight is a company friendly to the environment. Though it is difficult to quantify their effect in hard numbers, it suggests continued dissemination of attitudes favorable to the company. These groups publish newsletters, author books, and otherwise communicate with current and potential customers for

Church & Dwight's products. They indirectly promote the company's products.

In the remaining chapters of the book, we turn our attention to firms in the financial services community. We explore how stakeholder models similar to Church & Dwight's can help professional services firms to exploit their hidden stock of reputational capital more systematically.

Penny wise, pound foolish.

—*Robert Burton*
   The Anatomy of Melancholy

The
Deal
Makers

BANKERS BANK on their reputations. They regularly get clients to part with their wealth and advise them how to invest it. To do so, bankers invariably claim a commitment to the highest standards of honesty, credibility, and trustworthiness. After all, who among us would invest a lifetime's savings with someone whose integrity was in doubt? In many ways, then, banks are much like other professional service firms—law firms, accounting firms, and consulting firms among them—in that the measure of their success is their ability to maintain strong and favorable reputations. Which is what has made the rash of blunders by investment banks in recent years so startling. This chapter explores reputation building in financial services firms. In particular, it examines recent cases of meltdown at investment banks and the reputation-management issues that these crises and scandals raise.

DIRE STRAITS

In the last few years, it became apparent that during the go-go decade of the 1980s, brokers at Prudential Securities, a subsidiary of the mammoth Prudential insurance company, enticed many elderly investors to buy partnership shares in what they were led to believe were safe investments. In fact, a good number of those investments involved oil and real estate assets, high-risk deals. When the investments went bust—as risky investments often do—investors were dismayed to learn that they had lost their nest eggs. They brought suit. After a drawn out investigation, in October 1993, the investment bank reluctantly admitted widespread fraud and settled charges with regulators. They set up a $330 million fund to pay out claims to the hundreds of investors that had been deceived. Not only had the rogue brokers violated ethical norms, they had dealt their company's reputation a critical blow. Yet it wasn't until March 1994 that Prudential's chairman, Robert Winters, publically took responsibility for the lapse of control in the company's brokerage subsidiary. As he put it: "The public image of the Prudential has suffered on my watch, and I feel the weight of that burden. Any action that was taken that was not in the best interest of our customers was wrong. We have hurt too many of our customers. We are committed to taking care of these customers, and that commitment extends well beyond that $330 million."[1] A few months later, he would publically admit to the company's criminal actions and agree to settle criminal charges to the tune of yet another $330 million.

Although the scandal at Prudential briefly eclipsed the major Wall Street crimes of the 1980s, it would itself be dwarfed by dramatic losses in the derivatives markets that occasioned highly publicized lawsuits against prominent bankers Merrill Lynch and Bankers Trust in 1995 and the collapse of the venerable British investment house of Barings PLC.

In fact, most of these banking scandals share common features. They can ultimately be traced to a combination of (a) rogue behavior by individual bankers and (b) institutional failure to infuse sound judgment and secure compliance from employees. They suggest the necessity for companies to install key internal systems to monitor and maintain reputational capital.

Take Drexel Burnham Lambert. The bank's dramatic collapse in the late 1980s can be traced not only to the dubious practices of its entrepreneurial bankers, Dennis Levine and Michael Milken, but to the whole laissez-faire culture of Drexel that CEO Fred Joseph had sanctioned. Left to his own devices, Milken generated extraordinary profits from his junk-bond operation, blinding the firm to the reputational risks it was taking.[2] As journalist Connie Bruck observed, "Milken would in effect create his own firm within the firm of Drexel Burnham, one which its members would refer to simply as 'the department.' He laid the groundwork for that autonomy in 1973."[3]

As a prominent banker also told me, however, the Milken machine was itself a form of self-promotion: "Mike Milken's marketing was fantastic. Everyone called him a genius. But he was really selling a cancer. As far as the Drexel Burnham company was concerned, he was just another con-artist." In falling victim to the promoter's spiel, Drexel Burnham failed to create a system that could safeguard its reputational capital.

Another casualty of 1994 was the once-proud securities firm of Kidder Peabody. The firm and its parent company, General Electric, had both suffered heavily from the reputational loss incurred when Martin Siegel, Kidder's former takeover star, pleaded guilty in 1987 to two felony counts of tax evasion and conspiracy to violate securities laws and paid $9 million in civil fines. At that time, Siegel proved to have been deeply involved in trading on inside information with risk arbitrageur Ivan Boesky. Publically embarrassed by the indictment, GE vowed to clean house and rebuild Kidder from the ground up, filling it with presumably better-trained managers from GE—only to find itself eating those words when in April 1994 Kidder announced another scandal. The firm had been obliged to discharge its chief government bond trader after uncovering a bond trading scheme that had artificially inflated the firm's profits by some $210 million. This development did little to help Kidder Peabody's standing in the competitive securities industry and explains why GE opted to sell off Kidder's investment banking division to rival PaineWebber in October 1994 for a paltry $650 million.

In 1985 it was broker E. F. Hutton that scandalized Wall Street by pleading guilty to 2,000 felony counts of defrauding its banks of millions of dollars through a massive check-kiting operation. The revelation was jarring. As one reporter put it:

> For decades a powerful mythology had surrounded Hutton as the home of Wall Street's shrewdest and classiest professionals. When Hutton talked people listened—the advertising line had been so successful because, to millions of investors, and the brokers at Hutton, it had seemed a simple statement of fact. That made it difficult for many to accept that the firm would try and pull off such a sleazy scam.[4]

Hutton never recovered from the scandal. Within years, the firm's tarnished assets were sold and absorbed into the Shearson brokerage empire and have now fused into Primerica's Smith Barney operations. And the once-proud Hutton name has vanished in all but memory from the industry.

In 1991, Salomon Brothers was rocked by scandal. The premier bond trader in the industry was charged with systematically violating auction rules over a two-year period and of cornering the market in various new issues of U.S. Treasury bonds. The charges were serious. The bank's parent company lost about $500 million, or 15 percent, of its market value in the scandal's immediate aftermath. Much of the blame for that scandal would get placed on rogue behavior by the point man in charge of the bank's government bond-trading desk, Paul Mozer. As most analysts concluded, it seems Mozer simply got caught up with winning at any cost in the high-stakes lotteries at which Salomon and 13 other leading banks regularly compete as primary dealers for securities of the U.S. Treasury. His errant behavior seriously jeopardized the bank's reputation and its very survival.

Because of their complex and high-stakes financial dealings, investment banks face such reputational risks on a regular basis. Many banks, including the upstanding Goldman Sachs, were dragged into the insider trading scandals of 1986 and 1987. Facing ambiguous situations, employees allowed themselves to be enticed by producing bigger numbers, all too often at the expense of doing what's right for the firm as a whole and its reputation.

Of the banks that manage risks better than others, Goldman Sachs may be among the more vigilant. Over the years, the closely held partnership has proved highly adroit at protecting its reputational capital from erosion. In large part, its success is due to widespread recognition within Goldman Sachs that at heart securities firms rely heavily on their reputations to compete. We'll take a closer look at Goldman Sachs after a quick tour of the close-knit community of investment banking.

BANKING ON REPUTATION

Investment banks mediate between buyers and sellers of assets. They bring in their revenues by issuing new securities, trading old securities, managing financial assets, or deal making—advising client companies about possible mergers and acquisitions. Since investors are reluctant to buy securities from unknown dealers, the industry is concentrated. Investment banks are few in number and high in clout. Table 13-1 lists the small group of companies that dominates the market in which securities are bought and sold in the United States. The volume of business that each bank does in the major product areas of the industry is a significant indicator of its reputation.

Naturally, all of these banks compete against each other for visibility and status with corporate clients. Those with stronger reputations, however, enjoy a relative advantage in generating business with better-regarded clients. A bank's reputation signals to a client company the likely success of the bank's counsel, whether for pricing a new issue of the company's stocks and bonds or for negotiating a buyout. A corporate financial officer is therefore likely to give greater latitude to a bank with a solid reputation. In a book about investment banks, two Harvard professors rightly observe that:

In selecting an investment bank, the customer must base expectations about future performance on past experience, the experiences of others, and

Table 13-1 THE TOP UNITED STATES INVESTMENT BANKS

	Amount ($millions)[a]	Rank
Merrill Lynch	$173,783	1
Goldman Sachs	127,265	2
Lehman Brothers	115,977	3
Kidder Peabody	94,441	4
Salomon Brothers	91,179	5
CS First Boston	90,374	6
Morgan Stanley	67,717	7
Bear Stearns	56,237	8
Donaldson, Lufkin & Jenrette	36,911	9
PaineWebber	29,890	10
Prudential Securities	28,336	11
J. P. Morgan	22,614	12

[a]Total of all domestic issues by investment banks in 1993, with full credit given to lead manager.

impressions gained from marketing presentations. Reputation has a strong influence on these expectations and impressions. And because reputation extends to particular people, customers will sometimes select an investment bank if they are guaranteed that certain people will work on the deal.[5]

Banks are also regularly rated by specialized magazines like *Institutional Investor,* and the rankings are widely disseminated. Every year, for instance, the magazine ranks leading investment banks on the quality of their research. To do this, it sends out a questionnaire to the director of research or head of investments of about 750 money management groups as well as to corporate clients and a sample of analysts and portfolio managers. Respondents are interviewed, and the opinions of a total of almost 2,000 people are tapped to produce the "All-America Research Team."

Table 13-2 summarizes the reputational rankings of these banks based on surveys of the quality of their research between 1991 and 1993. The ranks are adjusted for the relative size of each bank's research departments. Topping the list are Donaldson, Lufkin—number 1 since 1990—and Wertheim Schroder. Although both are far smaller than rivals like Merrill Lynch and Goldman Sachs, they earn consistent praise for their research. Since Merrill stands at a lowly eleventh place in the ranking, it's safe to conclude that research is not the backbone of Merrill Lynch's reputation. Although its research is well regarded, the bank is more labor intensive and therefore much less productive than its rivals.

In the underwriting business, reputation is critical. When a bank agrees to help a company raise capital by issuing new shares of stock, it normally cooperates with rival banks to sell those securities to appropriate investors. Since no investment bank has enough brokers of its own to sell out a large corporate issue, rivals act like retail outlets. They share with the issuing bank the management and commission revenues derived from actually selling the securities.

Banks announce a newly issued security by placing ads in financial newspapers like the *Wall Street Journal.* Although these standardized ads register the "birth" of a security, they are paradoxically described on Wall Street as "tombstones." Listed on every tombstone are all the banks that have agreed to collaborate in distributing the security; they constitute the "syndicate."

If you pool all the tombstones issued in any one year, you'll find that the order in which syndicate members are listed on the tombstone reflects

Table 13-2 WHO'S TOPS IN RESEARCH?

Bank	Relative Rank 1991	1992	1993
Donaldson, Lufkin & Jenrette	1	1	1
Wertheim Schroder	11	4	2
Goldman Sachs	2	2	3
Morgan Stanley	4	6	4
PaineWebber	9	5	5
CS First Boston	8	7	6
Lehman Brothers	5	8	7
Sanford Bernstein	15	10	8
Prudential Securities	3	3	9
Smith Barney, Shearson	7	9	10
Merrill Lynch	10	11	11
Salomon Brothers	13	13	12
Kidder Peabody	12	14	13
Cowen & Co.	6	12	14
C. J. Lawrence	16	15	15
Dean Witter Reynolds	14	16	16
Montgomery Securities	19	17	17
Oppenheimer & Co.	18	19	18
Bear Stearns	17	18	19
NatWest Securities	20	20	20

Source: Adapted from various issues of *Institutional Investor*. Rankings reflect the number of nominations to a bank's analysts for their research excellence, adjusted for the total number of research analysts working in the bank.

their position in the hierarchy of banks in the industry.[6] Reputation has implications for which banks get invited, how much of an issue each bank gets to distribute, and how large a cut of the fees each one gets. Given the financial implications of getting "bracketed" at a particular level, banks argue about the order in which their names appear in tombstone ads: "High-status firms want to reinforce their status by maintaining the rank order, whereas lower-status firms seek to improve their status by moving up. . . . In some cases, firms will not participate in a deal rather than have themselves listed below other firms they consider of lower status."[7]

Tombstones invariably remind both banks and their clients what the pecking order is—who's on top and who isn't—and they raise some valid questions. Where do these rankings come from? How do banks earn top billing in the minds of customers, whether for their underwriting, trading, advising, or research? How do they acquire the reputations that entitle them to preeminence in the eyes of their peers? And how can investment banks safeguard against reputational loss from rogue behavior?

REPUTATION AND IDENTITY

In the financial business, there are essentially two types of institutions: specialists and generalists. Specialists build reputation by staying small. They focus on delivering a unique service to corporate clients quickly and capably. Often these specialist firms can do a better job for a corporate client in a particular transaction than can a big-name generalist. Indeed, throughout the 1980s and into the 1990s, large banks often lost ground to speedier, more focused, and more aggressive specialists. In contrast to specialists, top-tier investment banks improve their reputations by enlarging their service offerings. To do so, they grow their capital base and expand their distribution network. As you might expect, the premier investment banks—the so-called bulge-bracket banks—are all very big. They're generalists.

THE SPECIALTY BANKS

The industry provides safe haven for a large number of smaller securities firms that specialize in delivering a unique service to corporate clients. These specialist firms build reputation in distinctive ways.

Consider Herzog, Heine & Geduld (HHG), a securities firm that specializes in trading stocks in the over-the-counter (OTC) market. Most of its clients are institutional funds. In reputational surveys of the OTC market, HHG ranks among the leading firms, in close competition with its two archrivals Alex Brown and Montgomery Securities. Though smaller, these specialist banks regularly vie with top-tier powerhouses like Goldman Sachs to entice institutional investors to invest in the stocks of smaller OTC companies rather than those of the larger companies traded on the major exchanges.

Spear, Leeds & Kellogg (SLK) is another type of specialist firm. Since 1931, SLK has provided other banks with trading services by maintaining a market in the securities of some 230 companies on the New York and American stock exchanges, including top names like Boeing, Mobil, and Motorola. Over the years, the firm has built a reputation for being among the best of market makers. It also has a reputation for being frugal with its own money. The spartan facilities I visited on lower Broadway reflect that attitude. As one of the firm's 30 partners told me:

> *To a specialist firm, the basis of a good reputation is financial. You can schmooze all you want, but if you don't have the capital, financial history, and performance, you won't make it. Your reputation depends on how your clients see your management. We have a reputation for being well-managed, not overly aggressive. We stick to our knitting. We're also known to be very conservative. We have to be conservative because we're in some of the riskiest businesses of all—risk arbitrage.*

As a specialist, SLK competes principally with the likes of MJ Mien and Henderson Brothers on size—the bank's total capital base. In the OTC market, its principal rival is none other than Herzog, Heine & Geduld. One way SLK retains its reputation is by always putting its customers first: "The firm maintains close rapport with the companies in which it specializes. Regular communication is required in order to assure that management is satisfied with the trading of the company's stock."[8] As one of the partners added:

> *We try to help customers through their bad times. For instance, if we get information about a transaction, we'll make sure our customers get it first, even if it means one of our partners loses. Because we're part of a very small community, that kind of story gets around and boosts our reputation. For us, communication is key. That's why I'm on the phone regularly with our customers. You never want a customer or banker to find out something negative from a third party.*

Given the high stakes involved in making markets, the firm puts a lot of stress on industry apprenticeship—a recurring theme in the industry. Its 800 employees continually take classes inside and outside the firm. As a partner put it: "People stick around for a long time at SLK, but before an employee will make partner, you want to make sure he has the proper mindset."

Neuberger & Berman is yet another type of specialty firm. Founded in 1939, the company has built an enviable reputation as a specialist in money management. Its in-house analysts do corporate research on more than 700 companies. Their analyses enable the firm's money managers to act like entrepreneurs in building portfolios of stocks and bonds for wealthy individuals, corporate pension funds, and school endowments. Today, Neuberger & Berman manages more than $20 billion in mutual funds, pension funds, and individual funds. As a member of the firm recognized: "For us, reputation is key. When people leave their money with you, it's more than a heart transplant. Clients will tell their money managers more than they tell their doctors or lawyers."

The company is known for being bright, customer oriented, careful, and conservative; it is *not* known for being on the cutting edge. In part that's because Neuberger & Berman prefers to hire older money managers—the average age of employees is more than 50 years. "We hire only people who have been through a bad market cycle. We're very cynical about having younger people manage our funds. That's because we believe that if you've been through a down, you'll take less risk. Another way to put it is that we're plain vanilla."

Despite continuing technological and economic challenges, the firm's specialist identity has remained impervious to change over the years. Past attempts to diversify into other products and markets were quickly undone, and under founder Roy Neuberger's streetwise leadership, the firm has opted to stick to its knitting. According to one long-time employee: "We're very internally focused. We don't trade real estate, art, rare coins, commodities, or tax shelters. We don't want to diversify. We tailor our operations to the people we have instead of the other way around."

Consistent with its conservatism and internal focus, Neuberger & Berman maintain an introverted facade. It avoids strategic efforts to shape its own reputation. Most emphatically, for instance, the firm refuses to advertise to recruit customers. Like many prestige-oriented businesses, they expect new business to come in through a network of referrals and by word of mouth. At the same time, caution dictates an arm's-length relationship with the media. That's why no one in the firm has direct contact with the press. The official policy is to avoid publicizing the company's opinion on any financial matter. As a senior employee put it: "We're always quoted out of context, so we avoid giving quotes. We regularly turn down invitations to speak out for fear of looking sensationalistic."

In exceptional situations, the firm does take ads in major papers to comment on what it considers to be "alarming" industry trends. The big debate on program trading that took place in the aftermath of the stock market crash of 1987 was a case in point. On that issue, the company decided to express itself in a high-profile ad published in October 1989 in the *New York Times*, the *Wall Street Journal*, and *Investor's Daily*:

> *We're angry at what is happening to the American investor. The issue is program trading, especially what's known as stock-index arbitrage. . . . In short, program trading is nothing more than a numbers racket in which those running the numbers win, while individual investors, corporations, and the American economy lose. . . . We usually stay out of the limelight and work quietly to increase our clients' financial well-being. But program trading is such a threat to everything we find positive about investing in America's future that we believe action must be taken now.*

As these examples suggest, specialist firms share a common concern with continually defining and refining their target market. They build reputation by developing a strong set of relatively narrow skills that give them a competitive advantage against their larger rivals. Specialist firms also favor lower public profiles and seem to delight in their introverted postures. Not unlike specialists in other industries, they rely heavily on word-of-mouth advertising and avoid direct involvement in actively shaping their external images.

THE GENERALIST BANKS

Unlike specialists, major investment banks build reputation by enlarging their scope of operations. They work hard to encompass the full gamut of securities and strive to create new sources of revenue by introducing ever more innovative financial instruments and services. Increasingly these top-tier banks operate globally. They maintain branches outside the United States and trade securities on the exchanges of countries like Japan, England, France, and Germany.

Because of their wide reach, strong capital base, and breadth of offerings, generalist firms find it difficult to differentiate themselves from one another. As one banker said: "Most Wall Street firms don't really do anything different from one another. There's high overcapacity in the industry. You could probably shrink each one of them to 10% of what they are without losing much." Another senior banker concurred: "Most new products are short-lived and our services are commoditized, so there's no real difference between the handful of firms that can provide them. These companies can only differentiate themselves based on (1) how hard they work, (2) how fast they are, and (3) how ethical they prove to be." Differentiation among generalist firms is accomplished largely by their carefully managing the way clients perceive them—by engaging in active efforts to build, sustain, and defend their reputations.

To explore the corporate reputations of generalist banks, in 1992 I surveyed some 725 of their major corporate clients. The questionnaire asked the chief financial officers of these companies to nominate the banks for which they had the most respect and with which they did most of their business. Exhibit 13-1 lists the top 20 banks that got the most votes from the 268 companies that replied. These generalist banks are clearly the most active in the industry.

What factors influenced a bank's reputation? A statistical analysis of the reputational rankings in Exhibit 13-1 suggests that four factors differentiate the high-visibility bank from the low-visibility bank:

1. *Capital base:* A bank's visibility to clients was significantly—and positively—related to the bank's total capital position.

2. *Growth rate of capital:* Banks expanding their capital base at a faster rate were less attractive to clients. The growth rate of a bank's capital position appears to signal to clients that the bank may be overreaching, which significantly dampens the bank's visibility.

3. *Number of branches:* The number of branches a bank operates throughout the United States, an estimate of its strength in distribution, proved to be *inversely* related to the bank's attractiveness to clients.

4. *Number of agents:* Agents constitute a measure of retail distribution. Large corporate clients appear less interested in banks with a large network of agents.

Overall, then, clients ascribe better reputations to banks that can provide higher-quality services. A strong capital base is key, but banks that grow their capital base too quickly worry clients. Strengths in distribution through branches and agents appear to have a negative affect on

1. Goldman Sachs
2. Merrill Lynch
3. Salomon Brothers
4. Morgan Stanley
5. CS First Boston
6. Shearson Lehman
7. J. P. Morgan
8. Kidder Peabody
9. Smith Barney
10. Bear Stearns
11. Keefe, Bruyette & Woods
12. Dillon Read
13. PaineWebber
14. Lazard Freres
15. Citicorp
16. Donaldson, Lufkin, & Jenrette
17. Alex Brown
18. Prudential-Bache
19. Montgomery Securities
20. Piper, Jaffray & Hopwood

a bank's external image with corporate clients, because it seemingly suggests a stronger commitment to retail brokerage activities than to financial deal making.

In 1992, generalist banks fell into a three-tiered hierarchy. At the top were the "premier banks," dominated by big names like Goldman Sachs, along with Merrill Lynch, Salomon Brothers, Morgan Stanley, CS First Boston, and Shearson Lehman. They were followed by a second tier of "select banks," led by J. P. Morgan, Kidder Peabody, Smith Barney, and Bear Stearns. Finally, in the third tier were the smaller, high-profile, "niche banks," including Alex Brown; Lazard Freres; Donaldson, Lufkin & Jenrette; Dillon Read; and Prudential Securities. All of these investment banks are generalists, with varying degrees of diversity and aggressiveness.

Moving between the top tiers of the industry is difficult. There are significant barriers that derive from perceptions of the bank by clients and from self-perceptions within banks. For one, clients recognize the hierarchy of prestige of the banks and are unwilling to alter existing relationships. At the same time, bankers themselves often participate in recreating the established order, at the cost of occasionally shooting themselves in the foot when they insist, say, on lead-bank status on a new issue, despite defections by rival banks.

Historians like to point out how an archetypal rivalry between upstarts and blue bloods is actually woven into the historical fabric of investment banking. They remind us that at the turn of the century the industry was dominated by the House of Morgan, the ancestral parent of J. P. Morgan and Morgan Stanley. It was "the establishment," and upstarts fed on the scraps from the Morgan table. As one historian put it: "Goldman Sachs specialized in commercial paper, Lehman in commodity trading. Around 1900, they began underwriting shares for companies that were spurned by the gentile firms as too lowly—retail stores and textile manufacturers, for instance. Among them was Sears Roebuck, introduced by Goldman Sachs and Lehman Brothers in 1906."[9] In due course, a new "establishment" was born that included former upstarts Goldman Sachs and Lehman Brothers along with the pedigreed successors of the House of Morgan—J. P. Morgan and Morgan Stanley. Jointly they came to dominate the prestigious and profitable underwriting business that derived from school ties and the "old boy network."

The rivalry between establishment and upstart would recur, however. Salomon Brothers was launched as a bond-trading house in large measure because of its outsider roots. The now-prestigious Bear Sterns was founded in 1923 as a rough-and-tumble trading firm, with no connections to the corporate establishment. In the late 1970s, the recently merged Philadelphia-based firm of Drexel Burnham, like its upstart predecessors, found it difficult to attract first-rate companies as clients because of the brash, outsider image that one partner, Burnham & Company, had brought to the other—the older, more genteel Drexel Firestone.

The rivalry between rednecks and blue bloods, between moneyed upstarts and the establishment, would also take root at Lehman Brothers in the 1980s. As trading became strong enough to rival banking as a profit center in the bank, traders sought parity with the bankers who had looked down on them. In the end, the firm virtually exploded from the internal conflict between traders and investment bankers and was absorbed into the rapidly expanding Shearson retail empire.

Over the years, these generalist banks have become well known to one another and to corporate clients for their historical strengths in particular markets and products. Among premier investment banks, for instance, Goldman Sachs and Morgan Stanley now owe their sterling reputations to phenomenal strength in underwriting—the ability to sell out a new issue of securities. In contrast, Salomon Brothers derives its reputation from the bond-trading side of the house, and the aggressive, gun-toting image that the traders project. Different still are the first-rate reputations of firms like Merrill Lynch and Shearson (absorbed in 1994 into the Traveler's Smith Barney subsidiary), which draw heavily on client awareness of their powerful retail distribution networks. All of them try to exploit their reputations to build linkages across the different financial markets in which they all participate.

The second-tier "select banks" have reputations for dealing with smaller and less prestigious client companies than premier banks. They are known principally for their historical strengths in serving the complete needs of clients in focused markets: Smith Barney for its established strength at retailing financial products to middle-market firms; J. P. Morgan for its blue-chip clientele in wholesale banking; Kidder Peabody for its underwriting business; and Bear Stearns for its scrappy and aggressive trading.

The third tier is dominated by niche players like Alex Brown, Lazard Freres, and Dillon Read. Niche firms have reputations for doing a better job than generalists in focusing on key products and so attract more "transactional" clients. For instance, Alex Brown is widely known for its strength in IPOs (individual placement offerings), Lazard and Dillon Read for their advisory business in mergers and acquisitions, and Donaldson, Lufkin & Jenrette for its involvement with middle-market firms and its strength in issuing IPOs.

Ultimately, however, what underlies every bank's reputation is money. As a prominent banker put it, with only a hint of cynicism: "In this business, there's only one thing that builds reputation: How good are your deals, and how much you make for your clients. The only thing you can really use hype for is to get into the advisory business—that's where friendships can really count."

RENTING A BANKER'S REPUTATION

In the process of mediating flows of capital, investment bankers build an extensive network with firms, investors, and rivals. Historically, bankers developed close, almost proprietary, relationships with their clients, few of whom would ever dream of betraying their banker by associating with a rival.

Things changed in the 1980s. Much has been written about the decline of "relationship banking" in those years. The globalization of the securities markets combined with technological developments in funds transfers and a booming economy to fuel rivalry between investment banks. Rivalry, in turn, dissolved many established relationships between clients and bankers, as clients shopped around for better deals and as newcomers to the industry aggressively promoted their innovative products. An era of transactional banking had seemingly arrived. As one senior banker with whom I spoke at the former American Express subsidiary Shearson-Lehman recognized: "Companies now do a lot of competitive bad-mouthing in this industry as a way of selling their own products. We're highly sensitive to the kinds of commentary competitors make about us to governments and corporations. During the Salomon crisis, you had Goldman, Lehman, and others bad-mouthing Salomon, telling issuers that Salomon was dead."

Despite growing rivalry, some 46 percent of the 268 major companies that responded to my survey still claimed to maintain a primary relationship with their banker—a relatively high proportion. Statistical analyses showed that it's the more profitable companies that favor relationship banking, whereas less profitable clients shop around for the "right" banker at every transaction. Not surprisingly, perhaps, transactional clients reported having more frequent contact with their temporary bankers—a reflection of their relative lack of familiarity with the banks and their greater need for advice. Indeed, transactional clients reported being less centralized in their decision making about financial matters, which also helps to explain why they parse out their business to different banks.

In sum, the study showed that banks' reputations play an important role in affecting a client's decision of which bank to hire. It suggests that when companies call on an investment bank, they are in effect "renting" the bank's reputation. Better-regarded client companies associate with high-reputation banks to signal their common membership in an elite private club. Lower-status companies may hitch themselves to better-regarded banks in an effort to benefit from the banker's reputational halo.[10]

The hostile takeovers launched in the 1970s also built lasting reputational halos around banks for representing either aggressors or defenders. As often happens, Morgan Stanley and Goldman Sachs stood on opposite sides of the issue:

> *Representing the restless, mature giants who wished to diversify into other fields, Morgan Stanley took the offense. Associated with the more medium-sized and retail firms likely to be prey, Goldman Sachs would refuse to represent aggressors, although it would sometimes offer them advice. Gradually Wall Street divided into two camps—the offensive (Morgan Stanley, First Boston, Drexel Burnham, Merrill Lynch, and Lazard Freres) and the defensive (Goldman Sachs, Kidder Peabody, Salomon Brothers, Dillon Read, and Smith Barney).*[11]

Once established, such reputations influence the kinds of clients each firm chooses to represent.

PREVENTING ROGUE BEHAVIOR

A bank's reputation also matters to potential employees. They interpret reputation as a signal about the bank's internal practices and recognize what it implies for their work lives, personal income, and careers. As two industry observers note: "If potential hires think a firm is in the 'second tier' or 'unethical,' they will be concerned about the firm's future and their own personal reputation and will be less likely to join it if they have other opportunities."[12]

The reputations of investment banks therefore coincide closely with their internal character and identity, and develop in part from each bank's recruitment, training, and compensation practices. A senior banker described to me the importance in recruitment of achieving "fit" with his bank's trading culture: "We don't look for basic skills when we recruit. Instead, we look to see whether a person fits into the culture. And that means whether he's aggressive, quick-moving, quick-acting, quick-thinking, results-oriented, something of a braggart, thumbing their nose at everyone. We ask: Is this guy or woman tough enough to take it?"

Bear Stearns operates with just such a street-smart, maverick culture. During the 1980s, the bank's well-known CEO Alan "Ace" Greenberg circulated a memo in which he described the firm's recruitment philosophy: "Our first desire is to promote from within. If somebody applies with an MBA degree, we will certainly not hold it against them. But we are really looking for people with PSD degrees. PSD stands for poor, smart, and a deep desire to become rich."

Even if a bank does a good job at recruiting, however, the record suggests that people will still look out more for their own interests than for the interests of the bank. It therefore magnifies the importance of designing intensive training experiences and creating foolproof monitoring systems to ensure compliance with the bank's operating philosophy. As a senior banker told me: "When you believe a particular idea is going to drive the business, you've got to communicate it and create policies to support it. You've also got to set an example: When you've got voracious man-eaters at the top, that's the kind of company you get. Around here everyone sees what I'm doing."

Before he stepped down as CEO of Bear Stearns, I spoke with Alan Greenberg by phone. The cantankerous CEO surprised me when he asserted that reputation building was nothing more than one simple thing: "Managing by example." He seemed to believe that whatever he did, the rest of the firm would invariably copy. A good reputation simply meant that you personally were doing the right things.

In premier banks, there's no doubt that recruiting and example setting play a key role in managing reputation. Training, however, counts more. At highly rated J. P. Morgan, from the bank's earliest days

new management trainees underwent a rigorous six-month training program meant to acculturate them to the bank. Rarely did 23 Wall [the original headquarters address] recruit from outside, and it spent millions annually on free lunches to promote camaraderie. There remained an ethic of not stealing credit or upstaging colleagues. "The Morgan feeling of collegiality is the most important thing we've got," said former Morgan president Rod Lindsay.[13]

Training programs have grown more important as leading banks struggle to diversify their product portfolios. When underwriting became a more mundane activity in the 1970s, generalist banks committed themselves heavily to the lucrative takeover business. To compete, premier institutions expanded quickly, bringing newly minted college graduates into positions of significant responsibility, with minimal training. To prevent information leakage between their advisory and trading functions, banks erected so-called Chinese Walls between departments. Simultaneous participation in underwriting, trading, and acquisitions, however, created potentially thorny conflicts of interest and ethical issues. It called for more intense training, more profound consideration of ethical issues:

> *Morgan Stanley tried to throw the fear of God into merger specialists and monitored their activities closely. Briefed on legal and ethical issues, young professionals had to sign statements that they understood house rules. To foster a healthy paranoia about using inside information for personal gain, scare memos listing grounds for dismissal were circulated periodically. . . . Every fortnight, security officers conducted electronic sweeps and projects were camouflaged with the names of English kings or Greek philosophers. Staff members weren't permitted to discuss them in halls or elevators and weren't supposed to know each other's deals. Stock research people couldn't even browse in the library's corporate-finance section.*[14]

Finally, most top investment banks like to pay relatively modest salaries, with high pay-for-performance bonuses. To encourage teamwork across departments and identification with the bank's overall interests, many have moved away from paying bonuses from a departmental pool to paying bonuses out of an aggregate pool. By sharing in company-wide success, the bonuses have decreased the likelihood that individual traders or bankers would show excessive zeal in ways that might jeopardize the bank's reputation.

Unfortunately for Drexel, that wasn't the case in the mid-1980s. Under Michael Milken's tutelage, the bank's high-yield department operated in virtual secrecy and with complete autonomy—an abnormal practice for which Drexel's shareholders and other employees ultimately paid the price. As reporter Connie Bruck documents:

> *Milken told his boss . . . that he wanted to create an autonomous unit, with its own sales force, its own traders and its own research people: the high-yield and convertible-bond department. . . . From the very beginning, Milken made it mandatory that a certain portion of his people's profits were reinvested in trading accounts which he ran. It was a system of forced savings, in which these salesmen and traders were able to watch—from a distance—their wealth accumulate. With the kind of return Milken got, no one really had much to complain about. On the other hand, if one decided*

to leave him on less than amicable terms, as one trader would, there might be difficulty getting one's money out. It was a powerful disincentive to taking any secrets from Milken's operation to a rival firm.[15]

The combination of excessive autonomy without accountability and acculturation proved costly, first to Drexel's reputation and then to its survival. In large measure, the issue was revisited time and again in the early 1990s: first at Prudential Securities, where the quest for higher volume-based bonuses encouraged misrepresentation of particular securities by sales staff; then at Salomon Brothers, when the bank and one of its top traders were found guilty of violating auction rules in trading government bonds; next, at none other than Bankers Trust, the fast-growing newcomer to investment banking in the 1980s, with a corporate culture founded on individualism, entrepreneurialism, and autonomy.

In the early 1990s, Bankers Trust found itself charged by former clients Gibson Greetings (the card maker) with misrepresenting the risk of various "derivatives"—a set of complex financial instruments used mostly by sophisticated corporate investors to manage their interest costs on outstanding debt. According to government investigations in the case, Bankers Trust staff lied to Gibson about how much money it was losing in these transactions. Unfortunately for Bankers Trust, the lies were actually recorded on tape as part of an internal system set up by the bank itself to monitor trades. So much for the bank's ability to build an ethical culture in an individualistic environment motivated by greed that rewarded growth.

Finally, nowhere was rogue behavior made more visible perhaps than in March 1995 when Barings PLC, the British investment bank, was driven into bankruptcy by an overzealous trader in "derivatives" for the bank's own account. The evident lack of corporate controls and the bank's inability to prevent unbridled speculation by a lone trader in its Singapore office still puzzles most observers.

Since then, the tide has turned on Wall Street. As premier institutions have faltered, they have worked to reinforce internal systems for recruiting, training, paying, and monitoring traders and bankers in an effort to prevent rogue behavior. Their struggle backs the importance of enacting a *coherent* set of recruitment, training, control, and compensation systems that crystallize the bank's shared values and magnify for all employees the reputational as well as the financial risks of their activities.

THE MEDIA FACTOR

The struggles of the financial services industry illustrate the role of the media in reputation management. As indicated in chapter 6, most banks shun celebrity and favor a more introverted posture. As one banker told me, they prefer that their products act as their PR. In his prize-winning biography, *The House of Morgan,* author Ron Chernow recognizes banking's historical inclination to secrecy:

> Though the world's prestige investment bank, Morgan Stanley seldom appeared in the press. It didn't promote itself and conscientiously avoided publicity. . . . To advertise would be "kind of cheap. . . ." Investment bankers subordinated themselves to clients and tried to keep their profiles low. . . . This aversion to publicity was related to the restrained style of competition: if you couldn't raid other firms' clients, why bother to advertise? Morgan Stanley's goal was to freeze the status quo.[16]

In the 1970s and 1980s things changed, and many banks found themselves thrust into the fray. As one banker reminded me: "If you go back 15 years, there were probably no PR or media people in the industry. They started doing it in the 1970s and 1980s, and that generated incredible interest in investment banking that wasn't there before. It helped boost the salaries and prestige of bankers and attracted an aggressive new breed into the industry." Broker E. F. Hutton was among the first to shape an aggressive image through the televised media. Its arrogant tagline—"When E. F. Hutton talks, people listen"—became one of the most widely known mottos of all time. It was designed to support the company's large retail network of brokers in their efforts to reel in individual investors.

The avalanche of media attention, although initially flattering, quickly turned deadly as reporters uncovered scandal after scandal and used them to deride the industry. Various watershed articles stand out for their attacks on the premier banks and the implicit signal they gave that all banks were fair game.

Morgan Stanley Trips

In 1978, the *Wall Street Journal* broke a story centered around Morgan Stanley that launched extensive debate about client-banker confidentiality. The incident in question involved Morgan Stanley's improper sharing of information obtained from one client with another client during a takeover battle. The article strongly suggested ethical violations at Morgan Stanley. It was followed by other articles that demonstrated the ineffectiveness of Morgan Stanley's Chinese Walls: While one department of the bank was pursuing takeover discussions with a client, the bank had taken a large stake in the target, giving it a vested interest in the outcome. In 1981, the first criminal indictments ever brought against investment bankers were handed down. They produced jail terms and fines for a former Morgan Stanley banker. The charges of insider trading did significant damage to the bank's reputation and foreshadowed the Ivan Boesky debacle.

DREXEL COLLAPSES

Throughout the 1980s, secrecy had been crucial to the operation of Michael Milken's junk-bond machine. From the start, he shunned publicity, convinced that it had no upside and a considerable downside. Having been ignored, the press would have a field day uncovering Mr. Milken's maneuvers and the stores of data his department had kept from the public. The publicity would not serve the other parts of the Drexel empire well. In its last years, the bank tried to revive its sagging fortunes with televised ads that promoted Drexel's populist image of helping "the little guy." By then, of course, it was too little good press, too late.

GOLDMAN SACHS STUMBLES

Goldman Sachs treasures privacy and discretion. It's not a firm that likes to see its name in the press. In 1987, however, the firm got dragged into the public eye when Robert Freeman, a senior partner in charge of risk arbitrage, was found to have ties to arbitrager Ivan Boesky and to others accused of insider trading at Kidder Peabody and Drexel Burnham. After a drawn out negotiation, Mr. Freeman pleaded guilty in 1989 and resigned from the firm, leaving its reputation a tad sullied.

SALOMON'S GREED

In August 1991, it was Salomon's turn to fall. In a flurry of damaging revelations to the press, the bank admitted guilt in attempting to corner the market in five separate auctions of Treasury securities. In an attempt to manipulate the prices at which those securities sold and thereby make a profit, Salomon's rogue banker Paul Mozer had not only exceeded bidding limits at the regulated auction but submitted false bids on behalf of clients without their consent. A barrage of negative publicity greeted the announcement, and Solly's market value dropped by some $500 million, more than 15 percent (see chapter 15).

KIDDER COLLAPSES

Joe Jett may have fabricated paper profits of $250 million in 1993, but it was media exposure from the scandal that turned a lapse in control into a public relations nightmare for Kidder Peabody's conservative parent, GE. Unable to cope with the damaging effects of the scandal, in October 1994 GE essentially dissolved the Kidder name by selling off the bank's investment banking unit to PaineWebber for $650 million, a fraction of its original investment.

ANY LESSONS?

As these public beatings suggest, managing the press looms as an ever larger concern for investment bankers. One industry insider justified the reactive posture of most leading investment banks as follows: "You can't deal with the press in the middle of a crisis. Where reporters are concerned, ideally we'd like to play offense, but most of the time we're playing defense." Still, the introverted facade that banks maintain clearly has more downside risk than was ever anticipated. In the struggle to maintain reputation, introversion may be unwise. Some banks are recognizing the danger of remaining outside the community of journalists involved in print and television that regularly monitors the industry. In my conversations with different bankers, it struck me that many banks, especially the bigger, potentially more vulnerable generalists, were coming to grips with the need to build stronger relationships with constituents *other than clients* to protect their reputational capital. As the next chapter suggests, J. P. Morgan is among the more active of the top banks in reaching out to one of its key constituencies: New York City.

CHAPTER FOURTEEN

A man always has two reasons for doing something:
A good reason, and the real reason.

—*J. P. Morgan*

Doing Good, the Morgan Way

COMPANIES THAT rate well in reputational surveys demonstrate consistent attention to constituents other than clients. J. P. Morgan is among the premier banks in the United States. It regularly appears on top-10 lists of the best-managed companies. This chapter explores some of the bank's efforts to demonstrate corporate citizenship. The bank focuses on "doing good" in the community with which its employees most closely identify, the city of New York. I argue that J. P. Morgan's sterling reputation derives in no small part from the bank's efforts to create a symbiotic link with the city that accounts for most of its revenues. Acts of corporate citizenship are taken seriously by most of the bank's employees, if only because everyone recognizes that doing good is, quite simply, good business.

COMMUNITY ACTIVISM

On June 11, 1992, I joined a group of 40 teachers and principals from two New York public schools at J. P. Morgan's headquarters to celebrate a major transition. An independent program, designed with support from Morgan to improve teaching quality in public schools, was being adopted by the city's Central Board of Education to be put into effect throughout the school system—a clear sign of success. The professional development laboratory had grown out of a private initiative begun in 1988 to improve public education by providing teachers with growth opportunities and peer feedback on teaching methods. The program brought together representatives from New York's Board of Education, the United Federation of Teachers, the Manhattan Borough President's Office, the City Council President's Office, and banker J. P. Morgan.

Within Morgan, Hildy Simmons, head of community relations and public affairs, convinced the bank to contribute more than $900,000 of funding. She also mobilized some of the bank's staff to hold skill-building workshops for teachers. After two city schools had been selected as test sites, a number of Morgan volunteers were picked as school liaisons, and groups of teachers were put through staggered four-week cycles during which they left their classrooms to observe more experienced teachers and to work on skill building and professional development. At the cocktail celebration, everyone I spoke to testified to how the PDL pilot program had been both a personal and an organizational success.

A month later, on July 25, 1992, I joined yet another celebration sparked by Morgan. This time we were far away from the bank's post-modern headquarters, in one of New York's more colorful but poor neighborhoods. Gourmet ice cream gurus Ben Cohen and Jerry Greenfield, who had arrived from their Vermont headquarters along with a busload of employees, grinned proudly. News cameras rolled, spectators gawked, music blared, children skipped rope, dancers frolicked, and everyone crowded around to sample free ice cream up and down New York's 125th Street in Harlem. The occasion? A block party celebrating the opening of Ben & Jerry's first Partnershop, a revolutionary alliance between the well-regarded Vermont ice cream maker, a Harlem entrepreneur by the name of Joe Holland, and HARKhomes, a nearby homeless shelter founded by Holland. Joe Holland's idea? To create a viable business in a distressed neighborhood, capable of providing disadvantaged residents with employment opportunities and job training. As Mr. Holland put it: "The challenge is to meld the profit-making goals of a business enterprise with the social mission of HARKhomes and the economic development needs of a courageous comeback community. My greatest hope is that, by setting a sustainable example, we will encourage other companies and organizations to establish similar programs for doing well by doing good."

In realizing the project, no one proved more valuable than J. P. Morgan's Oliver Wesson, president of the Morgan Community Development Corporation. Since early 1991, he and the bank's subsidiary had helped both to structure the deal and to identify viable lending sources for start-up and operating expenses. In 1992, Morgan itself turned investor by purchasing some $65,000 in preferred stock from the scoop shop. With ice cream in hand and family in tow, Wesson obviously had much to celebrate on that sunny July afternoon in Harlem.

Both of these events demonstrate the range of contributions that prominent companies like J. P. Morgan regularly make to sustain their reputations.

J. PIERPONT MORGAN'S LEGACY

Morgan sustains its first-rate reputation in New York by "doing good" in two principal ways: It donates considerable sums of money and time to needy nonprofit groups, and it invests in community development. Much of the bank's commitment to good citizenship harks back to the philosophy of "enlightened self-interest" propounded by its influential founder, Pierpont Morgan.

Mr. Morgan became interested in philanthropy at an early age. Unlike such other noted philanthropists as John D. Rockefeller and Andrew Carnegie, however, Pierpont Morgan never developed a philosophy of giving; he simply gave to the causes and institutions that pleased him most, especially to religious, cultural, and educational institutions that were private and elite, whether the Wadsworth Athenaeum in Hartford, the Harvard Medical School, St. Paul's Cathedral in London, or a hospital in Aix-les-Bains. In New York, he made large gifts to St. George's Church on Stuyvesant Square, St. Luke's Hospital, the American Museum of Natural History, the YMCA, the Cathedral of St. John the Divine, and the Metropolitan Opera. His greatest love, however, was art, and Mr.

Morgan played a leading role in organizing and funding the Metropolitan Museum in 1871, serving as its president from 1904 until his death in 1913.

His considerable charitable contributions aside, Pierpont Morgan is also well remembered for the sense of institutional responsibility he demonstrated at critical times. In October 1907, for instance, the failure of Augustus Heinze, a well-known copper speculator who controlled a chain of banks, touched off widespread panic. When one bank subsequently failed (the Knickerbocker Trust Company), other institutions trembled in anticipation of an assault by frightened depositors. Since they were allowed to operate with low reserves, a run on the unregulated trusts could have created a financial crisis that would have damaged the national economy. Morgan personally stepped in and organized the presidents of the solvent institutions to meet the threat. For two weeks, financiers wrangled in the rooms of Mr. Morgan's library to raise enough capital to save the trust companies, the stock exchange, and the city of New York. As historian Frederick Lewis Allen comments, "In an emergency that threatened the national economy, the crucial leadership did not come from the president of the United States or from the secretary of the Treasury. It came from Morgan. Morgan served as a one-man Federal Reserve Bank."[1]

Many times since then, the bank's top executives have played a leading role in averting contemporary financial panics. A recent example was in 1984, when J. P. Morgan's top managers were key players following a global run on the Continental Illinois Bank and Trust Company. With speculation of Continental's imminent collapse widespread, the Federal Reserve Bank appealed to Morgan's chairman, Lew Preston, to help assemble a $4.5 billion credit line for Continental. Although the U.S. government ultimately had to step in, Morgan's leading role in mobilizing the banking community to safeguard the monetary system is widely acknowledged.

This tradition of answering to a higher calling continues to pervade the company. Morgan's current chairman, Dennis Weatherstone, is a member of many national advisory groups such as the Business Roundtable, a high-profile network of chief executives of the largest American corporations. He also sits on multinational study groups that contemplate and analyze the safety and soundness of the financial system worldwide. The Group of 30 is one such group, its principal objective being to ensure the free flow of capital to productive uses around the world. Indirectly, these actions sustain the bank's reputation.

CONSTANCY IN THE MIDST OF CHANGE

In the late 1920s, the financial services industry was dominated by the House of Morgan, the jewel in financier J. Pierpont Morgan's crown. Fearful of overconcentration, the U.S. Congress passed the notorious Glass-Steagall Act in 1933 to separate commercial banking from investment banking. As a result, the House of Morgan was forcibly divided into two companies: J. P. Morgan & Company, a commercial bank, and Morgan Stanley & Company, an investment bank.

Since 1933, Morgan has operated mainly as a wholesale bank, providing banking services and loans to blue-chip companies, governments, and institutions throughout the world as well as to individuals with a high net worth. Throughout the post–World War II era, Morgan held a dominant position in blue-chip lending. In 1956, the Bank Holding Company Act precluded the bank from acquiring more than 5 percent of companies engaged in nonbanking activities and limited its involvement in the securities business. As deregulation progressed in the 1970s and 1980s, Morgan faced growing threats from clients themselves, who began borrowing more cheaply by issuing their own commerical paper or tapping the bond markets, getting transactional assistance from other, more innovative banks.

Threatened by aggressive rivals, Morgan moved into investment banking with determination. Throughout the 1980s, the bank focused its efforts on Europe, where it became a prominent underwriter of new securities. In the mid-1980s, to get into the securities business in the United States, CEO Lewis Preston even considered having Morgan abandon its commercial banking charter, which would have meant sacrificing some of its traditional business. It proved unnecessary. Between 1988 and 1990, industry deregulation spurred the Federal Reserve into giving Morgan progressive authorization to underwrite and deal not only in Treasury and municipal bonds but also in corporate bonds.

In June 1992, Morgan brought to market for the first time in 62 years a $172 million initial public offering of equity securities for Riverwood International. The stock placement opened a new chapter in U.S. financial history, making Morgan the first commercial bank to exercise a full range of securities powers since 1933. Today, although Morgan remains, technically speaking, a commercial bank, its increasingly visible involvement in mergers and acquisitions and securities underwriting places it ever closer to competing with top investment banks like Goldman Sachs and Salomon Brothers as well as its prominent sibling, Morgan Stanley.

In terms of strategy, the company retains a strong focus on disciplined diversification. Its clients are relatively few in number, distinguished not by size but by quality and scope of activity. The need for sophisticated financial services defines the market that the bank strives to serve on a global basis. Although early in the company's evolution Morgan made some judicious acquisitions, most notably the Guaranty Trust Company in 1959, since then the company has grown largely by capitalizing on the skills and creativity of its employees and diversifying from within. The results have been impressive. In 1992, Morgan's 13,000 employees brought in more than $10 billion in revenues. With $102 billion in total assets, the company ranks fifty-ninth in market value among *Business Week*'s top 1,000 and first in banking, ahead of Citicorp and Bank America.

Morgan is generally characterized as having a fortress-like mentality: a conservative, relatively low-risk posture in its lending practices; a cautious stance in investing its own portfolio; and, most emphatically, a preference for maintaining a low profile in the media. Throughout the 1980s, it was frequently chastized by analysts and competitors for lacking aggressiveness. It shouldered few Third World loans, shied away from high-yield debt financing, and grew steadily, if somewhat unspectacularly. The bank's cautious style, however, has proved highly effective as more aggressive institutions like Citicorp have had to shoulder the huge burden of low-performing loans.

Growing rivalry in the financial services industry created a new pool of competitors in the 1970s and 1980s that shunned the more traditional relationship-based orientation to banking in favor of a one-shot, transaction-based outlook. Increasingly under assault was Morgan's historical reliance on a network of stable relationships with large, established, blue-chip companies.

Despite numerous flank attacks throughout the years, the bank remains true to its roots. As chairman Dennis Weatherstone emphasizes:

Our company's character is woven through J. P. Morgan's evolution as a global financial intermediary. First, we seek relationships of trust with clients who have challenging financial needs. We are international, in per-spective and ability. We don't avoid risk, we manage it. We stress thorough research and analysis. We believe in personal responsibility, accountability, and teamwork. Finally, we aim for sound performance and leadership over the long term.[2]

The growing importance of investment banking in Morgan's portfolio has, however, created some tensions in the bank between the more tradition-bound lending side, oriented to relationship banking, and the more risk-prone securities side, which has a more transactional outlook. As the business mix has continued to evolve, J. P. Morgan has found itself facing something of an identity crisis and has been forced to communicate more aggressively with its outside publics.

Internally, the bank recruits top talent, trains for specialized skills, and rewards professionalism. But it prides itself on teamwork. In contrast to the individualism stressed in many rival banks, especially Citicorp, Morgan's culture strongly supports cooperative relationships; team assignments bring together an eclectic group of professionals to meet client needs.

Both creativity and common sense flourish when people with diverse points of view get together. We see it vividly in working with people of different nationalities, since we have a long history of international orientation. We purposely look for diversity of experience right through to the Corporate Office, the senior governing group at Morgan. We've got four accents among the five of us, and a mix of business backgrounds as well. But as much as we believe in teams, we equally believe in getting the best and brightest on the teams. And we've got to have people who can balance sound principles with competitive drive and brilliance.[3]

The well-greased workings of the internal culture give J. P. Morgan an external reputation for being fair in its dealings with clients, employees, competitors, and other stakeholders. As one manager told me: "We have a reputation for probity, depth, responsibility, international scope, long-term client-oriented focus, and quality in every possible sense of the word. We are a responsible participant in business finance, in the world monetary system, in communities, and in the way we deal with employees. And we care about that reputation, we care a lot."

In June 1992, J. P. Morgan announced that it would participate in a debt-for-nature swap with Bolivia. By donating its holdings of Bolivian debt to support the country's environmental programs, the company became the largest private donor to benefit a single country. The debt had a face value of $11.5 million and would be converted to approximately $2.8 million in cash. The funds were to be used by the Nature Conservancy and the World Wildlife Fund to support projects ranging from the maintenance of national parks to the training of Bolivians in natural resources management skills. The swap is representative of the many efforts Morgan now makes to convey the sense of a social conscience, which in turn fortifies its first-class reputation.

Officially, Morgan's outlook is phrased as follows:

Our overall philanthropic objective is to improve the quality of life in the communities in which we live and work. We focus our efforts on increasing the capacity of people and organizations to help themselves, and stress long-term solutions to problems rather than short-term remedies. We are often able to supplement and multiply the beneficial effect of our financial contributions in other ways.

Historically, the bank's senior executives have routinely encouraged employee involvement in the community. Following Morgan's fusion with the Guaranty Trust Company in 1959, for instance, then chairman Henry Clay Alexander made an explicit and often-repeated exhortation to employees of the merged company: "I hope that a lot of our people will take part at the precinct level or otherwise in the affairs of their community. Make a better citizen and in turn a better banker, if I may say so."[4]

A June 1992 memo from Sandy Warner, J. P. Morgan's president, reminded employees about the merits of corporate giving and of Morgan's matching gifts program:

A commitment to community responsibility and involvement is part of our institutional heritage; a similar personal commitment on the part of many of our people is one of the things that makes Morgan special. . . . I salute those of you who have used [the matching gifts] program in the past and urge everyone to consider taking advantage of it. It's a great way to make a difference and put Morgan's resources to work for the organization of your choice.

Rooted in the tradition of noblesse oblige that the Morgan family itself grew up with, the values of philanthropy and citizenship permeate the institution and powerfully inform its reputation.

THE LEGISLATIVE IMPERATIVES

In 1977, the U.S. Congress passed the Community Reinvestment Act (CRA) to encourage banks to lend more to the poor and to minorities in areas where they maintain branches. Even though Morgan does not operate retail branches or make mortgage loans it must comply with the CRA because it is chartered as a commercial bank. The CRA requires banks to live by the spirit of a broad mandate: to look at lower-income neighborhoods as potentially profitable markets and to apply systematic market planning in these areas.

In December 1989, the laws got tougher with passage of the Financial Institutions Reform, Recovery, and Enforcement Act. Accordingly, since July 1990 all regulated financial institutions are now monitored and assessed by examiners who then publish an overall rating of each institution. Like other banks, Morgan maintains a CRA log that documents internal discussions about community development. Every 18 months or so, government evaluators visit Morgan and conduct an in-depth review of the bank's compliance with CRA requirements. Regulators scrutinize logs, records, and documents, from which they compile a report that provides feedback to the bank about its community performance, including an overall rating on a scale of 1 (outstanding record) to 4 (noncompliance). In its 1992 performance review, Morgan received a rating of 2, indicating a "satisfactory record of ascertaining and helping to meet the needs of its entire delineated community in a manner consistent with its resources and capabilities." As the examiners wrote: "Morgan has been able to establish a good working relationship with government and private sector representatives and to identify opportunities for becoming involved in community development lending programs."

Are these community-based efforts purely a result of the need to comply with legal constraints? Not really. As one manager told me:

Certainly we're doing a little bit more, maybe a little bit differently because of the way the CRA has been interpreted. We're spending money differently not because of the CRA but because it's made us rethink how we could use our money. The CRA committee has involved more people within the firm. I hear a lot of positive comments from people who like to see that Morgan is doing something responsible in the local community in a way that draws on our strengths and fits our strategy. It makes sense, and people here feel very good about it.

CITIZENSHIP PROGRAMS

Morgan sustains its first-class reputation through the activities of two principal groups: community relations and public affairs (CRPA) and the Morgan Community Development Corporation (MCDC). Together, CRPA and MCDC strive to fulfill J. P. Morgan's official mandate: "to ascertain community funding needs and implement community development lending, investment and charitable programs appropriate to the activities of a wholesale bank."

The citizenship activities of the bank are officially monitored by a committee established in 1989 to coordinate the bank's CRA program. The nine-member CRA committee is chaired by one of Morgan's vice chairmen and includes Morgan's general counsel, Morgan's CRA compliance officer, the president of MCDC, and representatives of the CRPA and four other Morgan departments.

Oliver Wesson, MCDC president since 1990, explains the CRA committee's relationship to the community development corporation in this way:

We generally go to them and say this is what we want to accomplish this year. For instance, we want to deal with entrepreneurs who want to open up businesses in Harlem and Bedford-Stuyvesant. We'd like to see $300,000–400,000 equity investments made in these companies, and we'd like to grow the assets by this much. We ask them if this makes sense for Morgan as a whole. After they give us their input and stamp of approval, we implement it through our own board.

Jack Ruffle, the head of the CRA committee, points out that the ground rules for success in community development require searching for committed individuals who stay with a project. "Successful community effort occurs," he argues, "only when the people themselves feel some kind of ownership in the process, and when we can encourage that, we can have an impact. The trick for us is to figure out how to do it intelligently and within our means. Again, it's consistent with the idea of adding value—just as we do for all clients."

Besides community investments, J. P. Morgan's citizenship activities include charitable grant making, community development, volunteerism, networking, and communications. Through volunteer activities and board memberships, bank employees are networked into a plethora of local nonprofit organizations, where they encounter employees of other companies located in the New York area.

CHARITABLE GRANTS

Charitable grants are made by a staff of five CRPA program officers led by VP Hildy Simmons. Grant making is determined through team reviews of more than 1,500 proposals received annually.

In community development, Morgan benchmarks itself most closely against investment banks. As one senior employee points out, "In the U.S. we tend to compare ourselves more and more with Goldman Sachs and Morgan Stanley. One of our more traditional peers is also Bankers Trust. We look less to Citicorp and Chase, although in some businesses they are our rivals. . . . Overseas, we compare ourselves to Warburg in the U.K. and Deutsche Bank in Germany—in other words, to the premiere banks in those countries, the ones that have a specialized high-quality wholesale business in particular."

Comparisons with peers are difficult to make as Morgan moves more aggressively into investment banking. "We used to look at the money-center banks," says Simmons, "but that's become more problematic, since there are fewer of them now due to mergers. Although we never felt that we had to base our numbers precisely on what any one of those institutions were doing, it used to give us a range for what competitors were up to. As we've evolved in the last few years, we don't even see most of those institutions as competitors anymore, so it's less useful to look at their numbers."

J. P. Morgan's charitable contributions consist of: grants, matching gifts, and volunteer funds. The CRPA in New York distributes 78 percent of the grant-making budget. The remaining 22 percent is distributed locally by subsidiaries located principally in London, Paris, and Delaware.

In 1990, 2,490 of J. P. Morgan's 12,000 employees made charitable donations that were matched by the company. In 1991, the number of employees making donations grew by 60 percent to 3,963. Since many of the 2,000 different organizations receiving funding through the matching-gifts program are fledgling nonprofit organizations that rely heavily on individual contributions for their survival, the near doubling of individual contributions from Morgan extends the bank's outreach dramatically and makes it a powerful voice in the community. This explains why the corporate office encourages employee participation and makes it likely that the number and size of Morgan's matching gifts will continue to grow. Table 14-1 shows that the bank's total pool of funds available for grant making is constituted of direct corporate contributions, matching gifts, and volunteer gifts.

SUPPORT OF NONPROFITS

The CRPA allocates Morgan's annual contributions budget to nonprofit programs and projects of its choice. In 1991, funds were allocated to organizations involved in six principal areas: the arts (20 percent), education (50 percent), health care (19 percent), international affairs (10 percent), urban affairs (33 percent), and environmental issues (4 percent).

Of the 1,500 or so requests for funding received in 1991, 379 programs were funded by the CRPA. Consistent with the needs of the city, the largest number of grants were given to nonprofit groups involved in urban affairs, the arts, and education. Among the recipients of the largest grants made in 1991 were the New York Downtown Hospital ($330,000), the Fund for Public Schools ($200,000), Lincoln Center for the Performing Arts ($100,000), and Educators for Social Responsibility ($100,000). Some of these funds came from a special allocation made at the end of the Persian Gulf War to support a nursing internship and a program on confict resolution in public schools.

In fact, education receives a disproportionate share of Morgan's charitable grants. One educational program that has received extensive commitment from J. P. Morgan in terms of both financial resources and the involvement of Morgan employees is the professional development laboratory (PDL). The program was launched in 1989 as a collaborative public/private venture with the goal of sharing skills that characterize excellent teaching practice across the public school system. In two differ-

Table 14-1   SOURCES OF FUNDS FOR CHARITABLE GRANTS

Year	Charitable Grants	Subsidiary Grants	Matching Gifts	Volunteer Fund	Total
1990	$6,231,400	$1,835,000	$2,008,010	$22,000	$10,096,410
1991	$6,671,350	$1,824,000	$2,256,089	$34,500	$10,785,939

ent New York school districts, teachers volunteered for PDL "sabbaticals" of three to four weeks, which they spent in the classrooms of oustanding teachers. They observed their coaches in action, consulted with them, and actually practiced new skills in the classroom. Meanwhile, adjunct teachers were hired to replace those teachers who were involved in PDL training.

As mentioned earlier in the chapter, the PDL program brought together some powerful collaborators in education and local government. The annual budget was $1.2 million, toward which Morgan contributed $200,000 for the first two years, an additional $200,000 in 1991, and $500,000 more for 1992 and 1993.

Morgan, however, did more than provide funding for the program. The bank's human resources department played a key role in helping to design an interviewing process to select the project coordinator and other project staff. The training group sponsored various sessions to train teachers in presentation skills, facilitation skills, and communication skills. The human resource department also helped to design an outcome-based evaluation system for teachers. Morgan liaisons worked with teachers to design goal-oriented, action-plan workbooks that encouraged individual accountability and facilitated the design of new performance appraisals that are now being used for teachers.

Morgan also helped the PDL network with relevant audiences. For instance, some of the adjunct teachers substituting for those undergoing PDL training were hired from the financial services industry. As the program coordinator, Mary Ann Walsh, recalls, "I had thought that we might be able to find some unemployed people in the industry with a teaching license. Morgan invited the top employment agencies the bank deals with to a luncheon, and we ended up hiring a number of businesspeople as adjunct teachers."

During the early life of the PDL, J. P. Morgan hosted a dozen luncheons during which teachers and Morgan staff could share professional experiences. At every lunch, one Morgan employee sat with two teachers from different districts. "After an initial icebreaker," says Walsh, "we had them share ideas about nurturing professionalism, and it was incredibly instructive for teachers to hear what people from the business culture did, what they read, and how they formed networks. As a result of these luncheons, teachers from different schools made contact, shared ideas, and formed networks to continue the process of professional development."

Two years after the PDL was first introduced, more than 100 teachers had participated and 5,000 students had been exposed to the program's results. An evaluation study demonstrated that PDL produced impressive results. Teachers had mastered more effective teaching strategies and learned to collaborate with peers; they also reported feeling increased confidence in themselves as professionals and closer rapport with students.

According to Walsh, "A major reason PDL proved so successful was that, throughout the program, it never was Morgan doing for us, it always was Morgan doing with us—a really successful collaboration." In mid-1992, with the program widely perceived as a success, PDL and its project coordinator moved under the umbrella of the Central Board of Education of New York's public school system. The bank had done its part.

SOME DIFFERENT KINDS OF ASSISTANCE

Besides providing financial and human resources, Morgan periodically donates office furniture, computers, and other equipment to needy groups in the community. First choice is typically given to holders of community grants. In 1990, Morgan donated used equipment to more than 25 organizations.

Morgan employees also participate in popular local food collection programs. Canned food is collected annually and distributed to 900 programs in the New York City area through one of the bank's grant recipients, Food for Survival. In 1990, the food drive collected 2,809 pounds of food for the needy. In 1991, the drive brought in more than 3,449 pounds.

Like many other well-regarded companies, J. P. Morgan also provides computerized payroll deductions as a means to contribute to the United Way. In 1991, however, increasing interest in environmental issues prompted Morgan to offer employees the opportunity to contribute to Earth Share, an environmental group as an alternative to the United Way campaign. Total contributions remained comparable to prior years at about $552,000.

Finally, J. P. Morgan regularly offers community groups—and especially grant recipients like PDL—free use of meeting facilities in its Wall Street headquarters building. The bank frequently hosts social gatherings either to facilitate information exchange or to provide training in management and communication skills for nonprofit groups that it funds.

COMMUNITY DEVELOPMENT

Various regulatory amendments instituted in the Bank Holding Company Act of 1970 allowed bank holding companies like J. P. Morgan to engage in some activities that were, technically speaking, nonbanking activities. One of these happened to be community development, specifically: "Making equity and debt investments in corporations or projects designed primarily to promote community welfare, such as the economic rehabilitation and development of low-income housing, services, or jobs for residents."[5]

The Morgan Community Development Corporation, launched in 1971, was the first such organization created by a bank holding company. The subsidiary's purpose was to provide equity interest in joint ventures with developers of small apartment dwellings that qualified for federal assistance. It encouraged equity investments in projects that essentially promoted social welfare.

In 1989, the federal regulatory agencies got more vigilant about enforcing the Community Reinvestment Act of 1977. MCDC president Oliver Wesson points out that:

As the criteria for evaluating a bank's CRA performance got tougher, MCDC shifted its focus to respond to the new CRA guidelines, yet still did things in a Morgan-like way. The CRA committee targeted nonprofit financial intermediaries as a good vehicle for reaching out into the community. Through them, we could funnel capital to low and moderate segments of the community, and get very involved in areas that one would not automatically identify with J. P. Morgan.

Since 1990, the J. P. Morgan subsidiary has helped community organizations to construct and renovate low- and moderate-income housing, to fund small business, and to promote economic and community development and welfare in New York City's neighborhoods. Unlike community relations and public affairs, which focuses on charitable donations, the MCDC focuses on generating returns for Morgan.

According to Jack Ruffle,

We have a special role to fill because we're not a retail institution with branches in those communities. So we find other viable alternatives, such as providing $250,000 in seed capital for the Community Capital Bank in Brooklyn, or lending $300,000 at below-market rates to the National Federation of Community Development Credit Unions, an umbrella organization for nonprofit, community-based credit unions that provides capital and basic financial services in low-income neighborhoods.

The MCDC is legally structured as a separate corporation, distinct from its parent company J. P. Morgan. Since its inception in 1971, the subsidiary has built up an equity base of more than $25 million. This equity base, together with short-term financing from parent J. P. Morgan, enables the MCDC to make commitments to the community in excess of $60 million. It operates with a small staff of three officers but draws on the legal, accounting, and marketing resources of its parent.

Rather than fund programs directly, the MCDC tends to make loans to large intermediaries that have more intimate knowledge of the local area and the skills needed to deliver and monitor programs. On May 5, 1992, for instance, Jack Ruffle announced that via the MCDC, Morgan had pledged $10 million to the New York Equity Fund, a limited partnership jointly funded by Morgan, Bankers Trust, and Republic National Bank. The purpose of the equity fund is to revitalize neighborhoods by financing rehabilitation and providing low-cost housing. "The equity fund's commitment to New York City," said Ruffle, "goes well beyond bricks and mortar and reaches into the community."

A good example of the kind of venture support MCDC favors is the Ben & Jerry's Partnershop that opened in Harlem in July 1992. In the fall of 1990, New York–based entrepreneur and Harvard Law School graduate Joe Holland approached the MCDC. According to Wesson:

Joe had decided that what he wanted to do was to start a business that would actually employ some of the local teenagers as well as some of the men from HARKhomes [the local shelter for the homeless founded by Holland]. He had heard about Ben & Jerry's desire to promote economic development of inner-city areas through socially responsible investments. He discussed the idea of a Harlem franchise with managers at Ben & Jerry's, and they indicated interest in assisting him in establishing a franchise. Ben Cohen, a cofounder of Ben & Jerry's, agreed to work with Joe on a marketing plan for the store and agreed to donate their franchise fee if Joe was able to get financing to establish an ice cream parlor on 125th Street in Harlem.

Joe came to us with a proposal: We would lend HARKhomes $175,000 to $200,00 for five years to establish the business. After looking at the projections, we realized that they were very optimistic: It was unlikely the company would be able to support much debt in its early years. However, since we liked what Joe was trying to do, we wanted to help him. In conversations with another client, we had learned that the New York Urban Development Corporation [UDC] had established a lending program to assist minority entrepreneurs. Under the UDC program, New York State lends up to two dollars of debt for each dollar of equity put into the business. We described the program to Joe and indicated that if he got approval for the loan, we would help him with the equity. We also agreed to put up $65,000 of the bank's capital as an equity investment.

Based on the equity and the donated franchise fee, Joe was able to secure a commitment from UDC to provide a $100,00 medium-term loan. The commitment also enabled him to get a construction loan from Community Capital Bank, a community development bank in which Morgan had also invested.

When Joe Holland opened his Ben & Jerry's Partnershop on July 25, 1992, to a barrage of local publicity, Oliver Wesson preserved Morgan's traditional low profile, avoiding press interviews. In none of the press releases widely distributed to the reporters and officials present was J. P. Morgan's name even mentioned.

VOLUNTEERING

Another activity that sustains Morgan's reputation in the local community is the Volunteer Center. Established in 1971, the program is designed to help community organizations benefit from the skills and talents of Morgan employees. The Volunteer Center acts as a clearinghouse for matching interested employees with organizations in need of assistance.

The files of the center indicate that about 350 of Morgan's 9,000 or so New York-based employees volunteered time in 1991. Unlike other companies, Morgan does not keep a detailed record of volunteers. As one of the center's program officers put it, "We respect their privacy. We don't want them to feel like Big Brother is looking over their shoulder. Even if we know from the agency that they are volunteering, we don't necessarily go back to them. What employees do on their own time is up to them." Volunteering occurs largely from employee responsiveness to announcements made in the company newsletter or from fliers that are widely distributed and posted.

Morgan supports two large programs on company time: Junior Achievement and Project Live. Project Live is sponsored by the Children's Aid Society. "We pay for transportation," says Morgan's program coordinator, "to take children from a seventh grade class in Washington Heights to the bank for tutoring on a one-to-one basis with Morgan volunteers. They're at the bank from 4 P.M. to 6 P.M., so it's an hour of bank time and an hour of employee time. We have the Project Live library, where books and computer programs are made available for the tutors to work with the children."

In the nationally coordinated Junior Achievement program, employees volunteer to go into the public schools and work with a class of third, sixth, or seventh graders. According to a Morgan administrator, "The programs that Morgan works with run from five to eight weeks, and their aim is to encourage kids to stay in school. The volunteers usually bring their class to the bank to show them the world of work. Most of these kids come from low-income areas and have never been in a company like this. Children tend to associate banking with tellers. They don't realize that there are kitchens, with chefs that work in those kitchens, that we have a building department, with painters and spacklers, and that there are many other careers in a bank other than tellers."

NETWORKING

Although business has become more competitive and work more time-consuming, senior executives do considerable volunteer work. Morgan president Sandy Warner sits on the board of Sloan-Kettering. Dennis Weatherstone is president of the Royal College of Surgeons. Various other employees sit on nonprofit boards that provide Morgan with informal links to a wide variety of organizations in the New York area. As Table 14-2 indicates, Morgan's top managers, directors, and officers serve as board members for more than 144 nonprofit organizations.

The staff of the CRPA and the MCDC are also members of various networks of nonprofit professionals that meet regularly to exchange information about various programs at one another's companies. For instance, Morgan is a member of Corporate Volunteers for New York, and members of the bank's CRPA meet once a month with representatives of other banks and companies to exchange information about nonprofit groups. "At those meetings," says Morgan's volunteer center coordinator Mary Stuart, "I hear about what other banks are doing, and I tell

Table 14-2 J.P. MORGAN SERVICE ON NONPROFIT BOARDS

Group Type	Number of Boards Employees Sit On
Education	42
Culture	28
Urban affairs	22
International	30
Health	19
Environment	3
Total	144

them what we're doing." Volunteer networks like these help to amplify Morgan's reputational standing in the community.

COMMUNICATIONS

Morgan employees are low key and reserved in dealing with publicity. "That stance suits our institutional character, with its stress on discretion and seriousness of purpose," says Jack Morris, former head of public relations in the corporate communications department. Public shyness carries over from the business side and affects how the bank publicizes its community development efforts. As Laura Dillon, Morgan's managing director of communications, explains:

> We haven't communicated our philanthropic efforts quite as aggressively as we could have. It's part of a natural reticence about blowing one's own horn. We've gone about building relationships in the community the way we have gone about dealing with clients, carrying on a corporate tradition of privacy—quiet diplomacy, if you want to put it that way—without too much fanfare. We feel that it's seemly to take a low-key approach. We don't want to boast about doing good.

The bank publishes many brochures and notices to communicate with employees and outside groups. Internally, they help to build a common bond among employees. "Once an organization gets to be as large as ours," adds Dillon, "you have to be more aggressive in communicating what the organization does so that people who work for you identify with your approach. So part of our communications efforts are focused internally to help people understand what the company does to be responsible in the community, from pure philanthropy to organizing volunteer networks."

The principal newsletter circulated throughout the bank is the monthly *MorganNews,* in which announcements of ongoing events and activities are made, including requests for volunteers. In 1990, the CRPA launched a specialized biannual publication called *Capital Ideas* to illustrate how Morgan invests to strengthen the community. The elegant newsletter details specific activities engaged in by different parts of the bank that benefit the community. Each newsletter focuses on particular organizations that may be grant recipients or clients of the MCDC. It is distributed to all of Morgan's U.S. employees, community groups, and interested government officials.

Externally, publications help Morgan to meet the regulatory mandate imposed by the Community Reinvestment Act that requires bank holding companies to publicize their activities. Various publications are also distributed that describe Morgan's citizenship activities. One is entitled "Community Development Initiatives" and describes the credit and investment products of the MCDC and the grants provided by CRPA. It is widely shared not only with Morgan employees but also with many not-for-profit community groups in New York City and with publically elected officials.

THE REWARDS OF GOOD CITIZENSHIP

In conversation, Morgan employees appear to be justifiably proud of their record of community involvement. They are often applauded at social functions, thanked by politicians, educators, hospital administrators, artists, and community organizers. Adds Laura Dillon:

> *I'm embarrassed to say that we keep no systematic records of awards we've received. But it's revealing, isn't it? We don't like to brag. It translates into the business sphere. You don't see Morgan trumpeting record financial performance, which we did turn in last year. We'll use the "best" and "most" citations in marketing and publicizing business activities, but at the corporate level we are reserved. I don't know if your parents ever taught you this, but I remember my mother saying very clearly: You don't brag about yourself; somebody else will if you deserve it. That's a clear strain in the Morgan ethic.*

J.P. Morgan was instrumental in helping to launch a teacher training program in the New York City school system. The elementary school children and teachers who benefited from the program acknowledged the company's support by sewing a quilt that now hangs at Morgan's new headquarters building at 60 Wall Street, pictured below. (© 1995 J.P. Morgan & Co. Incorporated.)

In July 1991, a multicolored quilt was presented to Morgan at a reception that marked the end of the first full year of the professional development laboratory. The quilt was sewn by grateful students and teachers from elementary schools in Manhattan, where the program was piloted. Today the quilt hangs in a prominent place at Morgan headquarters. To Hildy Simmons, "It's a very beautiful quilt. It's been beautifully framed, and put it in a place where all employees pass every day for lunch. It acts as a constant reminder of Morgan's good works. It's not a big thing, but it's certainly symbolic."

CAPITALIZING ON REPUTATION

There appears to be a pervasive belief among employees that corporate citizenship, as one employee put it, "is not merely a charitable act but is a form of 'enlightened self-interest.' " The convergence of goodwill and good business is perhaps best manifested in the bank's recent efforts to extend its business into the not-for-profit domain. By marketing its services to nonprofit groups, Morgan stands to capitalize on a heretofore untapped source of potential synergy between its line activities and its goodwill-generating citizenship efforts.

In August 1990, J. P. Morgan underwrote $54 million in tax-exempt bonds for the much publicized renovation of the Guggenheim Museum in New York. Coming after its $20 million in tax-exempt financing for the new, ecologically designed headquarters of the National Audubon Society in New York's Greenwich Village, the backing of the Guggenheim pointed to Morgan's entry into a new and promising line of business: financing for not-for-profit companies. The not-for-profit (NFP) group was formally constituted in early 1991 to assist in marketing Morgan's asset and liability management services to such nonprofit groups as foundations, health care institutions, and educational, environmental, religious, and cultural organizations.

The NFP group's explicit strategy is to identify all the not-for-profit clients now being served by various Morgan business groups, to determine which products and services those clients currently use, and to expand existing relationships into new areas. The group also tries to identify key prospects in each segment and develop new client relationships with them. Through the NFP group, not-for-profit organizations have access to all of the Morgan financial products and services available to major coporations, governments, and wealthy individuals.

The NFP group also develops financial plans, for both not-for-profit organizations and donors. Through Morgan's fiduciary services group, the bank helps wealthy individuals identify philanthropic objectives and establish appropriate legal and accounting structures to establish new charitable trusts and foundations and make long-term commitments of assets. Today, Morgan acts as the trustee or investment advisor for charitable accounts that total more than $3.1 billion.

In May 1992, the NFP group sponsored a seminar entitled "Philanthropy and the Family" at the Pierpont Morgan Library in New York. Some 60 clients and wealthy prospects came to hear experts in philanthrophy—including CRPA's Hildy Simmons—outline strategies for effective giving.

Most recently, the NFP group has tried to generate marketing contacts within Morgan itself. Employees who participate in the management of not-for-profit organizations are encouraged to contact NFP if they feel their group might benefit from Morgan's advice or services. "It's nothing fancy, just the basic 'blocking and tackling' of relationship management," says Sandy Smith who heads NFP. "We want to make the organization as seamless as possible to clients so that we can capitalize on business opportunities that otherwise might fall through the cracks."

Although difficult to quantify, it's clear that throughout the bank citizenship activities are thought to sustain the bank's reputation and bring in business. That's doing good, the Morgan way.

*The more you are talked about, the less powerful
you are.*

—*Benjamin Disraeli*

Song of Salomon

NOT ONLY must top-flight companies like J. P. Morgan regularly sustain their reputations, but they must occasionally defend it against attack. In 1991, the venerable trading firm of Salomon Brothers faced a crisis unprecedented in its history: Charges of rigged bidding and rogue behavior by its trader of government bonds quickly escalated and threatened the firm's survival. In many ways, the circumstances Salomon encountered epitomize those of the entire financial services industry in the late 1980s. Salomon was hardly the first company on Wall Street to take a fall. Few, if any, banks emerged from the 1980s with their reputations unscathed. Today, the industry is littered with the scattered remains of once-prominent companies like E. F. Hutton, which succumbed to indictment for mail and wire fraud, and Drexel Burnham Lambert, which eventually collapsed from charges of insider trading in 1990.

This chapter examines the actions taken during 1991 and 1992 by Salomon Brothers, where a savvy group of managers skillfully postured the bank both publicly and privately so as to defend its reputation, sustain its character, and regain economic value and a sense of self.

SALOMON ON THE BRINK

In March 1991, the esteemed investment bank Salomon Brothers moved out of its old stonefaced structure at the tip of lower Manhattan and into a nearby building: the never before occupied corporate headquarters of Drexel Burnham Lambert. Today, most of us remember Drexel as the junk-bond house sullied by charges of insider trading and bankrupted by stock fraud. It was to be an ironic and oddly prophetic move for Salomon. A few months after the move, John Gutfreund, Salomon's mighty chairman, publicly admitted that its government desk had placed illegal bids in some 30 of the 230 auctions of government securities in which it had participated since 1986. Shortly thereafter, both Gutfreund and Thomas Strauss, Salomon's president, resigned, and the U.S. Treasury Department suspended Salomon from bidding for its clients at future Treasury auctions.

At the time, Salomon was without doubt the most powerful broker on Wall Street and a top-gun trader of government securities. The disclosure threatened not only to shatter the firm's hard-won franchise and pristine reputation but to eviscerate its culture by striking at the heart of the bank's character and identity. This was surely the worst scandal to hit the company in its 81-year history, and it would take exquisite managerial skill and timing to weather the storm.

Although no one could have predicted the precise form that a crisis would take—or its timing—most industry observers believe that something like this was bound to happen to Salomon Brothers someday. Among the preconditions that made a crisis likely were, on one hand, the firm's aggressively "macho" culture and, on the other, the lax regulatory and increasingly competitive environment that Salomon's traders faced. Like kindling, these two sets of factors helped to ignite unethical and illegal behavior in the bank.

BACKGROUND

Salomon, Inc., is a holding company with assets of $147 billion (1992) held in two major operating units: Salomon Brothers and Phibro Energy. Phibro is the largest oil-trading company in the world. In early 1991, however, the crown jewel of the Salomon empire was clearly Salomon Brothers, the investment bank with the reputation for masterful trading in the $2.4 trillion global market for U.S. government securities.

About 80 times a year, the U.S. Treasury auctions bonds to raise money for the government. An elite club of some 40 leading investment banks are granted status as primary dealers at these auctions, giving them the exclusive right to buy the government's securities and the power to influence not only a bond's original offering price but its resale price in the secondary market. Three investment banks walk especially tall at these auctions: Salomon Brothers, Morgan Stanley, and Goldman Sachs.

At every auction, the Treasury allots bonds first to the highest bidder and then to each successive bidder until the issue is sold. Treasury rules limit each bidder to acquiring no more than 35 percent of the issue. But since banks buy bonds for clients as well as for themselves, they often enter multiple bids and can sometimes end up controlling more than 35 percent of an issue as both principal and agent. In 30 of some 230 auctions held since 1986, Salomon had actually acquired close to 50 percent of the securities offered.

THE CRISIS

In June 1990, Paul Mozer, managing director of Salomon's government bond desk, bid for more than 100 percent of the four-year notes up for auction. Soon after, a concerned Treasury official warned Mozer about excessive bidding. Despite the warning, two weeks later Mozer again bid for more than 100 percent of a 30-year bond issue in an effort to buy more than his share. An angered Treasury rejected the bid and reaffirmed the 35 percent rule.

To circumvent the limit, in December 1990 Mozer submitted bogus bids in the names of uninformed customers at an auction of four-year Treasury notes. The unauthorized bids gave Salomon effective control of 46 percent of the securities, once again breaching the Treasury's 35 percent rule. Unbeknownst to Treasury officials, Mozer repeated the practice at eight other auctions in 1991 in which Salomon ended up illegally controlling more than 50 percent of an issue by submitting false bids from clients.

In April 1991, Mozer informed Vice-Chairman John Merriwether about the illegal bidding and, through him, Salomon's top team of John Gutfreund and Thomas Strauss. Incredibly, no action was taken. To explain why he delayed reporting the violation, Gutfreund would later claim he had not been told that the infraction was part of a sustained pattern.[1]

But Mozer did not stop there. In a rash display of arrogance—and doubtless heady from his previous successes—he bought effective control of more than 94 percent of a $12 billion issue of two-year notes at a May 1991 auction. Angered by the exorbitant prices Salomon made them pay to buy the notes they needed, dealers whose bids had been unsuccessful rose up en masse and charged the bank with monopolizing the issue. Following the auction, the Treasury officially invited the Securities and Exchange Commission to investigate. In June 1991, the seriousness of Mozer's actions hit home when the SEC and the Justice Department both issued subpoenas to Salomon and some of its clients.

Surprisingly, it wasn't until August 1991—a full three months later—that Salomon itself released a gingerly worded statement that admitted to committing "irregularities and rule violations in connection with its submission of bids in certain auctions of Treasury securities." By year's end, the bank found itself accused of having submitted a total of 10 false bids between August 1989 and May 1991 totaling $15.5 billion, $9.5 billion of which were illegally acquired. In bottom-line terms, the returns to Salomon were not startling. Net profits from those illegal bids totaled no more than $19.7 million, including a $13.8 million loss from a February auction. Losses to other firms affected by the "May Squeeze," however, were estimated at more than $100 million.

As a result, the company faced 46 lawsuits charging: (1) fraud in trading securities, a violation of antifraud provisions of the SEC Act of 1934; (2) price manipulation by purchasing Treasury securities above the legal limit, a violation of antitrust laws and the Racketeer Influence and Corrupt Oganization (RICO) Act; and (3) misrepresentation, for stating in its March 1991 proxy statement that "management has no knowledge of any business other than that described herein." It had not been a good year for the institution affectionately known as Solly and widely regarded as the preeminent trader on Wall Street.

BACKDROP TO THE CRISIS

Investment banks are of two sorts: relationship oriented and transaction oriented.[2] The business of underwriting new corporate securities has traditionally been dominated by the more prestigious relationship bankers, who call on their close personal ties with the captains of industry to do business—the old boy network. Morgan Stanley and Goldman Sachs dominate that market. It's a sober world of three-piece suits, school ties, antique clocks, and old money.

In contrast, traders like Salomon grew up in a world dominated by transactions, one concerned less with relationships and more with matching all possible buyers and sellers and collecting on the interest rate spread. In the early 1980s, the dynamics of trading changed dramatically when the Federal Reserve instituted floating interest rates. Since bond prices are tied to interest rates, suddenly they too were free to fluctuate. As Michael Lewis, author of the wildly popular *Liar's Poker,* puts it, "Bonds became objects of speculation, a means of creating wealth rather than merely storing it. Overnight the bond market was transformed from a backwater into a casino."[3] And all sorts of bonds were created to finance the huge budget deficit run up during Ronald Reagan's presidency and to fund the massive acquisition binge of consumers and businesses. Salomon made a killing throughout the 1980s by packaging and trading on that debt.

THE SALOMON MYSTIQUE

Salomon was started in 1910 by brothers Arthur and Percy Salomon to arrange bank loans for Wall Street firms and to trade bonds. Twenty years later, it was among Wall Street's most prominent traders. Rather than deal with individual investors, Salomon Brothers concentrated its efforts on institutional investors (like pension funds and big companies) that bought and sold bonds in large blocks. In the 1960s, the company diversified into stock trading and quickly became known as a partnership capable of handling any deal, no matter how large.

A partnership stucture breeds collegiality at the top of a company and encourages loyalty among younger bankers. Since retired partners depend on the next generation of employees to safeguard their accrued wealth and to deliver their pensions, a partnership structure makes them careful to leave the firm in safe hands. When Salomon Brothers sold itself to commodity trader Phibro Corporation in 1981 for the seemingly astronomical sum of $550 million, it gave up, with its partnership structure, a part of the glue that had held the company together.

Salomon is known for its "street fighter" mentality. Since its founding, "the squabbling, the internal competition, the buccaneering spirit—all became part of the Salomon culture."[4] Graduates of the bank's training programs have likened the experience to "Green Beret training: They teach you the business; then they drop you in the Amazon with the weapons to fight your way out." Appearances to the contrary, "the ones who succeed at Salomon are not the nice ones. They're the ones who scream and rant and rave; who kick butt." Mr. Gutfreund's legendary instructions to trainees were to come to work ready to "bite the ass off a bear." Adds another associate: "This is a very macho place. No one holds your hand and tells you what to do. You have to live by your wits." And that can create tension: "If you're covering a client and that client does a deal with Morgan Stanley or First Boston, you're going to get incredible heat, no matter how thorough a job you've been doing. And they don't care where they chew you out—often it's right in front of everyone."[5]

Through the years, the company's competitiveness and innovativeness was fueled by a corporate structure that decentralized decision making and gave ambitious young traders the chance to start a new department or package a new security. Lewis Ranieri joined Salomon in 1966 as a $70-per-week night clerk. After spearheading the growth of mortgage-backed securities, he was made general partner in 1978, becoming in 1984 the youngest member of the executive committee. Stories like his were commonplace as staffers were given both autonomy and resources to make money for the bank. Whereas careful hiring and training to produce shared values are characteristic of relationship-oriented banks like Morgan Stanley and Goldman Sachs, at Salomon, "They just don't care if you don't look, talk and act like the typical investment banker, as long as you are good at what you do." According to wunderkind Lewis Ranieri, "It has to do with identity. No one gave us what we have. We got where we are today through sheer guts. You don't get where we are by being someone else's equal, but by being better."[6]

A mix of ambition, individualism, and autonomy encourages innovation. Indeed, most of Salomon's extraordinary profits throughout the 1980s can be traced to popular new instruments like zero-coupon bonds, interest rate swaps, and Ranieri's highly profitable mortgage-backed securities.

To stimulate competition and innovation, Salomon always paid extremely high bonuses. Ranieri, for one, was paid $2–5 million a year in each of the golden years between 1982 and 1986. By 1990, 106 employees each took home $1 million or more. At $1.6 billion in 1992, compensation remained the heftiest expense on Salomon's books. Although consistent with the bank's trading outlook, these bonuses only tied pay to the bank's short-term performance, encouraging staffers to achieve quick results but discouraging them from appreciating how their actions might affect the bank's long-run reputational capital.

In early 1990, John Gutfreund made a secret deal with one of the bank's most profitable fiefdoms—risk arbitrage—to let them retain 15 percent of the group's profits that year. To everyone's surprise, the group's performance improved dramatically. By year's end, that meant outsized bonuses for the group's top traders. One bond trader pocketed a cool bonus of $23 million, exceeding all prior compensation rules that unofficially denied paying commission. Not surprisingly, news of the extraordinary bonuses of the arbitrage group infuriated traders like Paul Mozer, doubtless fueling his fraudulent bidding activity.

All this, of course, because Gutfreund couldn't see his way clear to disciplining the different businesses of the bank. As one reporter commented in the mid-1980s:

> An organization so dominated by internal competition is less managed or run than it is guided and manipulated. Any overt attempt by a single personality to impose its will—whether over the feuding barons of the executive committee or the hungry spear-carriers on the battlefields of trading, sales and corporate finance—would stifle the dynamic of conflict and tension that has made the firm so successful. Stability in the form of a rigid, autocratic management system would be anathema to a firm whose very essence is instability and opportunism. Turmoil must to some degree be constant; egos must be allowed to clash so that, like the two dogs in the room, they become "meaner and tougher."[7]

Which is exactly what Gutfreund did throughout the 1980s. Rather than force discussions of budgets, strategies, and other critical trade-offs, the man that *Business Week* had dubbed the "King of Wall Street" back in 1985 elected to decentralize operations and thereby avoid conflicts between the bank's profitable fiefdoms. As one observer puts it: "In John Gutfreund's Salomon, nobody much wanted to supervise departments that were making money; in Ronald Reagan's and George Bush's administrations, nobody much wanted to regulate anything that was making money. Greed was good; more greed was better. Fraud was undesirable but only a frictional inefficiency, and, after all, the best people were doing it."[8]

Not surprisingly, Salomon's costs ballooned as bonuses skyrocketed to reward and retain star performers, provoking ever more internecine conflict between the bank's different businesses. Growing competition and declining profits in the early 1990s made clear the fact that Gutfreund had done little to improve the bank's operations but had instead so delayed addressing its core problems that the bank was in jeopardy.

After the scandal broke in 1991, a *New York Times* editorial put a moral caveat on the bank's aggressiveness. It characterized Salomon as a company that celebrated clever evasion of rules and trampled anyone standing in the way of profit and as a company governed by a "culture of greed, contempt for government regulations, and a sneering attitude toward ethics or any other impediment to earning a buck."[9] Not someone you'd necessarily want to do business with.

CATALYSTS OF CRISIS

Although Salomon's internal character pushed individualism and set the stage for one employee's rogue behavior, various external conditions also contributed to the bank's violations in 1991. They were of two sorts: lax regulators on one hand and an increasingly competitive environment on the other.

The Treasury Department sells its new issues through the offices of the Federal Reserve Bank of New York. The Fed supervises the auctions and ensures that primary dealers comply with Treasury rules. The close-knit relationships between the two government agencies and the primary dealers, however, may well have contributed to escalating the violations to crisis proportions. For one, the Treasury is an organization like any another, and many of its career officials have strong ties to Wall Street; most were once employees of the primary dealers that they now regulate. They come into regular contact through the weekly auctions.

Even among dealers, collusion and price fixing appear to have been routine in the $2.5 trillion market for the Treasury's securities. Although officially the companies denied having participated in any form of collusive behavior, in anonymous interviews with the *Wall Street Journal* traders from Salomon, Morgan Stanley, First Boston, Citicorp, Daiwa Securities, and Greenwich Capital Markets admitted to having shared information. By exchanging information, dealers could avoid bidding too high for an issue and reduce the risk of losing millions from overpricing. Although illegal, information sharing is standard procedure, according to a former top Salomon trader: "This is the way business has been conducted forever, and that's why it hasn't changed."[10] Could neither the Fed nor the Treasury possibly have noticed?

In fact, the Federal Reserve routinely saw information detailing Salomon's huge positions at auctions throughout 1990. In and of themselves, the bids should have prompted an internal investigation. As one observer noted:

> Salomon did cheat, and disgracefully, but a lot of the blame for what happened rested with the government agencies that failed to supervise this market at precisely the time when it most needed supervision. . . . [By] 1991 the Federal Reserve Bank of New York had become essentially part of the audience for the auction and the subsequent trading of the bonds and notes. What supervisory process survived had become pro forma, vestigial from previous administrations of the bank.[11]

Despite Salomon's disclosure of auction violations, in mid-August 1991 the Fed still claimed it saw no need for new regulations. In this, the agency adhered to policies set by Chairmen Paul Volcker and Alan Greenspan, who both endorsed loose auction regulations because they believed that laissez-faire policies would bring in the best prices. Critics of this system, however, view it as insufficiently open. Narrowing the flow of investors to the 40 primary dealers creates incentives for collusion, they say. A more competitive auction would open the way for other large institutions to bid, possibly electronically, and function much as the over-the-counter market does.

Instead of the Federal Reserve, it was the Treasury Department that took action in May 1991, under a barrage of complaints by dealers squeezed out of the May auction. The Treasury extended an unprecedented invitation to the Securities and Exchange Commission to investigate the apparent violations. Having responded to the immediate pressure, Treasury officials opted to postpone until August a review of possible changes in auction rules that might prevent overconcentration of an issue in the hands of a few dealers.

The limited response of the Treasury Department was consistent with its reputation for maintaining loose regulations and caving in to the requests of primary dealers. The Treasury drew most of the criticism for meek monitoring. Records of a meeting between Fed and Treasury officials on May 1, 1991, show that the Treasury knew of Salomon's violations well in advance of the May auction but did nothing to prevent it.

Clearly, then, the regulatory apparatus of the industry contributed to aggravating the crisis. As often happens, social proximity seems to have disarmed regulatory officials and compromised their willingness to take preventive action at the first signs of Salomon's rule violations. After all, this was not Salomon's first such scandal. In October 1991 Salomon paid $30 million to settle with Revco, and in December 1991 Salomon and two other securities firms settled a suit by First Republic Bank Investors for $42.2 million. Documentation on those two deals suggests that regulators and officials were all too willing to overlook problems.

At the same time, the financial services industry of the late 1980s had grown increasingly competitive. Declining interest rates, fewer deals, and a moribund global economy put pressure on traders and bankers to generate profits for the bank. A generation of bankers and traders raised in the go-go era of acquisitions and leveraged buyouts found it difficult to adjust to the postcrash conditions of the market. With their own pay contingent on the short-term performance of their area, traders like Mozer sought ways to dampen the loss of profits from declining interest rates, emboldening them to take larger positions in the higher-priced bonds.

If competition was a dark cloud hovering over Salomon in the late 1980s, Paul Mozer served as the barometer of the industry's ills. Likely as not he fell victim to the very competitiveness and aggression that the industry had instilled in him as a condition of success.

WEATHERING THE STORM

Not only did conditions internal and external to Salomon propel the violations, but the reactions of important constituents of the bank helped shape the way the crisis unfolded.

COMPETITORS' RETRIBUTION

Rival dealers affected by the May Squeeze were estimated to have lost more than $100 million. They did not take it lightly. Their vociferous complaints provoked the early investigation by the Fed and the Treasury. As one observer states: "What did damage to Salomon was not regulation but the fury of the participants in the market who had lost money. These participants screamed for the cops."[12] The threat from rivals was great. They stood to gain dramatically from crippling Salomon's trading ability in the Treasury market.

REGULATORY PROBES

The investigations launched by the SEC in June 1991 and the Justice Department were without doubt the forces that drove the violations into the open. They were the result not of regulatory initiative but of complaints by Salomon's rivals for the exhorbitant prices they were forced to pay at the May 1991 auction.

Salomon only publicly admitted its guilt in August 1991, when warned that it would be barred from bidding for clients in future auctions. When the Treasury shut out Salomon on August 18, 1991, it threatened the very existence of the firm. Many thought the bank might permanently lose its status and franchise as a primary dealer. Everyone realized that Salomon would face huge fines and penalties.

States can also revoke licenses to operate in their jurisdictions, and considerable pressure was put on state government agencies to do so. On August 29, 1991, Missouri's secretary of state announced a national commission to investigate Salomon. By September 18, 33 states were involved in the investigation. Salomon risked losing more than just its primary dealer status in Treasury auctions.

Media Frenzy

The media reveled in the crisis. Figure 15-1 shows that between August 1990 and December 1990 coverage of Salomon Brothers by the *Wall Street Journal* was limited to 26 articles, whereas between August 1991 and December 1991 coverage multiplied fivefold to 126 articles. Much of it was negative publicity and did damage to Salomon's reputation. Salomon had to act swiftly to prevent continued erosion of the company's intangible assets.

Investor Anxiety

The reaction of investors was swift and devastating. Figure 15-2 depicts Salomon's market value before and after its public confession. In early August 1991, the price of Salomon's shares dropped from an immediate precrisis high of about $29 to a postcrisis low of $24, representing a loss of more than $500 million, or some 15 percent of the company's market value—and all of its $350 million in reputational capital. Indeed, many analysts contend that the overall market drop for the entire week was a ripple effect induced by the Salomon scandal. It wouldn't stop there: The following week saw more of the same, including a drop of another 5 percent in Salomon's market value on August 20.

The danger to the firm from stockholders was twofold. First, there was the threat that speculative panic could drive massive sell-offs,

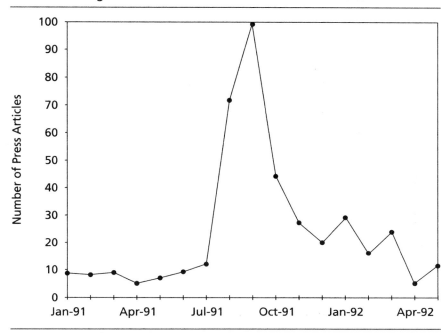

Figure 15-1   MEDIA INTEREST IN SALOMON

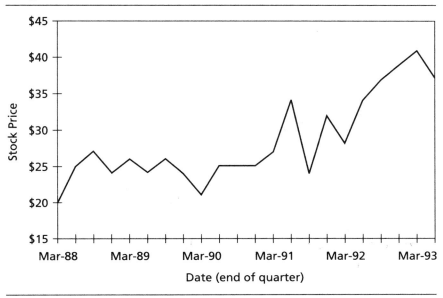

Figure 15-2   INVESTOR REACTION TO SALOMON'S VIOLATIONS

destroying the bank's market value. In turn, the loss of value would not only increase the bank's cost of capital—its borrowing power—but completely destroy the bank's credibility with customers and paralyze its ability to function in its other activities. A second fear was that the loss of reputational capital could fuel shareholder law suits charging market manipulation.

Soon after the scandal broke, credit regulators launched reviews of Salomon's debt. Late in August 1991, Moody downgraded Salomon's debt rating from A2 to A3. Standard & Poor's followed suit by lowering the bank's long-term debt rating from A+ to A−, its subordinated debt from A to A−, and its preferred stock from A− to BBB+. Lower ratings meant significantly higher borrowing costs and would seriously hinder Salomon's ability to function in its different markets.

CONCERNED EMPLOYEES

Employee reaction to the impending changes in the bank would be pivotal to its successful rebirth. Early signs were not good. Low morale coupled with expectations of a precipitous decline in future compensation frayed employee loyalty. Since staff members remaining at Salomon till the end of December 1991 would share in a $100 million bonus pool put in place before the crisis, it was expected that most would stick around till then.

By the end of 1991, in fact, industry-wide bonuses for investment bankers jumped by 25 percent. At Salomon, however, bonuses dropped by 25 percent from the previous year. A significant voluntary exodus of Salomon staff was expected in 1992.

CUSTOMER REACTIONS

Many customers initiated legal action against Salomon. Dozens of state pension funds and international customers suspended their dealings with the firm. Their initiatives dramatized the events, fueling panic about the bank's future prospects. Exhibit 15-1 lists client reactions to Salomon's August 1991 revelation.

Once activated, a scandal like the one faced by Salomon invariably triggers an informational stampede that can prove difficult to stop. Regulatory actions create a crisis of confidence. As the company loses market value, clients defect and credit ratings drop. Defections and credit

Exhibit 15-1 CRITICAL EVENTS

August 16	The State of Wisconsin Investment Board (Public Employees Pension Fund, $26 billion in assets) suspends business.
August 19	Various European institutions reduce their trades.
August 21	California Public Employees Retirement System ($63 billion) withdraws funds.
August 22	The World Bank, Massachusetts, California, and Connecticut defect. The British Treasury announces that it is reevaluating its business.
August 27	Colorado suspends trading.
August 28	Texas suspends trading.
August 30	New York adds Salomon to list of dealers providing day-to-day service to the state.
Sept 10	Loses business of Pacific Co., with $2 billion under management.
Sept 11	World Bank continues assessment of Salomon.
Sept 12	After three-month suspension, World Bank resumes business with Salomon.
Sept 17	California votes to resume ties with Salomon.

downgrades paralyze work activities, generate more bad publicity, and so propel a downward spiral that can quickly drive a company to bankruptcy. Arresting the process is difficult, and this is what Salomon's board had to do in August 1991 after confessing to the company's violations.

SALOMON'S SELF-DEFENSE

There were seven key elements in Salomon's self-defense: accepting responsibility, selecting esteemed leaders, disclosing information candidly, rebuilding confidence, restructuring for credibility, revising pay systems, and dodging bullets (especially those delivered in the form of criminal charges). In combination, these initiatives appeased regulators, placated investors, and mollified the public. They also secured renewed respect for Salomon with the public.

STEP 1: ACCEPTING RESPONSIBILITY

Following Salomon's board meeting in early August 1991, the company publicly disclosed violations of several Treasury auctions. Action was swift. The board suspended Paul Mozer, head of the company's government desk, as well as the key members of his team who had helped him make the bogus clients bids in different auctions.

It soon became clear that Gutfreund, Strauss, and Vice-Chairman John Merriwether had known about the illegal bids since April, yet had failed to act. The board viewed this as a display of unreasoned arrogance by Solly's top team and accepted their resignations. After his departure, Gutfreund reportedly told executives at a closed-door meeting: "I'm not apologizing for anything to anybody. Apologies don't mean [expletive]. What happened, happened."[13] In the board's judgement, this was obviously not the kind of attitude that would earn kudos in the court of public opinion.

STEP 2: SELECTING ESTEEMED LEADERS

At a shareholder meeting a few days later, Salomon's board appointed one of its own directors, Warren Buffett, to act as interim chairman. As chief of Berkshire Hathaway, Buffett represented the bank's largest shareholder, with a 16 percent stake in Salomon valued at some $700 million.

Buffett was an inspired choice. The vaunted "sage of Omaha" had a solid reputation for conservative, long-term investing; he was a custom-made antidote to the get-rich-quick schemes Salomon was being charged with. He was also known as a master at manipulating the media, something he had done skillfully in building his own image as a nice, down-to-earth, grandfatherly sort of guy, and definitely "Mr. Clean." That personal reputation for integrity proved extremely useful to Salomon. After dropping 38 percent since the scandal broke, Salomon's stock fell no more than the market after Buffett took over, and quickly rebounded by 15 percent.

From the start, Buffett recognized the value of the bank's intangible assets. As he told a group of managers: "If you lose dollars for the firm by bad decisions, I will be very understanding. If you lose reputation for the firm, I will be ruthless."[14] The *Wall Street Journal* concurred: "Salomon's bigggest hurdle is to convince customers and creditors that it is worthy of keeping their trust and that it is a creditworthy institution."[15]

In his first move as chairman, Buffett named Deryck Maughan, an eight-year veteran of Salomon's Tokyo office, as the company's chief operating officer. Hailed as "Mr. Integrity" and the "savior from the East," he was credited with building Salomon's Japanese business unit into a major force. He would play insider to Buffett's role as outsider.

Buffett also quickly appointed Los Angeles lawyer Robert E. Denham as the bank's general counsel to replace Donald Feuerstein. Feuerstein resigned at Buffett's request for failing to ensure full disclosure of the violations in the four months since he had known about them.

STEP 3: DISCLOSING INFORMATION CANDIDLY

In July 1991, before the crisis broke, Gutfreund had asked Wachtell, Lipton, Rosen & Katz, the bank's outside counsel and well-known Gutfreund allies, to conduct an internal review of the alleged violations. Under Gutfreund's leadership, neither Wachtell nor Salomon was willing to disclose the contents of the report, angering regulators who had anticipated the bank's cooperation after the uproar over the May auction.

In contrast, Buffett was keenly aware of the importance of accepting responsibility for the crisis if Salomon was to regain the trust of investors and clients. He viewed full disclosure and cooperation with regulators as necessary first steps to preventing further reputational drain. As he told reporters: "The most important job we have is to come clean in an aggressive way to regulators. . . . My job is to clean up the sins of the past and capitalize on the enormous attributes that this firm has."[16]

In his first days as chairman, Buffett candidly discussed with the press and with regulators what the company's own reviews of the auctions had revealed. Concerned about Martin Lipton's ties to Gutfreund and their joint strategy of making piecemeal disclosures to the press about the crisis since April 1991, Buffett asked the Wachtell firm to resign. He replaced them with Cravath, Swaine & Moore.[17]

STEP 4: REBUILDING CONFIDENCE

Crisis management is about rebuilding confidence. Although Arthur Andersen, the bank's accounting firm, was not faulted in any way, Buffett hired Coopers & Lybrand in August 1991 to conduct "a comprehensive internal control and compliance review of our U.S. securities trading operations." He conveyed poise by seeking an independent review from a company with no prior connection to Salomon. Shareholders approved of his assurance that the bank would implement any recommendations made.

Early in the crisis, Salomon had hired a new public relations firm, Kekst & Co. As with Wachtell, however, rumors of close personal relationships with Gutfreund led Buffett to fire the firm in August 1991 and to bring in Burson-Marsteller, the company that won wide acclaim for its handling of J&J's public relations after a woman died from taking a cyanide-laced Tylenol capsule in 1986.

Some key customers were marshalled to demonstrate Salomon's trustworthiness. On August 26, 1991, Laurence Tisch, chairman of CBS and Loew's—and a close friend of Buffett—bought 1.5 million shares in Salomon. To further regain the confidence of shareholders, Buffett sent them a letter sharing his analysis of Salomon's situation and his plan for turning things around. He personally assured smaller investors and the public of Salomon's fundamental integrity and pronounced the bank's future good. The two-page open letter was widely published in major dailies on October 29, 1991.

Finally, in a symbolic show of support for Buffett's leadership and for Salomon's role as a major employer in New York State, in late August 1991 Governor Mario Cuomo put Salomon on the bidding lists for the state Treasury and the Urban Development Corporation. As economic and political allies rallied around the beleaguered bank, the public grew more confident in its stock and share prices rose steadily from their postcrisis low of $24 a share to about $31, a level approaching the company's precrisis high of $33.

Step 5: Restructuring for Credibility

To convey credibility in a crisis of this sort, a firm must convince the public that drastic actions are being taken to remedy the problem. Buffett did just that. The restructuring addessed three areas: personnel; control systems; and financial systems. This restructuring accomplished several things simultaneously.

Personnel Changes. The purge of top managers was drastic. Only three of the bank's top nine managers remained with the firm following the scandal. Although some of these moves were only indirectly related to the crisis, many reflected Buffett's commitment to mute what he saw as Salomon's overaggressive culture. Some 15 percent of Salomon's senior investment bankers were forced out and the bank's real estate department was chopped in half. In December 1991, Salomon appointed 22 new managing directors, reinforcing its new focus on the core bond business. All told, more than 140 bankers, stock traders, and security analysts were dismissed as part of the restructuring. The personnel changes achieved three purposes: They cleaned house of those involved in the scandal; proved that Salomon was serious about preventing a similar scandal from ever recurring; and, politically, removed those who opposed the restructuring.

Control Systems.   Buffett heavily ascribed blame for the scandal to an improper structure that placed the investment banking subsidiary of Salomon, Inc., in an overly powerful role vis-à-vis its parent. As he put it: "In recent years both Salomon Inc., the parent, and Phibro Energy have been treated by top management as adjuncts to Salomon Brothers. That was understandable, given that the managers of the parent came from the securities unit. Now, however, we are viewing Salomon Inc. as the owner of two indepenent and substantial businesses, each of which will be measured by return on the equity capital it requires."[18]

In November 1991, Buffett amended the power structure of the investment subsidiary by naming an executive committee composed of nine Salomon executives to take charge of all of the company's daily operations. In an effort to reduce risk-taking in the firm, Salomon also tilted power towards the bond units and away from the riskier stock units. Buffett also set up a compliance committee of the board to monitor Salomon's trading activities.

Eager to demonstrate its rebirth, Salomon returned to the municipal market for the first time since 1987 with the largest offering of nontaxable bonds ever made. Despite the success of the offering, Salomon's market share for underwriting tumbled from 11 percent to 2 percent. To boost Salomon's underwriting presence, Berkshire Hathaway (the company chaired by Buffett) filed a secondary offering of $163.5 million jointly with Salomon.

Financial Systems.   Before the crisis, Salomon claimed $150 billion in assets and excellent credit ratings. To shore up its capital position, just before the crisis the bank sold off $40 billion in assets, the most rapid balance sheet reduction in Wall Street history. Beefing up cash would help Salomon cope with tightened credit resulting from likely downgrades in its ratings. Salomon also increased its internal borrowing rate, forcing traders to rethink their market positions. With its commercial paper coming due at the end of August, the bank needed lots of cash. Rolling it over in the aftermath of the crisis would cost millions. Instead, the bank substituted 90 percent of its commercial paper with more flexible, short-term repurchase agreements backed by securities. Impressed with the financial condition of the firm, Citicorp and J. P. Morgan committed to lending Salomon $2 billion in October 1991.

STEP 6: REVISING PAY SYSTEMS

Warren Buffett wanted to soften the swashbuckling image of the Salomon of old. To do that, he prodded the bank to sell off some big blocks of stock and take losses. The $301 million sale of the bank's shares of ConAgra recorded a $10 million loss, while the sale of Sun Microsystems produced a 17 percent loss. It sent to all traders a signal that Salomon was no longer interested in high-risk wait-outs, that the bank would no longer act as a bully trader, that it would assume a less aggressive stance in the market. If the old Salomon had been like John Wayne, known for its swagger, the new Salomon was to become more like Ozzie Nelson, nice and low key, neither so strong nor so effective.

Arguably the most controversial step Buffett took to force cultural change was his concerted attack on the pay structure. As he claimed, "The problem at Salomon Brothers has been a compensation plan that was irrational in certain crucial respects." Buffett went on to say that:

> One irrationality has been compensation levels that overall have been too high in relation to overall results. For example, last year the securities unit earned about 10% on equity capital—far under the average earned by American business. . . . But the overall result made no sense: Though 1990 operating profits before compensation were flat versus 1989, pay jumped by more than $120 million. . . . A related irrationality is connected to the lopsided way in which Salomon has earned its profits. . . . The data . . . show that Salomon's lackluster overall profits of recent years resulted from a combination of excellent earnings in a few areas of the business—operating in an honest and ethical manner, it should be added—with inadequate or non-existent earnings at the remainder. Yet the compensation plan did not take this extreme unevenness into account. In effect, the fine performance of some people subsidized truly out-sized rewards for others.[19]

Mr. Buffett favored a closer link between pay and performance. To this end, he scrapped all special pay pacts. To align the interests of owners and managers more closely, Buffett offered equity-partnership plans. He drained $110 million from the 1991 bonus pool and began paying employees in Salomon stock. By July 1993, employees held 12 percent of Salomon, up from 5 percent in 1990. Under the new scheme, employees are obliged to hold the shares the company pays them for at least five years. Senior managers thus have a more significant portion of their wealth invested in Salomon shares, which should alter their concern for the bank's overall welfare and enable the bank to recapture some of the advantages of its old partnership structure without sacrificing its ability to tap the capital markets.

Step 7: Dodging Bullets

The biggest threat to Salomon's survival clearly came from the regulators. To avoid the fate of E. F. Hutton and Drexel, Salomon would have to dodge the criminal charges that might be brought forward. Intense lobbying by Salomon and the swift action of its new leadership reassured regulators that the bank was making the necessary changes. The Treasury was persuaded to allow Salomon to continue to participate in government auctions, if only for its own account.

To Salomon, however, the SEC's investigation was the most threatening of all. The crucial development was this: In the months following the crisis, the SEC came to believe that Salomon's infractions were rooted in individual excess rather than in systemic abuse. The SEC's chairman publically praised Salomon's management team for its swift action in purging the company of its rogue elements and quickly turned to the broader question of regulatory negligence and the possibility of dealer collusion. Within days, the SEC issued 100 subpoenas throughout the industry, diverting attention from the immediate problems at Salomon.

Salomon's reforms not only impressed the SEC and allowed the bank to dodge the proverbial bullet but also appeased a Congress busily revisiting securities laws. Warren Buffett's credibility helped a lot. At a September congressional hearing on the Salomon violations, in fact, Buffett was received like a messiah. "Mr. Buffett . . . get in there and kick some butt," intoned a representative from Ohio. Clearly, by renting Mr. Buffett's reputation for integrity, Salomon had avoided facing a Congress customarily intolerant of large-scale financial offenses.

PRACTICING CORPORATE JUDO

Salomon's crisis could have been anticipated. It was precipitated by characteristics of both the bank and its institutional environment. In recent years, few banks on Wall Street have been more closely identified with the mentality of short-term trading. Salomon was successful and its traders autonomous. If you combine the power and capabilities of the largest firm on Wall Street with heightened competition and a loosely regulated environment, you have a sure recipe for disaster.[20]

As Exhibit 15-2 indicates, the Salomon saga presents a vivid example of how managers can actively return from the brink and rebuild reputational capital damaged by a scandal. Like Johnson & Johnson before them, Salomon's adroit self-defense demonstrates that crises need not permanently depreciate a company's reputation. Because all established companies face challenges to their reputations at one time or another, managers need to be prepared to defend them.

From Salomon's experience we can derive some instructive advice. First, leadership. As one commentator put it: "If Warren Buffet had not been available to lead Salomon Brothers in August 1991, the firm would have gone under that fall." Buffet's personal relationships with politicians and regulators, his credibility to investors, and his carefully cultivated image of scrupulous benevolence were tailor-made to the situation.

Exhibit 15-2 RESTORING REPUTATION

Step 1:	Take immediate and public responsibility for what happened.
Step 2:	Convey concern to all stakeholders.
Step 3:	Show full and open cooperation with authorities.
Step 4:	Remove all negligent incumbent managers.
Step 5:	Appoint credible leaders that represent all interests.
Step 6:	Dismiss suppliers and agents tied to the incumbent managers.
Step 7:	Hire independent investigators, accountants, counsel, PR.
Step 8:	Reorganize operations to ensure greater control.
Step 9:	Establish strict procedures.
Step 10:	Identify and target the practices that stimulated infractions.
Step 11:	Revise internal practices and pay systems.
Step 12:	Monitor compliance.

Second, every crisis needs a fall guy, a scapegoat. A company's managers must quickly accept responsibility for a scandal and punish those responsible. Buffett's purge of top personnel expressed the company's moral outrage at their ethical lapses. It sent a clear message to regulators and investors that the company recognized its delinquency and would take whatever steps were necessary to avert a recurrence.

Third, far-reaching structural, cultural, and financial reforms were instituted that reduced the incentives to cheat the system. They signaled the company's willingness to follow through on its commitment to perform drastic surgery on internal practices. In a highly competitive marketplace, Buffett made clear that to rely on the self-control of individuals when stakes are high is at best unwise and likely as not foolish. Decentralization without control invites anarchy.

Fourth, Salomon's well-publicized efforts to address the root causes of the scandal clearly muted the reprisals it might have faced from institutional authorities. As much as anything else, it was the stonewalling, the negative publicity, and the steady barrage of civil lawsuits and settlements that eventually sank Drexel in February 1990. Many observers suggest that it was Drexel's notorious defiance and uncooperative posture that probably provoked regulators to scrutinize it so closely and to levy heavy penalties. In contrast, Salomon successfully deflected the blows that regulators might have inflicted. The substantial steps taken by Buffett reduced the need to punish.

Finally, all stakeholders need reassurance that their positions are being aggressively defended and want information about how changes will affect them. Buffett kept everyone focused on Salomon's future prospects rather than on its past wrongs. Through open letters to shareholders published in the media, stepped-up staff meetings, and constant contact with customers, Salomon reassured investors and employees and helped secure Salomon's turnaround.

In the end, Mr. Buffett proved that it was wiser to take tough measures early and suffer in the short run than to run the risk of loosing the hard currency of a good reputation. Had John Gutfreund acted forcefully in April 1991 when he was informed of Paul Mozer's violations of auction rules, there would probably not have been a scandal. Although no company will ever eliminate the possibility of rogue members breaking the law, under Buffett's leadership, Salomon has shown us how to deal with them in a way that protects the company's most valuable asset—its reputation.

THE AFTERMATH

Less than two years after the trading scandal brought Salomon to the brink of collapse, the bank was back with a vengeance. In 1992, Salomon Brothers earned $1.4 billion before taxes, an all-time peak and a 34 percent gain over 1991. By March 1994, the company's stock price had jumped to a high of $50 per share from its low of $24 in June 1991, and its market value had grown to a healthy $5.5 billion.

In May 1992, Salomon agreed to pay $290 million in civil fines and damages, in return for which it would not face the kinds of criminal charges that had felled E. F. Hutton and Drexel. Instead, the company agreed to dole out $122 million for civil securities law violation, to pay $68 million in forfeitures to the Justice Department for settlement of antitrust and other claims, and to create a $100 million fund for restitutions in private damage claims. With considerable relief, the company also agreed to a two-month suspension of its primary dealership, to payment of legal costs of $12.5 million for private claims, and to $54.5 million in payments to holders of the company's stock and bonds. In March 1994, Salomon settled the remaining class-action lawsuits brought by rival bond traders claiming injury for an estimated $30 million in additional payments.

The joint investigation initiated by 33 individual states largely followed the lead of the federal agencies. Although these actions had the potential to be devastating, they did not amount to much in either fines or penalties, and no state has permanently banned Salomon from operating in its jurisdiction.

In December 1992, John Gutfreund agreed to never again run a securities firm and to pay a $100,000 fine as part of a settlement of civil charges stemming form the firm's illegal bidding. Thomas Strauss, Salomon's former president, agreed to a fine of $75,000 and suspension from associating with a Wall Street firm for six months. John Meriwether, a former vice chairman, agreed to a three-month suspension and a fine of $50,000.

In September 1993, Paul Mozer, the trader at the center of the Treasury scandal, was allowed to plead guilty to two felonies stemming from his submission of illegal bids when he was head of government bond trading for Salomon. He faced a maximum prison term of 10 years and a $500,000 fine. By December 1993, he had been sentenced to a four-month term in a minimum-security prison and fined a mere $30,000.

In justifying his lenient sentence, U.S. District Court judge Pierre Leval praised Mozer's "valuable cooperation" in testifying against others. He also called Mozer's crime an "extremely foolish, arrogant, insouciant offense."[21] The closing chapter on the 1991 bond auction scandal was written on July 15, 1994, when Mozer agreed to pay a $1.1 million fine and accepted a permanent ban from the securities industry.

On June 3, 1992, in a surprise move, Salomon named its general counsel, Robert Denham, to replace Warren Buffett as chairman of Salmon, Inc. An outsider, Denham had been brought in only nine months before to shepherd the company through the long investigation that culminated in the $290 million settlement. Deryck Maughan was subsequently named chairman and chief executive of Salomon Brothers, while Buffett remained on the parent company's board and continued to chair its executive committee.

Competitors have taken advantage of the diminished role Salomon has been forced to play. Shortly after the crisis broke, Salomon ranked fifth among investment banks, down from first just before the crisis. Salomon's skillful handling of the crisis and revitalized reputation make long-term effects less clear. Today, Salomon is still Wall Street's largest bank and among its most influential players.

Shortly before the scandal broke, John Gutfreund was asked about the future culture of Salomon. The man who throughout the 1980s personified Salomon's culture of aggressive bullying and who inspired fear and respect on Wall Street had this to say: "I'd like to see a return to more collegiality, more camaraderie. And I think this will come about, because I expect over the next few years that more ownership will revert to employees. Then there will be a community of interest that will change the interpersonal relationships again."[22]

Under Buffett's artful maneuvering, that's precisely where Salomon seems to be headed, its reputation bruised but healthy, its stock once again flying high. On August 17, 1993, the well-known holding company that Buffett controls, Berkshire Hathaway, announced that it had sought permission from antitrust regulators to raise its stake in Salomon to between 15 percent and 24.9 percent. Investors clearly welcomed the news: Salomon's shares spurted $2.25 to close at a healthy $48, near its 1986 high of $53—a remarkable recovery.

C O N C L U S I O N

Fame is a bee;
It has a song, it has a sting;
ah, too, it has a wing.

—*Emily Dickinson*

The Burden of Celebrity

CORPORATE REPUTATIONS are both products and by-products of competition. They are *direct products* of competition because companies strategically manipulate the images they project to gain favor with constituents. Internally, companies adopt managerial practices that are more or less employee friendly. Externally, companies actively project their most attractive features—to customers through advertising, to communities through social and environmental projects, and to investors through profitability. The result is that some companies treat their employees better than others, some make better products, some are better investments, some more responsive, some more environmentally sensitive—and their reputations partly reflect these identity traits.

Reputations are also *indirect by-products* of competition because they crystallize from the assessments generated by reporters, analysts, and the rumor mill. These images are not under a company's control. Rather, a reputation forms from these disparate images much like a reflection in a broken mirror.

Clearly, corporate reputations fulfill an important role in the competitive process. For one, they inform constituents about the merits of a company's products, jobs, and strategies. For another, companies held in higher regard attract more and better resources than rivals. Their products entice more customers, their jobs lure more applicants, their stock offerings draw greater demand.

Reputations are rent-producing assets—they create wealth. In particular, they are a form of capital that goes unrecorded on corporate balance sheets. One take-away from these observations is therefore that creating shareholder value involves not only exploiting the financial and human capital of a company to maximum benefit but extracting value from the company's *reputational capital*. To build and safeguard reputational capital, managers must hone their skills in observing constituents and in recognizing the importance of constituents' perceptions and interpretations in the competitive process.[1]

Ultimately, reputations have economic value to companies because they are difficult to imitate. Rivals simply cannot replicate the unique features and intricate processes that produced those reputations. Reputations are therefore a source of competitive advantage. To sustain that relative advantage requires a commitment to the ongoing management of a company's reputation—that is, the extent to which the images a company projects coincide with and reinforce its identity.

This chapter explores some of the gaps between reality and perception that occasionally appear when managers *mis*manage a company's reputation. As companies diversify their products and disperse their operations around the globe, they are challenged as never before to ensure the convergence of image and identity, to exploit more effectively their hidden stock of reputational capital.

REPUTATION AND REALITY

Reputations are not only a boon, but a burden. King Midas's gift of the golden touch had a downside. Whatever he touched turned to gold—including his food! All too soon the wealthy but starving monarch found himself wishing his gift would simply go away. Companies that achieve preeminent standing face a similar challenge. Because they perform in the limelight, their every move is subject to close scrutiny, interpreted and reinterpreted; their every action—like Midas's every touch—has significance. The reputations they earn from doing some things particularly well sit on the slippery ground of their constituents' fickle interpretations. Managing those interpretations requires considerable savvy.

Intel provides a vivid example of a company that got caught in a crisis of perception in fall 1994. Intel's managers were caught unprepared—and stumbled badly as a result—when the company's pristine reputation for engineering excellence came under attack after a fundamental flaw in its highly touted Pentium chip was first identified by the mathematician Dr. Thomas Nicely of Lynchburg College in Virginia. Specifically, the chip sold in the latest models of personal computers since May 1993 miscalculated by a very small amount when it performed some simple divisions—making a so-called floating point error. This was a serious charge. Moreover, it was being levied against a company with such a widespread reputation for quality that its name lent distinction to PC makers themselves: For years they had boldly emblazoned their machines with the label Intel Inside to attract customers.

Initially, Intel's managers publically denied the charge. But after Dr. Nicely's memo was circulated on the gossip channels of cyberspace—the Internet—an initial hum turned into a veritable explosion of speculation, rumor, and innuendo as users, researchers, computer nerds, and scientists first confirmed and then struggled to assess the relative significance or insignificance of the flawed chip. Reacting to the rapidly spreading rumor and the growing sense of panic in a user community that was investing thousands of dollars in new machines, Intel's Andrew Grove sent out a message on the electronic network in November 1994, part of which follows.

This is Andy Grove, president of Intel. I'd like to comment a bit on the conversations that have been taking place here. First of all, I am truly sorry for the anxiety created among you by our floating point issue. I read thru [sic] some of the postings and it's clear that many of you have done a lot of work around it and that some of you are very angry at us. Let me give you my perspective on what has happened here. . . . We held the introduction of the chip several months in order to give [OEM] more time to check out the chip and their systems. We worked extensively with many software companies to this end as well. We were very pleased with the result. . . . In the summer of '94, in the process of further testing (which continued thru [sic] all this time and continues today), we came upon the floating point error. . . . We started a separate project, including mathematicians and scientists who work for us in areas other than the Pentium processor group to examine the nature of the problem and its impact. This group concluded after months of work that (1) an error is only likely to occur at a frequency of the order of once in nine billion random floating point divides, and that (2) this many divides in all the programs they evaluated . . . would require elapsed times of use that would be longer than the mean time to failure of the physical computer subsystems. In other words, the error rate a user might see due to the floating point problem would be swamped by other known computer failure mechanisms.[2]

Consistent with this official, engineering point of view, Intel invited only those customers with exceptional needs to apply for a replacement chip. In an attempt at damage control, Grove asked for patience from the user community:

We would like to find all users of the Pentium processor who are engaged in work involving heavy duty scientific/floating point calculations and resolve their problem in the most appropriate fashion including, if necessary, by replacing their chips with new ones. We don't know how to set precise rules on this so we decided to do it thru [sic] individual discussions between each of you and a technically trained Intel person. We set up 800# lines for that purpose. It is going to take us time to work thru [sic] the calls we are getting, but we will work thru [sic] them. I would like to ask for your patience here. . . . We appreciate your interest in the Pentium processor, and we remain dedicated to bringing it as close to perfection as possible.[3]

Despite mounting concern expressed by large PC distributors like IBM, Gateway 2000, Packard Bell, and Dell, as well as end users, Intel's top managers insisted on examining requests on a case-by-case basis. To the consternation of most proud Pentium owners, in fact, the company stuck to its official technical position: that the flaw was trivial. Intel put it this way in a public release:

Earlier this year, as a part of Intel's ongoing testing and product development work, a flaw was discovered in the floating point unit (FPU) of the Pentium processor. This flaw affects the accuracy of the floating point divide instruction for certain combinations of input operands (i.e. certain combinations of specific numbers). The impact of the flaw is that for one in nine billion possible independent divides, the precision of the result is reduced. . . . Intel has assessed the likely impact of the flaw on three types of applications that might be run on a Pentium processor-based system. These include: (i) commercial PC applications on desktop and mobile platforms running MS-DOS, Windows, and OS/2; (ii) technical and workstation applications, such as engineering and scientific, advanced multimedia, educational and financial applications. . . ; and (iii) server and transaction processing applications. . . . [In conclusion] . . . the flaw is not meaningful for the vast majority of commercial PC applications. The flaw is not likely to be meaningful over the usable life of the processor for the remainder of these commercial applications and most workstation applications. . . . The flaw has no effect on server applications.[4]

Hardly a reassuring statement. Among the major users of Intel chips, however, it was IBM (with about 9 percent of the market) that reacted the most aggressively. IBM's researchers vehemently disagreed with Intel's assessment of the severity of the flaw. In a memo distributed on the Internet, they reasoned as follows:

IBM Research focused on the likelihood of error on the Pentium chip in everyday floating point division activities. Intel has analyzed the probability of making an error based on the assumption that any possible 64 bit pattern is equally likely to occur in both the numerator and the denominator. . . . Our analysis shows that the chances of an error occurring are significantly greater when we perform simulations of the types of calculations performed by financial spreadsheet users, because, in this case, all bit patterns are not equally probable. . . . [After extensive computations, the authors conclude that,] on a typical day a large number of people are making mistakes in their computation without realizing it.[5]

Of course, IBM had mixed motives for reacting this way. After all, it was coproducer with Apple of a rival chip (the Power-PC) targeted to the same market as Intel's. To IBM, then, Intel's loss would mean a gain for the Power-PC. The battle over the Pentium's flaw masked a more fundamental battle for reputational standing between IBM and Intel.

Many weeks into the crisis, Intel still maintained a public posture that inadvertently trivialized users' fears. Bit by bit, Intel's engineering facade crumbled under the onslaught of publicity only to reveal an arrogant company relatively distant from customers' anxieties about the fallibility of its machines. By mid-December 1994, IBM had stopped selling Pentium-based PCs. A rash of articles in the *New York Times,* the *Wall Street Journal,* and consumer-oriented technology magazines and news-letters recommended holding off on Pentium purchases. The Gartner Group, an information services consulting firm, suggested that its corporate clients also delay their purchases.

Despite the negative publicity, in the last weeks of 1994 Intel's CEO and senior officers arrogantly defied the interpretations of customers. Speaking to newscaster Ted Koppel on NBC's *Nightline*—and to the many customers who had tuned in to the broadcast—Andrew Grove defended the company's point of view: to wit, that all chips have flaws, that the Pentium chip is simply the best engineered product of its kind, that this particular flaw was trivial, and that the fuss being made about the chip's flaw was much ado about nothing.

It was to be Grove's last gasp. Within days of the *Nightline* interview, Intel succumbed to pressure from the growing army of disgruntled users. In an about-face, the company announced that it would replace flawed Pentium chips for *every* buyer who wanted one free of charge. Replacement chips would cost Intel millions of dollars. The overall crisis would wind up costing Intel even more in lost sales for the months during which customers delayed purchasing new machines. Moreover, ungauged would be the hidden reputational loss to the company, its once pristine image for engineering excellence and customer responsiveness sullied by the crisis. As Grove concluded from the debacle, Intel learned an important lesson: that although the company's products were sold far and wide, Intel didn't know how to speak the language of the consumer: "We decided what was good and what was not good when we had to replace the Pentium. It turns out that consumers highly resent it when a company presumes to judge the quality of its products on their behalf."[6]

On the Internet, discussion groups around the world also indulged in jokes about the crisis, for example:

QUESTION: What's another name for the "Intel Inside" sticker they put on Pentiums?

ANSWER: The warning label.

QUESTION: How many Pentium designers does it take to screw in a light bulb?

ANSWER: 1.99904274017; that's close enough for non-technical people.

Most were insightful in confirming the inappropriateness of Intel's response to what had been from the beginning not a crisis of reality but one of perception.[7] Yet despite the drama and the financial costs to Intel, the story ends on a slightly humorous note. After agreeing to a full replacement of all of its installed chips, the company supplied the flawed Pentiums to a manufacturer of costume jewelry for use as earrings.

WHAT AFFECTS REPUTATION?

As I've emphasized throughout this book, reputations deserve greater attention from both practitioners and researchers because they create economic value. Two sets of factors affect a company's ability to realize value from its reputation: the company's *strategy* on one hand, and its *corporate practices* in identity shaping and image making on the other. Insofar as both fit well together—they reinforce each other—then constituents experience stronger and more coherent images of the company. In turn, coherence induces better reputational ratings from constituents and builds reputational capital. Figure C-1 summarizes the logic through which companies realize economic value from their reputations.

STRATEGIC FACTORS

First and foremost, a company owes its reputation to its uniqueness in delivering products and services to constituents. In corporate parlance, reputation derives from a company's ability to differentiate itself from rivals. Differentiation creates perceived advantage among customers about the company's merits. Insofar as the company pursues and consistently differentiates itself from other constituents as well, then it rein-

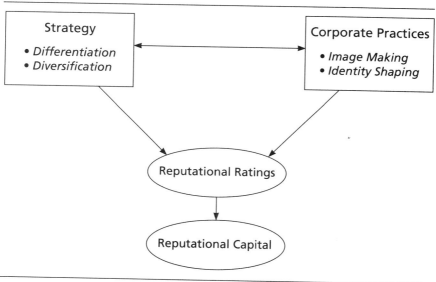

Figure C-1 REALIZING VALUE FROM REPUTATION

forces perceptions of uniqueness by those constituents and creates economic value. In a crowded field of rivals, however, differentiation is sustainable only when a company's reputation sits on a solid foundation of corporate practices that reinforce and promote its uniqueness to constituents.

For each of a company's businesses, maintaining uniqueness suggests the following value proposition:

- *Value proposition 1:* The more a company pursues a strategy that differentiates it from rivals with each of its major constituent groups, the more likely are constituents to ascribe a strong reputation to the company, and the greater the company's reputational capital.

When companies diversify either into new product arenas or new geographic areas, new issues arise. Insofar as diversification dilutes a company's perceived distinctiveness, it is also likely to erode the company's reputation. It explains the frequently observed reticence of investors to ascribe high market value to conglomerates—hence their reduced stocks of reputational capital compared with more focused companies. There are exceptions, however. General Electric is a highly diversified company that is consistently among the most admired companies in the United States. Since 1980, with Jack Welch at the helm, the company's market value and reputational capital have soared. Consistent with our view, however, wealth creation has largely resulted from Welch's efforts at reducing GE's diversity and intensifying its focus.

One reason for expecting lower reputations from highly diversified companies is the relative opacity of multibusiness companies to outside scrutiny. Observers have much greater difficulty understanding a conglomerate's operations and so give it lesser ratings in reputational surveys. In a statistical analysis of *Fortune*'s reputational ratings, my colleague Mark Shanley and I found that companies with more diversified portfolios of businessess fared less well than more focused companies. Moreover, we also found that constituents drew on a wider range of informational inputs to interpret the actions of more diversified companies. They were influenced not only by accounting and market measures of performance but also by press reports, advertising, and charitable contributions as they struggled to resolve their sense of ambiguity about a company's diversified operations.[8] Consequently, we arrive at

- *Value proposition 2:* The more a company pursues a diversification strategy around a core competence, the more likely constituents are to ascribe a strong reputation to the company, and the
greater the company's reputational capital.

CORPORATE PRACTICES

Strategic factors alone do not account for the creation of value from
reputation. Also vital to the value proposition are corporate practices.
To reinforce their uniqueness and differentiate their business, companies
need to develop systematic identity-shaping and image-making programs
that also work together. Externally, programs designed to build better
customer relations, investor relations, community relations, government
relations, and competitior relations should also be assessed for their
effectiveness at producing reinforcing images with constituents. Internally, programs that target employee relations should strive to build a
sense of identity among employees that helps to reinforce the company's
strategic differentiation and uniqueness. Identity shaping and image making should work together and become visible in naming practices, advertising, annual reports, and other corporate self-presentations.

Diversification presents interesting challenges to a company's identity
and image. Cross-cultural differences make it difficult for a company
to maintain coherent identities and images with geographically diverse
constituents. Legal constraints often impede a company's ability to promote singular images and to develop a shared identity and reputation
across countries. Banks are a case in point. Bank holding companies are
generally restricted from integrating the operations of their member
banks located in different countries. In the United States, the Glass-
Steagall Act has long prohibited a fusion of investment services with
commercial banking.

There are also cultural impediments to integrating identities and
images across national boundaries. Take Seattle-based Nike, the maker of
athletic shoes and apparel. Without considerable effort and expenditure,
employees of its Asian factories are unlikely to perceive the company in
the same terms as its Seattle-based managers. The imagery with which
the company promotes its products can also prove difficult to translate
around the world. Nike relies on uniquely American sports imagery and
on endorsers like basketball's Michael Jordan and tennis's Andre Agassi
to project an aggressive and dynamic image of the company and its

products. Some images travel well, others do not. An important question for diversified companies to address is the extent to which their unique but locally developed images and identities translate globally.

Although we've discussed image making with customers—the marketing angle—parallel questions should be asked about the images projected to suppliers, distributors, employees, and local publics. How similarly should the company position itself vis-à-vis each of these constituents in different countries and regions? Should the company's many products and businesses rely on the same corporate naming and image-making practices in all countries? As we discussed in chapter 11, diversification tends to encourage companies to develop fragmented identities and dilutes their reputational capital. It takes considerable effort and expenditure to maintain a monolithic identity in a diversified company. I therefore suggest:

- *Value proposition 3:* The more a company adopts identity-shaping systems and image-making practices that reinforce its strategic position, the more likely are constituents to ascribe a strong reputation to the company, and the greater the company's reputational capital.

REPUTATIONAL MATTERS

Questions of reputation invariably elicit discussion and debate. I comment below on some selected issues that are likely to be of widespread interest to readers.

DO COMPANIES HAVE ONE REPUTATION OR MANY?

Some observers claim that companies have *many* reputations. They suggest that it may be meaningless to speak of a single corporate reputation. Throughout this book, however, I have argued in favor of looking at reputation as a net assessment of many individual appraisals of a company by its constituents. The argument is predicated on reasoning that parallels the arguments made by students of public opinion. Much as they aggregate individual opinions to crystallize "the public's" point of view, so have I proposed that we should conceive of corporate reputations.

That's not to say that constituents cannot hold different points of view about a company. It's entirely possible for a company to be well known for making high-quality products yet still have a terrible reputation for the way it treats employees. The better informed observers are about a company, in fact, the more likely they are to know about the company's different images and so to have a complex view of the company's performance.

Nonetheless, each individual observer balances pros and cons, positives and negatives, to form a *net* assessment of a company. When we aggregate these net assessments across constituents, we create a reputational profile. I therefore defend the merits of looking at a company's overall reputation rather than its underlying components.

How Should Reputations be Measured?

Opinion researchers rely on polls to gauge public opinion. We may well want to construct reputational profiles and rankings of companies in quite similar ways. Consistent with the suggestions made for conducting a reputational audit in chapter 8, the following process would result:

- Carefully identify each of the company's key constituent groups.

- Sample constituents from each group.

- Solicit their nominations of well-regarded firms.

- Obtain ratings of those firms on relevant dimensions.

The better represented are *all* of a company's constituents in the reputational audit, the more valid is the reputational profile that it generates. The main concern is with constructing samples of constituents that will not bias results. To achieve a representation of the population at large, political pollsters advocate random sampling: "Respondents . . . are not selected because of their typicality or of their representativeness. Rather, each sampling area and each individual falls into the sample by chance and thus contributes a certain uniqueness to the whole. It is only when these unrepresentative elements are added together that the sample should become representative."[9]

Insofar as corporate ratings accurately reflect the multiple images of a company that are being disseminated, they provide a useful tool for assessing the company's overall performance. For some companies, the fragmented images will converge, producing strong reputations. For other companies whose actions produce contradictory images with different audiences, weaker overall reputations will result.

Currently, the only large-scale reputational surveys of companies are those sponsored by *Fortune* and *Business Week*. Neither one is comprehensive, however, and both could be significantly improved with minor modifications in methodology. *Fortune*'s survey of corporate reputations, for instance, has steadily grown in size and reach over the years. Each year, more respondents are included, as well as more industries. Although the survey asks respondents to nominate and evaluate companies on different dimensions, studies of these ratings find that they are in fact highly correlated and load on a single factor.[10] Appropriately, then, the magazine now reports ratings and rankings based on an index of overall reputation rather than on individual dimensions.

As pointed out in chapter 7, however, a serious limitation of *Fortune*'s survey remains its near total reliance on a single evaluating group: senior executives, directors, and analysts. *To do so is to misrepresent the company's images with employees, customers, and local communities.* There's no good reason for perpetuating such a managerialist bias. The magazine now surveys some 9,000 executives—a number that far exceeds the sample size needed to develop an accurate representation of a company's reputation *with all of its constituents.* Much as public pollsters warn that a poll's validity hinges on randomness, so do I suggest that *Fortune*'s survey would gain in validity by targeting the full range of constituents.

Much of the dispute surrounding rankings of business schools (discussed in chapter 10) also derives from the different constituents sampled and the disparate criteria that these groups apply. *Business Week* samples recruiters and alumni but excludes faculty, students, donors, and the local communities in which the schools operate. *U.S. News & World Reports* surveys business school deans but no one else (although the final ranking does incorporate a wide range of archival measures that partly reflect the judgments other groups might make). To fully crystallize the reputations of these institutions, more representative sampling should be done that includes not only business school deans, corporate recruiters, and alumni but also current students, faculty, and community groups. The resulting rankings would better capture the multifaceted missions in education, research, and service that business schools are intended to fulfill.

Who's Responsible for Managing Reputation?

If reputations are valuable, who should be accountable for managing a company's reputational capital? In chapter 8, I concurred with others who have suggested that companies appoint a chief reputation officer, or CRO, to act as guardian of their corporate reputation. A CRO would regularly call attention to the implications of a company's decisions and actions on its reputation. The CRO would also examine how resource allocations might affect reputation and systematically explore ways to build up reputational capital.

The danger of having a CRO is that the position could be used as a scapegoat for corporate crises and scandals. For accountability to make sense, however, a CRO would have to be provided an equal measure of responsibility for maintaining reputational capital. That means *equal membership* on the top management team—with access to the chief executive officer comparable to that of the functional heads of finance, manufacturing, marketing, and product development.

Ultimately, there is disagreement over who should be held responsible and accountable for reputational gains and losses. In the United States, CEOs appear more than willing to accept praise for gains but not for losses. At a recent presentation, for instance, General Electric's well-known CEO Jack Welch admitted that he had never contemplated quitting over the scandal at GE's Kidder Peabody subsidiary. Yet in all probability a Japanese CEO faced with a similar profit-draining scandal would have resigned.

In chapter 15, I showed how the decisive steps taken by Salomon Brothers actually saved the company and stemmed its reputational free-fall in 1991. In that case, however, the board of directors clearly placed responsibility and accountability squarely on the shoulders of the bank's top team—and fired its members for their failure to prevent rogue behavior in subordinates.

Doubtless having a CRO would have helped Salomon and other financial institutions in recent years to anticipate and address the kinds of crises likely to stem from rogue behavior by individual traders and bankers. It should never be a substitute, however, for ascribing complete accountability for reputation management to *all* members of a company's top team. Since projecting and cohering identity-consistent images is at the heart of reputation management, members of the top management team should be clearly the ones to carry the burden of defending the interests of all the company's constituents. Making reputation management in all its different facets a centerpiece of the top team's activities should therefore be a central ingredient of all good strategic management.

CAN REPUTATIONS BE USED AS PERFORMANCE MEASURES?

All too often managers fail to consider their firm's reputation as a valuable asset until forced to do so—that is, when a crisis hits. Then and only then do miscreant managers seem interested in discussing reputational matters and in decrying the lack of systematic attention to such intangibles. By then, of course, it's too late to be discussing positive ways to manage reputational capital.

In fact, I suggest that reputation is a potentially powerful means of measuring a company's overall performance in a marketplace made up not only of customers but of employees, investors, suppliers, distributors, and other observers. By drawing attention to a company's relative success at meeting the common interests of all its constituents, a reputational audit provides a useful vehicle for simultaneously gauging a company's economic, financial, social, and environmental performance.

Moreover, when reputations are aggregated into relative rankings against rivals, they provide a viable means of auditing the performance of an entire corporate sector. The growing popularity of reputational ratings in the business press actually offers the tantalizing possibility that well-constructed reputational surveys could adequately capture the corporate sector's ability to meet society's broadest expectations. Imagine what would happen if these rankings were to become institutionalized. They would constitute an attractively decentralized mechanism capable of channeling managers' activities in socially desirable directions. No mean feat.

To achieve those lofty aims, we'll need to strengthen the process by which rankings are actually constructed and reported. Valid rankings can serve as the foundation of a performance measurement system only if information is systematically collected, the comparison process is standardized, and the system is institutionalized.

When ratings are reported in the press, for instance, they draw attention. Publicly reported audits are therefore a key mechanism for developing rankings as a guidance mechanism. Another way to strengthen the attention-generating role of rankings would be to present them not only in the press but in the annual reports that companies release to shareholders. Now annual reports only describe an independent auditor's assessment of the company's *financial* results. As discussed in chapter 4, U.S. accounting rules unfortunately prohibit the reporting of accumulated goodwill or the value of brand names on a firm's balance sheet. To explicitly capitalize reputations in financial statements, however, would be to encourage managers to more carefully maintain these invisible assets.

Still, *extra-balance sheet reporting* of reputational ratings and rankings could be done. For instance, auditors could also assess and report on how key constituents—other than financial analysts—evaluate a company. Efforts in this direction are evident: A growing number of firms now voluntarily and systematically report in their annual statements the results of employee surveys in the belief that investors care about the company's *human capital*. The same might be done with customers, suppliers, dealers, and other constituencies. If well-regarded companies were to report their relative reputational standings in their annual statements, they might induce others to follow suit. Prospective employees, investors, and other constituents would doubtless pay attention to these ratings as a gauge of the company's *reputational capital,* forcing lesser-ranked rivals to imitate the practice and to work toward improving their own reputations. In matters of reputation, however, it's best not to confuse wishes with reality.

N O T E S

INTRODUCTION

1. See Phyllis Fine, "Juggling the Stars," *Travel Agent*, July 26, 1993.
2. James Villas, "Connaught in the Act," *Town & Country*, April 1994, 96.
3. David Aaker, *Managing Brand Equity* (New York: Free Press, 1991).
4. Peter Reuter, "The Value of a Bad Reputation: Cartels, Criminals, and Barriers to Entry" (Paper presented at the Annual Conference of the Association for Public Policy Analysis and Management, Minneapolis, October 1982).
5. Rahul Jacob, "Corporate Reputations," *Fortune*, March 6, 1995, 54.
6. For a similar view of how uniqueness defines excellence, see Michael Treacy and Fred Wiersema, "How Market Leaders Keep Their Edge," *Fortune*, February 6, 1995.
7. Roberto Goizueta, quoted in *Fortune*, March 6, 1995, 56.

CHAPTER 1

1. As for Tonya Harding, after the 1994 winter Olympics she returned to Oregon, where she pled guilty to "obstructing" the police investigation into the attack on Nancy Kerrigan. Harding agreed to pay a $100,000 fine and resigned from the sport. Her reputation in tatters—and despite her eighth-place finish at the Olympics—she was later denied a dinner invitation to the Clinton White House with the other Olympic athletes.
2. H. S. Becker, *Art Worlds* (Berkeley: University of California Press, 1982), 25, 35, 361.
3. Gita Siedman, ed., *World of Winners* (Detroit: Gale Research, 1989), viii.
4. Daniel Chambliss, "The Mundanity of Excellence: An Ethnographic Report on Stratification and Olympic Swimmers," *Sociological Theory* 7 (1989): 70–86.
5. Ibid., 73.

6. Ibid., 77, 81.

7. Sherwin Rosen, "The Economics of Superstars," *American Economic Review* 71 (1981): 845–858.

8. In *The Discipline of Market Leaders* (Reading, Mass.: Addison-Wesley, 1995), authors Michael Treacy and Fred Wiersema show that successful companies all create economic value by making their own unique contributions: "Our research shows that no company can succeed today by trying to be all things to all people. It must instead find the unique value that it alone can deliver to a chosen market" (*Fortune,* February 6, 1995, 89).

9. "Small British Companies: Family Values," *Economist,* December 25, 1994, 79–82.

10. *The Insider's Guide to Law Firms,* compiled and written by Harvard Law students (Boulder, Co.: Mobius Press, 1993).

11. Quoted in Erwin Cherovsky, *The Guide to New York Law Firms* (New York: St. Martin's Press, 1991) 1.

12. Ibid., 2.

13. Bill Starbuck, "Keeping a Butterfly and an Elephant in a House of Cards: The Elements of Exceptional Success," *Journal of Management Studies* 18 (1993): 1–32.

14. Richard Tedlow, *New and Improved* (New York: Basic Books, 1990).

15. John Kay, "Keeping Up with the Market," *Economist,* September 11, 1993, 65–69.

16. Peter Drucker, *The Effective Executive* (New York: Harper & Row, 1985), vii.

17. Thomas Dowdell, Suresh Govindaraj, Prem Jain, "The Tylenol Incident, Ensuing Regulation, and Stock Prices," *Journal of Financial and Quantitative Analysis* 27 (1992): 283–301, and Clark Johnson, "A Matter of Trust," *Management Accounting* 71 (1989): 12–13.

18. Bruce Harrison, "Assessing the Damage: Practitioner Perspectives on Valdez," *Public Relations Journal* 45 (1989): 40–45.

19. John McDonald, "Sears Makes It Look Easy," *Fortune,* May 25, 1964, 120.

20. Max Bazerman, *Judgment in Managerial Decision Making* (New York: Wiley, 1994), 3rd edition.

21. Arthur Ashe, *Days of Grace* (New York: Alfred Knopf, 1993), 3.

CHAPTER 2

1. Edwin McDowell, "Helmsley Palace Succession: Brunei Royalty Buying Hotel," *New York Times,* November 1, 1993: D1, D3.

2. See Stuart Albert and David Whetten, "Organizational Identity," in *Research*

in Organizational Behavior, ed. L. L. Cummings and B. Staw (Greenwich, Conn.: JAI Press, 1985), 7:263–95.

3. See "Chairmen Starring as Spokesmen May Eventually Lose Their Luster," *Wall Street Journal,* February 12, 1992, B5.

4. Appeared in the *New York Times,* September 10, 1993, D3.

5. Alexis Lichine, *New Encyclopedia of Wines and Spirits,* 5th ed. (New York: Alfred Knopf, 1987), 75–78.

6. Quoted in Jerry Gray, "What's in a Name? If It's New Jersey, Not Much," *New York Times,* May 3, 1992, 49.

7. Kimberly McLarin, "Rutgers Seems to Like Its Stately, Stateless Image," *New York Times,* February 19, 1994.

8. Advertisement in the *New York Times,* September 22, 1992, A19.

9. See Anne Raver, "Audubon Society Pursues an Identity beyond Birds," *New York Times,* June 9, 1991, 1, 22.

10. Stephanie Strom, "Image and Attitude Are Department Stores' Draw," *New York Times,* August 12, 1993, D1.

11. Albert and Whetten, "Organizational Identity," 263–95.

12. Gerald R. Salancik and James Meindl, "Corporate Attributions as Strategic Illusions of Management Control," *Administrative Science Quarterly* 29 (1984): 238–54.

13. C. Schwoerer and B. Rosen, "Effects of Employment-at-Will Policies and Compensation Policies on Corporate Image and Job Pursuit Intentions," *Journal of Applied Psychology* 74 (1989): 653–56.

14. The complete study of the Port Authority is described in Jane Dutton and Janet Dukerich, "Keeping an Eye on the Mirror: Image and Identity in Organizational Adaptation," *Academy of Management Journal* 34 (1991): 517–14.

15. Craig Weatherup, quoted by Richard Lyons in *New York Times,* June 18, 1993, A16.

CHAPTER 3

1. In fact, even a bad reputation can serve to strengthen a competitive position. One study of the Mafia-controlled garbage industry in New York City observed how prosecution acts perversely to strengthen the bad reputation of the industry and discourages honest entrepreneurs from entering it, thereby increasing the market power of organized crime in that sector. See Peter Reuter, "The Value of a Bad Reputation: Cartels, Criminals, and Barriers to Entry" (Paper presented at the Annual Conference of the Association for Public Policy Analysis and Management, Minneapolis, October 1982).

2. T. Hall, "Striving to Be Cosmetically Correct," *New York Times*, May 27, 1993, C1, C8.

3. Susan Strange, *Casino Capitalism* (London: Oxford, Blackwell, 1986).

4. John Taylor, *Circus of Ambition* (New York: Warner Books, 1989).

5. Economists have proposed various models to analyze these investments as dynamic games. See B. Klein and K. Lefler, "The Role of Market Forces in Assuring Contractual Performance," *Journal of Political Economy* 89 (1981): 615–41. See also, Paul Milgrom and John Roberts, "Price and Advertising Signals of Product Quality," *Journal of Political Economy* 94 (1986): 796–821.

6. Herbert Baum, quoted in "What Makes a Brand's Image Valuable?" *Sense 91* (Lippincott & Margulies) 1989.

7. See Robert Wilson, "Auditing: Perspectives from Multiperson Decision Theory," *Accounting Review* 58 (1983): 305–18.

8. *Moody's Rating Process* (A publication of Moody's Corporate Department), 1989.

9. David Kearns, quoted in "Corporate Identity as a Marketing Tool," *Sense 90* (Lippincott & Margulies), 1988.

10. Ralph Larsen, quoted in "Tomorrow's Image: How Some Leading Companies View Image Management as a Corporate Priority," *Sense 92* (Lippincott & Margulies), 1990.

11. Ibid.

12. For a discussion of the difference between search goods and experience goods, see P. Nelson, "Information and Consumer Behavior," *Journal of Political Economy* 78 (1970): 311–29.

13. Rita Reif, "Record Price in a Sale of Art Owned by Streisand," *New York Times*, March 4, 1994, C3.

14. See Richard Beatty and J. Ritter, "Investment Banking Reputation and the Underpricing of Initial Public Offerings," *Journal of Financial Economics* 45 (1986) 213–32.

15. Ibid.

16. George Stigler, "Information in the Labor Market," *Journal of Political Economy* 70 (1962): 49–73.

17. Michael Spence, *Market Signaling: Informational Transfer in Hiring and Related Screening Processes* (Cambridge: Harvard University Press, 1974).

18. David Kearns, quoted in "Corporate Identity as a Marketing Tool."

19. See Klein and Lefler, "Role of Market Forces," 615–41, and Paul Milgrom and J. Roberts, "Price and Advertising Signals," 796–821.

20. Andrew Grove, quoted in Jacob, "Corporate Reputations," 56.

21. Sandy Weill, quoted in "What Makes a Brand's Image Valuable?"

22. Richard D'Aveni, "Top Managerial Prestige and Organizational Bankruptcy," *Organization Science* 1 (1990): 121–42.

23. Richard Caves and Michael Porter, "From Entry Barriers to Mobility Barriers," *Quarterly Journal of Economics* 91 (1977): 421–34.
24. Gary Becker, *Human Capital* (Chicago: University of Chicago Press, 1975).

CHAPTER 4

1. Howard Becker, *Art Worlds,* 23.
2. Svetlana Alpers, *Rembrandt's Enterprise: The Studio and the Market* (Chicago: University of Chicago Press, 1988), 105.
3. Warren Buffett, quoted by Jonathan Fuerbringer in *New York Times,* August 27, 1991, D1.
4. See *Fortune*'s special issue reviewing efforts to quantify a company's intellectual assets, October 3, 1994, 68–74.
5. Donald Kieso and Jerry Weygandt, *Intermediate Accounting* (New York: John Wiley & Sons, 1992), 598.
6. See Michael Wines, "Assets Intangible? Congress Has an Idea for You," *New York Times,* July 15, 1993, 1, A18.
7. For instance, see Joseph Corry, "Accounting Aspects of Takeovers," *Management Accounting,* September 1990, 47–51.
8. A comment by Michael Ozanian as part of an article by Alexandra Ourusoff, "What's in a Name? What the World's Top Brands Are Worth," *Financial World,* September 1, 1992, 40.
9. Based on data provided by Information Resources and reported in the *New York Times,* April 24, 1993: 37, 44.
10. Herbert Baun, quoted in "What Makes a Brand's Image Valuable?"
11. See Alfred King and James Cook, "Brand Names: The Invisible Assets," *Management Accounting,* November 1990, 41–47.
12. See Peter Farquhar, "Managing Brand Equity," *Marketing Research,* September 1989, 24–34.
13. This is the prevailing technique used by British consulting firm Interbrand. See Laurel Wentz and Geoffrey Martin, "How Experts Value Brands," *Advertising Age,* January 16, 1989, 24.
14. Ourusoff, "What's in a Name?" 47.
15. The ratio of market value to book value is popular among analysts and is known as *Tobin's Q.* I favor the reputational capital measure only because most people don't think in terms of ratios; also, a dollar value highlights the economic worth of a company's reputation.
16. What I have termed *reputational capital* John Swanda defends as a company's moral standing in "Goodwill, Going Concern, Stocks and Flows: A Prescription for Moral Analysis," *Journal of Business Ethics* 9 (1990): 751–59.

17. See Charles Fombrun and Mark Shanley, "What's in a Name? Less and Less," *Business Week,* July 8, 1991, 66–67.

18. Carol Simon and Mary Sullivan propose two methods for estimating a firm's brand equity. The first is based on the brand's advertising budget, market share, age, and order of market entry and relies on a cross-sectional regression model of those factors for a set of 638 firms—a cumbersome method for which data are generally lacking. The second estimates changes in brand equity using stock market prices. Simon and Sullivan conclude that marketing factors are reflected in Wall Street's stock prices, thereby justifying the use of a measure of reputational capital such as ours. See Simon and Sullivan, *A Financial Approach to Estimating Firm-Level Brand Equity and Measuring the Impact of Marketing Events* (Report #92-116, Marketing Science Institute, Boston, June 1992).

19. Alexandra Ourusoff and Meena Parachakesen, "Who Says Brands Are Dead?" *Financial World,* September 1, 1993, 40–52.

CHAPTER 5

1. Robert Levering, Milton Moskowitz, and Michael Katz, *The 100 Best Companies to Work for in America* (New York: New American Library, 1983).

2. This idea builds on the concept of stakeholder management described by R. E. Freeman in *Stakeholder Management: A Stakeholder Approach* (Boston: Pittman, 1984).

3. This is the argument made by Treacy and Wiersema in *The Discipline of Market Leaders.* They suggest that companies build their uniqueness and identity by pursuing operational excellence, product leadership, or customer intimacy.

4. Robert Levering, *A Great Place to Work* (New York: Random House, 1988), 45.

5. *The Transformation of IBM: A Market-Driven Quality Reference Guide* (Document #G325-0670-00, IBM Corporation, Stamford, Conn., June 1992), 32.

6. Levering, Moskowitz, and Katz, *100 Best Companies,* 11–14.

7. "Takeovers," *Sense 87* (Lippincott & Margulies, Inc., 1985).

8. Eugene F. Fama, "Efficient Capital Markets: A Review of Theory and Empirical Work," *Journal of Finance* 25 (1970): 383–417.

9. Robert S. Kaplan and R. Roll, "Investor Evaluation of Accounting Information: Some Empirical Evidence," *Journal of Business* 45(1972): 225–57.

10. Richard Brealey and Stewart Meyers, *Principles of Corporate Finance* (New York: McGraw-Hill, 1988), 165; Steven Ross and Richard Westerfield, *Corporate Finance* (St. Louis: Times Mirror/Mosby, 1988), 172.

11. Brealey and Meyers, *Principles of Corporate Finance,* 564.

12. *Moody's Rating Process.*

13. Susan Antilla, "Gang That Couldn't Pick Straight," *New York Times,* August 10, 1992, D1, D3.

14. Beth Mintz and Michael Schwartz, *The Power Structure of American Business* (Chicago: University of Chicago Press, 1985).

15. Doron Levin, "Stubborn Taurus Tramples on the Heels of the Accord," *New York Times,* 13 September 1992, 5.

16. *Transformation of IBM,* 16.

17. W. Edwards Deming, "Improvement of Quality and Productivity through Action by Management," *National Productivity Review* 1 (Winter 1981–82): 12–22.

18. See the biography of Deming by Andrea Gabor, *The Man Who Discovered Quality* (New York: Random House, 1990).

19. Philip Crosby, *Quality Is Free* (New York: McGraw-Hill, 1979). See also Joseph M. Juran, *Quality Control Handbook* (New York: McGraw-Hill, 1974).

20. "Corporate Identity as a Marketing Tool."

21. Peter Kinder, Steve Lydenberg, and Amy Domini, *Investing for Good* (New York: HarperBusiness, 1993), 183.

22. Mary Scott and Howard Rothman, "Companies with a Conscience," *World Monitor,* October 1992, 16.

23. R. E. Freeman, *Strategic Management.*

24. Donna Wood contrasts three sets of principles consistent with a long-run outlook: social legitimacy, public responsibility, and managerial discretion. See "Corporate Social Performance Revisited," *Academy of Management Review* 4 (1991): 691–718.

25. *Ben & Jerry's on Caring Capitalism* (Company brochure).

26. Lod Cook, quoted in *Principles of Excellence in Community Service: A Message to America's Business Leaders* (Points of Light Foundation, Washington, D.C., 1992).

27. H. B. Atwater, quoted in *Principles of Excellence,* 7.

28. *Principles of Excellence,* 5.

29. David Lewin, "Community Involvement, Employee Morale, and Business Performance" (Paper presented at IBM Worldwide Social Responsibility Conference, 1991).

30. Jane Dutton and Michael Pratt, "Merck's Mectizan Donation Program" (University of Michigan Working Paper, October 1992).

31. Al Gore, quoted in *New York Times,* 15 June 1993, C4.

32. Paul Shrivastava, "The Greening of Procter & Gamble" (Bucknell University Working Paper, October 1992).

33. "Who Cares, Wins," *Economist,* May 16, 1992, 19–20.

CHAPTER 6

1. *New York Times,* February 11, 1993, A1, A21. See also *New York Times,* February 12, 1993, A14.
2. See *Business Week,* August 9, 1993, 29.
3. Daniel Boorstin, *The Image* (New York: Random House, 1964), 12.
4. Ibid., 248–49.
5. Quoted in Peter Collier and David Horowitz, *The Rockefellers* (New York: Holt, Rinehart, and Winston, 1976), 152.
6. "Edward Bernays, 'Father of Public Relations' and Leader in Opinion Making, Dies at 103," *New York Times,* 20 March, 1995, B7.
7. *The Power of Communication,* Corporate brochure, (New York: Hill & Knowlton 1994), 6.
8. Quoted in John T. Flynn, "Edward L. Bernays: The Science of Ballyhoo," *Atlantic Monthly,* May 1931, 562–71.
9. "Corporate Image Ad: A Powerful Survey Works for Dell Computer," *Marketing Computers,* 12 (January 1992), 21.
10. S&P spokesperson, cited in "S&P to Speed Ruling on Chrysler Upgrade," *New York Times,* June 2, 1993, B1.
11. See Robert S. Kaplan and G. Urwitz, "Statistical Model of Bond Ratings: A Methodological Inquiry," *Journal of Business* 52 (1979): 231–261. Also Brealey and Meyers, *Principles of Corporate Finance,* 564.
12. Eric Berg, "The Bad Boy of Insurance Ratings," *New York Times,* January 5, 1992, sec. 3, 1.
13. Barbara Presley Noble, "A Downgraded Detroit Cries Foul," *New York Times,* November 3, 1992, D1, D4.
14. Robert Eccles and Dwight Crane, *Doing Deals: Investment Banks at Work* (Boston: Harvard Business School Press, 1988).
15. Stephanie Strom, "Apparel Industry Money Men Thrive," *New York Times,* December 16, 1991, D3.
16. Ibid.
17. Barry Rehfeld, "Cashing In on Old Friends in High Places," *New York Times,* August 15, 1993, 4.
18. The study of opinion leadership began with Paul Lazarsfeld and is extended and well documented by Everrett Rogers and Floyd Shoemaker in *Communication of Innovations* (New York: Free Press, 1971).
19. Early work on the spread of rumors was done by social psychologists who saw social networks as key to predicting the path a rumor would take. See John L. Moreno, *Who Shall Survive?* (Washington, D.C.: Nervous and Mental Disease Publishing Co., 1934).

20. John Kenneth Galbraith, *A Short History of Financial Euphoria* (New York: Whittle Books, 1993).

21. Charles MacKay, "The Tulipomania," In *Extraordinary Popular Delusions and the Madness of Crowds* (1841; reprint, New York: Bonanza Books, 1981), 89.

22. Ibid., 95.

23. Keynes's argument was pointed out by columnist Floyd Norris in his interesting story on Andrea Electronics, "The Spectacular Boom in Andrea Electronics," *New York Times,* July 11, 1993, Magazine section, 39–56.

24. See R. Ball and P. Brown, "An Empirical Evaluation of Accounting Income Numbers," *Journal of Accounting Research* 6 (1968): 159–77. 1968; Kaplan and Roll, "Investor Evaluation of Accounting Information."

25. Frederick Koenig, *Rumor in the Marketplace* (Westport, Conn.: Auburn House Publishing, 1985).

26. Described in "Anatomy of a Rumor: It Flies on Fear," *New York Times,* June 4, 1991, C1, C5.

27. William Meyers, *The Image-Makers: Power and Persuasion on Madison Avenue* (New York: Times Books, 1984), 98.

28. Eric Abrahamson and Lori Rosenkopf, "Institutional and Competitive Bandwagons: Using Mathematical Modeling as a Tool to Explore Innovation Diffusion," *Academy of Management Review* 18 (1993): 487–517.

29. Thomas Garbett, *How to Build a Corporation's Identity and Project Its Image* (Lexington, MA: Lexington Books, 1988).

30. Charles Fombrun, "Producing Organizational Configurations," *Journal of Management Studies* (1991).

31. Michael Kelly, "The Game and the Show," *New York Times Magazine,* November 20, 1993, 97.

32. Erving Goffman, *Stigma: Notes on the Management of Spoiled Identity* (New York: Simon & Schuster, 1963).

CHAPTER 7

1. Siedman, *World of Winners,* vii.

2. Sheila Rule, "Two Cities That Want Grammys," *New York Times,* March 10, 1993, 13.

3. According to Gita Siedman, ed., *Awards, Honors, and Prizes,* 10th ed. (Detroit: Gale Research, 1992).

4. J. Douglas Bates, *The Pulitzer Prize* (New York: Birch Lane Press, 1991).

5. See Ray Laakaniemi, William Green, and Laurence Jankowski, "Common

Traits of Award Winners," *Newspaper Research Journal* 13, nos. 1–2 (1992): 138–45.

6. Leonard Klady, "Oscar Pays in Lotsa Ways," *Variety,* February 22, 1993, 1, 245.

7. Bernard Weinraub, "First Comes a Junket, Then a Golden Globe; Hollywood Is Buzzing," *New York Times,* February 8, 1993, C11.

8. Tom Pollock, quoted in *New York Times,* February 10, 1994, C18.

9. "Buyer in the Wings for Clio Awards," *New York Times,* January 29, 1993, D16.

10. "Awards Presented in Direct Marketing," *New York Times,* February 26, 1993, D15. p. 15.

11. Anne-Marie Schiro, "Fashion's Night to Preen," *New York Times,* January 31, 1993, sec. 9, p. 9.

12. Richard Klein, "HBO Leads Pack with CableAce Awards," *Variety,* 25 January 1993, 33.

13. "1993 Car of the Year Winner: Ford Probe GT," *Motor Trend,* January 1993, 82–83.

14. Barbara Davies, "Artists Reap Rewards from B'Board B'Cast," *Billboard,* December 26, 1992, 12, 96.

15. Alessandra Bianchi, "Well Said," *Inc.,* January 1993, 98–99.

16. Tessa Melvin, "A Yonkers School Earns a Blue Ribbon," *New York Times,* March 14, 1993, 1.

17. Eugene Carlson, "Enterprise: Baldrige Fever Spreads to State, Local Levels," *Wall Street Journal,* March 9, 1993, B1.

18. John Grettenberger, quoted in John Holusha, "The Baldrige Badge of Courage—and Quality," *New York Times,* 21 October 1990, 12.

19. Jennifer J. Laabs and Allan Halcrow, "Optimas Winners Chart New Frontiers," *Personnel Journal* 72, no. 1 (1993): 50ff.

20. "IACP and Motorola Announce Quality in Law Enforcement Award Program," *Police Chief* 60, no. 1 (1993): 13.

21. Steve Lydenberg, Alice Tepper Marlin, and Sean O'Brien Strub, *Rating America's Corporate Conscience: A Provocative Guide to the Companies behind the Products You Buy Every Day* (Reading, Mass.: Addison-Wesley, 1986). See also Myra Alperson, Alice Tepper Marlin, Jonathan Schorsch, and Rosalyn Will, *The Better World Investment Guide* (New York: Prentice-Hall, 1991).

22. Peter Nulty, "The National Business Hall of Fame," *Fortune,* April 5, 1993, 108–16.

23. Adapted from a survey of U.S. executives, reported in "Most Innovative Companies," *Fortune,* December 13, 1993, 11.

24. Peter Kinder, Steven D. Lydenberg, and Amy L. Domini, *Investing for Good.*

25. Baila Zeitz and Lorraine Dusky, *The Best Companies for Women* (New York: Simon & Schuster, 1988).

26. See Jennifer Reese, "America's Most Admired Corporations," *Fortune,* February 8, 1993, 44.

27. Mark Shanley and Charles Fombrun, "The Market Impact of Reputational Rankings" (New York University, Stern School of Business Working Paper, June 1993).

28. Ibid.

29. Christopher Hitchens, "These Glittering Prizes," *Vanity Fair,* February 1993, 20–24.

CHAPTER 8

1. Alan Towers, "Realizing the Benefits of a Good Name," *New York Times,* June 16, 1991.

2. Charles Fombrun, Noel Tichy, and Mary Anne Devanna, *Strategic Human Resource Management* (New York: John Wiley & Sons, 1984).

3. James E. Grunig, "Image and Substance: From Symbolic to Behavioral Relationships," *Public Relations Review* 19 (1993): 136.

4. Paul Sweeney, "Polishing the Tarnished Image of Investor Relations Executives," *New York Times,* April 3, 1994, 5.

5. Ibid.

6. The same fragmentation characterizes the academics who study business. Management knowledge is largely created by specialists who work in departmental silos like economics, finance, strategic planning, marketing, human resource management, and so on. Academic specialization limits our ability to generate a truly integrative understanding of corporate reputations.

7. Freeman, *Strategic Management,* 48.

8. J. D. Aram, "The Paradox of Interdependent Relations in the Field of Social Issues in Management," *Academy of Management Review* 14 (1989): 266–83. See also Klein and Leffler, "The Role of Market Forces," 615–41.

9. See Paul Milgrom and John Roberts, "Informational Asymmetries, Strategic Behavior and Industrial Organization," *American Economic Review, Papers & Proceedings* 77 (1987): 184–93.

10. Kaplan and Roll, "Investor Evaluation of Accounting Information," 225–57.

11. Fombrun, Tichy, and Devanna, *Strategic Human Resource Management.*

12. Donna Wood, *Business and Society* (New York: HarperCollins, 1994).

13. Amitai Etzioni, *Capital Corruption* (New York: Harcourt Brace Jovanovich, 1984).

14. Boorstin, *The Image.*

15. In fact, economists focus almost exclusively on the reputations that develop between competitors in their models of strategy making. See Keith Weigelt and Colin Camerer, "Reputation and Corporate Strategy," *Strategic Management Journal* 9 (1988): 443–54.

16. Eric Abrahamson and Charles Fombrun, "Forging the Iron Cage: The Production of Macrocultures," *Journal of Management Studies* 29 (1992): 175–94.

17. *Wanted: Chief Reputation Officer,* Corporate brochure (Alan Towers Associates, New York, July 1991).

18. Clive Chajet, *Image by Design* (Reading, Mass.: Addison-Wesley 1991), 98–99.

19. Ibid., 102.

20. Ibid., 46–47.

21. *Crisis Communications,* Corporate brochure (Hill & Knowlton, New York, 1994).

22. Tim Wallace, "Crisis Management: Practical Tips on Restoring Trust," *Financier* 15 (1991): 13–16.

23. Richard Beckhard, *Managing Organizational Transitions* (Reading, Mass.: Addison-Wesley 1978).

CHAPTER 9

1. Daniel Boorstin, *The Decline of Radicalism: Reflections on America Today* (New York: Random House, 1969).

2. Stephanie Strom, "Braving Fickle Fashion," *New York Times,* August 16, 1993, D1, D4.

3. John Fairchild, *Chic Savages* (New York: Simon & Schuster, 1989), 12.

4. Richard Morais, "What Is Perfume but Water and a Bit of Essence?" *Forbes,* May 2, 1988, 90–95.

5. Nicholas Coleridge, *The Fashion Conspiracy* (New York: Harper & Row, 1988), 283–90.

6. Steven Gaines, *Simply Halston* (New York: Putnam, 1991), 238–40.

7. Ibid., 251.

8. Caroline Rennolds Milbank, *Couture: The Great Designers* (New York: Stewart, Tabori, & Chang, 1985), 341.

9. See "Bressler: Montana Still My Man," *Women's Wear Daily,* September 2, 1990, 6.

10. Martha Duffy, "Mais Oui, Oscar!" *Time,* February 8, 1993, 69.

11. For instance, see "Dawn Mello: Revamping Gucci," *Women's Wear Daily,* May 29, 1992, 6–7.

12. Godfrey Deeny, "Looking at Lanvin: A 'Flagship' Treads Water," *Women's Wear Daily,* September 12, 1991, 1, 6.

CHAPTER 10

1. The list excludes some prominent MBA programs offered by state-run institutions, such as the University of California, Penn State, and North Carolina. Their lower tuition, heavy reliance on servicing local communities, and state funding mean that these institutions face circumstances different from those facing the private schools that dominate most rankings of business schools.
2. Stephen Cole "The Hierarchy of the Sciences," *American Journal of Sociology* 89 (1983): 111–139.
3. Rosen, "The Economics of Superstars," 845–58.
4. Robert Hayes and William Abernathy, "Managing Our Way to Economic Decline," *Harvard Business Review,* July/August 1980, 66–77.
5. Earl Cheit, "Business Schools and Their Critics," *California Management Review* 27 (1985): 43–62.
6. In a survey of 60 deans and directors of executive education programs conducted by *U.S. News & World Reports,* March 23, 1992, 64.
7. Internal memorandum of Richard D. West, New York University, Stern School of Business, October 19, 1990.
8. Mukul Pandya, "At Wharton, They're Practicing What They Teach," *New York Times,* March 5, 1995, F7.
9. "Harvard B-School: An American Institution in Need of Reform," *Business Week,* July 19, 1993, 58–66.
10. Neil Rudenstine, quoted in "Reinventing Harvard: A New President Tries to Unite Its Schools," *New York Times,* February 10, 1993, B10.
11. Remarks of George Rupp at his inauguration ceremony, Columbia University, September 18, 1993.
12. William Honan, "A Decade and $1 Billion Put NYU with the Elite," *New York Times,* March 20, 1995, 1, B4.
13. Meyer Feldberg, quoted in "A Harder Sell for MBA's," *U.S. News & World Reports,* March 23, 1992, 63.

CHAPTER 11

1. *Brief Cases* (Lippincott & Margulies, June 1993).
2. *Brief Cases* (Lippincott & Margulies, November 1993).
3. Wally Olins, *Corporate Identity* (Boston: Harvard Business School Press, 1989), 157.
4. Olins, *Corporate Identity,* 158.
5. "The Corporate Name: To Change or Not to Change," *Sense 85* (Lippincott & Margulies, 1984), 4.
6. Olins, *Corporate Identity,* 160.

7. Ibid., 161.

8. "Corporate Name," 14–17.

9. Olins, *Corporate Identity,* 161.

10. Ibid., 162.

11. Wayne Calloway, quoted in "Corporate Identity, as a Marketing Tool."

12. "Employees and Image," *Sense 93* (Lippincott & Margulies, 1990), 4.

13. "Today's Decisions, Tomorrow's Image," *Sense 92* (Lippincott & Margulies, 1990), 5.

14. Olins, *Corporate Identity,* 106.

15. Gordon Lippincott, quoted in "Image Management in a Global Economy," in *Sense 92* (Lippincott & Margulies, 1990), 19.

CHAPTER 12

1. From a speech by Dwight Minton, "Why Environmental Literacy in Management?" (Church & Dwight, 1994).

2. The original work in this area was done by sociologist Paul Lazarsfeld in his studies of mass communication. He found that people are influenced by the media in a two-step process mediated by opinion leaders. See Elihu Katz and Paul Lazarsfeld, *Personal Influence* (Glencoe, Ill.: Free Press, 1955).

3. Walter Coddington, "Local Graffiti Removal Business Proposal" (Church & Dwight, June 2, 1994).

4. Walter Coddington, "Give Water a Hand" (Project Status Report #W92293-H, Church & Dwight, September 21, 1994).

CHAPTER 13

1. Robert Winters, quoted in Kurt Eichenwald, "Prudential Chief Takes the Blame for Scandals," *New York Times,* March 3, 1994, D5.

2. Connie Bruck, *The Predator's Ball* (New York: Penguin Books, 1989).

3. Ibid., 32.

4. James Sterngold, *Burning Down the House* (New York: Simon & Schuster, 1990), 18.

5. Eccles and Crane, *Doing Deals* 110.

6. Samuel Hayes, "Investment Banking: Power Structure in Flux," *Harvard Business Review,* March/April 1971, 136–52, and "The Transformation of Investment Banking," *Harvard Business Review,* January/February 1979, 153–70.

7. Eccles and Crane, *Doing Deals,* 92.

8. Company brochure (Spear, Leeds & Kellogg, undated).

9. Ron Chernow, *The House of Morgan* (New York: Atlantic Monthly Press, 1990), 89.

10. Robert Wilson suggested that this idea would apply to accounting firms in "Auditing: Perspectives from Multi-Person Decision Theory," *Accounting Review* 58 (1983): 305–18.
11. Chernow, *House of Morgan,* 600–01.
12. Eccles and Crane, *Doing Deals,* 116.
13. Chernow, *House of Morgan,* 704.
14. Ibid., 628.
15. Bruck, *Predator's Ball,* 32–33.
16. Chernow, *House of Morgan,* 516.

CHAPTER 14

1. Frederick Lewis Allen, *The Great Pierpont Morgan* (New York: Harper & Row, 1965).
2. Dennis Weatherstone, from remarks made at the annual meeting of stockholders, May 13, 1992.
3. Dennis Weatherstone, from remarks made at Columbia University, Graduate School of Business, New York, January 28, 1992.
4. Henry Clay Alexander, speech at officer's meeting, May 25, 1959.
5. From regulation Y, section 225.25, Bank Holding Company Act of 1970.

CHAPTER 15

1. See Peter Grant and Marcia Parker, "Hurtling toward Scandal," *Crain's New York Business,* June 1–7, 1992, 3ff.
2. Eccles and Crane, *Doing Deals,* 155f.
3. Michael Lewis, *Liar's Poker* (New York: Norton, 1988).
4. Judith Ramsey Ehrlick and Barry J. Rehfeld, *The New Crowd: The Changing of the Jewish Guard on Wall Street* (New York: HarperPerennial, 1990), 65.
5. Brokers quoted in Beth McGoldrick, "Salomon's Power Culture," *Institutional Investor,* March 1986.
6. Ibid., 74.
7. Ibid., 75.
8. Martin Meyer, *Nightmare on Wall Street* (New York: Simon & Schuster, 1993), 71.
9. Editorial, *New York Times,* August 22, 1991, A26.
10. See "Collusion, Price Fixing Have Long Been Rife in Treasury Market," *Wall Street Journal,* August 19, 1991, 1.
11. Meyer, *Nightmare on Wall Street,* 236.
12. Martin Mayer, "Antitrust the Real Issue in Salomon Scandal," *Wall Street Journal,* August 22, 1991, A13.

13. John Gutfreund, quoted in the *Wall Street Journal,* August 19, 1991, 1.
14. Fuerbringer, *New York Times,* D16.
15. See "Sullied Solly: Hubris Led to the Downfall," *Wall Street Journal,* August 19, 1991, 1.
16. Ibid.
17. See Laurie Cohen and Michael Sicosolfi, "Salomon Forces Wachtell to Resign as Outside Counsel," *Wall Street Journal,* September 3, 1991, 1, C9.
18. See Warren Buffett, "Salomon Inc.: A Report by the Chairman on the Company's Standing and Outlook," *Wall Street Journal,* October 29, 1991, 4–5.
19. Ibid.
20. See Clifford Smith, "Economics and Ethics: The Case of Salomon Brothers," *Journal of Applied Corporate Finance* 10 (1993): 23–28.
21. Susan Antilla, "Ex-Salomon Trader Gets Four Months," *New York Times,* December 15, 1993, D2.
22. John Gutfreund, interviewed by Gilbert Kaplan in *Institutional Investor,* February 1991, 54.

CONCLUSION

1. For a more elaborate discussion of how reputation factors into competitive dynamics, see Violina Rindova and Charles Fombrun, "The Dynamics of Competitive Advantage: Moving Targets on a Shifting Terrain" (New York University, Stern School of Business, Working Paper, March 1995).
2. Andrew Grove, Internet letter, November 27, 1994.
3. Ibid.
4. Faxback Intel Support #51, "Intel Pentium™ Processor: Floating Point Unit Information," December 6, 1994.
5. IBM, Internet West Site, Horace, December 12, 1994.
6. Andrew Grove, quoted in Jacob, "Corporate Reputations," 64.
7. Dwight Lemke compiled these jokes from the Internet.
8. Fombrun and Shanley, "What's in a Name?"
9. Charles W. Roll and Albert H. Cantril, *Polls: Their Use and Misuse in Politics.* (New York: Basic Books, 1972), 77.
10. Ibid.

I N D E X

Beene, Geoffrey, 222–223
Bellah, Robert, 58
Bell Atlantic, 44, 289
Bell Helicopter, 175
BellSouth, 135, 289
Ben & Jerry's, 129, 135, 138, 340
   Partnershop, 354–355
Benchmarking competition, 23, 27–28
Benetton, 224
Bergdorf Goodman, 52, 218, 225, 230,
   235, 236
Bergen, Candice, 230, 235
Berkshire Hathaway, 152, 189, 376,
   379, 385
Bernays, Edward, 143–144, 145
Best Cheese Award, 167
Best Companies for Women, The
   (Zeitz & Dusky), 182
Better Business Bureau, 50
Better World Investment, The (Council
   on Economic Priorities), 176
Beverage industry
   awards and ratings in, 183, 184, 188
   reputational capital in, 98–99, 106,
      107, 120
   shaping identity in, 270, 272, 286
   shaping image in, 157–158, 159
Bill Blass, 34, 35, 214, 216, 223, 224
Billboard magazine, 172
Biotechnology industry, reputation
   capital in, 105
Bird, Larry, 23
Birdsall, Connie, 285
Black, Susan, 145–146, 147
Black Enterprise magazine, 176
Blockbuster Entertainment, 152, 153
Bloomingdale's, 123, 221, 225
Blue Ribbon Schools of Excellence, 173
BMW, 4
Body Shop Company, 58, 129, 136,
   137, 160
Boeing, 24, 135, 172, 324
   awards and ratings of, 183, 184,
      188, 189
   reputational capital of, 99, 104
Boesky, Ivan, 337
Bonds
   Salomon's crisis in trading, 363,
      364–365, 366, 367–368
   specialists in trading, 363–364

See also Stocks
Bonfire of the Vanities, The (Wolfe), 58
Bonwit Teller, 218
Boorstin, Daniel, 140, 141, 214–215
Booz Allen & Hamilton, 256
Borg, Bjorn, 23
Boston Chicken, 75
Bousel, Art, 167
B. P. Pipelines, 189
Brand equity, 4, 11
   assessing, 90–92, 96–97
   in leading companies, 97–105
   See also Reputational capital
Brand names, 4
   in affecting identity, 285, 286–287
   associating corporate names with,
      41–42
   capitalization value of, 85, 88–90
   promoting and protecting, 39–41
   See also Labels, fashion; Products
Brennan, Ed, 64
Bressler, Leon, 234
Bristol-Myers Squibb, 96, 102, 299
Brooke Group, 189
Browning Ferris, 135
Bruck, Connie, 317–318, 344–345
Buffett, Warren, 84, 152, 376–377,
   378, 379, 380–381, 382–383,
   385
Burge, Christopher, 74
Burson-Marsteller, 144, 303, 378
Bush, George, 178, 368
Business Enterprise Trust, 151, 179
Business Ethics magazine, 137, 176
Business schools, 12
   academic reputations of, 247–251,
      255–256
   awards and ratings of, 180–181,
      190, 238
   challenges facing, 264–267
   changing history of, 239–242
   competition besieging, 251–254
   growth of, 242–244
   new facilities and names of, 256–258
   reshaping identity of, 258–263
   scholastic and practitioner models
      of, 244–247
   self-interest promoted in, 57–58
   survey of assets of, 7–8
Business Week

General Foods, 159, 160
Generalist banks, 323, 326–330. *See
also* Investment banking industry; *names of specific generalist
banks*
General Mills, 35, 40, 88, 101, 131,
177, 184, 188
General Motors (GM), 8, 18, 27, 28
awards and ratings of, 172, 173,
175
identity traits of, 124, 125, 126, 127,
236, 288, 289, 290
reputational capital of, 76, 78, 96,
98, 102, 105
shaping image of, 139–141, 143, 159
Generic products, 39, 41
Gentlemen's Quarterly, 142
Georgetown University School of Busi-
ness, 254
Georgia-Pacific, 101
German companies, managing reputa-
tion in, 203
Gerrity, Thomas, 260
Gerstner, Lou, 105
Gianfranco Ferre, 216, 224, 234
Gianni Versace, 214, 216, 223, 224,
232, 235
Gibson Greetings, 335
Gillette Company, 173
projecting identity of, 269, 270
value of brands at, 88, 90, 91, 92,
96, 97, 102
Giorgio Armani, 214, 216, 218, 222,
223, 225, 231
Girbaud, 224
Giuliani, Rudolph, 307
"Give Water a Hand," 306, 308–310
Glass-Steagall Act (1933), 343,
Global 500 Roll of Honor for Environ-
mental Achievement, 178
Goizueta, Roberto, 11
Goldberg, Harold, 119, 150
Goldberg Moser O'Neill, 145
Golden Carrot, 167
Golden Globe awards, 170, 171
Goldman Sachs, 28, 117, 290
capitalizing on reputation at, 74, 75,
78–79

clients and rivals of, 329, 330, 331,
332, 344, 349, 364, 365, 367
managing scandals at, 319, 337
ranking of, 320, 321, 322, 328
in shaping corporate image, 151,
161, 162
Gold Medal for International Corporate Achievement, 178
Golub, Harvey, 45
Good Society, The (Bellah), 58
Goodwill, worth of, 11, 85–88
Goodyear, 90, 98
Gore, Al, 68, 133–134
Gore, Bill, 113
Gourman Report, The (National Edu-
cation Standards), 180
Government
Church & Dwight relations with,
306–312
consulting firms relations with,
279–280
corporate awards given by, 173–175,
177, 178
managing corporate relations with,
194, 195, 197, 201
regulation of Salomon crisis, 365,
369, 371–372, 381, 384–385
Graham, Katharine, 179
Graham, Martha, 230
Grammy Awards, 21, 168, 169, 171
Grand Metropolitan, 87, 286
Greenberg, Alan ("Ace"), 333
Greenfield, Jerry, 138, 163, 340
Greenspan, Alan, 370
Greenwich Capital Markets, 369
Grettenberger, John, 175
Gretzky, Wayne, 35
Groundwater Foundation, 309
Grove, Andrew, 77, 388–389, 391
Grunig, James, 193
GTE, 96
Guaranty Trust Company, 344, 346
Guare, John, 153, 154
Gucci, 216, 221, 224, 228, 231–232,
235
Guggenheim Museum, 34, 360
Guide to New York Law Firms (Cher-
ovsky), 26

value and importance of, 1–5
See also Corporate reputation
Reputational audit
  components of, 206–209
  in defending reputation, 202–206
  executive role in, 196–198
  identity programs in, 201–202
  managing constituent relations with, 194–196
  nature and definition of, 11–12, 192–194, 395–397
  in start-up and spin-off companies, 198–201
Reputational capital
  benefits derived from, 72–80
  brands in generating, 88–90
    assessment of, 90–92
  costs in damaging, 93–96
  definition of, 8, 10, 11, 92
  in fashion industry, 223–225
  in glitzy industries, 105–106
  goodwill in generating, 86–88
  of hot companies, 96–98
  identity traits generating, 117, 120–121, 123
  image in generating, 81–86
  short- and long-term, 98–105
  valuing, 106–108
Reputational risks, 13, 78–79
Responsibility
  community demand for, 68–69, 136
  as reinforcing factor, 71–72, 80
Retail industry
  awards and ratings in, 180, 183, 184, 188, 189
  building reputation in, 24, 27, 30
  fashion designers in, 217, 224–225, 226, 229–230, 234, 235
  identity traits in, 116, 117, 121, 122, 134, 135
  reputational capital in, 90, 95, 96, 98, 102–103, 106, 107, 117, 121
  shaping corporate image in, 158, 159
  symbolism of names in, 51–53
Revco, 371
Revlon, 230
Richardson, Jerry, 268–269
Richo, 173, 174
Riverwood International, 343–344

R. J. Reynolds, 79
RJR Nabisco, 88, 104, 135
Robert Mondavi, 48
Rockefeller, John D., 34, 341
Rockwell, 135
Roddick, Anita, 58, 129, 160
Rollerblade company, 39
Rothman, Howard, 128
Royal College of Surgeons, 356
Rubber industry, reputational capital in, 107
Rubbermaid, 49, 183, 184, 189
Rudenstine, Neil, 264
Ruffle, Jack, 348, 353–354
Rumors
  nature and side effects of, 154–158
  social networks in promoting, 151–154
Rupp, George, 264–265
Rutgers, the State University of New Jersey, 49
Ryland Group, 189

Saatchi & Saatchi, 274
Safety Award for Excellence (SAFE), 178
Saks Fifth Avenue, 123, 220
Salomon, Arthur, 366
Salomon, Percy, 366
Salomon Brothers, 9, 13, 151
  crisis at, 319, 337–338, 362–363, 364–366
    catalysts of, 369–371
    constituent reactions to, 371–375
    government regulation of, 381, 384–385
    managing, 78–79, 204, 375–378, 398
    restructuring after, 378–381
  history and culture of, 363–364, 366–369
  ranking of, 320, 322, 328
  reputational capital of, 84, 101
  rivals of, 330, 331, 332, 344
Sampras, Pete, 23
Samsung Group, 268, 269
Sanford Bernstein, 322
Sara Lee, 20, 96, 101
Scent of a Woman (film), 171
Schering-Plough, 103

ABOUT THE AUTHOR

Charles J. Fombrun is the research professor of management at the Stern School of Business, New York University, where he has been on the faculty since 1984. Previously, he taught at the Wharton School, University of Pennsylvania. Dr. Fombrun has written numerous articles on management topics and is the author of two previous books on how companies adapt to changing environments, most recently *Leading Corporate Change*. He sits on the editorial boards of *Administrative Science Quarterly, Strategic Management Journal, Human Resource Management*, and *Human Resource Planning*.